❀ ARCHITECTURE ❀

A SHORT HISTORY

ARCHITECTURE
A SHORT HISTORY

by Joseph Watterson

REVISED EDITION

NEW YORK

W · W · NORTON & COMPANY · INC ·

To the Memory of My Father,
William R. Watterson,
ARCHITECT

Foreword to the Revised Edition

A GREAT DEAL has happened in the world of architecture since these words were first put together nearly twenty years ago. It looked at that time as though the last skyscraper might have been built, as though the works of Gropius, Le Corbusier, and Mies van der Rohe might be the final expression of the revolt in architecture, and as though the architect might continue to be merely the decorator for the engineer and the entrepreneur.

Now, in 1967, two of the Old Masters are still living and producing works which are true to their original principles but have gone far beyond them, and there is a new generation of architects who are designing buildings which presage a new era in architecture. Skyscrapers are being built every day, and the architect is being called upon to rebuild the old cities and to design new ones on a scale never before dreamed of.

Furthermore, there is a new awareness of the broader responsibility of the architect. Social upheavals have made us realize that the individual building is only a small part of the background against which man lives. The environment is a whole made up of a very great many very small parts, and it is the whole which must be seen and planned for, not just the parts. The need is for an environment in which new generations of men can live and grow and find the good life. This is the future of architecture; this is the task which the architect faces today and tomorrow. Yet he cannot face it alone. As never before, he needs the accumulated wisdom of many other specialists in the sciences and the humanities, for more than any other of the arts, architecture is a social art.

The last chapter of this book has been completely rewrittten, many new illustrations have been added, and this new edition is dedicated to the new architecture of today and the new city of tomorrow, and to the architects and their collaborators who will design them.

J. W.

Washington, D. C.
April 1967

[v]

Preface

It has been my purpose in writing this book to pass on to others some of the enthusiasm and deep respect an architect feels for the great buildings of the past and the men who produced them. In these times when, we hope, a new architecture is forming, surely a knowledge and a deeper understanding of the architecture of the past will help people better to understand the architect and his problems. Architects need an informed public, and this volume is put forth with the humble hope that it will reach many people who have never before thought of architecture as anything more than a part of the background.

I have kept my discussion to the architecture of those portions of the Mediterranean area, of western Europe, and of North America which have had the most to do with the architecture that is our heritage today. It is a straightforward history of the architecture of the past, written in the conviction that only through a knowledge of the past can we understand the present, and hope to face the future with an intelligent confidence. I have tried to hew to one line, and that is to stick to that which has shaped and most directly influenced our own architectural heritage.

I am indebted to scores of gentlemen for most of the information which I have incorporated into this book. To name them all would be impossible, for they are the authors of a lifetime of reading. The small balance of information is the result of my own travels and observations. I am deeply indebted to Robert E. Farlow, Editor for the publishers, with whom I enjoyed many long discussions which greatly helped to make this book what it is. I wish also to thank my clients, who have been patient and forbearing while I have neglected their interests in order to meet my good publisher's deadline.

John Shute said in a few lines what I have been trying to say in many, in *The First and Chief Groundes of Architecture,* which he published in London in 1563:

> *But I the setter forth of this treatise in English, acknolage
> myself not to be a parfaict Architecte, nor yet Gramarian, and*

though I have put myself in prease, it is not through the depe knowlaige aboue rehersed, but I do it for to put in use an entraunce or beginning to them which be therein Ignoraunt, and desyre further Knowledge in these things, as hereafter appereth by the declaracion hereof.

JOSEPH WATTERSON

COMMACK, *Long Island, New York*

Contents

Illustrations

❀ ARCHITECTURE ❀

A SHORT HISTORY

❋ I ❋

Art and Science

A man that has a taste of musick, painting,
or architecture, is like one that has another sense,
when compared with such as have no relish of those arts.
    —JOSEPH ADDISON in *The Spectator*

ARCHITECTURE is the most universal of all the arts. It is also the most expressive of all the arts, expressive not only of the artist but of whole peoples and their times. Furthermore, it is the one art which touches everybody.

To enjoy the beauties of a fine building is an experience available to all men, for no one lives where there are no buildings, and good architecture is widespread. The beauty of a building has only to do with its form and its decoration, nothing else need enter into it, not its function nor its history nor its creator. But architecture is not only an abstract art, it is an intensely human art. Buildings are conceived by men, built by men, and used by men. To know something of the men and the times which produced them, why their buildings took the forms which they did, and how those forms originated is to add greatly to an intelligent enjoyment of them. A painting can be enjoyed without knowing who painted it, when it was painted, or why it was painted. But a building is not like that, for, except in the case of a few monuments, it is primarily utilitarian, and to see only its form and decoration is to see only half of it. To know its use and the problems of its construction, and to understand something of the

[3]

times and the people which produced it, is to get the fullest enjoyment
out of it.

Architecture is an historical art. Although it would appear
that today's architects have turned their backs upon history,
trying to create a new architecture, it is true that the older
men were raised in the historical tradition and have a strong
sense of their place in the development of architectural history.
A generation from now it will be seen that what they are
doing is a logical outgrowth from what has been done before.
This is not necessarily true of many young architects, whose only
desire is for originality—but those fellows rise and fall. It will
undoubtedly be seen by architectural historians of the future that
the conservative contemporary architecture of this generation is
an assimilation of the architecture of the past, rather than a denial
of it.

Architecture is always expressive of its times. An intelligent
understanding of the history of architecture is a key to an intelligent understanding of history. Aside from the written word, man
has rarely expressed himself better than in his buildings. Architecture is a part of the stream of history, "history in stone."

Architecture is not only an art, it is also a science, for first of all it
is *building,* and as building it must be understood. The form and the
decoration of a building grow from its function and its construction,
as well as from its historical background, and these must be understood in order to fully understand and appreciate the building itself.
Every building of the past was built for a purpose which was meaningful in its time, by methods which were the most advanced for its
time, and decorated in a manner which was the logical outgrowth of
the culture of its time.

We of our time are not the first great builders of the world; indeed by some comparisons we are puny. Many great buildings have
been built which are larger and more wonderful than anything we
build today, which as builders we can approach only in wonder and
profound respect. But perhaps we are the first to give thought to the
social significance of our building. A history of architecture is of
necessity a history of the buildings of kings and aristocrats, for there
has been no architecture of the common man, unless it be the
medieval cathedrals. Architectural forms and methods have always

originated at the top, socially speaking, and have thence trickled down to the level of the comman man, if they reached him at all.

So the history of architecture is the story of many great buildings and the men who designed and built them, and it is the story of the growth of the techniques of construction and the development of the arts of planning and design.

❋ II ❋

Egypt, Mesopotamia, and Crete

REHISTORIC MEN left little which
we could call architecture, yet the cave paintings, carved bones,
and rough stone structures found in western Europe show that even
twenty-five thousand years ago men were developing the skills which
ultimately were to result in great buildings.

For many thousands of years men's building efforts were ex-
pended principally upon temples and tombs, the dwelling places of
their gods and their dead. One of the best-known of these ancient
monuments is at Stonehenge, on Salisbury Plain in southern England. Whether it was a temple or a tomb we do not know, nor do
we know when or by whom it was built, although it is generally
supposed to have been built by the Druids about 1600 B.C. It is a circle
about 106 feet in diameter of upright hewn stones, with indications
that it was surrounded by outer circles of stones and earthworks, and
approached by an avenue. Each stone is about fourteen feet high and
three or four feet thick, and they were evidently connected by stone
beams at the top, like a gigantic fence. Inasmuch as monuments like
Stonehenge show an orderly and studied arrangement of parts to ful-
fill a certain function, they may be called the beginning of architecture, for they were planned, and planning is the basis of architecture.

The beginnings of what we call civilization were in Egypt,
Mesopotamia, and the islands of the eastern Mediterranean Sea, about
seven thousand years ago. While the inhabitants of these lands were

developing a settled agricultural life, acquiring customs, and building buildings, men north of the Mediterranean were still roving and living in caves and huts. The pyramids of Egypt are older than Stonehenge.

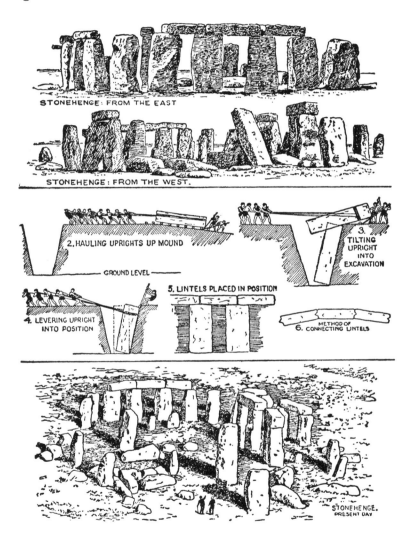

Stonehenge shows the beginnings of planning.

The most ancient of the monuments of Egypt is probably the Sphinx, that well-known symbol of mystery—and a mystery its history may always remain. Near it stand three pyramids, tombs built by the kings in which to preserve their bodies until the end of time, when, they believed, they would be needed again. The largest of these is the Pyramid of Cheops, built about 2570 B.C. It is 760 feet square and covers about thirteen acres, and was originally 482 feet high, which is the equivalent of a forty-five story building. A solid mass of stone except for two tiny chambers and their entrance passages, it is built of blocks of sandstone each weighing 2½ tons. It was originally covered with a smooth outer casing of limestone and granite, possibly in bands of different colors, little of which is left today since it has been used as a stone quarry for centuries. This accounts for its present stepped appearance.

Even more impressive than the size of the pyramid is the accuracy with which it is built. The stones are cut and fitted so perfectly that the joints are almost invisible, being less than one-fiftieth of an inch thick. Its sides are laid out so accurately that modern surveying instruments can detect no more than a half-inch error. When the Greek historian Herodotus visited Egypt in 450 B.C., he saw a great ramp leading from the river Nile up to the pyramid on the plateau above. The stones had been hewn from the cliffs across the river, floated across on barges, lashed to sledges running on a greased runway, and tugged up the mile-long ramp by thousands of men. Herodotus says it took a hundred thousand men ten years to build the ramp, and twenty years more to build the pyramid. Only the all-powerful ruler of an abject people could build such a tomb for himself.

The Egyptian Temple

THE PHARAOH AND THE PRIESTS RULED THE PEOPLE THROUGH A secret religion. Its inner mysteries were known only to them, the people knowing only that they must follow certain rites and obey certain laws. That is the key to understanding the form of the temple.

Although the temple of Horus at Edfu was built as late as the first century B.C., it is a typical medium-sized Egyptian temple and is

still standing in fair condition. It was originally approached by an
avenue lined with stone sphinxes which terminated at two obelisks,
slender tapering stone shafts nearly a hundred feet high. Behind   PLATE I
them, flanking the entrance to the temple, were colossal seated statues
of the pharaoh. The high entrance doorway is between two pylons,
tall masses of masonry with sloping sides and a flaring moulding

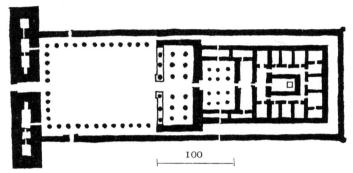

*The plan of the Temple of Horus at Edfu shows the progression
from large and open spaces to small and closed spaces.*

curling out at the top. Inside the entrance is an open courtyard surrounded by columns backed by a high wall. This is the court to which
the people were admitted. The columns across the rear of the court
are higher than the others and have a low wall between them, screen-
ing the space beyond from public view, but permitting light to pass in.
Between the central columns is the entrance to the first chamber, a
dim and lofty hall filled with columns, where only the priests and
their attendants were permitted. It is called the hypostyle hall, meaning a hall of which the roof is supported entirely by columns. The
traditional Egyptian method of roofing a building was by means of
stone beams and slabs, thus the columns and the walls had to be close
together, permitting no very large unobstructed floor spaces.

Beyond lies the sanctuary, low and dark, a small chamber which
only the pharaoh and the high priest could enter. Around it are
grouped small ceremonial chambers. These three units—the court,
the hypostyle hall, and the sanctuary—are enclosed by a high encircling wall extending back from the pylons. The building lacks
unity as a whole, and the wall was apparently an effort to tie the three

units together. Since the avenue of approach, the entrance, and the three main chambers are all on a single long axis, the temple has an aspect of having been meant to be viewed only from the front, which is an illustration in architecture of the most rigid of the Egyptian conventions in art, the *law of frontality,* so much more apparent in painting and sculpture. The progression from life in this world, through religion, into the afterworld is clearly implied in the progression along the avenue guarded by gods, through the narrow portal into the sacred enclosure, with the walled-off dwelling place of the gods beyond.

Larger temples have the same general plan as Edfu. The two temples of Amon, the great sun-god, are the largest and most famous. The temple of Amon at Karnak had a sacred lake within its grounds, extensive gardens, and palm-shaded avenues. It was connected to its sister temple at Luxor, two miles away, by an avenue lined with great stone rams. Each temple had several hypostyle halls, built at different times, the largest one at Karnak being 338 feet long and 170 feet wide, with 134 columns. The columns in the two central rows are 70 feet high and 12 feet thick at the base. The tops of the flaring bell-shaped capitals are 22 feet across—a hundred men could stand on one.

PLATE 2

This hypostyle hall is of particular interest because these two central rows of columns are about twenty-five feet higher than the others. Thus the central portion of the roof is higher than the roof over the sides. In the walls which connect these two roof levels, there are windows filled with pierced stone grilles, admitting light to the interior of the hall. This is called a clerestory. The Romans borrowed the idea centuries later, and its use followed through another thousand years to the Gothic cathedrals of western Europe.

These temples are now in a ruined and neglected state. They were not built as solidly as the tombs, and the shifting sands under their foundations have done much damage. Karnak is blocked up with mud-built villages, groves of palms, and great piles of debris. Part of Luxor was at one time converted into a Christian church, and it now has a Mohammedan mosque built within it and modern buildings backed up against its pylons.

Pyramid tombs passed out of fashion soon after the building of the Pyramid of Cheops, although many had been built before that— there are about forty along the Nile valley. Later pharaohs hollowed their tombs out of the cliffs, cutting artificial caves which extended sometimes as much as five hundred feet into the rock. Even there they followed the traditional temple plan, with the front of a temple carved on the face of the cliff and a hypostyle hall carved out of the living rock.

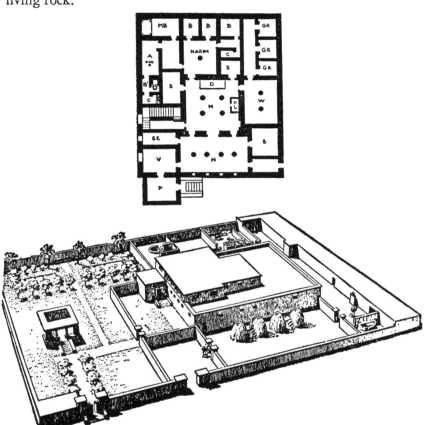

Home of an Egyptian nobleman.

b—*Bedrooms*

mb—*Noble's Bedroom*

b¹—*Bath Room*

h—*Hall (clerestory above)*

n—*Reception Room*

(From *Egyptian Architecture,* by E. Baldwin Smith, Appleton-Century-Crofts, Inc.)

The finest of these temple-tombs is that of Queen Hatshepsut at Der el-Bahri. At the base of the ragged line of cliffs, hundreds of feet high, are three long colonnades terraced one above the other, with a ramped approach from level to level. The terraces were originally planted as luxuriant gardens filled with plants from as far away as South Africa. The columns of the colonnades are relatively small and polygonal in shape, which together with the simplicity of the general design produces a strong resemblance to an early Greek temple.

The masses of the Egyptian people lived in huts built of reeds plastered with clay, huddled together by the thousands in cities of which few traces remain. The homes of the nobles and officials were built of wood or sun-dried brick, often three or four stories high, with many rooms opening from an interior covered court. The palaces of the pharaohs usually stood by the river, surrounded by gardens and a high wall. The walls were of brick, covered with stucco and brightly colored wall paintings.

Structural Methods

THE NATIVE BUILDING MATERIAL OF EGYPT WAS STONE. GRANITE and sandstone cliffs line the Nile river valley, but there are no forests, so wood is rare. Thus the ancient Egyptians developed a post and lintel system of building, that is, a post or column supporting a beam or lintel. In stone, this system requires that the supports be placed relatively close together, for a stone beam over twelve or fifteen feet long will break of its own weight, unless it be so large as to be too difficult to handle. That is why the hypostyle hall is so filled with columns as to hardly be a room at all; and that is why small rooms are long and narrow, so the slabs forming the roof can span from wall to wall.

The early builders of Mesopotamia, where there was neither stone nor wood, built with brick and invented the arch, which made it possible to span an opening without beams. The Egyptians were familiar with the use of the arch, for there is an occasional arch in their foundations and in hidden parts of their buildings. But in all their art forms they followed very rigid traditions, and the arch was not a part of their tradition, so it was never used as an architectural feature.

There have been many conjectures as to how the Egyptians built their massive buildings, for they were ignorant of the simplest mechanical devices. Even the wheel was almost unknown, or at least they seldom used it. Obviously they had no means of hoisting their massive granite blocks; furthermore, no hoists or other devices are shown in the wall pictures depicting temple-building. The French scholar Choisy has advanced the most plausible theory, fantastic as it may sound today. He says that they kept filling the building up with sand as they raised the level of the walls, course by course. Thus the workmen were always working on the ground. When the roof slabs were in place they dug the sand away. Considering that both sand and labor were cheap and plentiful, it seems a likely theory.

The column is the dominant feature of Egyptian architecture. There are three principal types. Each is cylindrical, rounded in a little at the bottom and with no moulded base, and tapering toward the top. It is chiefly in the capitals that they differ. One type of capital is the lotus bud, so called because it is carved in the form of a cluster of lotus buds. Sometimes the shaft of the column below is deeply grooved to look like a bundle of stems bound together at the top and the bottom. The second type is the papyrus flower, taking its form from the bell-shaped flower of the papyrus plant, from which the Egyptians made paper. The third type of capital is the palm leaf,

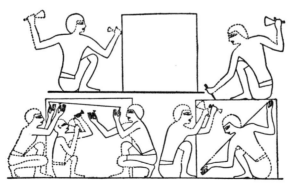

A fragment from an Egyptian wall painting showing stonecutters at work. (Courtesy Metropolitan Museum of Art.)

carved to look like a flaring circle of palm leaves bound about the top of the column.

The surfaces of nearly all walls and columns are covered with carvings in low relief. Relief means carving on the face of the stone. Low relief, or bas relief, is very shallow, like the relief on a coin. High relief is cut more deeply, with its figures standing out more fully from the stone. Full relief is cut so deeply that the foreground figures may stand entirely free of the stone. Egyptian reliefs are very low, and are cut entirely below the face of the stone, so that nothing projects beyond the surface of the wall.

The figures in the wall reliefs are curiously lacking in scale, some being very large and others being very small. They are represented as seen from the front, yet the heads and legs are in profile, and are always stiff and highly conventionalized. They are grouped to tell stories such as the lives of the gods, the exploits of the pharaoh, and the building of the temple. Originally they were painted in vivid red, blue, yellow, green, and brown, but only faint traces of color are left today. Paintings on the stucco walls of lesser buildings have the same characteristics as the reliefs.

The law of frontality is most evident in the large figure sculpture, for the figures have a rigid vertical axis, look stonily straight ahead, and appear to have been designed to be seen only from the front. The convention of frontality did not seem to apply to small and informal pieces of sculpture, for they are startlingly lifelike and fine in design, equal to the best work of any age.

Babylonia and Assyria

BABYLON, THE ANCIENT CITY OF THE WARLIKE CHALDEANS, LAY ON the banks of the Euphrates. Until archaeologists started digging there a few years ago, it had appeared to be no more than a gigantic mound. Having been built mostly of sun-dried brick, it had become a solid mass of clay again under the action of centuries of rain and sun. Only a few temples and palaces were built of an oven-baked brick, which was more permanent. The Chaldeans probably arrived at the arch through their development of the corbel, which is a more primitive form. It consists of a series of projecting courses of brick or stone, each extending a little farther than the course beneath it. When applied to the two sides of an opening in a wall, they are extended until they meet in the middle. It has its limitations, and can only be used over relatively small openings.

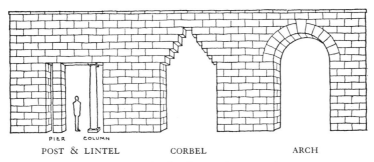

PIER   COLUMN
POST & LINTEL   CORBEL   ARCH

Ancient methods of covering openings.

The arch, on the other hand, turned out to have almost limitless possibilities, although the Chaldeans confined its use to comparatively small openings. A simple arch is a semicircular ring of bricks or stones, each slightly wedge-shaped. To build it, a temporary wood frame, called centering, is necessary to hold the masonry until all the members are in place. When the central stone, or keystone, is placed, and the mortar has set, the centering can be removed and used again. The members stay in place because their wedge shape prevents them from falling through. An arch will collapse, however, if it is not sufficiently buttressed at the sides, for it exerts a sideways push, called the thrust. An arch need not be semicircular. It may be a smaller arc of a circle, in which case it is called a segmental arch, or it may be elliptical or pointed. A large floor area can be covered by a continuous arch springing from the side walls. This is called a barrel vault. Thus the development of the arch was a great step forward in construction methods, for it freed building from the limitations imposed by the necessarily short length of beams.

Babylon was a vast and crowded city built on a great terrace to lift it above the floods which covered the plains every year, and enclosed by a belt of brick walls ninety feet thick and seventy-five miles in extent. The entire city was of a dull reddish color, being built entirely of brick, but there were gardens on many roofs and terraces—the famous "hanging gardens." Many stepped towers rose above the flat city, much like the skyscrapers of today. What is left of the walls and some of the larger structures has been uncovered. One of the buildings was a temple of Baal, consisting of a tremendous enclosure divided into several courts. Opening off the courts were rooms for priests and pilgrims, and in the largest court stood the ziggurat. This was a great tower built in a series of stages or terraces, the first two of which are still standing. It seems originally to have been over six hundred feet high, half again as high as the Pyramid of Cheops. In the shrine on top there is supposed to have been a statue of Baal of solid gold. The walls of the temple and of the ziggurat were decorated with vertical grooves, making perpendicular shadows in the brilliant sun, which glowed with the rich colors of glazed brick, for glazing was invented by the Babylonians. There was little sculpture, for stone was very scarce.

While Babylon was growing in the south of the valley of the Euphrates, another people, the Assyrians, were building their city of Nineveh in the north. Fierce and aggressive, they soon conquered the Chaldeans, and later swept through the whole country all the way to Egypt. They adopted the building traditions of the Chaldeans, but used stone from the near-by mountains to veneer the exteriors of their brick buildings.

Their greatest emperor, Sargon, built a city and a palace at Khorsabad. The palace covered 25 acres and contained about 700 rooms. Like the rest of the city, it stood on a terrace 50 feet above the plain. There was no danger of floods there, but the terrace had no doubt become traditional. The approach to the palace was by a double flight of steps, with a long ramp for vehicles, leading to a great archway between two towers. Standing guard at the gate were enormous stone PLATE 3 winged bulls with human heads. Within the palace were many courts from which opened the hundreds of chambers, and at one side stood the ziggurat, with a continuous ramp spiraling to the top. The plan of the palace appears to be utterly lacking in order, contrasting with the perfect symmetry of the Egyptian temple. Judging by the massive walls and long and narrow shapes, most of the rooms were roofed by barrel vaults, and there are indications in some of the reliefs that the Assyrians may have used the dome. The exterior walls were covered with glazed brick in brilliant colors and with stone reliefs. Their sculpture is vivid and naturalistic, subject to none of the conventions which bound Egyptian art.

Persia

THE CIVILIZATION OF THE CHALDEANS AND ASSYRIANS LASTED about twenty-five hundred years, but finally it was conquered by the Persians, who extended their empire from the Persian Gulf to Egypt. Having been originally a shepherd people, they had no building traditions of their own, so they borrowed from the nations they conquered. From the Egyptians they took the hypostyle hall, from the Chaldeans they learned the art of glazing tile, from the Assyrians they borrowed the winged bulls and other forms, and from all these nations they imported architects and artisans to build their buildings. With plenty of timber and stone from the mountains, they had no need for brick. They built wooden roofs, which permitted the use of slender columns widely spaced. They made no use of the arch, which thus passed out of general use until the fourth century B.C. Their borrowing of forms from other cultures is possibly the first historical example of eclecticism, a practice which became widespread during the nineteenth and early twentieth centuries.

During the height of their power the Persian kings built a number of palaces and halls at Persepolis and Susa. Persepolis is primarily an immense platform a thousand feet square, half-hewn out of the mountainside and half-filled in on the valley side, paved with granite slabs. The entrance is a broad flight of steps so gradual a horseman can ascend them. At the top is the ruin of a great gateway with winged bulls on either side. Scattered about the platform are the crumbled remains of several buildings, built at different times by different kings.

One of them is the "Hall of the Hundred Columns," built by Darius about 500 B.C., a vast audience hall 252 feet square. The hundred columns were 37 feet high and supported a timber roof. The single column which still stands reveals how lavishly the Persians applied their borrowed architectural details. At the top of the column, arranged to support the wood beams, are the foreparts of two Babylonian bulls. Below them are four double scrolls, a motive probably acquired in Asia Minor, the birthplace of the scrolled Greek Ionic capital. Below them is an Egyptian palm-leaf capital, and at the bottom of the shaft is a base composed of an Egyptian papyrus-flower capital turned upside down.

The Hebrews

SEVERAL CIVILIZATIONS GREW AND DIED IN THE AREA BETWEEN Egypt and Mesopotamia, some flourishing for several thousand years before they faded away or were conquered and passed their culture on to their conquerors. One of them was the civilization of the Hebrews in Palestine. They were never great builders, having been originally desert nomads, so when King Solomon wanted to build a temple at Jerusalem, he had to send to his Phoenician ally, King Hiram of Tyre, for materials and trained workmen. The temple was not built all at one time, but was added to, destroyed several times, and rebuilt. The building of the original temple is described in detail in the Old Testament in I Kings, Chapters 5, 6, and 7, and again in II Chronicles, Chapters 2, 3, and 4.

The details and construction of the temple were derived from both Egyptian and Babylonian sources. It was built on a terrace, and in its final form it consisted of three courts, one within the other, the Court of the Gentiles, the Court of the Jews, and the Court of the Priests. At the center stood the Holy of Holies, which held the Ark of the Covenant, the priests' trumpets, the seven-branched candlesticks, and the temple treasure. It was a heavy stone building roofed with timbers, its interior completely lined with gold. On each side was a corridor from which opened the priests' chambers, each lighted by a tiny window. The sanctuary itself was lighted only from the doorway, like that of an Egyptian temple. Little of this is apparent today except a portion of the terrace wall, the famous "wailing wall" of the Jews.

The Minoan Civilization

PRACTICALLY NOTHING WAS KNOWN OF THE ANCIENT CIVILIZA-tion of the Aegean Sea and the eastern Mediterranean until less than a hundred years ago, when a wealthy German amateur archaeologist named Heinrich Schliemann set out to prove the truth of the Greek legends. He excavated a mound on the coast of Asia Minor, which he believed contained the remains of Homer's Troy, and found there the ruins of nine successive cities, each one built upon the crumbled dust and debris of the former. He also found a cache of jewelry and objects of gold which were unlike known Greek workmanship, thus indicating the existence of a hitherto unknown civilization. Turning to Mycenae, in southern Greece, Schliemann uncovered massive fortress palaces, beehive-shaped underground tombs, and quantities of jewelry and utensils which seemed to be of the same workmanship as those found in Asia Minor. About 1900, Sir Arthur Evans started excavations in Crete, and to the astonishment of his native workmen he found, only a few inches beneath the surface of their fields, stone walls, pavements, and staircases. Ultimately, several towns were found, each with its palace. Here, then, was the center of this newly found ancient culture, which appears to have developed simultaneously with the cultures of Egypt and Mesopotamia, and then was completely and mysteriously destroyed about 1400 B.C.

About five acres of the palace of King Minos at Cnossos have been uncovered, revealing an unsymmetrical grouping of chambers, passages, and courts around one central court 90 feet by 180 feet. The site is sloping, so that some portions were two, and even three, stories high, the roofs of the lower parts forming terraces for the higher ones. The floors are paved with flagstones, even on the second story, where the stones were laid on wood beams supported by stone columns. The exterior walls are of solid stone, and the interior walls are of rubble stone faced with plaster, with wood door frames.

On the west side of the central court is a corridor two hundred feet long lined with huge stone oil-storage jars. On one side of the corridor are storerooms, built into the hillside, and on the other side are ceremonial chambers, facing on the central court. The stone throne still stands in the throne room. Across the court, and on a lower level, connected by a broad stone staircase, are the royal living apartments, situated so as to take advantage of the view across the river. A system of stone ducts and terra cotta pipes led the rainwater from the many courts and terraces to spouts in the outer walls. In the royal apartments there is a latrine which was flushed with rainwater from one

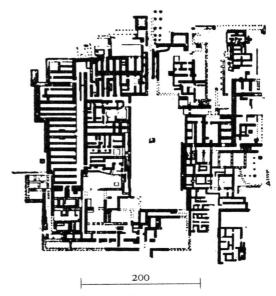

|———————————200———————————|

The Palace of Minos at Cnossos was truly a labyrinth.

of these pipes, while another pipe supplied water to a sunken bath. It was only necessary for the pipes to be cleaned out, and the drainage system functioned perfectly the next time it rained, after thirty-five hundred years.

More jewelry and trinkets of gold were found, as well as wall paintings of proud youths and statuettes of wasp-waisted women dressed in flounces and ruffles much like those worn during the 1890's. The paintings are vigorous and full of action, and the sculptures are refined and lifelike. Everything indicates that in Crete an aristocratic and pleasure-loving people lived a highly civilized life.

The Architect

THE ARCHITECT, IN THE SENSE IN WHICH HE IS KNOWN TODAY, DID not appear until relatively modern times, yet in all periods there were individuals who were not only highly skilled in the techniques of building, but who through natural gift and the training of experience were capable of designing buildings in the traditional manner of their time, with due regard for the fundamentals of order, scale, and harmony. These men usually came from the ranks of the building craftsmen, and should properly be called master builders. At the same time, many of them rose to high position and were held in great esteem, and were given titles and authority which correspond to those of the architect today. Another type of architect was the amateur, who may have been a prince or a priest, a sculptor or a gentleman of fashion, but who was endowed with the artistic ability and had acquired the scholarship to enable him to design buildings, which designs were then carried out by builders under his general direction. Master builders or gifted amateurs, if they designed and supervised the erection of their buildings, they were architects in the true sense of the word.

As is true of most ancient artists, the names of few Egyptian or Chaldean architects have been preserved, but there are frequent references to them in inscriptions and reliefs. We know them to have been learned persons held in high esteem, close to the court of the pharaoh and the inner circles of the high priests. Queen Hatshepsut's architect was Senmut, who erected two 97-foot granite obelisks at Karnak in honor of the thirtieth year of her reign. In Mesopotamia there was a prince named Gudea, whose capital was Lagash, who designed and built his palace and several temples. Some Egyptian drawings have been found, evidently intended for building purposes, which ingeniously contrived to show the plan, the elevation, and the section of a building all at one time.

Contributions of Ancient Architecture

THESE ANCIENT CIVILIZATIONS MADE THREE PRINCIPAL CONTRIBUtions to the development of architecture. One was the perfection of two structural systems, the post and lintel and the arch, and their use as decorative as well as structural elements. Another was a multitude of decorative forms and patterns, many of which passed into the architectural heritage of Western civilization and are still in use today. The third was the concept of orderly planning and the Egyptian temple plan in particular, which influenced the Greek temple plan centuries later. The most important of these contributions is perhaps the last, for plan is fundamental in architecture. From it grows the form of a building, and from the form and the method of construction develop the decoration. First, therefore, the plan must be appropriate to the function. The Egyptian temple plan grew from the ritual of worship, just as the plan of any building should be a logical development from the study of its function.

In the several thousand years covered thus far, architecture has matured from the rough monoliths of prehistoric man, shaped by his crude stone tools, to great monuments carved out by the keen metal tools of skilled stonecutters and erected by the labor of thousands. This suggests the thought that building keeps pace with techniques, that is, with man's invention of tools and methods, and that it is also limited by them. As these techniques become more complex, building becomes more complex. The building techniques of the ancient civilizations were relatively simple, so their buildings and their architecture are simple.

❊ III ❊

Greece

Our knowledge of the ancient Greeks begins with about the year 800 B.C., when they were already civilized and standing on the threshold of the greatest intellectual achievements the world had ever seen. They were apparently a mixture of two races, barbarians called Dorians who migrated from the north in search of sunny skies, and the Stone Age natives of the Grecian peninsula. They fell heir to the ancient culture of the Aegean Sea. Not that Greek architecture was a continuation of that of Crete, for there was a definite break of several hundred years, and the people were of different races. But the tradition of proficiency in the crafts had not died out, and the Cretans and the Mycenaeans furnished the early Greeks with skilled artisans, saving them generations of developing techniques.

In government, Greece became a group of democratic city-states bound together by many ties—by their common religion and their great religious festivals, by commerce with each other and with the rest of the world, by their common art, and by their Olympic games held every fourth year at Olympia. Later they formed the Athenian League to enable them to fight against their common enemy, the Persians.

The Greeks developed a civilization of the highest order. They became the Western world's greatest producer of goods, greatest traders, and greatest warriors. Their products were shipped from Britain to Persia; they planted colonies on the shores of the Mediterranean and Black Seas from Gibraltar to the Caucasus; their empire under Alexander extended all the way to India. The Greeks were the first to use money generally for all transactions, thus freeing trade to an extent hitherto unknown and making possible the economic freedom of individuals.

The Greek citizen was a new order of man. He was free, he was intelligent, he was accomplished. He had probably taken part at least once in the production of a drama, he knew much of Homer and the great poets by heart, he could play the lyre, sing and dance, he had served in the army or the navy and had built walls and fortifications, he was physically strong and had taken part in many games and contests, and if he was not an expert at vase-painting, bronze-working or some other craft, he at least could appreciate and criticize the work of the architects, sculptors, and painters with intelligence and understanding. "For we are lovers of the beautiful," said Pericles, "yet simple in our tastes, and we cultivate the mind without loss of manliness."

The peninsula of Greece is a rocky and mountainous country, yet with enough good land for an ample supply of grain and pasturage, and the lower slopes of the mountains are covered with olive trees. But Nature's greatest gift to the Greeks was an abundance of fine marble. Marble is the ideal building stone, and the marble from Mount Pentelicus was an inspiration to the sculptor and the stonecutter. Its straight fine grain could be cut to the sharpest edge, and its surface could be chiseled to the most delicate modeling, neither of which would be possible with a coarser stone. Yet it was hard enough not to weather away in the Greek climate, which is sunny and mild.

The tools and techniques of the Greeks were essentially the same as those of the ancient civilizations. Their stonecutting reached a higher state of perfection not only because they produced greater individual artists, but also because of the perfect material they had to work with. Thus it may be said that Greek architecture was really sculpture. It was, but it was more than that because it was good building too. It was the perfect alliance between architecture and sculpture.

The Doric Order

THE GREEKS BUILT MANY TYPES OF BUILDINGS, BUT IT WAS IN THEIR temples that they came the nearest to achieving perfection. The

Greek temple was not a place of assembly like the Egyptian temple, it was simply a shrine housing the statue of the god to whom it was dedicated. Thus there was no problem of enclosing a large space, there was rather the problem of focusing attention in outer space. Therefore the building was small and was designed with consideration first for exterior effect.

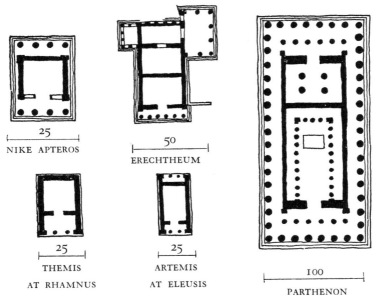

25
NIKE APTEROS

50
ERECHTHEUM

25
THEMIS
AT RHAMNUS

25
ARTEMIS
AT ELEUSIS

100
PARTHENON

Typical Greek temple plans.

The typical Greek temple was a rectangular building with columns on all four sides and a low pitched roof, standing on a low stepped platform. The triangular space in the gable ends, called the pediment, was usually filled with sculpture. Behind the surrounding columns was a continuous wall, with a door at each end. Sometimes small temples had columns only at the ends, with blank side walls, and sometimes still smaller ones had only two columns at the ends between the projecting side walls. But the peripteral temple, the type with columns all around, was the standard. The interior contained only one or two rooms, the naos or statue chamber, and often a treasury. These chambers were apparently lighted only from their doors, as were the sanctuaries of the Egyptian temples. Another link between the Greek temples and those of Egypt lies in the use of the column as the dominant feature, only in Greece they were used on the outside instead of the inside.

The Greeks possessed great originality, but cared little for novelty. They were familiar with the arch, but we know of only one instance where they used it. They chose to develop the post and lintel system to the highest possible degree toward perfection. They devised three types of columns, and spent generations improving and refining them rather than inventing new ones. A column together with its entablature, which is the beam and other horizontal members resting upon it, is called an order. There are three Greek orders: the Doric, the Ionic, and the Corinthian. The design of each order became more or less standardized, and their use has continued on and off through the centuries until the present day.

The first Greek order was the Doric, developed over a period of three or four hundred years to a point where it is generally considered to be one of man's most nearly perfect creations. The column is a simple fluted shaft, standing directly upon the platform without a base. The flutes are shallow grooves, usually twenty in number, meeting each other in a fine edge. Beginning at a point one-third of the way up, the shaft tapers slightly toward the top in a gentle curve, so that the upper diameter is one-sixth less than the lower diameter. This curving diminution is called the entasis, and its purpose is to correct an optical illusion, for if the column were the same diameter all the way up it would appear to be wider at the top. The shaft of the column is not monolithic, but is built of a series of drums. The uppermost joint, between the shaft and the capital, is cut into a groove, and above it are three or five tiny fillets, or flat mouldings. Rising in a subtle curve from the top fillet is the echinus, a moulding giving the effect of a cushion under the square block of the abacus above.

The entablature is divided into three parts: architrave, frieze, and cornice. The architrave is the lowest member, being the actual lintel which spans from column to column. It is separated from the frieze above it by a plain, square moulding. The frieze is a broad, flat surface, which on the Doric order is decorated with triglyphs and metopes. The triglyph (meaning three-groove) is a projecting surface divided by two grooves and edged by two half-grooves. They occur over each column and centered between each column. The square spaces between the triglyphs are the metopes, and they are usually decorated with sculpture in high relief.

The cornice is the overhanging member of the entablature, protecting the face of the building from the drip of rain and casting a

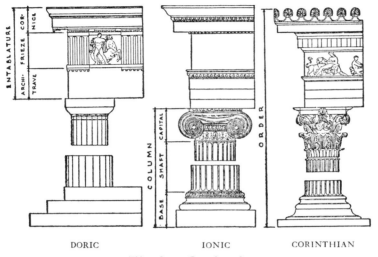

DORIC   IONIC   CORINTHIAN

The three Greek orders.

deep shadow. Its soffit, or under side, slopes upward slightly toward the building, and over each triglyph and metope is a block which has the appearance of a shallow bracket, called a mutule. The short vertical face of the projecting part of the cornice is called the corona. It is topped by a tiny moulding, and above it rises the cymatium, the uppermost member of the cornice. The contour of the cymatium is sometimes a cove, which has a hollow, rounded shape, and sometimes a full curve like the echinus; it is usually decorated with a conventionalized honeysuckle motive. The cymatium is really the gutter, for the back of it is hollowed out to catch the rainwater, and frequent holes, decorated with lion's heads, let the water out.

At the ends of the temple all the members of the entablature turn the corner and continue across the end of the building except the cymatium, which runs up the slope of the pediment, the other members of the cornice being repeated beneath it. At the corners of the roof and at the peak of the pediment there are standing ornaments called anthemions, which are usually formed of scrolls and honeysuckle motives. No Greek temple still has its original roof, but they seem to have been covered with flat tiles with ribs at the joints, of either marble or terra cotta.

The order described above is that of the Parthenon, which represented the culmination of at least three hundred years of development. The forms of the Doric order were well established as early as the seventh century B.C., and subsequent changes were limited to the refinement of the proportions of the various members and of the whole. Early examples are heavy and squat, and the development was toward a greater lightness and perfection of proportion. When the Romans adopted the Greek orders they formulated rules for their proportions which governed the relative size of every member. The unit of measurement was the lower diameter of the column. Thus a correct Greek Doric column should be 5½ diameters high, and its entablature 2⅙ diameters high. These rules, although often deviated from, have formed the standard for two thousand years.

The Doric order has been dissected in such detail for two reasons: First, to introduce many words and their use with which even the casual student of architecture should be familiar; and second, to demonstrate the fact that classic architecture is an architecture of rules and formulas which can be deviated from only by a designer who has first mastered them. Every member of a classic order has its definite place in the whole, and according to classic standards, little freedom of arrangement is allowed.

Many of the forms in the Doric order were undoubtedly derived from early wooden buildings. The fluted columns may have been an outgrowth of the polygonal columns, such as those at the tomb of Queen Hatshepsut, or they may have been derived directly from tree-trunk columns, grooved for decoration. The triglyphs look very much like the grooved ends of wood beams resting on the lintel, and the mutules look like wood rafter ends.

The ancient Greeks never saw their buildings marble-white, as they have usually been reproduced. The mouldings and the sculpture were picked out in brilliant red, blue, green, yellow, black, and gold. On a typical Doric temple the echinus of the capital was red and the abacus above it was blue. The triglyphs were blue, and the background of the metopes was red, with the sculpture painted in life colors. The carved ornament of the cymatium was green and yellow, separated by gilded edges. The larger than life-size sculpture in the pediments was painted in full flesh tones with highly colored draperies. Only traces of these colors are left today, and for centuries it was assumed that Greek architecture and sculpture was always white. Hundreds of public buildings have been built in the Greek style in dazzling white marble. The colored terra cotta temple that houses the Philadelphia Art Museum is a modern attempt to bring the color back to Greek architecture.

The architecture of Egypt might be said to be an architecture of decorated surfaces, whereas the architecture of Greece is an architecture of mouldings. Mouldings are an architect's means of playing with light and shade on the surface of a building. The Greeks developed many types of mouldings, which have continued in use in all classical architecture to the present day. They studied their height, their projection, and their contour with the utmost care, so that each one contributed just the right amount of shade or shadow to the design. Greek mouldings are soft and subtle in their contours, for Greece is a land of brilliant sunshine. In northern countries where gray skies are common, mouldings must be deeper and fuller to create enough shadow to give the desired effect.

The Parthenon

THE PARTHENON IS THE TEMPLE OF ATHENA WHICH STANDS ON THE Acropolis, the fortified citadel overlooking the city of Athens. It was built about 450 B.C., when Pericles was the political leader of the city. The Athenians were going through a period of great prosperity and national pride after their victory over the Persians, who had invaded Greece and burned their city. Pericles set out to build a new Athens, making it not only the most beautiful city in the world, but the center of all learning. Whether great periods produce great men, or great men produce great periods, certain it is that from time to time during history, when the stage was set for great works, great men appeared to perform them. During the Age of Pericles architects, sculptors, painters, philosophers, poets, and scientists such as the world had never before known were available to Pericles in his ambitious undertaking. The citizens at first supported him, but as his vast program required higher and higher taxes they gradually turned against him and he finally died in poverty and in sorrow.

Like many ancient buildings, the Parthenon has had hard treatment through the centuries. It has been used as a Roman church, a Greek Orthodox church, and a Mohammedan mosque. About 1690, when the Venetians were besieging Athens, the Turks turned the rocky crown of the Acropolis into a fortress, using the Parthenon as a powder magazine. A well-aimed Venetian cannon ball landed in the middle of it, and the explosion tore the building in half, as it is seen today. About 1800, Lord Elgin obtained permission from the Turkish government to take some of the remaining sculptures to England, where he sold them to the British Museum.

The master artist of the age was Phidias, a sculptor, whom Pericles put in charge of all the work, until he was unjustly accused and imprisoned as a part of the persecution of Pericles. The Parthenon was but one of the many buildings built under Phidias' direction, and its architects were Ictinus and Callicrates. The sculpture of the
PLATE 4   metopes, the pediments, and the continuous frieze that runs around the top of the wall behind the columns was done by Phidias' assistants. He personally created the great statue of Athena which stood in the naos. It was 40 feet high, made of sheets of gold and ivory over a wood core.

The building is 228 feet long and 101 feet wide, and the columns are a little over 34 feet high. Like most Greek buildings, it is small compared with some of the structures of antiquity or with later Roman buildings. The interior of the statue chamber was apparently treated as a two-story room, with a gallery on three sides supported by Doric columns, and a second tier of columns supporting the roof.
PLATE 5   The roof of the treasury was supported by four Ionic columns extending the full height. Some archaeologists believe that there was an opening in the roof over the statue of Athena, but it is generally believed that the only source of light was the open door, as was traditional in the sanctuaries of the ancient temples.

The Parthenon clearly illustrates the extreme care with which the Greek architects studied every aspect of their design. Measurements have revealed a number of intentional irregularities, which are called the "refinements" of Greek architecture. Their purpose was the

correction of optical illusions. Since a series of parallel horizontal
lines will have the appearance of sagging in the middle, the entire
structure of the Parthenon, from the platform to the roof, humps upward in the middle. The platform and the entablature curve gently
upward so that they are 4½ inches higher in the middle than at the
corners of the building. Furthermore, the columns are tilted slightly
inward, to prevent them from appearing to bulge outward, as they
might if they were vertical. The entasis, too, is a refinement. The
corner columns are a little thicker than the rest, because they are seen
somewhat isolated from the others and might look too slender when
silhouetted against the sky. To create still further the appearance of   PLATE 6
strength at the corners, the corner columns are spaced a little more
closely to their neighbors than the typical spacing. By means of such
meticulous attention to minute details, the Greek architects achieved
such satisfactory results.

The Ionic and Corinthian Orders

WHILE THE DORIC ORDER WAS BEING PERFECTED ON THE MAINLAND
of Greece and in her colonies in southern Italy and Sicily, a different
order was being developed in Asia Minor and on the islands of the
Aegean Sea. This is called the Ionic order, because the people living
in that region were descendants of the Ionians. It is lighter and more
elegant than the Doric, and a growing taste for richness led to its
use in Greece proper, where it gradually replaced the Doric.

The Ionic column is more slender than the Doric, being eight or
nine diameters high, and it has a richly moulded base. Its flutes are
deeper and more numerous, and they do not meet in an edge, but
have a narrow fillet between them. The capital, however, is the dis-
tinctive feature. Its principal decoration is a double volute or scroll
which sweeps across the top of the column with a graceful dip and
then curves down on each side and around in an ever diminishing
spiral. It is the same front and back, and from the sides it looks like a
scroll of paper tied with a ribbon. Some think this to have been its
origin, but it is more likely of Eastern derivation, for similar forms
have been found in Mesopotamia. The echinus below the volute is

decorated with ornament known as the "egg and dart," which has become the most common form of decorated moulding.

The Ionic entablature is much lighter than the Doric, being 2½ diameters high, or approximately one-fourth of the height of the column, whereas the Doric entablature is nearly one-half. The architrave is divided into three bands, each projecting slightly beyond the one beneath it. The moulding separating it from the frieze is ornamented, and the frieze itself is usually decorated with a continuous band of figures in relief. Beneath the projecting corona there may be a band of little blocks which give an interesting play of light and shade in the shadow of the cornice. They are called dentils, because they look like teeth.

The finest examples of the Ionic order are found in the porticoes of the Erechtheum, a small building on the Acropolis near the Parthenon. It is irregular in plan, for it was not only built on three different levels, but also had to cover several sacred spots, and furthermore, it apparently was never completed. There is a full portico at the east end, but the columns of the west end are built into a wall. Such partially projecting columns are called "engaged" columns. On the north PLATE 7 side there is another portico, standing on a lower level, overlapping beyond the main building as though something more were to have been built there, and on the south side is the famous caryatid porch. The entablature of this small porch is supported by six sculptured female figures, called caryatids, instead of by columns. They stand at ease, with one knee slightly bent, as though to show no strain under the load of marble which they carry on their heads. The folds of their draperies fall in sweeping vertical lines, suggesting the columns which they replace.

PLATE 8   At Ephesus, in Asia Minor, was a great Ionic temple dedicated to Artemis, the twin sister of Apollo. It used to be ranked as one of the Seven Wonders of the ancient world, and served not only as a temple, but also as a treasury, a museum, and a bank. Built during the fourth century B.C., when the Greeks were striving for grandeur rather than perfection, it was nearly 360 feet long and over 180 feet wide, and its double rows of columns were 54 feet high. The lower drums of the columns were decorated with reliefs, and there were enormous sculptured pediments. The entablature apparently had no frieze. This is the temple referred to in the New Testament, Acts

19:27, when Demetrius the silversmith attacked the Apostle Paul for destroying his business and bringing the temple into disrepute. It later furnished columns and building stone for the Christian cathedral which the Roman emperor Justinian built at Ephesus, and eight of its dark-green marble columns found their way into his great church of Haghia Sophia in Constantinople.

The third Greek order is the Corinthian. Its entablature is practically the same as that of the Ionic, but its column is ten diameters high and its tall capital is decorated with leaves of the acanthus, a thistle-like weed common in Greece. The capital occurs in many forms, but most of them have a moulded abacus which curves outward at the four corners, under which there are small volutes, which look like curling tendrils rising from the acanthus foliage below. Its big advantage over the Ionic capital is that it looks the same from all four sides. There are no temples standing in Greece in which the Corinthian order was used externally, except one which is primarily Roman. The order was developed late in Greece's history, and received little use before the Roman conquest. Its elegance perfectly suited the Roman taste, however, and they came to use it almost exclusively.

Athens once was filled with monuments to her heroes and her victorious athletes. The only one remaining is the Choragic Monument of Lysicrates, built in 334 B.C. by Lysicrates to commemorate the victory of his company of dancers in the Choric dances held in PLATE 9 honor of the god Dionysus. Standing on a high square pedestal, it is a small circular structure, only about eight feet in diameter, with six Corinthian columns engaged in its wall. At the peak of its low conical roof is a large scrolled ornament with three branching arms which originally supported the bronze tripod which was the actual trophy.

On the plain below the Acropolis stands the ruin of the great temple of the Olympian Zeus. Built after the Roman conquest, it was designed by a Roman architect, so it is hardly a Greek building. Only fifteen of its giant Corinthian columns remain. They are nearly 57 feet high, and the temple was 362 feet long and 145 feet wide, larger than the hypostyle hall at Karnak. Its very size marks it as more Roman than Greek.

The Greeks improved little on the methods of construction of the ancient civilizations, but for precision and accuracy the Greek temples are unrivaled. The marble was ground to such perfectly smooth surfaces that the two blocks met with an almost invisible joint, and no mortar was used between them. Instead, iron or lead clamps were used to secure one block to another, and wood dowels tied the drums of the columns together. Earthquakes are not uncommon in Greece, and a building which is elastic enough to sway a little is less apt to collapse than one which is rigid. The blocks of marble were carved on the ground, and projecting lugs were left on them to which to secure the hoisting ropes. When the blocks were in place, the lugs were cut off. The flutes were carved only on the top and bottom drums of the columns before they were set in place. When the entire column had been set, the flutes were cut through from top to bottom, thus assuring perfect alignment. An unfinished temple at Segesta, in Sicily, still has its unfluted columns and the hoisting lugs on some of the blocks of stone. In colonies where fine marble was not obtainable, the temples were sometimes built of a coarser stone which was then covered with stucco made of fine marble dust, in order to obtain a smooth surface suitable for painting.

Theaters and Houses

THE RELIGIOUS PROCESSIONS OF THE GREEKS EARLY DEVELOPED to the point where they were more in the nature of performances. In the fifth century B.C. the poet Aeschylus fused the song and pantomime into a play, trained actors, and gave to each a part. Thus the drama was born. The Greek theater was an open semicircular bowl, placed on a hillside whenever possible, like some of today's amphitheaters. In the center was a circle or a semicircle, enclosed by a stone ring called the orchestra. Here the chorus danced and sang, accompanying the actors who performed on the stage behind them. The stage was a long, narrow platform with a permanent architectural background called the skene, hence our word "scene." Behind it were dressing rooms. The tiers of seats were cut into the hillside, sometimes faced with marble, surrounding the orchestra in a little more than a semicircle. Every city and town had at least one theater, but most of them were so altered by the Romans

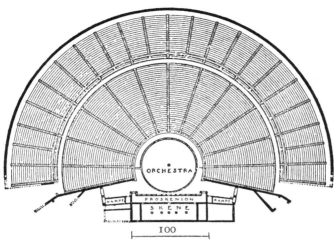

The theater at Epidaurus.

as to be no longer Greek. The best-preserved, at Epidaurus, was
designed by the great sculptor Polyclitus. Its orchestra is 66 feet in
diameter, and the entire theater is 373 feet across. PLATE 10

There are few remains of Greek houses, since they were built
primarily of sun-dried brick. They were low and flat, only a few
having a second story. The typical city house was built around a
central court open to the sky, with no windows on the street front.
It was entered from the street by a long passage at one side leading directly to the court, from which opened all the rooms of the
house. At the rear of the court was a wide opening leading to a foyer,

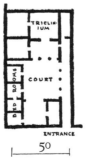

This plan of a Greek house at Priene is typical.

which in turn led to the largest room of the house, the triclinium, serving as both living and dining room. The sleeping rooms were tiny chambers opening off the court, receiving their only light and air through their door. There was no water supply nor drainage. Water was brought in vases from the well or spring which stood at nearly every street corner. There were no palaces, for the wealthy and powerful lived in houses only a little larger than those of their neighbors.

Greek Architects

LITTLE IS KNOWN OF THE ARCHITECTS AND THEIR DUTIES BEFORE the Age of Pericles. Of even Callicrates and Ictinus, the architects of the Parthenon, we know very little—possibly because they were overshadowed by the great figure of Phidias. It is evident, however, that they were given considerable freedom in designing the building, and it is known that they made many models while studying it. Many buildings were designed by sculptors, such as the theater at Epidaurus and a circular temple there, which was also designed by Polyclitus. The Corinthian capital is supposed to have been originated by Callimachus, who was a sculptor and metalworker. The temple of Artemis at Ephesus was designed by Alexander the Great's architect, Dinocrates, who also planned the city of Alexandria which the emperor built in Egypt. That city planning was early considered within the scope of the architect's work is indicated by the work of Hippodamus of Miletus, who wrote a book on city planning in 450 B.C. He introduced the principle of broad, straight streets intersecting each other at right angles—a principle which he applied in some cities without regard for the natural contours of the land, with the result that some streets consisted of flights of steps.

The Greeks not only invented the grammar of conventional forms upon which all subsequent European architecture was based, but also set a standard of perfection which has nearly always governed architectural taste and criticism. The principles of Greek architecture are based upon balance, symmetry, and proportions which are mathematically correct and emotionally satisfying. Only one structural principle was used, thus greatly contributing to unity and repose. Every part of a temple shows definite purpose, there is no sham; every member expresses its function honestly, and there are no members which purport to have a function they do not. Elaborate decoration is confined primarily to those parts of the building which have, or appear to have, no structural strain laid upon them, such as the tops of walls, the metopes, and the pediments.

This state of near perfection was achieved during the fifth century B.C., after several centuries of constantly refining growth. Later Greek architecture indicates a decline of taste in its increasing dependence upon ornamentation and its striving for magnificence. Sculpture exhibits the same decline from a noble and almost abstract serenity to a vivid and emotional realism. This decline parallels the breaking up of democratic ideals and the loss of freedom of the city-states, culminating in the empire of Alexander in the fourth century and the ultimate conquest by the Romans in the second. The Age of Greece was over, but the forms and the ideals which it produced are still living.

The three greatest periods of art, Greece during the fifth century B.C., western Europe during the thirteenth century A.D., and Italy during the fifteenth century, occurred when architecture, sculpture, and painting, the three great visual arts, were most nearly fused into one, and when the practitioners of each of these arts were skilled in all three. A Greek temple, a Gothic cathedral, or a Florentine chapel, without their sculpture and color, would not be the great works that they are. The work of the sculptor and the painter was conceived as an integral part of the design, not merely as decoration applied to an already complete whole. Thus the designer of a building, the architect, must have the vision of a painter when thinking of surface decoration, and the vision of a sculptor when thinking of three-dimensional form, in addition to the spatial vision of the architect when thinking of three-dimensional volume enclosing space. Add to this the purely structural elements of architecture, and its functional and social requirements, and it will be seen that architecture is by far the most comprehensive of all the visual arts.

❋ IV ❋

Rome

At some time in the prehistoric period a race of people drifted down into northern Italy and settled, intermingling with the Stone Age natives already living there. They are called the Terramare people because they seem to have come from a swampy country and built their houses on piles. This mixed race became the Latins, living in Latium on the south bank of the river Tiber, with Rome as their chief city. They learned to build with huge blocks of stone, and remains of their city walls are still to be found on the Palatine Hill beneath the palaces of the Roman emperors.

During the tenth century B.C., another race migrated to northern Italy, coming probably from Asia Minor, and settled on the north bank of the Tiber. They are called the Etruscans. Half Ionic Greek and half oriental, they were highly civilized and were always in close touch with Greece, both commercially and culturally. Although they were ultimately conquered and destroyed by the Romans, a good deal is known about them, for they were tomb builders.

The Etruscan tombs were underground chambers carved out of the rock. They had beams and rafters in imitation of wooden houses, and were decorated with wall paintings. These people cremated their dead, but buried images, so there is an abundance of sculpture. They were skilled in bronze-working, and finely made utensils, weapons, furniture, and even a chariot have been found. There are ruins of walls, aqueducts, and temples, the latter showing a definite Greek influence. They made use of the arch in their construction, and the Cloaca Maxima, a great arched drain under the Roman Forum, built by the Etruscans during a brief period when they occupied Rome, still carries the storm water to the Tiber.

The powerful and ambitious Romans conquered the Etruscans some time before 300 B.C., and in a hundred years more they occupied the entire Italian peninsula. Continuing their conquest and colonization, by 50 B.C. the Romans extended their domain to include all Asia Minor, Syria, Palestine, Egypt, the north coast of Africa, Spain, France, and Britain. Thus in less than three hundred years a small and comparatively uncultured nation swept through most of the Western world, conquering and absorbing civilizations, many of which were far more advanced than its own.

In government Rome developed from a small city-state under chosen kings into a republic, which it became about 500 B.C. However, through the years of conquest and expansion power tended increasingly to fall into the hands of a few wealthy and patrician families, culminating in the virtual rank of emperor being bestowed upon Augustus in 27 B.C. His reign of forty-one years, the Augustan Age, was for Rome what the Age of Pericles was for Athens. He boasted that he had found Rome a city of brick and left it a city of marble, which was very nearly true. Following him was a line of emperors who built prodigiously, principally Nero, Vespasian, Trajan, and Hadrian, and Septimius Severus, Caracalla, Diocletian, and finally Constantine, who ruled from 306 to 337 A.D. The ever increasing raids upon Italy by the Teutonic barbarians from northern Europe, and the corruption and chaos in internal affairs, were greatly weakening the strength and prestige of the empire. As a security measure, Constantine moved the capital to Byzantium, an ancient Greek city on the Bosporus, at the gateway between Europe and Asia. He renamed the city New Rome, but it was known for centuries as Constantinople, and is now called Istanbul.

The Romans were better governors abroad than they were at home. When they conquered a territory they extended full Roman citizenship to the new subjects and established a strong government under a local governor. Many foreigners thus rose to high position in the empire, including that of emperor. The Romans built large cities in all their provinces in true Roman style, connecting them by a vast system of paved roads and bridges, many of which are still in use. There are Roman baths in Britain, aqueducts in France, bridges in Spain, walls in Germany, and temples in Syria. Wherever the empire extended there are the remains of Roman buildings. Great builders as they were, their architecture, as a system of decoration, was based entirely upon the orders of architecture which they borrowed from the Greeks.

Vaults and Domes

THE ROMAN ARCHITECTS WERE GREAT BUILDERS, DECORATORS, AND planners. They devised great new techniques in construction, but architecture was to them merely a means of decorating what they had built, whereas to the Greeks, architecture and building were one. In most Roman buildings, except the early temples, the architecture was a veneer applied to the face of a structure to which it bore little or no relation. The similarity in principle to the architecture of the early twentieth century is obvious. The modern bank, with its marble front of Corinthian columns and sculptured pediments, is really built of brick, concrete, and steel. Its classical front is merely an archaic mask.

The development of the use of concrete was one of the Romans' most important contributions to the art of building. With it they were able to build enormous structures using relatively cheap and crude materials which could be found almost anywhere, and employing unskilled labor, such as soldiers, captives, and slaves. The basic difference between Roman concrete and modern concrete lies in the fact that modern concrete is reinforced with steel rods. Roman concrete achieved great compressive strength by means of sheer mass; modern concrete achieves both compressive strength and tensile strength by means of the steel rods embedded in it.

Another of Rome's great contributions was the further development of the arch and the dome. Long before they evolved the use of concrete, the Romans took the arch, and the primitive vault and dome as they found them in Syria, and improved them to the point where they were able to cover a great space 200 feet long and 80 feet wide with a roof of stone 100 feet above the floor, without columns or obstructions of any kind.

The constructive genius of the Romans thus brought a new element into architecture, the element of space. For the first time, the architect was free to design not only in terms of exterior mass, but also in terms of interior space. The shape and proportions of enclosed space, and the relation of one space to another, thus became elements of equal importance to the actual treatment of the masses which enclosed the space. The great genius of the Roman architects evidenced itself chiefly in this feature of spatial design and in the axial plan, which is the grouping of spaces on an axis or center line, and on secondary axes, so as to achieve the greatest monumental and dynamic effect.

The barrel vault of the Assyrians could roof only a narrow chamber. The Romans built barrel vaults spanning areas up to one hundred feet wide which, however, required tremendously massive walls

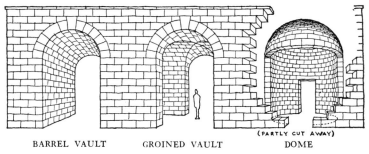

BARREL VAULT   GROINED VAULT   (PARTLY CUT AWAY) DOME

Methods of covering spaces with vaults and domes.

for support of the sheer weight and the great outward thrust of the stone vault. Openings in the walls had to be low, below the spring line of the vault, and being set in such thick walls, they admitted little light to the interior. Roman engineering genius solved these difficulties by cutting through the barrel vault with a second barrel vault at a right angle to the first. This opened up large semicircular areas above the side walls where the cross vault intersected them; these were filled with clerestory windows. The side walls under the cross vault no longer had to be massive, for they supported nothing. The entire weight and thrust of the two vaults were brought to the four corners, where four massive piers carried all the load. This not only made possible light and airy interiors, but saved over half the masonry in the side walls. Such a vault is called a groined vault, and the diagonals in which the two vaulted surfaces intersect are called the groins. With the increased use of concrete, it was found that the groins could be built as independent arches of brick or stone, and the vaulted surfaces between could be filled in with concrete. This principle is of great importance, for upon it were based most of the structural developments of the next thousand years, culminating in the great Gothic cathedrals of western Europe.

The dome is based upon the same principle as the arch and the barrel vault, applied to a circular base. The stones are not only wedge-shaped, but are also cut radially so they can be laid in rings. Thus each circular course projects beyond the course beneath it, until those near the top are hanging out over space, held in place by their own wedge-shaped sides. The true dome thus exerts a thrust all the way around it, requiring a heavy wall or drum for support. Few Roman domes, however, are of true dome construction. Ingenious and more economical methods of building dome-shaped roofs were developed by means of combinations of corbels and internal arches. The Romans actually made much less use of the dome than of the groined vault, possibly because of the space wasted in fitting circular chambers into rectangular plans. They never completely solved the problem of placing a circular dome on a square base. That remained for the late Roman architects of Byzantium to perfect three or four hundred years later.

Since the walls and vaults of most Roman buildings were built of concrete, brick, or rubble stone, or a combination of those base materials, the designers felt that it was necessary that they be faced with finer materials. For this purpose they used marble, brick, or stucco. Marble was applied to the exterior in blocks, held to the masonry with mortar and bronze clamps. The interior walls were similarly veneered, or with thin slabs of rare colored marbles. The marble most used on the exterior was travertine, which is of a creamy color and has a "worm-eaten" texture which is very beautiful. Some concrete buildings were veneered with brick, the Roman brick being very long and thin, laid up with a thick mortar joint. Houses and small buildings were stuccoed or veneered with small stones, brick, or tiles, often laid in patterns, producing a variety of textures. Floors and pavements in public buildings and fine homes were usually decorated with colored marble mosaics laid in geometrical patterns, and glass mosaics were occasionally used on walls and vaults.

During the early republic the Romans built with large blocks of stone without mortar, borrowing the use of the orders from the Greeks and the use of the arch from the Etruscans. With the development of the use of concrete, they continued to use these forms, even though they had lost their true functions. The orders were applied to the faces of their buildings, often superposed one on top of another, suggesting a system of construction which was not really present. Arches and domes, when formed out of concrete, ceased to be true arches and domes, except in appearance, for concrete is monolithic, as though hewn out of one piece of rock. This had the practical advantage, however, of permitting lighter supporting walls, for a concrete dome exerts no more thrust than a teacup turned upside down.

In adopting the Greek orders the Romans altered them to suit their taste and their production methods, and added two new orders. They made the Doric order lighter, put a moulded base on the column, and added dentils to the cornice. They created the Tuscan order by simplifying their version of the Doric, making it heavier, and omitting flutes, triglyphs, and all ornament. They greatly simplified the subtle volute of the Greek Ionic order, reducing it to a geometric spiral, and also devised a capital with angle volutes, presenting the same appearance on all four sides. The Corinthian order they enriched by adding a row of carved brackets, called modillions, beneath the corona, by carving ornament on nearly every moulding, and by applying a continuous scroll and leaf ornament to the frieze. By adding the angle volutes of the Ionic to the capital of the Corinthian, they later created the Composite order, which was even more richly decorated. All the orders were frequently set on pedestals, in order to increase their height. The Romans also made extensive use of pilasters, which are flat projections with the proportions of a column but without entasis, treated with capital and base, and giving apparent support to an entablature above.

The Romans enriched the orders, and at the same time simplified them. They removed all subtleties from the contours of the mould-

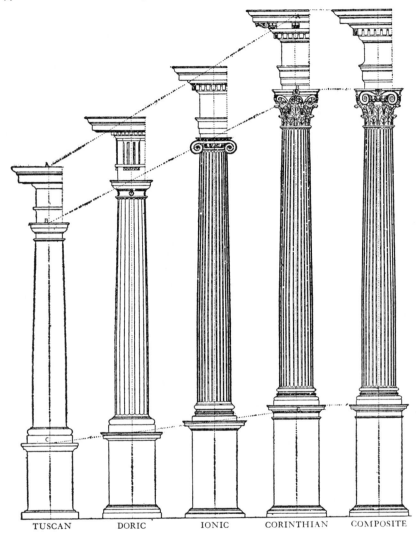

The five Roman orders, after Vignola

ings, reducing them to quarter-circles and combinations of arcs,
so they could be laid out with compasses and carved with less skill.
Although their ornament was adapted from Greek ornament, it
had none of the latter's delicacy and grace, being harsh and wiry

in appearance. It was reduced to a few standardized forms which could be turned out in quantities. Greek ornament was the work of sculptors; Roman ornament was the work of stonecutters.

During the reign of Augustus an architect by the name of Vitruvius wrote a book which he called *The Ten Books of Architecture,* in which he detailed the four orders (the Composite had not yet been devised) and laid down rules for their proportions. He also set rules for the spacing of the columns, their superposition, and every manner of grouping them. Fifteen hundred years later, during the Renaissance, this work was one of the source-books for the scholarly architects of that period.

Basilicas, Temples, Theaters, and Baths

ROME IS STILL A GREAT AND BUSY CITY, AS IT WAS TWO THOUSAND years ago. Everywhere in its ancient areas are the remains of old buildings, surrounded by and built into more modern buildings. Some of the churches were once pagan temples or parts of public baths; many of today's apartments are in palaces built by Roman noblemen five hundred years ago. Digging the foundation for a new building is an archaeological event, for every spadeful may turn up an ancient statue or the base of an old building. Here and there the accumulation of buildings of the past sixteen or seventeen centuries has been cleared away, revealing the broken columns and crumbled walls of imperial Rome. Much of ancient Rome may never be seen, for it underlies the modern city. The largest of these cleared areas is the Roman Forum. Every Roman city had at least one forum, which was a square surrounded by fine buildings, serving as the center of business and political activities. The Roman Forum is the oldest of Rome's several forums. In it are the ruins of many temples, monuments, arches, and basilicas.

One of the most important Roman buildings was the basilica, which served as both a court of justice and a business exchange. The usual plan consisted of a long and high central space, called the nave (from the naos of the Greek temple), with one or two rows of columns on each side forming single or double aisles. The roof over the aisles was low, permitting clerestory windows in the upper part of the nave walls. The ceilings of both nave and aisles were typically of wood construction. The entrance was usually at one end, and at the other end was a semicircular recess with a raised floor, called the apse, which contained the tribunal and seats for the magistrates. In front of the apse was an altar, where a sacrifice was offered before transacting business. There was sometimes a screen of columns or a balustrade separating the tribunal from the public space. Every Roman city had at least one basilica, often the most imposing building on the forum.

The Basilica of Constantine, which adjoins the Roman Forum, is not a typical basilica, for its roof was vaulted, but it illustrates how masterfully the Roman architects dealt with the new requirement that had been laid upon architecture, the need for space. It

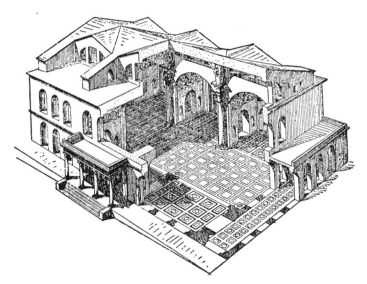

A sectional view of the Basilica of Constantine.

was begun by the Emperor Maxentius and finished by Constantine in 313. The nave is 265 feet long and 83 feet wide, and the width across the aisles is 195 feet. The nave roof was an immense groined vault 120 feet high, in three sections or bays, each groin being supported on a 60-foot monolithic column standing free of the side walls. The aisles were formed by three barrel vaults at right angles to the nave vault, and lower so as to permit clerestory windows above. All that is left today is one of the aisles, with its great barrel vaults 76 feet across, and a portion of the nave vaulting still hanging in midair. The rough brick and concrete interior now exposed was originally sheathed with fine marbles and mosaics, travertine, and alabaster. There were niches and recesses in the walls filled with Greek sculpture, and the mouldings and cornices were richly carved and colored. The exterior, however, was apparently a simple functional mass, faced with brick.

The vaulting of the aisles of the Basilica of Constantine illustrates another structural principle which the Romans discovered, and which reached its peak of development over a thousand years later in western Europe. The thrust of the nave vault is buttressed by the cross walls of the aisles which support the barrel vaults, and the thrust of each barrel vault is counteracted by the thrust of the ad-joining barrel vault, except at the ends of the building, where there is a massive wall for support. This illustrates the principle of "thrust and counterthrust," meaning that if two arches can be made to push against each other, no other lateral support is needed.

The temples of Rome were derived from both the Etruscans and the Greeks. They stood on a high moulded base called a podium, with steps at the entrance end between extended arms of the podium

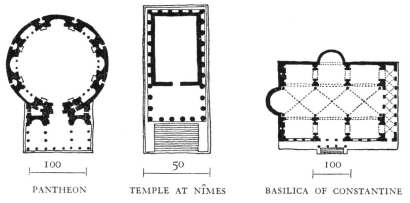

| PANTHEON | TEMPLE AT NÎMES | BASILICA OF CONSTANTINE |

Although their temple plans were generally conservative, in their vaulted structures the Roman architects showed great daring.

leading up to a portico three or four columns deep. At the sides and rear the walls extend out to the columns, making them engaged columns. Thus the Roman temple had a definite front, which faced the forum, from which it was meant to be viewed. The interior was one chamber, called the cella, which usually had a timbered ceiling. The best-preserved temple of this simple type is the one known as the Maison Carrée, at Nîmes in southern France, erected in 16 B.C.

PLATE 11 Circular temples were occasionally built, consisting of a ring of columns surrounding a circular cella. The Temple of Vesta, at Tivoli near Rome, perches picturesquely on a rocky precipice above a waterfall. Its Corinthian order stands on a circular podium ten feet high, and is surmounted by a low conical roof.

The only large Roman building standing whole and in use today is the Pantheon. Now a church, it was built as a temple by Hadrian in 124 A.D. It is circular in plan, with a great Corinthian portico 110 feet wide and 60 feet deep. Its concrete walls, 20 feet

PLATE 13 thick, are faced with brick on the outside, which was originally covered with Pentelic marble. The interior is 142 feet in diameter, surmounted by a dome of the same height. A Corinthian order 43 feet high runs around the interior, with columns carrying the entablature over the eight recesses and niches in the thickness of the wall. The circular wall above the order was originally faced with marble pilasters and paneling. Above that rises the great dome, the

PLATE 14 surface of which is decorated with coffers, which are deeply sunk panels. There are no windows. The interior is lighted by a circular opening 27 feet in diameter at the apex of the dome, admitting sufficient light for the entire interior. The magnificent unity gained by the use of one dominant structural feature, the flood of light from a single source, and the great size and fine proportions of the space enclosed, make the Pantheon one of the great buildings of the world.

After a conquest the victorious emperor paraded through the streets of Rome with his legions, his prisoners, and his trophies. The streets and buildings were decorated for the occasion with garlands, and a triumphal arch of flowers was erected. Afterward, the emperor built a permanent triumphal arch to commemorate his victory. The Arch of Septimius Severus has a central arch 22 feet wide and 40 feet high, with a smaller arch on each side. There are four

The Arch of Trajan, at Beneventum, after Vignola.

free-standing Composite columns on each face, standing on pedestals, and above the entablature is a high story, or attic, which carries
the inscription of dedication. The walls above the side arches are
covered with reliefs illustrating the campaign, and there was originally a four-horse chariot on the top, containing statues of the emperor and his two sons. Trajan built a different type of monument,
possibly inspired by the obelisks of Egypt. It is a giant column 147
feet high, with a spiral band of reliefs winding up its entire height,

PLATE 12

telling a picture story of his war against the Parthians and the Dacians. The column still stands as he erected it in 114 A.D., having miraculously escaped damage, except that a bronze St. Peter has replaced the pagan emperor on top.

Roman theaters were essentially like those of Greece, being semicircular, open to the air, and having a permanent stage and background. The semicircle which was occupied by the chorus in the Greek theater was given over to seating for senators and other officials. When a hillside was not available, the tiers of seats were supported by an elaborate system of arches and vaults with entrance and exit passages running through them. The theater at Orange, in southern France, is fairly well preserved. Its great auditorium, 340 feet across, held 7,000 spectators, and its stage is 203 feet wide and 45 feet deep. The architectural facing of the scena (the Greek skene) is gone, but it apparently consisted of three tiers of superposed orders framing niches filled with sculpture. The projecting walls at the ends of the stage indicate that there may have been a wooden roof over the stage. The outer façade of the scena had arched openings at the ground level, and the wall above, 116 feet high, was ornamented with arches built flush into the wall and with stringcourses, which are cornice-like mouldings. There are stone brackets which supported masts from which an enormous awning covering the entire auditorium was suspended.

The grandest ruin in Rome is the Colosseum, or Flavian Amphitheater. It was built by the Emperors Vespasian and Titus between 70 and 80 A.D. for the gladiatorial combats and fights between men and wild beasts with which they entertained the populace. In plan it is an ellipse 620 feet by 513 feet, with an elliptical arena 287 feet by 180 feet. The arena is surrounded by a wall 15 feet high, from which the banks of seats rise to a height of 157 feet, accommodating 50,000 people. The Colosseum is a marvel of engineering, honeycombed with stairways, ramps, and passages, with its four great arched stories supporting the seats, while beneath the arena are the vaulted dens which housed the wild animals. It is the prototype of the modern football stadium.

The architectural treatment of the exterior of the Colosseum illustrates the manner in which the Romans used the orders. Its wall is four stories high, each story except the uppermost being pierced

by arches about twenty-two feet on centers. Between the arches of
the ground floor are engaged Tuscan columns with an entablature
above, upon which rest the pedestals of the Ionic order of the second story, upon which in turn rests the Corinthian order of the
third story. The fourth story, which was added one hundred and
fifty years later, has blank walls with small windows, and is treated
with Corinthian pilasters. Between them are brackets which supported the masts carrying the vast awning that covered the entire
amphitheater. As used here, the orders are pure decoration. The
arches represent the true structure of the building, the columns and
entablatures that frame them are merely a marble facing bearing
no relation to the actual structure—even the architraves are not
lintels, but are built of small blocks embedded in the wall behind
them. The ingenuity and structural skill which it evidences, its
great size, and the magnificent sweep of its elliptical form, make
the Colosseum another of the greatest monuments that man has
built. Its present ruined state is not due entirely to neglect and decay, for during the Renaissance the Colosseum was used as a quarry,
and much of its travertine found its way into many Roman palaces
and churches.

Of all the buildings which the Roman emperors built to win
the favor of the public, the baths were the most spectacular. They
served not only as bathing establishments, but also as centers for
sport, lectures, and social life. In general, the baths consisted of a
main building standing upon a raised platform or terrace which
was sometimes a quarter of a mile square. Around the edges of
the platform were lecture halls, libraries, shops, and shaded alcoves
for conversational gatherings. The area surrounding the central building was laid out with gardens, fountains, and mosaicked pavements.
The main building centered around the tepidarium, or warm lounge,
a huge vaulted room magnificently decorated. Adjoining it were
the calidarium, or hot room, and the frigidarium, or cold plunge.
Surrounding them were private bath rooms, hot baths, rooms for
massaging, gymnastics, and games, and more libraries and lounges.
The walls and vaulted ceilings of all the chambers were richly
decorated with applied orders of gigantic scale, colored marbles,
paintings, and copies of Greek sculpture. Beneath the building was
a labyrinth of vaulted passages and storerooms, while beneath the

hot rooms were furnaces in which fires were kept burning by slaves, the heated air being passed through ducts in the floors and up through the walls to heat the chambers above.

There are ruins of baths in all Roman cities, even as far away as Silchester, in England, and there are several in Rome. The Baths of Diocletian are the largest, standing today in the heart of the city, opposite the railroad station. It accommodated 3,200 bathers, and as many more at recreation. The tepidarium is 200 feet long, 80 feet wide, 90 feet high, and it still stands, for in 1563 Pope Pius IV ordered Michelangelo to remodel it into the church of Santa Maria degli Angeli. Other portions of the Baths have been absorbed into modern Rome: one little domed hall is the church of San Bernardo, another part contains an art museum, and the semicircle of the theater encloses a busy public square.

On the edge of the city lie the ruins of the Baths of Caracalla. Its terrace, 20 feet high, is a fifth of a mile square, and it has a stadium across the rear which could accommodate a quarter-mile track. The main building covered nearly seven acres. Perhaps the greatest beauty of these baths is the beauty of their monumental plans. The chambers are grouped with functional logic and a fine sense of space. The major and minor axes are strongly emphasized, which produced magnificent vistas from room to room. The bathers passed from a large high chamber to a small low chamber, from a brilliantly lighted space to a dimly lighted space, from a longitudinal axis to a cross axis. Many interior columns supported balconies and low roofs around open courts, and framed the vistas from space to space. The PLATE 15 tepidarium of the Baths of Caracalla was roofed by a concrete groined vault 108 feet high, in three bays, with clerestory windows. The groins were supported on eight granite columns, standing free of the walls, with isolated pieces of entablature above them. This chamber was the model for the main concourse of the Pennsylvania Railroad Station in New York City, which was almost a copy of it, except that its "vaulting" was of steel and plaster.

It took tremendous quantities of water to supply the baths, to say nothing of the needs of the populous cities themselves. Older cities had been dependent upon wells and springs, which were usually polluted and often dry. The Romans built aqueducts to bring a plentiful supply of pure water from the hills and highlands. One

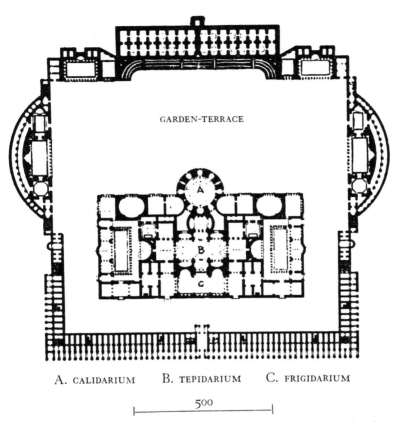

GARDEN-TERRACE

A. CALIDARIUM   B. TEPIDARIUM   C. FRIGIDARIUM

500

*The plan of the Baths of Caracalla illustrates the highest develop-
ment of axial planning and contrasting spaces.*

of those at Rome, the Anio Novus, was sixty-two miles long. Originating in high country, the aqueducts sloped gradually toward the
city, often circling miles out of their way to maintain a gradual pitch.
Normally they ran in concrete channels on the ground or were
carried above ground on miles of stone arches, but when necessary
they tunneled under hills or bridged rivers. Within the city the water
flowed in underground channels and through lead or bronze pipes
up into the buildings. In the time of Augustus there were nine aqueducts supplying Rome, two of which are still in use. The famous
Pont du Gard, in southern France, is part of the aqueduct that supplied Roman Nîmes with water, and at Segovia, in Spain, a portion

of the Roman aqueduct still crosses the heart of the city on arches high above the roof tops. Undecorated and strictly functional in design, these aqueducts are imposing proof that straightforward, honest building can also be fine architecture.

Palaces, Villas, and Slums

THE PALATINE HILL IS COVERED WITH THE RUINS OF THE PALACES of the emperors of Rome. Augustus built the first one there, and succeeding emperors added their own, until an area of twenty-five acres was covered with great courts, halls of state, dining chambers, libraries, gardens, a stadium, and hundreds of living and service rooms. The plan of the area shows the ingenuity of the architects in tying together with axes and vistas the various units of the group, built at different times, and their skill in disguising irregularities by means of circular rooms and semicircular niches. At Tivoli are the ruins of Hadrian's summer palace, spreading over 170 acres with villas, terraces, colonnades, pools, and gardens. There were living quarters for the scholars and artists of his court, a theater, a library, and a gymnasium. Hadrian took an architect with him on his travels over his empire to make drawings of the fine buildings he saw, some of which he reproduced at his villa. Thus there is exhibited at Tivoli nearly every building material and method used by the Romans.

A few years before Constantine officially moved the capital of the empire to Byzantium, Diocletian took the first step in that direction by building a summer palace at Spalato, across the Adriatic Sea, safe from the barbarians who constantly threatened Rome. The palace is an eight-acre rectangle, surrounded by high walls with many towers. It is divided into four quarters by two arcaded streets crossing in the center, with fortified gates where they pass through the walls, except on the south side, which overlooks the sea. Two of the quarters were occupied by the chambers of the imperial household and staff, and two were devoted to temples, baths, and the emperor's mausoleum. Across the southern side, with a long loggia overlooking the sea, were the chambers of the emperor.

The architecture of this fortified palace shows the evolution that was taking place in the use of the orders, and foreshadows what was to come. Under the pediment of the entrance to Diocletian's own chambers the entablature resting on the two center columns curves abruptly upward to form an arch, thus losing its structural significance as a lintel. At the northern gate, the arches rest directly upon the capitals of the columns, with no entablature between, as was done in Romanesque times seven hundred years later. During the Middle Ages a town grew up within the palace walls, and today it is the Yugoslavian city of Split. Its buildings are tucked in between the arches of the palace, and its cathedral is the former mausoleum.

The contrast between Diocletian's palace and Hadrian's villa shows the great change that had taken place in the state of the Roman empire. The villa, built about 124, covered acres of the sunny countryside with its gardens, courts, and fountains, with all the easy confidence of an unchallenged empire. Spalato's grim walls, 7 feet thick and 60 feet high, built only two hundred years later, reflected the constant fear of invading barbarians and a crumbling empire.

The town house of the well-to-do Roman was in general similar to that of the Greek. It turned a blank wall to the street, although larger houses sometimes had rented shops and apartments which

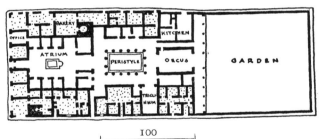

Plan of the House of Pansa at Pompeii, showing the shops and apartments opening onto the street and the family rooms facing the interior.

opened on the street front. A central entrance door led to the atrium, a small open court surrounded by alcoves and offices where the master of the house transacted his business. A shallow pool in the center of the floor caught the rain water. From the atrium a short passage led to the peristyle, which was a large open court with another pool and often a fountain. This was the center of the household life. It was surrounded by columns supporting the wooden roof of a passage on all four sides, from which opened the various rooms of the house. There were no doors in the openings, curtains being used when privacy was desired. At one side was the triclinium or dining room, and at the rear was the oecus or reception room. The oecus opened on a portico which overlooked a terraced and walled garden. At one side, where they could open from the street, were the kitchen, bakery, and wagon house. The houses were usually planned on a symmetrical axis, with a vista from the entrance through to the garden. The principal rooms and the peristyle were handsomely decorated with marble columns, bronze furniture, Greek sculpture, and rich wall paintings.

The poor quarters of Rome were much like the poor quarters of any crowded modern city. The high price of land forced landowners to build tenements five and six stories high. Building laws were needed then as now, to set limits to the congestion. Augustus limited the height of buildings to 68 feet, Trajan reduced the limit to 58 feet. The ground floors of the houses were occupied by shops and warehouses, with stairways in interior courtyards leading to the apartments above. There were many balconies, but there were no toilet rooms or chimneys, and curiously enough no evidences have been found of kitchens. The rooms were apparently dark, damp, and unsanitary. Small wonder Rome was so often swept by plagues, such as the one in 77 A.D. when 10,000 people died in a single day. Several emperors tried to do something to improve the city's slums, but it was too big a problem. When Augustus built his forum he built a wall 100 feet high behind his temple of Mars Ultor, to shut out the filth and the stench of the slum behind it. The great fire which occurred during Nero's reign was of some benefit to the city for it destroyed some of the worst districts.

New Roman cities, such as Silchester in Britain, Timgad in Africa, and many others throughout the provinces, were laid out with characteristic Roman regularity and precision, following the gridiron plan established by the Greeks. Near the center of the city, space was left for the forum, with the basilica, the temple, and other public buildings—in Silchester there was a Christian church. There were always baths, usually a theater, and outside the city walls an amphitheater. The provincial houses were generally of a rather simple type, and unlike those in Italy, were often detached, each house standing in its own garden, with stables and outbuildings. Otherwise they

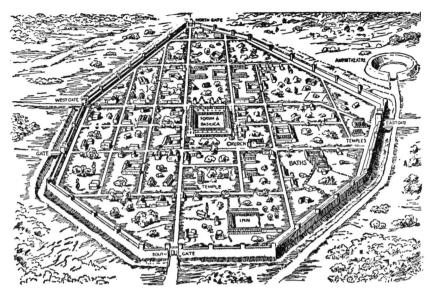

View of the Roman provincial city of Silchester, laid out with military regularity and precision.

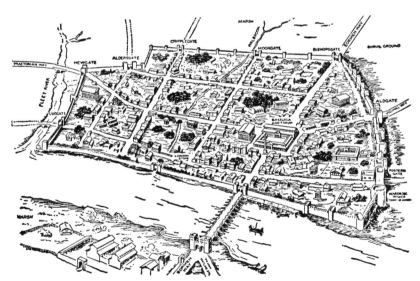

A bird's-eye view of Roman London shows a typical Roman city in the provinces.

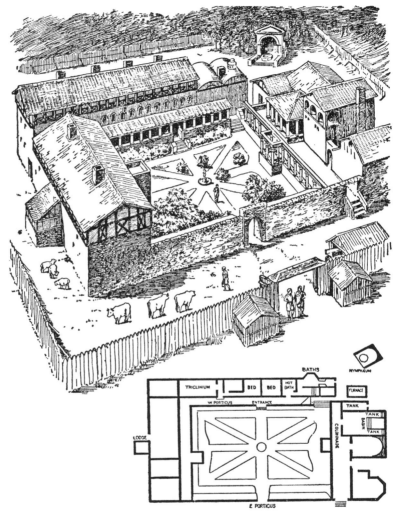

A typical Roman villa in the provinces.

were typically Roman, with their mosaic floors, wall paintings and, in northern climates, basement furnaces with hot-air ducts passing through the floors and walls. The Romans had achieved a high standard of living, and they maintained it wherever they went.

Pompeii

ABOUT FIFTEEN MILES SOUTH OF NAPLES, ON THE SUNNY SLOPE OF Mount Vesuvius and overlooking the blue waters of the Gulf of Naples, was the ancient city of Pompeii. By the first century A.D. it had become a thriving provincial Roman city with a population of about 25,000, and a summer resort for many wealthy Roman families. In 63 A.D. it was badly damaged by a severe earthquake which necessitated rebuilding most of the important buildings of the city, and before some of the work was finished, in the year 79, an eruption of Vesuvius covered it with a layer of cinders and dry volcanic ash fifteen to twenty feet deep. Most of the people had time to escape, but about 2,000 perished, chiefly those who had sought safety in cellars. The city was so completely buried that it was abandoned, some survivors returning only to tunnel down to retrieve their valuables.

During the Middle Ages the existence of Pompeii was forgotten, but early in the seventeenth century, excavations for an underground aqueduct accidentally revealed that there was a city beneath the grassy slope. It was 1748 before the excavation for the aqueduct was carefully examined, however, and it was not until 1763 that systematic excavation was begun. The French government carried on the work off and on until the middle of the nineteenth century, when the new kingdom of Italy took over. Pompeii stands now about two-thirds excavated, its streets and walls bared to the sun. Roofs and upper stories of the buildings are gone, but the walls and pavements trace out their plans, and give us an almost complete picture of a prosperous Roman city.

Pompeii is fairly regular in layout, with the streets at right angles to each other, except in the oldest part of the city. The principal streets are from twenty to thirty feet wide, paved with large polygonal blocks of stone, with raised sidewalks and raised stepping stones for pedestrians at the street intersections. As in all Roman cities, civic life centered about the Forum, which had covered porticoes on three sides, and was surrounded by monumental buildings. At the north end stands the temple of Jove, ruined by the earthquake; on the east side is a large market, next to that an official city sanctuary, and beyond that a spacious building used as a cloth exchange; across the south end are three halls which contained the council chamber and city offices; and on the west side are the basilica and a temple of Apollo. Ruined as they are, it is apparent that these buildings formed a handsome grouping around the civic square, which was paved with marble and dotted with statues and monuments.

Five other temples have been found, one of them an ancient Greek temple dating back to the sixth century B.C. It was apparently a building of special veneration to the Pompeians, for it stands apart in its own triangular "square," surrounded by Doric colonnades. There is also a temple of Isis, which shows the broad tolerance of the Roman governors, for although forbidden officially in Rome, this Egyptian cult had many Roman followers. There are three public baths, of which the smallest is well preserved. There are two theaters, the larger one being built partially on the side of a hill, with seats for 5,000 people. The smaller one was roofed, and seated about 2,000. The amphitheater lies outside the excavated area, but has been uncovered, revealing an oval bowl 460 feet by 345 feet, hollowed out of the ground, with stone seats accommodating 20,000 spectators. It is the oldest Roman amphitheater known, earlier ones having been temporary structures of wood. A barracks for the gladiators stands on the other side of the city, adjoining the theaters. In it were found armor and weapons, and sixty-three skeletons. The last mortal remains of three recalcitrant gladiators were found in the stocks, where they had obviously been placed for punishment.

These are the principal buildings, but they are surrounded by a city of homes, of which several hundred have been uncovered. They vary from the three or four rooms of the humble artisan to the veritable palace of the patrician. Whatever their size, they follow the general plan of the Roman house already described, which was the "House of Pansa" in Pompeii. The principal streets are lined with shops, which are small and open at the front, with wooden shutters. At the rear of the shop is a living room, and some had a sleeping room on a second floor. Many goods and utensils were found almost intact, so that their use could easily be identified. There is a blacksmith shop almost fully equipped, with many tools which had been brought in for repair; a food store, with remains of corn and bread, and preserved fruit in glass jars; dyers' shops, tanneries, silversmiths' shops, surgeons' offices, and a sculptor's studio with half-finished statues.

Most of the buildings are built of concrete or of inferior grades of local stone faced with small stones or stucco, sometimes with brick trim. The principal buildings are faced with marble. Many of the blank street walls are decorated with scenic paintings and some with advertising; even idle wall scribblings are preserved. The principal decoration of the finer houses is wall painting, of which there are many fine examples. Some seem to have been executed by Greek artists, and they form one of our chief sources of knowledge of Greek painting. The walls are divided into panels by painted columns and cornices, often highly exaggerated in form and in detail, and some-times drawn in perspective to give an illusion of distance. They are PLATE 16 garlanded with painted flowers and fantastic architectural orna-ments, and within the panels are landscapes and mythological com-positions peopled with nymphs, fauns, and gods. The colors are deep and rich, yet gay. Black is used a great deal, and a deep red known today as "Pompeian red." The interior architecture of the houses is exceedingly varied, showing no strict adherence to formal rules, and all three Greek orders are found, but used with an almost whimsical freedom. One of the characteristic treatments is that of filling up the flutes of the columns with stucco for about a third of the height, form-ing a smooth surface which was then painted.

About halfway between Pompeii and Naples is the smaller city of Herculaneum. The eruption covered it to a much greater depth, varying from 85 to 100 feet, and the action of water turned the ash to a soft stone, so much less excavation has been done there. Herculaneum was first discovered in 1738, and the Naples Museum is filled with its beautiful sculpture. Of particular importance was the discovery of a library, with nearly two thousand priceless papyrus manuscripts, con-taining the works of some of the greatest Roman philosophers.

Roman Architects

LITTLE MORE IS KNOWN ABOUT THE ARCHITECTS OF ROME THAN OF those of Greece. The scholarly Vitruvius spent most of his time de-signing artillery and composing his famous books. No building of his design is known, except for one which he describes in great detail. Architecture ranked as one of the learned professions, for which men of good birth and good education were considered to be best suited. There was one architect who was a senator, and another who was a consul, and there were also some who were slaves—Roman slaves were captives who may have been princes or scholars in their homeland. On the whole, Rome seems to have given her architects and engineers all due honor.

The architect about whom the most is known is Apollodorus of Damascus, an oriental Greek who accompanied Trajan on his military expeditions and supervised the building of bridges and fortifications, and also designed his forum and probably his column. But the most interesting architect, if indeed he may be called an architect, is the Emperor Hadrian. It is not known just how much of an architect he actually was, and how much merely a talented and educated amateur. Some ancient writers say he was very accomplished in "arithmetic, geometry, painting, and every department of art." If that be true, then he is to be credited with the design of some noble buildings built during his reign, such as the Pantheon. The same ancient authorities say he designed his own mausoleum, his villa at Tivoli, the temple of Venus and Roma at Rome, the baths of Agrippa, the baths of Trajan, and many other buildings. Architect or not, he was a busy and enthusiastic builder and an ardent student of Greek art, sending many young sculptors to Athens to study. He himself visited Athens several times, and rebuilt many buildings there. He was a prodigious traveler and visited every corner of his vast empire. From his travels he brought back statues and other works of art, and ideas for his villa. He is one of the most versatile and gifted figures in Roman history.

Hadrian and Apollodorus did not get along very well. When the emperor-to-be was still a young man, the famous Greek architect snubbed him in the presence of the Emperor Trajan, telling him to "go away and paint pumpkins." Hadrian apparently swallowed the insult, for later when he was himself emperor, he sent his design for the temple of Venus and Roma to Apollodorus for criticism. The elder architect pointed out abruptly that his design was out of scale, for if the statues of the seated gods in the temple were to stand up they would bump their heads on the roof. It was doubtless a fair criticism, but it was one too many for Hadrian, and it later cost the tactless Apollodorus his head.

As the power and prestige of the Roman empire declined, the purity of its architecture declined too—that is, its purity as judged by the classical standard and as defined by Vitruvius. Actually, however, architecture was going through a transition, as it usually has after an historical period has reached its height. The Roman use of the orders and the Roman concept of the monumental plan died out, until they were revived by the architects of the Renaissance about 1500. Today the cities of the United States, and to a lesser extent the cities of western Europe, are filled with columns and pediments in the manner of ancient Rome. During the early days of the American republic, Thomas Jefferson introduced the architecture of republican Rome as a suitable style for the public buildings of the new republic he had helped to create, and ever since then the Roman orders have enveloped the façades of most federal buildings and state capitols. The use of the Roman style received a new impetus during the early years of the twentieth century, when American architects again turned to the "grandeur that was Rome" to lend grandeur to their banks, railroad stations, and office buildings made possible by the new age of steel. The incongruity of it occurred to few; most were content to dig deep into their source-books, producing newer and more brilliant monuments to finance and industry, clothed in the magnificent trappings of ancient Rome.

V

Byzantium

When the power of imperial Rome was at its height the small bands of Christians which formed here and there were tolerated by the governors, as were other provincial sects. But as the followers of Christ became more numerous they also became more lawless, from the official point of view, for they would not pay homage to the image of the emperor nor would they serve in the Roman armies. Finally, to put a stop to this treason, Nero banned Christianity and started the systematic persecution of the Christians which continued for nearly two hundred and fifty years. In spite of that, however, the faith spread so rapidly throughout Rome and the provinces that before long even Rome's enemies, the German barbarians, were converted. The persecution was stopped by Constantine in 306, and a few years later, after he had won a crucial battle with the cross of Christ on the shields of his soldiers, he proclaimed Christianity the state religion of the empire. It was a wise move on the part of a shrewd emperor, for he knew that the empire was weakening and needed new ideals. If the passionate devotion of the Christians could be turned to work with it rather than against it, the empire might be saved. Christianity did not save the empire, but it prolonged its life and brought about a great new art.

Before Constantine died he divided his empire between his two sons, to rule jointly, one in Rome and one in Byzantium. Several short-lived attempts were made by later rulers to reunite the empire, but it remained divided into a Western Empire and an Eastern Empire. Rome was still being threatened by the Germans, and they finally captured it in 410. A few years before, however, the Western emperor, Honorius, had moved the capital to Ravenna, a little city on the eastern side of the Italian peninsula. But in 475 even Ravenna fell to the barbarians, and their leader set himself up as the emperor of Rome. In the sixth century the Eastern emperor, Justinian, succeeded in reconquering Italy and reuniting the empire for a while, with Ravenna as its Western capital, but his successor was overthrown by the Lombards. Thus for several centuries Italy was the scene of constant warfare and pillage. Through all this the Church stood firm, and its power and prestige increased. Since most of the tribes which invaded Italy were already Christian, the Church was willing to give its blessing to any leader who could muster a powerful army. The bishop of Rome had become recognized as the head of the Church by the sixth century, so it was the Pope who was the real ruler of Europe. His position as absolute head of a universal church gave him an authority and prestige no mere emperor could aspire to.

In the Eastern Empire, however, the emperor became the head of the Church, and remained so until the conquering Turks killed the last of the emperors on the steps of Haghia Sophia in 1453. Lying in the heart of what had been the empire of Alexander the Great, the Eastern Empire became less and less Roman and more and more Greek, and Greek soon replaced Latin as the state language. After centuries of theological disputes, the church of Rome and the church of Byzantium formally split in 1054 into two separate churches, the Western or Roman Catholic Church and the Eastern or Greek Catholic Church.

Constantinople became a great and beautiful city, and all the wealth, the learning, and the art of the Western world centered there. For over a thousand years it was the cultural center of the European world. Even as late as the Middle Ages, Constantinople was looked to by France and England as the source of all learning and luxury, for while scholarship and art seemed lost forever in the turmoil that engulfed western Europe before the year 1000, the schools and libraries of Constantinople kept alive the flame of classic culture. When it finally fell to the Turks in the fifteenth century, its artists, scholars, and philosophers fled to the West, where their influence was one of the factors which contributed to the rebirth of classical art and scholarship which we call the Renaissance.

The Early Christian Church

THE FIRST EARLY CHRISTIAN ART WAS PROBABLY THE PAINTING ON the walls of the catacombs of Rome, where the hunted Christians worshiped in secret. At first the paintings were very much like the decorations of the baths and palaces of the pagan city, for the mere act of conversion had not furnished the painters with a whole new repertory of motives. So for the first hundred years they continued to paint the same cupids, birds, and flowers they had painted as pagans. Gradually, however, new meanings came to be read into these forms and Christian morals were drawn from pagan fables, and thus the art of Christian symbolism arose. The hidden meanings were apparent only to believers; to official Roman eyes the forms looked innocent enough. The dove came to represent peace and the resurrection of Christ, the anchor represented faith, the fish became the symbol of Christ, and the phoenix and the peacock also stood for the resurrection. Gradually the artists began to represent the apostles and the leaders of the Church, and finally Christ Himself. The earliest representations of Him were as a graceful and beardless youth, not unlike a Greek god. It was not until the fourth century that He came to be shown as the grave and bearded figure so familiar today.

When Constantine established Christianity officially, he turned over to the Church many temples, baths, and basilicas. But the form of Christian worship had already grown into an elaborate ritual, and the fathers of the Church were not long content with second-hand buildings. Thus a wave of church-building started all over the empire, and the plan of the basilica was adopted as the most suitable for the purpose.

The typical Early Christian church is a three- or five-aisled basilica, with the altar placed in the apse. A small wing was usually added at each side to make more space for the priests, giving the church its cruciform plan. This cross-space is called the bema, and it was the forerunner of the transept of the Gothic church. As the number of priests increased and the ritual grew more elaborate, it became necessary to extend their area, called the choir, out into the nave. It was raised a few steps and separated from the public space by a rail, with a pulpit on each side. These rails were called *cancelli,* from which comes the word "chancel." In the earliest churches the columns separating the aisles from the nave were very close together, being connected by stone entablatures. Later they were connected by arches so they could be spaced more widely. The walls above the columns ran up to a high timber roof, and the nave was lighted by clerestory windows. It was customary for the men of the congregation to stand in one side aisle and the women in the other. In front of the church was a colonnaded atrium, derived from the atrium of the private house. The side of the atrium adjoining the church is called the narthex, which served not only as a vestibule, but as a meeting chamber for the church council. In the center of the atrium was a well or a fountain where the people were required to wash before entering the church. This was the origin of the holy-water stoup which stands in the narthex of every Roman church today.

The Early Christian builders used many materials from old Roman buildings, particularly sculptured ornament. Most of the colored marble columns were taken from temples, and they were used regardless of whether or not they were of the same color or even of the same order. If they were too short, a section was added; if they were too long, the base was cut off. The half-dome of the apse and the main arch separating the bema from the nave, called the triumphal arch, were richly decorated with glass mosaics, and if the church could afford it the mosaics were carried entirely around the clerestory walls. In the apse there was usually a gigantic head or figure of Christ on a background of gold. The other figures were austere representations of the saints and apostles. The timber ceilings were richly carved and gilded, and the floor was covered with colored marble mosaic. The exteriors of the churches were usually plain brick, although once in a while the front was covered with mosaics.

In the year 324 Constantine ordered the erection of two churches in Rome. One was to be built over the tomb of St. Peter and the other over the tomb of St. Paul. St. Peter's was a huge basilica with an enormous atrium and many surrounding buildings. According to ancient drawings and records it was magnificently decorated, but it was pulled down in the sixteenth century to make room for the great

Renaissance church of St. Peter that stands there today. All that remains of the old St. Peter's is a handsome bronze pine cone that stood in the atrium, which is now in the Giardino della Pigna of the Vatican.

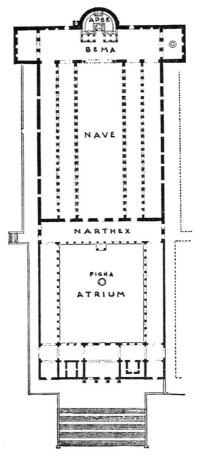

Plan of the old Basilica of St. Peter in Rome. Destroyed to make way for the present St. Peter's.

St. Peter's was not then the home church of the Popes. It was not until the new church was built that it became the headquarters of the Roman Catholic Church.

Constantine's other church is known as St. Paul's Without the Walls, for it stands a mile or so outside the city walls on the road to

Ostia where St. Paul was killed. The original church was quite small and was soon replaced by an immense building, which burned down about a hundred years ago. It was rebuilt on the original plan, and still has the undamaged fifth-century mosaics in the apse and on the

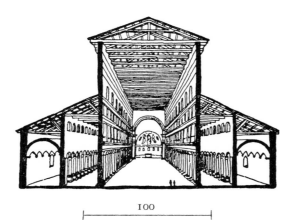

100

Sectional view of the old Basilica of St. Peter in Rome, showing the high timbered nave and the double aisles, one of which may have been barrel-vaulted.

triumphal arch. It is a magnificent church, and one of the great sights of Rome.

The early home of the Popes was the Basilica of St. John Lateran and the adjoining Lateran Palace. The basilica was given to the Church by Constantine and was remodeled to its new use; it was so thoroughly remodeled again during the Renaissance that nothing of the Early Christian church remains today except the baptistery. This little round building was built by Constantine, and still stands, the first of the circular or polygonal baptisteries.

There were thirty-one basilican churches in Early Christian Rome, and a surprising number of them are still standing. Few, however, escaped remodeling by the Renaissance Popes and their architects, so most of them have only the old mosaics of the apse left, the rest of the church being covered with the plaster finery of the late Renaissance. Santa Maria in Cosmedin is one church which more nearly has its original appearance, for the plaster ornament has been removed, revealing the simple and dignified interior of the ancient building.

Throughout Asia Minor, Syria, Palestine, and north Africa are many Early Christian churches. Christianity was not Roman by origin, but only by adoption, for it originated in the East and gained its first footholds there. Realizing the impossibility of suppressing it, the Roman governors of the eastern provinces permitted the Christians to build churches long before Rome came to that point. Indeed, it is thought that these eastern churches set the style for later Christian art, and as culture declined in Italy artists were brought from the East to do the decorative work formerly done by Romans. Diocletian's palace at Spalato shows definite Eastern influences, and most of the early experiments with domes which led to the perfected Byzantine style took place in the now deserted churches of the Syrian plains. So it is not at all unlikely that Early Christian and Byzantine art were fundamentally Eastern, grafted onto the stem of Roman tradition.

Haghia Sophia

IN SYRIA, ARMENIA, AND PERSIA ARE THE MANY BUILDINGS WHICH, coupled with the lessons learned from Rome, taught the builders of Byzantium how to construct a round dome on a square base. This problem had been bothering builders for centuries, as is indicated by the many different attempts at its solution. The problem was this: A circle drawn within a square leaves a sort of triangle in each corner. It was the support of this triangle which caused all the difficulty. The easy way out was to lay a beam across the corner, thus making an octagonal base for the dome, an octagon being so close to a circle that a circular dome could then be built upon it. Many buildings were built this way, and the method was further improved upon by building a corbel in the corner, or by throwing an arch across it instead of a beam—the latter method being called a squinch. These solutions served the purpose structurally, but they were compromises and they did not look well.

The perfect solution was finally reached in the great church of Haghia Sophia in Constantinople, built by Justinian in 532. The troublesome triangles were treated as portions of the surface of a dome *larger* than the square space beneath it. In other words, the circle was drawn outside the square instead of inside it. Since the base of this imaginary dome lay outside the square space, each of the four walls intersected it in an arch running from corner to corner. The top

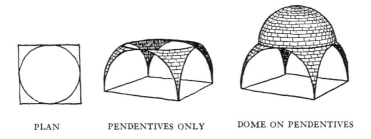

PLAN   PENDENTIVES ONLY   DOME ON PENDENTIVES

The dome on pendentives.

of this imaginary dome was then cut off just above the crown of the four arches, providing a circular base for the actual dome, apparently hanging in space above the floor. Because of this appearance of hanging in space, the curved triangles in each corner, which are all that actually exist of the imaginary dome, are called pendentives. This simple and ingenious method was satisfactory both structurally and artistically, for it was not only stable and secure but was a delight to the eye.

Justinian stands out as the greatest of the Byzantine emperors since Constantine. He sent out military expeditions which reconquered for the empire much of the lost territory in north Africa, Sicily, Italy, and southern Spain. Although he closed the school of philosophy founded by Plato at Athens, he founded a university in Constantinople, and he issued the code of Roman law which became one of the foundations of modern law. He was ambitious, a good organizer, and something of a scholar—although his Greek accent was always poor—and his wife, the Empress Theodora, was a woman of equal ability, even though she had been an actress in her youth. He was an intelligent and enthusiastic builder, so when he determined to build a great church in Constantinople he called in the best brains of his empire.

It is called the church of Haghia Sophia, which means "Divine Wisdom." The emperor sent to marble quarries all over the empire for specifications of the finest marbles obtainable in both slabs and columns. He appointed Anthemius of Tralles as chief architect, with Isodorus of Miletus as his assistant. Both were men of exceptional ability and both, it is interesting to note, were semi-orientals from Asia Minor. Work was started in the usual Byzantine manner. The walls and piers were built of concrete faced with long flat bricks. The four main piers supporting the central dome, each about twenty-five feet square, were built of blocks of hard limestone to withstand the great weight and thrust. The dome was built of special brick from the island of Rhodes, so light that five of them weighed no more than one ordinary brick. This entire mass of masonry, comprising the structural shell of the building, was allowed to dry and settle thoroughly before any of the marble veneers were applied to the interior, to avoid cracking them. Meanwhile Justinian had commanded his provincial governors to send him the finest materials of every kind. He had a temporary residence erected on the site so he could watch the progress of the work from day to day.

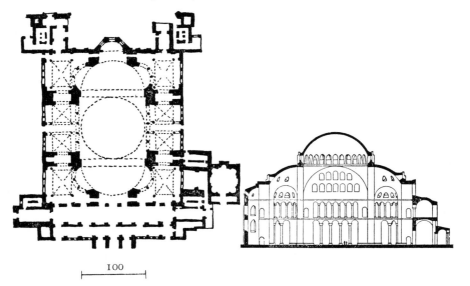

100

Plan and section of Haghia Sophia at Istanbul, still the greatest of all domed structures.

The building centers about the dome, 107 feet in diameter, which rests upon pendentives above the square central floor area. Around the base of the dome is a row of windows which not only light the interior, but considerably lighten the weight of the dome. The crown of the dome is 180 feet above the pavement—a sixteen-story building could be built inside with room to spare. To the front and rear of the central dome are two lower half-domes, and each half-dome is further enlarged by three semicircular niches. Thus there is a great oval interior space 214 feet long and 107 feet wide—high, clear, and unobstructed. On each side there are wide, two-storied aisles, and across the front an inner narthex and an outer narthex. In 558 an earthquake caused the central dome to fall, but it was immediately rebuilt, with a slightly higher curvature than the original one.

The interior walls are covered with slabs of fine marble, extending up to the spring line of the arches. The columns of the balconies and the narthexes are also of varicolored marble, with capitals of white marble carved with the delicacy of lace. The arches, domes, and pendentives are covered with glass mosaics in gold and rich colors. The effect is gorgeous beyond description, yet the decoration is always subordinate to the great dome, the dominating feature to which all lines lead. "I have surpassed thee, O Solomon," cried Justinian. Paulus Silentiarius, the court poet, wrote a poem to commemorate the opening of the church on Christmas Day, 537. Describing the interior, he says:

PLATE 17

"Who shall describe the fields of marble gathered on the pavement and lofty walls of the church? Fresh green from Carystus and many-colored Phrygian stone of rose and white, or deep red and silver; porphyry powdered with bright spots; emerald green from Sparta, and Iassian marble with waving veins of blood-red and white; streaked red stone from Lydia, and crocus-colored marble from the hills of the Moors, and Celtic stone, like milk poured on glittering black; the precious onyx like as if gold were shining through it, and the fresh green from the land of Atrax, in mingled contrast of shining surfaces."

The exterior of the church is a picturesque mass of shelving roofs and half-domes leading up to the central dome, which is considerably flattened in effect by the circular drum pierced with windows. The richness is all in the interior. The church became a Moham-

PLATE 18

medan mosque when the Turks captured the city, and although it still stands fundamentally as it was built, they did much to rob it of its splendor. The gold altar, the silver screen, and the marble, ivory, and silver pulpit have disappeared. For centuries most of the mosaics were covered with whitewash, and Islamic inscriptions disfigured the walls. After the recent formation of the Turkish republic the church was made a public monument, the whitewash was removed, and every effort was made to restore it to its original condition. It stands today as the greatest monument of the Byzantine era, 1100 years long; Haghia Sophia and the Pantheon are the greatest European buildings that have come down to us practically intact from ancient times.

The Spread of Byzantine

THERE ARE MANY EARLY CHRISTIAN AND BYZANTINE CHURCHES IN Greece, Asia Minor and farther east, and to the west there are still more. Constantine built two in Palestine, one being the Church of the Nativity in Bethlehem, a simple and dignified basilica erected over the spot where tradition says Christ was born. The other, the Church of the Holy Sepulchre in Jerusalem, built over Christ's tomb, has been greatly altered and defaced by Saracens and Christians alike.

When Ravenna was the seat of the Eastern government in the West, several Byzantine churches were built there. One is the octagonal church of San Vitale, a jewel box of glowing mosaics, built by Justinian to celebrate his recapture of the city. There are also two Early Christian basilicas, full of Byzantine craftsmanship. S. Apollinare in Classe, a basilica also built by Justinian, has a plain round brick tower beside it, one of the first of the campaniles, or
PLATE 19 bell towers, which were to become characteristic of Italian churches. Oldest of all is the tomb of Galla Placidia, sister of the Emperor Honorius. Its mosaics display the last traces of the classic realism of Greek and Roman painting, before this style was forgotten and replaced by the austere and archaic style of Byzantium.

The Palatine Chapel in Palermo and the cathedral at near-by Monreale were built in the twelfth century during the Norman rule in Sicily. Their workmanship is both Byzantine and Saracenic, and they are unrivaled in the beauty of their mosaics and marble veneers. The interior of the basilica at Monreale is severe and majes- PLATE 21 tic, yet incredibly rich and splendid in its glowing color and gold backgrounds. The wooden ceilings of both buildings show the Saracenic influence in their rich carving and coloring.

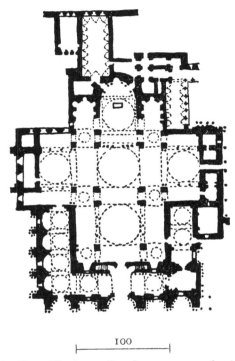

|———— 100 ————|

Plan of St. Mark's at Venice, a Greek cross covered with five domes.

In Venice there is the famous San Marco, or St. Mark's, which was built and rebuilt several times, most of what is seen today having been completed in 1063. In decoration it is a miniature Haghia Sophia, but in plan it is quite different, being in the form of a cross, with a dome over each arm and over the center, five all together. The interior is the most gorgeous in Europe, having never been despoiled. It still has its sumptuous gold and silver chancel furnishings, pulpits and altar are exquisitely carved of the rarest marbles, and beautiful mosaics gleam through the dim light from the tiny windows high

PLATE 20

in the domes. The exterior was originally as severe as most Byzantine churches, but succeeding generations added more and more decoration until it now has the fantastic and unreal appearance of a shimmering fairy palace. St. Mark's stands in a magnificent setting, at the end of a great piazza, lined on both sides with palaces.

At Périgueux, in southern France, is the church of St. Front, almost a copy of St. Mark's, although here the mosaics are gone. This church is of interest primarily because it ties French Romanesque in with the Byzantine heritage. The Frankish Emperor Charlemagne built a chapel for his palace near the Rhine in 800, at Aix-la-Chappelle or Aachen. It was copied from San Vitale at Ravenna, and some marbles and columns were brought from there. It still stands, incorporated into the later Gothic cathedral, miraculously preserved from destruction in World War II.

The churches of Russia were the step-children of Byzantium, for Russia was civilized and Christianized by the imperial court of Constantinople and the Greek Catholic Church. Older buildings, such as the interiors of the palace known as the Kremlin, at Moscow, are almost pure Byzantine. Buildings built after the fall of Constantinople in the fifteenth century, such as the Church of the Assumption, also at Moscow, show Armenian and Persian influences in their onion-shaped domes, and more strictly Russian characteristics in their great variety of complicated forms. Today the descendants of Byzantium are to be seen nearly all over the world, for Byzantine became the accepted style of architecture for the Greek Catholic Church. There is a Byzantine Greek church in almost every large American city, and among the shabby frame houses of many industrial districts there is often a little wooden Greek church, its bulbous onion-shaped dome painted yellow in imitation of gilding, a pathetic reminder of the glories of Byzantium a thousand years ago.

Byzantine Ornament

ARCHITECTURAL ORNAMENT UNDERWENT AS MANY CHANGES as did architectural form. The Eastern concept of ornamentation was over-all pattern, as opposed to the Western or classical concept of concentration of ornament in sculpture or on mouldings. Thus mouldings passed almost entirely out of use, sculpture became a minor art confined to details, and in their place appeared great areas of mosaics. Linked to the Eastern love for over-all pattern was the Eastern aversion to figure sculpture. One of the causes of the split between the Eastern and Western churches had been the fact that the Byzantine church forbade the use of the human figure in sculpture, although permitting it in painting or mosaic. When this rule was enforced in Italy it was resisted by the sculpture-loving Italians, who since their pagan days had not been able to separate some sort of image from their worship. This edict in the East had two direct effects upon art: It drove many sculptors to the West and forced others to evolve new forms based upon plant life and geometric figures. This new sculptured ornament was based upon the invention of the drill, with which deep holes were drilled in the stone to give the effect of a dark background. The surface was then carved in low relief, giving a lacelike appearance. This rich treatment was applied to capitals, rails, and screens with the same lavish hand that applied the mosaics to the walls and domes.

The design of the capitals had changed too. The concave contour of the Corinthian capital looked weak under the fat haunch of a Byzantine arch, so the architects and sculptors devised a capital with a convex contour, cleverly making the transition from the round column to the square abacus. It was the first new capital in a thousand years. Above the capital they often placed a block called an impost block. It may have been an echo of the Roman custom of inserting a piece of entablature between the capital and the arch, instead of setting the arch right on the capital; it may also have been a means of providing a larger surface for the thick brick arch to rest upon.

Byzantine architecture carried on the great Roman tradition of spatial planning, the concept of magnificent interior space. Coupled with this was the emphasis upon the central plan, that is, the plan centering about the central dome, sometimes carried to the point of complete cruciform symmetry. The Early Christian basilican interior emphasized horizontal lines, leading the eye with rows of columns, entablatures, and flat roofs to the apse, which was the dominant feature of the church. The Byzantine interior emphasized vertical lines, leading the eye upward by means of piers and half-domes to the dominating central dome.

Byzantine architecture saved the art from degenerating into mere decoration. It swept away the Roman method of applying meaningless columns and entablatures to buildings without relation to what lay behind them. It brought about a return to honest architecture, for the marbles and mosaics were frankly veneers, making no attempt to masquerade as constructive elements, and the columns were real columns actually supporting the loads above them. Byzantine art also showed that a great art need not be realistic. It was a far cry from the vivid realism of the reliefs on Trajan's column to the gaunt austerity of the mosaic figures in the apse of S. Apollinare in Classe, yet they are equally beautiful.

Byzantine art was the medieval art of the East, as Gothic was the medieval art of the West. Western Europe was in such turmoil before the year 1000 that Byzantine art got an earlier start, thus Byzantium became the center of the medieval art world, sending out artistic impulses all during the Middle Ages. As life in the West began to settle down, these scattered artistic impulses ran together here and there, and helped to produce the great art which the uncomprehending architects of the Renaissance were to call "Gothic," a term of contempt meaning "barbarous." This Gothic art was created by the races the Romans knew as northern barbarians, out of their own materials and suited to their own needs, based upon the art of the Rome they had conquered, and influenced by the art of the Byzantium they envied.

❈ VI ❈

Romanesque

BEFORE THE year 1000 the emperors in Italy and the kings in France had little real power, for they had no resources of their own and no armies, and if it had not been for the strength of the old tradition of the empire they would have had no influence at all. Control had passed into the hands of the feudal lords, the heads of the great families that owned vast estates which were worked by peasants who gave them part of their produce, and served in their armies. War was the law and the chief occupation of the barons. War against each other, against the king, and against the barbarians who constantly invaded from the east, the south and the north—the Slavs, the Hungarians, the Saracens, and the Normans. Yet government, trade, and craftsmanship were not entirely lost. The more powerful rulers carried on much of the old Roman governmental system, communication from town to town and with the East was comparatively easy, and the heritage of skills in the arts and crafts was never entirely lost.

The Church of Rome was the one great force that tied the Western world together. Although the Popes were occasionally weak men, tools of the powerful families of Italy, the local bishops increased in power and wealth to a degree that often gave them authority over civil governments and the power to appoint officials and even to wage war. Many of them were feudal lords in their own right. By

bequest, gift, and mortgage, the Church gradually acquired own-
ership of a fourth of all the land in Europe, becoming not only a
spiritual kingdom governing the souls of men, but a great temporal
state under a supreme head, with laws regulating the conduct of all
Christians, lords or serfs, and with the power to enforce them.

The rise of the monasteries was one of the sources of the power
of the Church. Although most of the monastic orders were founded
by devout priests who had become dissatisfied with the worldliness
of the Church and sought to return to the simple life led by Christ
Himself, they were human institutions and controlled by human
ambitions. So the orders increased greatly in wealth and their monasteries came to own and operate tremendous tracts of land. It was
principally in the monasteries that the learning of ancient times was
kept alive, and also the techniques of the arts and crafts. Each monastery aimed to be self-supporting, producing its own food, clothing, and implements. Thus many of them became manufactories,
selling and shipping their products all over the Western world.

Monks were the teachers of western Europe, teaching not only
religion but the arts of civilization. Many came into western Europe
from Italy, and many from Ireland. During the first centuries of
Christianity the Church fathers sent thousands of missionaries to
western Europe, and particularly to the British Isles. Later, as waves
of heathen invaders swept over the land, the work of these men
was almost wiped out, except in Ireland. Separated from the Continent, that little island was hardly disturbed. So when things began to quiet down again it was the Irish monks who set out to win
the new population to Christianity and to the ways of the ancients.
The influence of the Irish upon medieval art is of importance because the civilization which they taught was the Greek civilization
of the early Church, and because the romantic temperament of the
Irish and their art forms freely copied from nature helped turn
medieval art toward naturalism.

Among the invaders from the north who pushed their unwelcome way into Europe were the Normans, or Norsemen, who had
been raiding the coasts and rivers of northern France for a long time.
Finally, about 900, they persuaded the French king to give them
the northwest corner of France, in return for settling there and
becoming his Christian subjects. But the Normans were restless and

ambitious, and in 1066 a band under Duke William crossed the Channel and conquered England. This conquest was far-reaching in its results, for it carried Norman-French methods and traditions to the British Isles. Within a hundred years the nobility, the bishops, and the architects of England were Normans, and the dukes of Normandy were the kings of England.

During the eleventh and twelfth centuries the gradually increasing trade between the West and the East, and between different sections of the West, led to the growth of the cities as trading centers. Trade brought money, and money brought power. The fighting dukes and barons began to disappear, their power broken by the wealthy merchants, to whom they had mortgaged their lands as they previously had to the Church. City governments gradually took the place of feudal governments. Although nominally still subject to both king and Pope, the cities became practically independent states, collecting their own taxes, enforcing their own laws, and waging their own wars, often with each other. In Italy the greatest city-states were Venice, Genoa, Pisa, Florence, and Naples. In France there were Marseilles, Tours, Paris, and Bordeaux. In the north there were Ghent, Bruges, Antwerp, Bremen, and Nuremberg. And in England were London, Oxford, Cambridge, Southampton, and Dover.

The merchants and craftsmen of the cities were organized into guilds which established prices and standards, trained apprentices, took care of the aged and the sick, and prevented outside competition. There was great rivalry among the guilds for political power and favor, some of them ultimately becoming so powerful as to control the city governments. There were few manufactories in the modern sense, producing goods in quantities and selling them through retail stores. Most of the guildsmen were both manufacturers and merchants, making and selling their own goods.

Before the year 1000 few buildings were built aside from the monasteries. The monasteries, however, built great churches, with dormitories, offices, workshops, and many outbuildings. As trade and intellectual activity began to pick up, the lay pupils of the monks carried their knowledge out into the world, and gradually the precious heritage of how to make things and how to build was passed on to the people again. All medieval architecture was closely bound up with the crafts, with methods and materials, and with religious buildings. The forms of medieval architecture, although borrowed at first from ancient buildings, rapidly developed into new forms which were the logical outgrowth of the methods and materials employed. The roots of medieval architecture were firmly in the handicrafts. The architecture of the years between the rule of Charlemagne, around 800, and the thirteenth century is called Romanesque, which means "Romanish," because it was based at first upon the old Roman methods of building.

Early Romanesque

THE FEW ATTEMPTS AT CHURCH-BUILDING BEFORE THE YEAR 1000 show to what a low level the building arts had sunk. Their builders had half-ruined Roman buildings to turn to as models, but they did not have the skill or the wealth to follow them. Charlemagne's brilliant efforts were short-lived, and his chapel at Aix-la-Chapelle was in its time the most advanced building in western Europe. There is a legend that there was a guild of builders in Lombardy in the seventh century, known as the Comacini, the descendants of the master masons of Rome, who fled to an island in Lake Como when Rome was sacked by the Germans in 410, there keeping alive for generations the traditions of building vaults and domes. Certain it is that in northern Italy are found the earliest churches showing the gradual development of ribbed vaults, leading to the Romanesque style. It was not until the tenth century, however, that these and other attempts throughout western Europe, through generations of building by trial and error, began to take on the definite form which is called Romanesque.

The earlier churches are low, dark, and severe. The walls are very thick, usually of brick or small stones. Windows and doors are small and round-arched, and columns are heavy and squat, with clumsy capitals. They are generally of the basilica plan, with a semicircular apse, the Early Christian bema having been extended into full-fledged wings, giving the church a fully cruciform plan. The wings are called transepts. Many churches have timber roofs over the nave, with walls as high as the builders dared build them, in order to provide clerestory windows. The low aisles are usually vaulted with barrel or groined vaults, with a wooden roof above them. The space between the aisle vault and the roof was made into a narrow gallery with little arches opening into the upper part of the nave. This is called the triforium, and it became an accepted part of church design, soon appearing as a distinct stone gallery. Numerous efforts were made to vault the naves completely with masonry, to make them fireproof. The first are barrel vaulted, with stiffening ribs at each pier, the thrust being counteracted primarily by the massiveness of the walls, and to some extent by the vaulting of the aisles. Later naves are groin vaulted, with clustered piers sometimes replacing the single column. The clustered pier has the appearance of a series of colonnettes, or very slender columns, engaged in the main pier or column, each colonnette corresponding to a rib of the arches above.

The only interior decoration is the relatively crude carving of the Corinthianesque capitals, the many stepped or ringed mouldings of the arches, and the stringcourses separating the nave arches, the triforium, and the clerestory. There are traces remaining in some churches of painting on the plain surfaces of the walls. In the church of St. Benoît-sur-Loire, the lower portions are painted to represent draperies, and above are groups of stiffly Byzantine saints and angels—an attempt to capture some of the glory of mosaics. The exteriors are still more severe, except at the entrances, which have deeply recessed arches with many rings and colonnettes. The rings are carved with geometric and floral ornaments, and between the colonnettes are often figures of the saints and apostles. Sculpture was employed much more in Italy and southern France, where there were Roman models to follow, than in the north or in England.

Italian Romanesque

PISA IS NOW A DUSTY LITTLE ITALIAN CITY WHERE TOURISTS SHUFFLE wearily through the empty halls of its former grandeur. But in the year 1000 it was the greatest commercial and naval power in the Mediterranean, and in a burst of civic pride the Pisans built a cathedral, a baptistery, and a campanile. The architect of the cathedral was a man named Boschetto, who seems to have been a Byzantine, but who was obviously a great admirer of the Romans.

His cathedral follows the typical basilica plan with transepts. The nave has a timber ceiling, the aisles are vaulted, and there is a

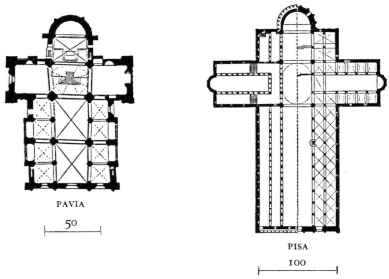

PAVIA

50

PISA

100

Plans of San Michele at Pavia and the cathedral at Pisa. (Courtesy University Prints.)

dome over the crossing, which is the intersection of the nave and the transepts. The exterior is of dazzling white marble, with occasional strips of red set in horizontal bands, and it is decorated with colonnettes and little arches in a manner which forms a sort of latticework over the entire building. Intentional irregularities have been introduced into the design, obviously to avoid an appearance of monotony and rigidity. The little arches are of slightly different heights and sizes, the long lines of the building curve upward in the middle, and the axis of the nave is slightly curved, reminiscent of the refinements of the Parthenon.

The baptistery is a circular building 129 feet in diameter, decorated with arcades inside and out similar to those on the cathedral, and covered with a high conical dome. During the Renaissance a second and spherical dome was built outside the old one, leaving the peak of the cone sticking through the top, which accounts for its peculiar silhouette. Beside the cathedral is the campanile, over one hundred and fifty feet high, the famous "Leaning Tower of Pisa." It, too, is decorated with the same delicate arcades which appear on the cathedral, each one representing a story in height. When construction reached the second story, the builders noticed that the foundation was beginning to settle on one side, causing the building to lean. They tried to straighten it as they built, and went on to the fourth story. It started to settle still more, so work was stopped for sixty years. Nothing further happening, they went on and completed it, compensating somewhat for the "lean" as they built. The Tower has continued to settle through the centuries. Today the top hangs fourteen feet out of plumb, and it is still settling.

PLATE 22

All over northern Italy are other churches which illustrate the gradual development of the Romanesque style. In Florence there is a baptistery which shows the influence of Pisa, and the old church of San Miniato. In Pavia is the church of San Michele, built about 1188. It is typical heavy Romanesque, yet its ribbed vaulting and clustered columns show kinship to the northern Romanesque churches in Caen and Durham, which were building at the same time. San Zeno Maggiore, in Verona, is another of the same type, but it never received vaulting. There is a projecting porch over the entrance, supported by two columns which stand on the backs of crouching lions, and above is a great wheel-like rose window. The barnlike bareness of the walls is relieved only by pilaster strips of slight projection and the characteristic little corbeled arches under the cornice. Even though these churches lack exterior grace and have some awkward features, since they represent a transitional rather than a perfected style, many of them attain great dignity and impressiveness.

French Romanesque

THROUGHOUT SOUTHERN AND CENTRAL FRANCE THERE ARE many churches large and small, built during the eleventh and twelfth centuries, showing the gradual growth of the Romanesque style

PLATE 24

PLATE 23

away from the low and dark to the high and light. At Vignory there is a little stone church with an interior that is almost cavern-like, and at Toulouse is the great church of St. Sernin, with a high, barrel-vaulted nave that gives a suggestion of the height and the light to come. Two of the finest examples of the architectural sculpture of the period are to be found in the portals of the church of St. Trophîme at Arles and the church at near-by St. Gilles, the latter a triple-arched entrance probably inspired by the Roman triumphal arch. The portal of St. Bartholomew's Church in New York City is a very beautiful modern use of this heavy but handsome style, taken directly from the portal at St. Gilles.

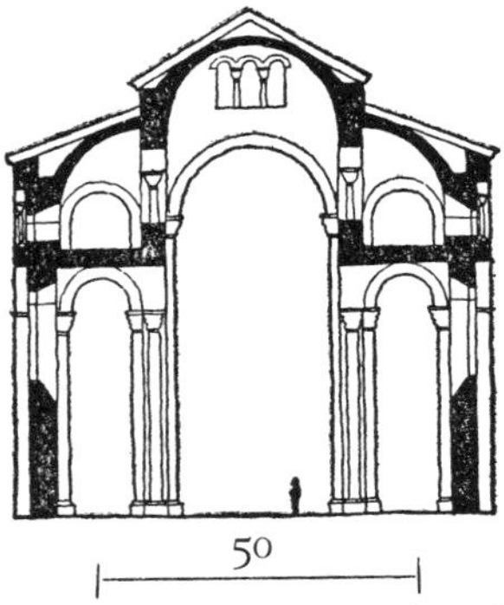

50

Section through the early Romanesque church of Notre Dame-du-Port at Clermont, showing the round nave arches buttressed by half-barrel vaults over the triforium.

When the Normans adopted the Romanesque manner of building, in their northwest corner of France, they rapidly made great improvements in it. Barrel and groined vaults required massive walls and piers to support their great weight and thrust. But massive walls were difficult and expensive to build in a country where large blocks of stone were unobtainable and labor had to be paid for in money. The Southern builders had tried to get around this by building walls of rubble stone faced with cut stone. But this was a weak and unsatisfactory method. The Normans were fortunate in having a plentiful supply of fine-grained Caen stone, which was abundant all over Normandy. The gray skies of northern France demanded large windows to let sufficient light into the vast interiors of the churches, and heavy vaulting would not permit big openings in the walls beneath. So the Normans carried to its logical conclusion the system of stiffening ribs which had been developed in the South. They built cross ribs from pier to pier, and then diagonal ribs from pier to pier. Each rib was a separate and complete arch, and together they formed a complete skeleton frame for the vaulting that was to come, resting on the piers, not on the walls. Then they filled in the triangular spaces between the ribs with a very light shell of thin stone vaulting, springing from one rib to another.

Two types of such vaulting were developed. In the simpler type the four piers of each bay are connected by cross ribs and diagonal ribs, thus dividing the bay into four parts. This is called quadripartite vaulting. In the other type two bays of the nave walls are grouped to make one bay of the nave vaulting. Thus there are six piers to each bay. They are each connected by cross ribs, but the diagonal ribs skip the center piers and cross from one corner pier to the other. This divides the bay into six parts, so it is called sexpartite vaulting.

It is not clear just where this system originated. Apparently the same solution was arrived at simultaneously in at least three localities—Normandy, Durham in England, and Milan in Italy—during the last years of the eleventh century. Doubtless all were the outcome of parallel developments, and doubtless, too, there was an interchange of ideas, since skilled artisans and mechanics traveled freely all over Europe.

By this method a complete stone ceiling was built, of light weight, not supported by the walls beneath it but by the piers upon which the ribs rested. The walls between the piers could be but thin curtain walls, with as many windows in them as desired, for they supported nothing. This may sound just like the solution the Romans arrived at a thousand years before, but it was not. The Roman groined vault, although supported by its piers and not the walls, was a solid masonry vault of immense weight requiring tremendous piers. The ribbed vault was of light weight and could be carried on very slender piers. It was the first step in the development of a new principle which was to free masonry construction of its great weight, making possible soaring vaults and expanses of glass such as the world had never seen before.

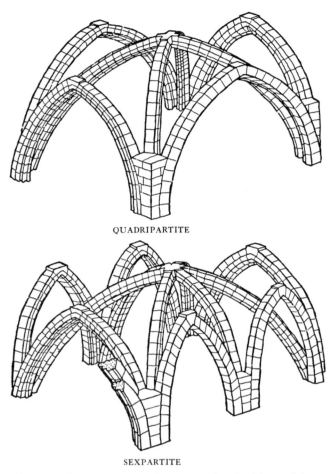

QUADRIPARTITE

SEXPARTITE

The two basic types of rib systems in Gothic vaulting.

Just before William the Conqueror set out for England in 1066 he commenced building two abbey churches in Caen, his principal city in Normandy, St. Étienne for men and la Trinité for women. Both churches are still standing, and are beautiful examples of the fine and rugged simplicity of the Norman Romanesque. La Trinité was severely damaged during World War II, but has been restored. St. Étienne, which escaped damage, is high and light, and has a very different aspect from the low and dark churches of the

South. The piers are clustered, each colonnette corresponding with perfect logic to a rib of the vaulting above. The low round arches between the nave and the aisles rest upon short columns which are engaged in the clustered colonnettes of the piers. There is a gallery

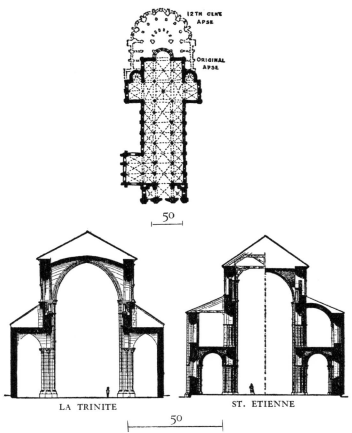

Sections of the abbeys at Caen, showing two methods of buttressing the nave vaulting. The plan is of St. Étienne.

over the aisles, roofed by a continuous half-barrel vault which stops the thrust of the nave vaulting by pushing directly against it. This is an application of the principle of counterthrust. The thrust of the nave vaulting in la Trinité was taken care of by the massiveness of

the walls and piers—the old principle of dead weight. On the out-
PLATE 26 side of la Trinité the wall was thickened a little opposite each interior
pier. This strip of masonry projecting from the wall is called a buttress. It furnishes additional support at the point where the thrust is
the greatest.

The interiors of the Norman churches are cold and bare today,
but they used to glow with color. The now bare spaces of the walls
were covered with pictures, painted on the stone in low-toned red,
yellow, and black, each with its story in verse low on the wall beneath where it could be read. The drawing was crude, but the color
PLATE 25 was rich and mellow. The floor was tiled in many colors and patterns, and the vaulting glowed with stars and emblems of gold and
silver. Above the altar were images of silver and gold, bronze, and
alabaster, and there were rich-dyed hangings and tapestries, em-
PLATE 27 broidered screens, and carved woodwork. Richest of all, the windows were filled with deep-toned stained glass, sparkling and jewel-
like. The churches were like the tapestries that hung on their walls,
rough and plain on one side but rich and glowing on the other.

The exteriors are very simple. There is little sculpture, even at
the portals. The doors and windows have receding arches, with colonnettes at the sides, or jambs, and under the eaves are tiny arches
resting on miniature colonnettes, one of the favorite Romanesque
motives. Both of the churches at Caen had two towers at the front
or west end. Thus the triple composition of the front expresses the
triple composition of the plan, the central nave with two aisles. The
transepts are no longer low wings, they have become as high and
as wide as the nave, thus definitely emphasizing the crosslike form
of the building. Both of William's churches had towers over the crossing, supported by four great arches and the four central piers. All
the towers of St. Étienne have spires, but they were added later.

In southern France and in Italy, where there is little rainfall
and no frost, the roofing tiles were usually laid directly upon the
stone vaulting. But in the North, where it rains a great deal and the
winters are long and freezing, it was found necessary to protect the
stone more carefully. So a wooden roof was built above the masonry,
pitched steeply to throw off the rain and snow. During the nineteenth century some of those of wood construction were replaced by
iron.

St. Étienne at Caen.

The man who seems to have had more to do with the development of Norman architecture than any other single individual was a Norman only by adoption; he was a Lombard Italian by birth. William of Volpiano went to the monastery at Cluny as a young monk, and although he was not actually trained in architecture, as were some monks, he knew a great deal more about building than did most people of his time. Put in charge of building a church at Dijon, he sent to Italy for "masters of divers arts and others full of science." As a result of his good work there he was invited to Normandy by the reigning duke, where he founded and built forty new monasteries and restored many old ones.

The Monasteries

SAINT GALLEN, A LITTLE CITY IN SWITZERLAND, CONTAINS THE ruins of one of the most ancient and most celebrated of all monasteries. It was founded by an Irish Benedictine monk named St. Gall in 614, and was extensively rebuilt by Charlemagne. In connection

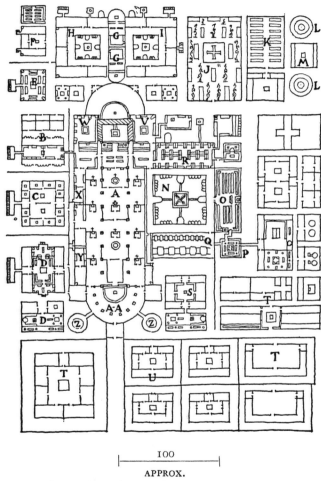

100

APPROX.

A tracing of the ancient plan of the monastery at St. Gall. (See opposite page for key to plan.)

with it is one of the most remarkable documents which has been preserved from the early Middle Ages. It is a plan of the entire group
of monastic buildings, drawn in red ink on two large sheets of
parchment. Quite possibly this is the very plan that Einhard, Charlemagne's architectural adviser, turned over to the abbot in charge of
the construction. Near the center of the group is the church, so
located that the public can reach it without penetrating the privacy
of the rest of the monastery. It has a long nave with two aisles, no
transepts, and a semicircular apse at each end. In the west apse is
the choir, with two belfries adjoining, and in the eastward apse is
the altar and the crypt, the vaulted cellar under the altar, which
contains the holy relics. On the south side is the cloister, with one
wall against the church. It is a covered walk enclosed by arches, surrounding an enclosed garden where the monks strolled and con-
versed. The buildings surrounding the cloister contain the chapter
hall, which was the meeting hall for the governing body of the monastery; the dormitory, a long and narrow hall where the monks
slept; and the refectory, which was their dining hall, with a pulpit
from which a brother read to them as they ate. Adjoining the refectory is the kitchen, with great ovens, each with its chimney, and

---

Key to the ancient plan of the monastery at St. Gall.

A-A	*Public Entrance*	M	*Cistern*
A	*Church*	N	*Cloister*
B	*Abbot's House*	O	*Refectory*
C	*Public School*	P	*Kitchen*
D	*Guest Houses*	Q	*Wine Cellar*
E	*Dispensary*	R	*Dormitory*
F	*Doctor's House*	S	*Public Hospital*
G	*Small Churches*	T	*Stables*
H	*Infirmary & Cloister*	U	*Barns*
I	*Novices' Residence & Cloister*	V	*Vestry*
J	*Cemetery & Orchard*	W	*Library*
K	*Vegetable Gardens*	X	*Schoolmaster's Residence*
L	*Granaries*	Y	*Porter's Residence*
		Z	*Towers*

near by are the wine presses, the brewery, and the extensive cellars.

Surrounding this group is a square of buildings and outbuildings—the abbot's residence, with its cloister, the library, also with a cloister, and adjoining them, the cemetery. There is an infirmary and a guest house, for the monasteries were always hospitable to travelers. There are stables and barns, mills and granaries, and workshops for various trades and crafts. Lying beyond these outbuildings are vege-

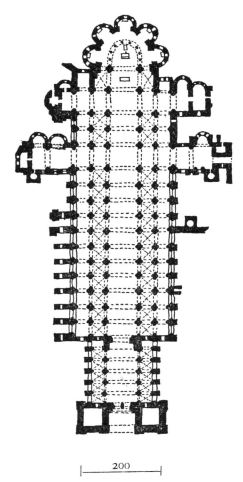

200

Plan of the Benedictine abbey at Cluny, the greatest church in Christendom in the eleventh century.

table gardens, and beyond them are rolling pastures. Like all medieval monasteries, it was an almost completely self-contained community, producing all that it needed. This same general plan has continued in use for Benedictine monasteries through all the centuries.

The headquarters of the Benedictine order was the abbey church at Cluny, which became the greatest church in Christendom in its

1. Church   2. Chapter House   3. Cloister Garth   4. Dormitory   5. Refectory
6. Kitchen   7. Cellar   8. Infirmary   9. Misericorde   10. Cemetery   11. Abbots
House   12. Well   13. Orchard   14. Prison   15. Fish Pond   16. Mill   17. Guest
House   18. Stables   19. Almonry   20. Barn

A typical Benedictine monastery in England.

time. In 1088 the little church which had long stood there was re-built and enlarged on a tremendous scale. The new church had a very long vaulted nave 99 feet high, with double aisles on each side and two transepts. The narthex was extended so that it formed a second church in front of the main church, making the entire length 615 feet. The apse was toward the east, which became traditional for all Christian churches, and was semicircular, with small chapels fitted in between the outer piers. The round apse with radiating chapels is called a chevet, and its circular aisle is called the ambula-tory. The chevet became a characteristic of nearly all French churches. The west front had a monumental carved and poly-chromed portal, with symbolic figures arranged in a great story-telling panorama. There were many classical touches in the mould-ings, capitals, and pilaster strips, and Saracenic influences in the decorative horseshoe arches of the triforium and the pointed arches of the aisles. It was perhaps the first church that attained the aspiring interior proportions seen in Gothic cathedrals two hundred years later. Truly a majestic building conceived on a grand scale, it was worthy of being the "capitol church of a monastic empire." It stood until the time of the French Revolution; now there is little left but a pile of crumbled ruins in a field.

English Romanesque

BUILDING TRADITIONS IN ENGLAND, AS IN FRANCE, DATE BACK to Roman times, but most of the Roman buildings were destroyed by the barbarian tribes which overran the island after the Romans withdrew about 420. When the Angles and the Saxons arrived from northern Europe a few years later, they brought no building tra-ditions with them, for they had none. But after St. Augustine, sent out from Rome, converted the King of Kent to Christianity in 597, monks came from Italy and building started up again. The earliest churches were built of wattles and mud—twigs woven together and plastered with clay. According to legend, the first was built "of twisted wands" by Joseph of Arimathea at Glastonbury. Here he is supposed to have buried the Holy Grail, which he had brought from the Holy Land. It was later rebuilt in stone, added to and enlarged again, and today the vine-covered ruins of Glastonbury Abbey stand there.

Remains of the Saxon stone churches and their towers dot the British Isles. They are heavy and crude, resembling two buildings

Saxon buildings in England seem to carry out in stone their original wooden forms as in these sketches of Earl's Barton.

placed end to end, the larger one being the nave and the smaller the chancel. Their earliest towers are round, no doubt adapted from the round fortress towers the monks built for protection against pirates and hostile unbelievers. At Earl's Barton, in Sussex, is a square Saxon tower attached to a much later church. It is built of rubble stone, with cut stone at the corners, and is decorated with strips of smooth stone set into the wall in obvious imitation of timberwork.

Just before the Norman conquest, Edward the Confessor, the last Saxon king, imported the Norman Romanesque style to England for the rebuilding of Westminster Abbey. After the conquest, Norman methods spread rapidly all over the land. The conquerors built new cathedrals and minsters, and rebuilt the old ones in their own style. The difference between a cathedral and a minster or an abbey is that a cathedral is the head church of a diocese, the seat of the bishop, while a minster is the church of an abbey or monastery. Many of the present English cathedrals were built originally as abbeys.

The English Norman style is similar in many ways to the Romanesque of northern Italy, for it is, of course, Romanesque. The

Some English Norman details.

cathedral at Pisa and St. Mark's in Venice were building at the same time that Duke William was building his abbeys in Caen, and setting himself up as king of England. Most of the Norman churches have a central tower rising over the crossing; some have ponderous pillars and massive arches of many rings, others have clustered columns and broad arches. Their walls are very thick, but rather poorly built, which has made it difficult to preserve some of them. Although they were obviously intended to have vaulted ceilings, it is doubtful if any of the vaults were built until about two hundred years later. Some of them were never vaulted and still have timber ceilings. The windows are small and the exteriors are very plain. No cathedral stands completely Norman today, for their construction extended over centuries, and each building shows the entire progress of English medieval architecture. Furthermore, most of the Norman churches were at least partially remodeled into later styles; sometimes the piers and arches were actually recarved into the more elaborate Gothic.

The cathedral at Peterborough has a Norman nave, with a very old timbered ceiling. Durham also has a Norman nave, with enormous round columns carved with flutes, zig-zags, and chevrons. Winchester has Norman transepts, and Norwich has a Norman choir. From these three parts one might form a complete picture of a Norman cathedral. There are other Norman buildings, however, which have not been altered so much.

PLATE 28

In the hamlet of Iffley, just outside of Oxford, there is a tiny parish church which has lost little of its original Norman character. It has no transepts, and a square tower rises in the center, separating the nave from the chancel, its rough gray stone walls undecorated except for two small round-arched openings on each face near the top and the little corbeled arches above them. The west front has a central arched entrance, each ring of which is decorated with heavy zig-zag "dogtooth" ornament which carries right down to the ground. Above it is a rose window, also surrounded by dogtooth, and in the stone gable are three round-arched windows with colonnettes, which are again surrounded by the inevitable dogtooth. The nave has a timber ceiling, and between it and the vaulted chancel are the heavy dogtoothed arches supporting the central tower. Some later Gothic windows undoubtedly admit more light than the narrow little building originally had, but even with them the interior is dark and cavernous.

The Romanesque System

TO SAY THAT ROMANESQUE IS A TRANSITIONAL STYLE IS TO DO IT AN injustice, for it achieved some noble monuments, and it is the style of most of the buildings erected in western Europe for six hundred years, from the fall of Rome to the end of the twelfth century. Yet Romanesque started as a crude assembling of Roman fragments and Roman structural techniques, from which the builders gradually found the key to a system of building, and developed through slow stages into a series of brilliant experiments with new structural principles, which in turn led to the perfection of the Gothic system of building. Thus it seems always to have been a style which was shaping itself toward a goal which was attained under another name. The Greeks early arrived at a simple structural system satisfactory to them and devoted their efforts to refining it architecturally. The Romans perfected several more complex systems and devoted their talents to decorating them. But the unknown master builders of the dark centuries when western Europe was struggling to re-civilize and re-Christianize itself did not achieve results which could be called a system until so late in their epoch that the ultimate flowering of their system belongs to another age.

The noble round-arched churches of the eleventh and twelfth centuries, however, can take their places with the finest of Europe's buildings. They began to achieve again that sense of fine interior space which had characterized the great Roman buildings, and which was to be one of the glories of Gothic architecture. And what they lack in unity and perfection they make up in original and interesting detail, sober dignity, and rugged simplicity.

❋ VII ❋

Gothic

THE THIRTEENTH CENTURY in western Europe was to the Middle Ages what the Age of Pericles was to Athens, and the Age of Augustus was to Rome. It was an age of remarkable artistic and poetic production, of unrivaled philosophical and legal wisdom, of military expeditions and great commercial and communal enterprises, and of a very genuine and widespread religious enthusiasm. All these factors contributed to a tremendous activity in building throughout the land, for there was a need for buildings everywhere—churches, city halls, guild halls, hospitals, fortifications, castles, and houses. Of these, the churches are the most spectacular and the most beautiful, and also the most important in the development of architecture, for it was in them that the structural experiments were made that made the Gothic system possible.

The Church, the cities, and the guilds were at the height of their power. The rivalry between the prosperous cities led them to race with each other to build the largest and the highest cathedral, the competition between the powerful guilds led them to vie with each other in contributing, and the religious fervor of the people led them to give generously of their money and their labor. Thus there was an era of church-building such as has never been seen before or since. In Henry Adams' priceless book on the Middle Ages, *Mont St. Michel and Chartres,* there is an estimate that during the hundred years from 1170 to 1270 eighty cathedrals were built in France, and five hundred great churches. That was the church-building of one century in one country, and the wave of building lasted for nearly three centuries all over western Europe.

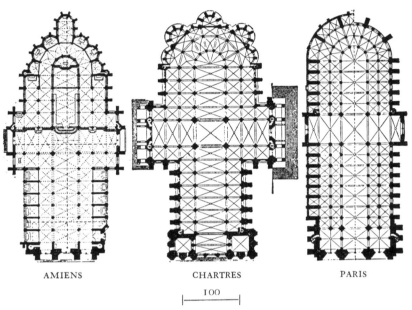

AMIENS   CHARTRES   PARIS

|———————100———————|

Plans of three great French cathedrals. (Courtesy University Prints.)

The fertile green area in the heart of France, surrounding Paris and south to the river Loire, which was most closely under the control of the king, has always been known as the Île de France. It was here, during the latter part of the twelfth century, that the Gothic system of building was born.

The nave arches of the Norman churches were round, so the diagonal arches had to be elliptical in order to cover the greater span in the same height as the cross arches. But the elliptical arch, being long and flat, was weak and unstable. So it was discovered that if the diagonal ribs were built as round arches, the cross ribs could be abbreviated into pointed arches. This was the first step in the development of the Gothic system. The pointed arch in itself was nothing new, for it had long been used decoratively in the East, but this application of it was an entirely new principle. Furthermore, the use of the pointed arch solved another problem, for round arches of different widths came to different heights, but pointed arches of any widths could be brought to any desired heights. Then came step number two. It was discovered that since all the weight and thrust was concentrated at the piers, there was need for a counterthrust only at those piers, and not along the entire length of the nave wall as at St. Étienne. So the shallow buttresses of the Normans were made much deeper, projecting far from the clerestory wall on the exterior of the building, often the full width of the aisle, in which case the aisle was arched under them.

The competitive race for the highest vaulting led to piers of great size, for they not only had to support the weight of the vaulting, but also had to resist the lateral thrust coming from such a great height, which meant they had to be very large at the base to prevent their overturning. Such piers occupied a great deal of floor space and necessitated much expensive stonework, so step number three was inevitable. Outside the wall of the side aisle a massive pier or buttress was built, carried up to about the level of the spring line of the nave vaulting. From this buttress a half-arch was built across to the rib of the nave arch, contacting the latter at the point where the thrust was the greatest. This is called a "flying buttress," and   PLATE 36
served as a bridge to carry the lateral thrust of the nave vaulting across to the outer buttress, which was massive enough to absorb the load. It might also be considered a prop which, leaning against the nave vaulting, kept the vaulting from pushing apart. Thus the piers of the nave could be very slender, for they now carried only weight, no longer having to resist any thrust.

In perfecting the buttress, the builders soon found that if it were weighted on top it did not have to be so massive at the base. Thus the pinnacles on top of so many buttresses are not only ornaments, they are weights. With the desire for more light in the interior of the cathedrals, and no doubt under pressure from the guild of stained-

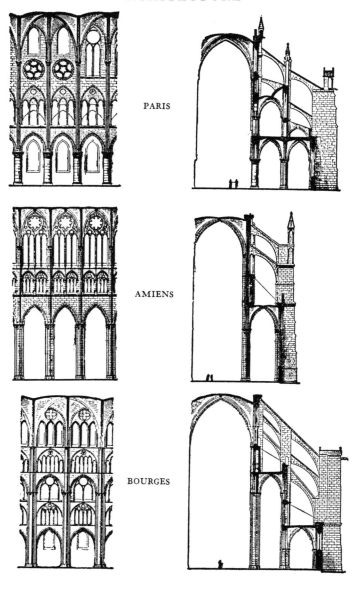

PARIS

AMIENS

BOURGES

50

Sections of three French cathedrals showing the intricate system of buttressing. (Courtesy University Prints.)

glass makers, the builders discovered that the entire clerestory wall, from pier to pier, could be window. Now that the real structure was a skeleton frame, like the steel frame building of today, the walls could be filled in with any material—stone or glass—as need and climate dictated.

One of the factors which made the Gothic system possible was the use of small pieces of building stone laid with thick mortar joints. This made the masonry sufficiently elastic to withstand the constant thrusts and strains. Monolithic columns, great masses of concrete, such as the older civilizations had used, would have been too rigid. There is little doubt that the early wooden churches of northern Europe, such as are still standing in the Scandinavian countries, were one of the influences which led to the development of the Gothic system. Wood is naturally flexible and the development of Gothic was the development of the means of making inflexible stone do the work of flexible wood. Building was done largely by trial and error. Structural engineering was not then the exact science it is today. An architect or master builder had a certain accumulated experience, his own and that of the tradition behind him, but innovations and improvements had to be tested for proof. As a result of the builder's daring, many a building collapsed before completion and had to be rebuilt heavier and stronger than before.

Structurally the Gothic cathedral is the opposite of the Greek temple. The post and lintel system is static, inherently stable, and obedient to the laws of gravity. Everything solemnly pushes downward, weight being the only force. But the Gothic system seems to defy the laws of gravity. It is dynamic, pushing in every direction, and every push is counteracted by another push from the opposite direction. The slender vertical supports depend for their stability upon being propped by the buttresses. Every part is dependent upon every other part. Theoretically, if one stone in any part of the skeleton frame were removed the entire structure would fall, arch by arch. Fortunately the fabric of a Gothic cathedral is not so fragile in actuality, in fact the reverse is true, due to its flexibility. World War II left many cathedrals and churches standing almost intact, while the area around them had been leveled by bombing, a tribute to the ruggedness of the apparently fragile Gothic buildings.

Since the pointed arch became the dominant form in the structural system, the designers, with their careful sense of logic, made it the keynote of the decorative system. All openings were covered with pointed arches, with an occasional flat lintel for contrast. Since the dominant line of the structure was vertical, it was emphasized wherever possible. The great nave piers often rise a hundred feet or more in sheer unbroken lines to the spring of the arches, formed of a cluster of colonnettes to emphasize their vertical sweep. As the windows grew larger and larger, they were broken up into smaller divisions by vertical stone shafts called mullions, which blossomed at the top into graceful curved tracery.

The early cathedrals were simple and often austere, but gradually richer and more fanciful forms of decoration were evolved, until by the fifteenth century the churches were lavished with flowing curved lines, carved figures and forms, and elaborate spires and pinnacles. The double-curved line, like a flattened letter "S," occurring in the tracery of late Gothic, has a flamelike appearance, from which comes the name "Flamboyant"; it is applied to late fourteenth- and fifteenth-century Gothic. The earlier churches are often finer than the later ones; their simplicity is one of the sources of their beauty and appeal. In the hands of architects of little taste and too much ingenuity the Flamboyant style easily became gaudy and overloaded with ornament, and it probably would have strangled itself with its own finery had it not been replaced by the new style of the Renaissance.

The interior of a Gothic cathedral conveys a sense of great spaciousness and immense height. The long, dim vista toward the apse draws the eye to the altar, and at the same time the soaring vertical lines of the piers give a sensation of great height overhead. The glimpses of chapels and windows through shadowy faraway arches arouse a feeling of mystery and awe. It seems as though there is worked into the very fabric of the walls an emotional and devotional quality that arouses the deepest reverence in the beholder. The trained eye will follow with delight the sweep of the lines of the piers, blossoming out into the fanlike vaulting above, then follow them downward again, noting the logic and order with which the thrusts are balanced and the loads carried to the ground. All the structural elements are exposed—the ribs, the piers, the buttresses—clean and strong, seldom cluttered with ornamentation.

They alone form the decoration, sculpture being limited, in the finest examples, to capitals and bases. Although long and narrow and high, the proportions are satisfying, often noble. It is space, beautifully proportioned and magnificently enclosed. The impression is not so much of one great unified whole, revealing itself all at once, as in Haghia Sophia, but rather of space extending in many directions, luring the eye far away and upward and around corners, always with the suggestion of more space and more beauties to be found.

The form of the exterior is the logical outcome of the form of the interior and of the methods of construction. The long ridge of the steeply pitched roof over the nave, intersected by the roof of the transepts, the high clerestory windows beneath, the shelving roof of the aisles under the flying buttresses, and the flaring buttresses around the chevet, are all the strictly functional expressions of the elements of the building. There is more applied decoration on the exterior than on the interior. The towers of the west façade, the portals between them, the frequent portals in the transepts, and the buttress piers are all richly sculptured with figures, floral forms, lacelike canopies, tracery, and spires.

Sculpture and Stained Glass

ARCHITECTURE IS always the "mother of the arts," but never was it more so than during the Middle Ages, and the Church was the mother of architecture. Great works were accomplished in sculpture and the crafts, but seldom for their own sake, for they were invariably accessory to architecture or to use.

Gothic sculpture developed rapidly from the stiff and archaic figures of Romanesque times. The art had had to be learned all over again, for few medieval sculptors ever saw any of the ancient works of Greece and Rome. The Byzantine influence which reached them set an ideal of abstract and decorative beauty, but it was of little help in their efforts to attain naturalism. Sculpture of the twelfth century was still archaic, and the figures stiffly architectural, as though partaking of the character of the building of which they are a part. Yet they have a dignity, charm, and grace which was only too easily lost when the art became more naturalistic. The Byzantine influence appears in the poise of the figures and in the treatment of the folds of the draperies. But they are youthful figures; Christ and the Virgin are young and sweet-looking, even the kings and prophets of the Old Testament have young faces under their curling beards. The figures of Byzantine mosaics and enamels are hoary with age.

A century later, sculptured figures were more natural and less stiff, but they had not yet lost the serenity and dignity of the early work. During the fourteenth and fifteenth centuries, however, as architecture became Flamboyant, sculpture became flamboyant too. It showed the development of a marvelous technical skill, but like the sculpture of later Greece, as it gained in physical perfection it lost in spiritual grace.

Although sculpture abounds on Gothic churches, it is principally limited to a few focal points of the exterior structure, such as about the portals and on the spires, and to the interior furnishings. Foliage and fanciful figures, in addition to the Biblical and historical characters, were the delight of Gothic sculptors, and they are found in twining forms of acanthus, oak and grape leaves, and birds, animals, and grotesque monsters. The stonecarvers were allowed full fancy, and there was no limit to their imagination, but they kept their decoration strictly subordinate to the structural lines of the building. It was when that sense of fitness began to disappear that the style began to deteriorate.

Nearly all medieval sculpture was "building sculpture," not "studio sculpture." It was carved of building stone, not of the finest marbles, and carved on the spot where it was to stand, not in the studio of an artist. The sculptor usually worked in a temporary building erected beside the church, but often it was necessary for him to work on a scaffolding high on the façade. Of all the hundreds of figures adorning the exterior of a cathedral, not one was too small or too far out of sight to be executed with the greatest care. Scores of figures are hidden away where no ordinary visitor could ever see them. Unsought and unpraised, these little-known masterpieces have stood for centuries exposed to the winds and rains of countless seasons.

Gothic sculpture was by no means limited to stone. No age in history has turned out so much and such fine woodcarving as the Middle Ages. Most of it was church furniture—choir stalls, altars, reredoses, organ lofts, screens, pulpits, and pews. They were decorated with all the details of Gothic architecture in miniature, tiny buttresses with pinnacles and finials, pointed arches with delicate tracery, little figures standing in tiny niches under exquisite canopies, and bands and clusters of grape vines, oak leaves, flowers, and animals.

The greatest craft of the Middle Ages was stained-glass making. Although great quantities of medieval glass have been lost through centuries of wars and weather, revolutions and Reformation, there are still thousands of great windows full of beautiful, glowing colors. A stained-glass window is a transparent mosaic formed of bits of stained and painted glass held together by H-shaped strips of lead. The knowledge of glassmaking was very ancient, but the use of glass in windows had been rare, although Justinian employed glassworkers to make windows for Haghia Sophia. The oldest known stained-glass window is in the cathedral at Dijon, and it has been traced back to 820. It was not until the twelfth century, however, that glazed windows became at all common, and then only in buildings of major importance.

The design of the early windows was simple; usually a single figure stood against a plain background, surrounded by a border of foliage. Gradually the figures became more elaborate, and suggestions of an architectural background were added, such as the niche used for Gothic sculpture. By the twelfth century there were two types of designs for lancet windows—a lancet is a single window PLATE 33 without tracery. One was the single large figure, the other was a series of small medallions, or groups of figures surrounded by circular or geometric borders, one above the other. Early rose windows had spokelike tracery radiating from the center, with medallions in the larger openings and spots of color in the small ones. The large windows of the fourteenth and fifteenth centuries were divided by stone mullions which branched into flowing tracery at the top, and the rose windows by flamboyant tracery of great beauty. As the glass-makers learned how to make larger pieces of glass, their designs became more free and naturalistic, with more dependence upon drawing on the glass and less upon the lead lines, so the figures lost much of their stiffness. But when complete naturalism was achieved, much beauty was lost, for color and its proper placing, regardless of realism, is the most important element in the design of a stained-glass window.

The northernmost of the three twelfth-century lancet windows

PLATE 32

in the west front of Chartres Cathedral is considered to be one of the most beautiful stained-glass windows in the world. It represents the Tree of Jesse, or the genealogy of Christ. Jesse, the father of David, lies on the ground at the bottom of the window. A tree which springs from his side grows up through the nine panels of the window in a conventionalized pattern, and upon its branches are the kings and prophets of Israel. Next to the top is the figure of Mary, and above her is Christ. The figures are surrounded by a pattern of curling and twining branches against a luminous blue background which ascends the full height of the window. The center panels are bordered by side panels containing minor figures on a red background, and there is a narrow border of floral and geometrical forms running around the entire window.

Thus the stained glass, and also the sculpture, was not meant for decoration alone. It carried a much deeper significance, for every figure and picture told a story. The pictures of the Early Christian painters had grown over a thousand years into a vast language of symbolism by which the people of the Middle Ages, few of whom could read, were taught the stories of the Bible, the parables of Christ, and the lives of the saints. The Creation, the Flood, the Annunciation, the Nativity, the Miracles of Christ, the Crucifixion, and the Resurrection are told over and over again—in stone, in wood, and in glass. Each saint has a symbol by which he can be distinguished, and it was a part of everybody's heritage to know these symbols. St. Paul has a scroll in his hand, St. Peter holds the keys of Heaven, St. Matthew has a purse, St. Catharine has her wheel of martyrdom, and St. Mark is accompanied by a lion. Not only religious stories were represented, for the Greek philosophers, the Roman emperors, and all the traditions and history of the past are also there. The symbolic decoration of a medieval cathedral is a pictorial encyclopaedia, a compendium of the knowledge of its time.

The Cathedral at Chartres

THE CATHEDRAL AT CHARTRES STANDS ON A LOW HILL RISING from the rolling plains of Orléanais. It dominates the low buildings of the town clustered about it, and its spires can be seen for twenty miles around. Thus is the sky line of every medieval town dominated by its cathedral, for the cathedrals were built as big and as high as men knew how to build.

The history of Chartres goes back to Roman times, for in the foundations of the cathedral there are traces of Roman city walls, and there was a Christian church there in the time of Constantine. Early in the eleventh century a fire destroyed the Romanesque church which stood on the site, and in 1194, as a new building was being completed (it was still filled with scaffolding and debris), another great fire swept through and destroyed all but the towers and west front. Again the townsfolk were called upon to give their money as their ancestors had before. Preachers traveled all over France gathering gifts; the wealthy gave money, jewels, and land; the peasants gave grain and vegetables; those who could give nothing gave their labor. It was a remarkable example of widespread communal effort. The rebuilding went along quickly, and by 1230 the cathedral was practically completed as it is seen today, an early Gothic building. Other cathedrals were to be bigger, others were to be higher, and still others were to be richer in decoration, but Chartres established the type of the great communal pilgrim's church. It is severe, rugged, and irregular, but it represents the highest expression of Gothic art. PLATE 31

A visitor's first trip to the cathedral should be on a gray day, for Gothic developed under the gray skies of northern France. In brilliant sunshine the broken surfaces of the exterior, with its many buttresses and arches and its sculptured figures and ornament, become a jumble of shadows and highlights. But by the soft light of a gray day the effect is one of serenity. Inside, too, the soft light is better. Yellow sunshine does injustice to the colors of the stained glass, for it also was PLATE 30 designed for the white light of gray skies. The interior seems dim when first stepping through the western door, but as one's eyes become accustomed to the subdued light one sees first the jeweled windows gleaming high in the distant apse, and then the great clustered piers rising to the pointed arches above, the delicate triforium, and the bold clerestory windows. The proportions are satisfying and there is great dignity in the simplicity of Chartres.

The plan of the cathedral is similar to the plans of the abbeys at Caen—in fact, the French cathedral plan became well standardized, differing only in details. When Chartres was rebuilt the last time, the old west front, which had escaped the fire, was taken down stone by stone and rebuilt flush with the front of the towers, thus adding nearly forty feet to the length of the nave. The inside length is 428 feet, and it is 150 feet wide across the transepts. It is said to hold 10,000 people without crowding. The quadripartite vaulting is 120 feet high at the crossing, and two feet higher at the west end because the floor slopes downward from the center. Crowds of pilgrims used to sleep in the church, and it was necessary to flush it out to keep it clean. The nave has but one aisle on each side, but the apse has two, the better to accommodate the pilgrims. There are Renaissance decorations in the choir, the work of ambitious churchmen of the eighteenth century, but they do not mar the effect of the whole.

The clerestory windows, above the triforium, are simple lancets in pairs, with a small rose above each pair. At the end of each transept and at the west end there is a gigantic rose window, with lancets below. Nearly all these windows still have their glorious thirteenth-century stained glass. During both World Wars it was all removed and stored away in the crypt, safe from bombs and shellfire. There are 124 of these great windows, and over 50 roses large and small, filled with glowing blood reds and sparkling azure blues.

As the glory of the interior is the glass, so the glory of the exterior is the sculpture. That of the west portal is from the original twelfth-century church. The figures flanking the entrances seem archaic, being long and thin, with stiff draperies, but they are purposely so, for they are architectural sculpture, partaking of the character of the colonnettes to which they are attached. At the same time they are graceful and thoughtful, and are considered to be the most beautiful in the church.

The porches of the north and south transepts are remarkable. They are about 120 feet wide and 20 feet deep, divided into three bays, each of which is covered with a pointed barrel vault. Beside the doors are exquisite figures of the saints and apostles, larger than life. Each PLATE 29 stands on a pedestal, with a stone canopy over his head. In the tympanum over each door are groups of Biblical figures in relief, and in the rings of the receding arches above are hundreds of tiny figures, portrayals of all the great of history. There are over seven hundred figures in each porch. These beautiful portals were the gift of the royal family of France, the north porch being dedicated to the Virgin

Mary and telling the story of the Old Testament, and the south porch being dedicated to Christ and telling the story of the New Testament and the saints.

Of the two western towers, only the one toward the south was completed according to the original design, and it is the finest tower in France. It slips from its square base to its octagonal spire so gracefully that one scarcely realizes the transition has taken place. The other spire was not built until the fifteenth century, and is in the Flamboyant style, thus being out of harmony with the severe dignity of the rest of the building. Nine towers were intended, but only two were completed. Very few medieval churches were ever completely finished.

Amiens, Beauvais, and Notre Dame

THERE ARE SCORES OF OTHER CATHEDRALS IN FRANCE, AND HUNDREDS of great churches, many of which are bigger and richer than Chartres. Amiens, Rheims, Bourges, Rouen, and Notre Dame at Paris are perhaps the best-known. Of these, Amiens is usually picked out as the PLATE 34 perfect French cathedral, for it was built almost entirely during the thirteenth century, the period during which French Gothic art reached its greatest height. The shimmering west front of Amiens has the usual triple portals, deeply recessed and filled with stone figures, with a separate pointed roof over each recess. Above is an open gallery and above that a row of great figures, probably the kings PLATE 35 of Judah, the predecessors of Christ. The rose window between the PLATE 36 towers is a very beautiful example of Flamboyant tracery. The towers are intentionally unsymmetrical, the north tower being a little higher and heavier than the south tower. The quadripartite vaulting of the nave is very high, 140 feet, and the clerestory windows extend fully from pier to pier. One of the great beauties of the church is the woodcarving of the choir stalls and chancel furniture.

The citizens of Beauvais tried in 1225 to build the highest vault over the greatest area of glass that had been attempted thus far. A choir with vaulting 157 feet high was finished, but a few years later it fell. It was rebuilt, heavier and stronger than before, and in the sixteenth century transepts were added, but the nave has never been built. The façade of the south transept is a beautiful example of the Flamboyant Gothic style. About 1560 a tower was built, with an openwork spire 500 feet high, the highest in France. Jean Vast, the architect, boasted that he was another Michelangelo, for that great architect of the Italian Renaissance had just designed the dome for the new church of St. Peter in Rome. The spire of Beauvais topped it by fifty feet. But five years later it fell too. Beauvais was the last attempt—a new style was already well on the way.

Notre Dame in Paris is probably the best-known of all the cathedrals of France. Built about the same time as Chartres, it stands on the little island in the river Seine which was the original city of Paris in Roman times. Over the portals of the west front is a gigantic row of kings, set in niches, and above them there is a wheel-like rose window in the center, with lancets on each side under the towers. Over the crossing is a slender spire called a flèche, meaning "arrow," built of wood and covered with lead. The nave is 110 feet high and 42 feet wide, and the axis of the church bends slightly to the north, whether by accident or as a "refinement" is not known. It has two aisles on

PLATE 37

each side, each 36 feet high, and beyond the aisles is a continuous row of chapels, built in between the outer buttresses. The piers of the nave are short round columns, with capitals suggestive of the Corinthian, which support the clustered colonnettes above. The four piers of the crossing have no such columns, but sweep upward in unbroken verticals 79 feet high. The triforium is a high and wide gallery, fully lighted by its own windows above the roof of the outer aisle. Like Chartres, Notre Dame has much of its original glass.

The grotesque figures and gargoyles of the cathedrals are well known, and the presence of such monsters on religious buildings has been the cause of much speculation. The explanation lies in the past, in the origins of the Franks and the Normans, and of the Gothic system. Grotesque woodcarvings, representations of demons and deities, were a part of the heritage of these northern forest dwellers. The wisdom of the early Church fathers permitted their converts to bring much pagan lore into the Church with them, so churches from the earliest Middle Ages in western Europe were decorated with the grotesque, side by side with the devout, for the use of these forms had become traditional.

As in the Romanesque churches, the Gothic interiors were

The radiating flying buttresses around the apse of Notre Dame suggest the dynamic restlessness of Gothic architecture.

painted, though there is hardly a trace of the color left now. Even the stone figures in the exterior porches were painted in lifelike colors, the backgrounds of their niches often being gilded, and the leafy ornament picked out with green, red, and blue. Inside, the columns and the walls were covered with painted patterns, the ornament colored and the ceiling painted perhaps a deep blue with gold and silver stars. The altars, choir stalls, pulpits, and screens were colored and gilded, and there were rich tapestries on the walls. Color has been almost lost to architecture since the decline of Gothic. Perhaps it is only now beginning to return.

English Cathedrals and Parish Churches

THERE ARE BASIC DIFFERENCES BETWEEN ENGLISH AND FRENCH cathedrals. Compared with the French, the English churches are long and low. The average French cathedral is about four times as long as it is wide, and three times as high. In England the average is about six times as long and twice as high. Winchester Cathedral is 560 feet long, the longest medieval church in Europe, yet the vaulting is only 75 feet high. Few are over 60 to 80 feet in height, many are lower. Consequently they have a very different aspect from the French churches. As the French architects accented the vertical lines, the English architects accented the horizontal. Much of the great length is in the choir, for most English cathedrals were originally built as monastic churches and had to accommodate the entire body of

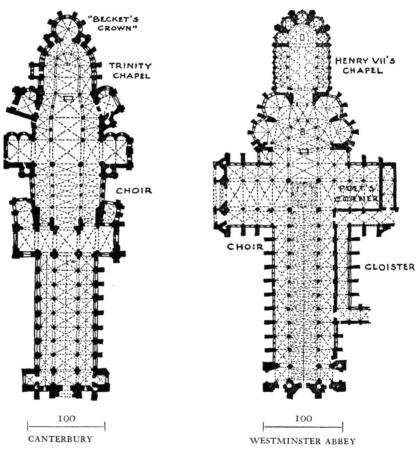

Plans of two English cathedrals.

monks in the chancel. Many of the cathedrals have two transepts, a form which originated in the monastic church at Cluny.

Another characteristic of the English cathedral is that the apse is generally square-ended. However, Westminster Abbey and Canterbury Cathedral were both designed in the French manner, and PLATE 40 Norwich and Peterborough both have semicircular Norman apses. English vaulting was seldom so daring as in France, being lower, and the supports were usually large and stable, so flying buttresses were uncommon. The Norman tradition of thick walls and heavy piers persisted, so props were unnecessary. Even more than in the case of the French cathedrals, the English cathedrals were built over long periods of time, and the differences in one building between the early Norman work and the late Gothic work are very great and readily apparent.

Probably owing to the persistence of the Norman tradition, nearly all the English cathedrals have a central tower over the crossing, which is the dominating feature of the building. Each English cathedral has its "Lady Chapel." Most French cathedrals were dedicated to the Virgin Mary, but in England it was customary to dedicate a separate chapel to her, located at the east end of the building. Since so many of the cathedrals were originally a part of monasteries, most of them still have the cloisters, priories, refectories, chapter houses, and other buildings of the monastic establishment. The monasteries usually stood in the country or in villages which grew up around them, so most English cathedrals today stand free of the buildings of the towns, surrounded by green lawns and gardens. There is a smallness of scale and a certain quality of urbanity to the cathedrals of England, which is a great contrast to the soaring, almost barbaric, grandeur of the French cathedrals. Their lines are quiet and more reposeful, and their decoration is for the most part modest and architectural, consisting mainly of mouldings rather than sculpture—with a few outstanding exceptions, such as the west fronts of Wells and Peterborough.

Local stone, cut into blocks or used as rubble with cut stone trim at corners and openings, was used for construction purposes where it was workable. From southwestern England came an excellent variety of limestone, and from the Isle of Purbeck came a marble which was used primarily for the piers and columns of the churches, as well as

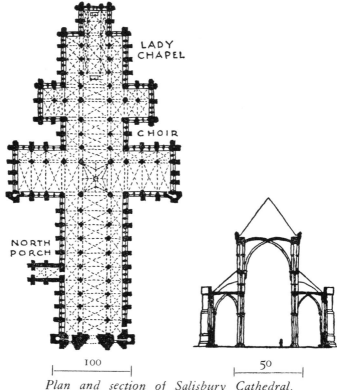

LADY
CHAPEL

CHOIR

NORTH
PORCH

100

50

Plan and section of Salisbury Cathedral.

for sculpture. For some buildings Caen stone was shipped across the Channel from Normandy, as at Canterbury Cathedral. Different materials in different parts of the country gave each local architecture a distinct character. The great oak forests of England produced an abundance of fine timber for many centuries, and oak was used freely for roof and ceiling construction in the churches, framing for the houses and minor buildings, and for church and household furniture and wainscoting.

PLATE 41   The English churches built during the thirteenth century are in what is called the Early English style. It is by no means so massive as the Norman, and is further lightened in appearance by a greater use of mouldings. The arches are pointed and the piers are formed of clustered colonnettes. The capitals are usually moulded, although

STANWICK, NORTHANTS

YORK

WESTMINSTER   LINCOLN   NETLEY ABBEY

YORK

WESTMINSTER

Early English Gothic details.

sometimes they have simple foliage. Quadripartite vaulting is the general rule, but sometimes an intermediate rib was introduced between the cross ribs and the diagonal ribs, as at Westminster Abbey. This necessitated the addition of a "ridge rib," a sort of stone ridgepole extending down the center of the vaulting, to brace the new intermediate rib. The windows are slender lancets, and the wall surfaces are sometimes decorated with an applied treatment of engaged

PLATE 38
PLATE 39 colonnettes and little pointed arches. Salisbury is a perfect example of the style of this period, for like Amiens it was built all at one time, according to a single design. The spire over its crossing is the tallest and most beautiful in England, being 408 feet high.

English Gothic of the fourteenth century is called the Decorated

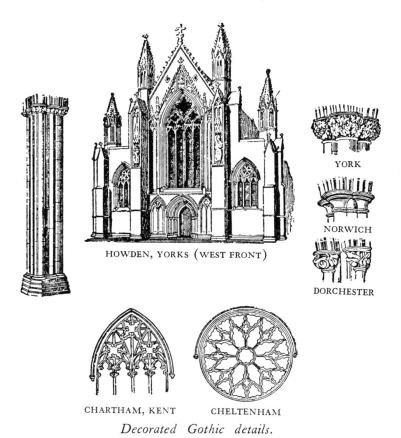

HOWDEN, YORKS (WEST FRONT)

YORK

NORWICH

DORCHESTER

CHARTHAM, KENT   CHELTENHAM

Decorated Gothic details.

style. The windows are larger, and curved and flowing lines were introduced into the tracery, a feature which led to the Flamboyant style when it spread to France. Capitals and ornament are generally of chastely carved foliage. Vaulting was enriched into a complicated pattern by the addition of many intermediate ribs. Short cross ribs were introduced, spanning from rib to rib, which are called lierne ribs. There are usually carved ornaments, or "bosses," at the many intersections of the ribs. The beautiful fanlike effect of much English vaulting results from this elaborate rib system. Exeter is an excellent example of this type of vaulting and of the Decorated style.

Meanwhile at Gloucester a third style was coming into being. Its use falls roughly into the fifteenth century and it is called the Perpendicular style. Part of the interior of the old Norman minster at Gloucester was being recarved with an elaborate surface decoration of repeating paneling, arranged in tiers. The tracery of the new windows, although still flowing, was divided into sections by perpendicular mullions. When this system of panel decoration was applied to the vaulting it resulted in some very beautiful, and occasionally some very cumbersome, effects. The choir and cloister at Gloucester and the chapel at King's College, Cambridge, are exquisite examples of this elaborate fan vaulting. It is interesting to observe, however, that as this fanciful decoration was spread over the vaulting it ceased to be a system of rib construction and became an applied decoration. The structure was really a solid stone groined vault, with the ribs carved on the under side of it. Later, the architects contrived daring and intricate vaults which seem to spring from great pendants. The pendants are carved knobs hanging down from the vaulting, from which spring a series of small ribs. Actually they are supported by being hung from the true structural ribs, which are practically concealed by the intricate pattern of false ribs.

Westminster Abbey is not a cathedral, for it is not the seat of a bishop, but it is probably the best-known of all the English churches, and in size, beauty, and importance it is second to none. It is French Gothic in style, but with a thoroughly British flavor. The present building was begun in 1245, as a new abbey for the Benedictine monastery in London. The architect, although English, seems to have traveled extensively in France before designing it, and it is quite likely that he had carefully studied the cathedral at Rheims, for it had just been completed and was considered to be one of the great sights of Europe. The Abbey has the highest vaulting in England, being 102 feet high. It also has a chevet in the French manner, and flying buttresses. The two west towers were not built until 1740, and their classic air comes from their having been designed by a Renaissance architect, Nicholas Hawksmoor. East of the apse is the famous Henry VII's

PLATE 42

Chapel. It is a remarkable example of the dazzling beauty of the late
Perpendicular style, with its immense mullioned windows and its
gravity-defying ceiling, apparently half-supported by the great stone
pendants amid a lacelike labyrinth of tiny ribs.

In England, the country of landed families, where each manor
had its dependent village, the parish churches are generally simple
little buildings accommodating only the townsfolk and the "great

*Plan of a typical English parish church, Carrington Church, Oxford-
shire.*

people" from the manor. There are about nine thousand of them, and
for the most part they are beautiful examples of an indigenous and
traditional architecture, standing in their churchyards, surrounded by
the tombs of the generations of families that built them and worshiped in them. Usually they consist only of a nave and a chancel, for
many have no aisles and few have transepts. The roof of the nave is
high and the roof of the chancel is low, in the Saxon tradition. The
older churches have broad sweeping roofs which come close to the
ground, their interiors lighted only by low windows in the side walls.
Later and larger churches with aisles and clerestories have nave arches
of stone, but very few have vaulted ceilings. Their open timber ceilings
are of great variety, and often carved and painted. A stone arch sep-
arates the nave from the chancel, and the floor of the chancel is raised
two or three steps, with two more steps at the altar. The choir stalls,
the seats for the clergy, pulpits, screens, and pews are of wood and
beautifully carved.

The principal entrance is usually through a little porch on the south side, but sometimes it is through the base of the west tower. The west towers are the dominating features of the churches, sometimes broad and squat, sometimes tall and slender. Early towers are simple, PLATE 43 with no decoration other than their few small openings. Later towers have ornamented buttresses, pinnacles, and Perpendicular panel work. The towers are usually very large in relation to the size of the church, and in the more prosperous towns they have tall stone spires.

Italian Gothic

DURING THE THIRTEENTH AND FOURTEENTH CENTURIES THE ARCHI-tects of Italy were influenced, more or less in spite of themselves, by the new Gothic system which had by then been perfected in France. They seem to have taken to it almost reluctantly, and they used it superficially, more as a means of decoration than as a system of construction. The old Roman traditions were too strong for them to understand this new manner of building, with its soaring lines and its complex principle of thrust and counterthrust. Nevertheless, they made use of it, and some of the results are very beautiful.

Like the cities of France, the cities of Italy each set out at some time to build the largest and finest cathedral in the world. Such was the ambition of the people of Siena when they started to build their cathedral in 1229, a magnificent structure of black and white marble PLATE 44 laid in alternating bands. The west front is a gorgeous screen of shimmering white marble and colored mosaics, but it bears no relation to the building behind it. The interior, with its painted vaulting and the black and white bands which run through all the walls and piers, and its rich incised and inlaid marble floor, is almost comparable to San Marco in its subdued glow of color.

Arnolfo di Cambio designed a cathedral of noble simplicity for the people of Florence in the thirteenth century, but died before it was completed. The great painter-sculptor-architect Giotto was chosen to finish it, and he added a handsome and unusual campanile before he died. It was early in the fifteenth century before the building was completed, except for the great octagonal dome over the PLATE 45 crossing, which had to wait a few years longer to be designed by

Brunelleschi, the first great architect of the Renaissance. The cathedral is Gothic in its construction, but it has little in common with the cathedrals of France. The exterior is covered with a flat surface decoration of black and white marble, and the interior is almost classic in

Giotto's campanile, like the cathedral in Florence, has black and white marble surface decoration.

its accents of horizontal lines. Classic, too, is the air of wide spaciousness and the emphasis upon the central dome as the dominating feature. The interior appears bare and cold, but it is likely that it was intended to cover the walls and vaults with frescoes, like the neighboring Gothic churches of Santa Maria Novella and Santa Croce, whose dim interiors glow with the rich colors of mural paintings. In Italy, where windows were small and the tradition of painting was strong, frescoes took the place of the stained-glass windows of the North, furnishing the color and doing the storytelling.

The people of Milan succeeded in building the greatest cathedral in Italy, in fact it was in its time the second largest in the world, for it is 480 feet long inside and 194 feet wide, with nave vaulting 148 feet high. It was begun in 1385, when the Renaissance was already under way in Florence. Beautiful as it is, it illustrates the Italian disregard for the principles of Gothic construction, for the two sides of the nave, instead of being buttressed sufficiently to keep them from spreading, are tied together with iron tie rods exposed high above the floor—a simple and effective means, to be sure, but not Gothic. The double aisles are very high, so the clerestory windows of the nave are tiny, and over the crossing is a domelike vault which was added in the sixteenth century. The exterior is a shining profusion of pinnacles and spires of pure white marble, and it is literally covered with sculpture, for there are more than four thousand giant marble figures on it. Construction of the cathedral was promoted by the Visconti family, the ruling dukes of Milan, and their French, German, and Italian architects practically completed the interior in a little over thirty years, although the exterior was not finally completed until the nineteenth century. It has a unity and completeness which many other medieval cathedrals lack, but it is overly ornate, and seems to lack the very ingredient—which can only be called a deep spiritual quality—that gives other cathedrals their true beauty.

The medieval Italians were decorators rather than builders. Byzantine tradition was still strong, and they chose to decorate a surface rather than to build in a manner which was its own decoration. In a Gothic building structural lines are the principal decoration, and any other decoration is subordinate to them. The Italians were concerned more with effect than with structure.

German Gothic

SOUTHERN GERMANY AND THE RHINELAND HAD BEEN IN CLOSE touch with Italy since Roman times, so the early medieval buildings of Germany bear a close resemblance to those of northern Italy. There

PLATE 46

are Romanesque cathedrals at Worms, Mainz, and Bamberg, and the Church of the Apostles at Cologne and St. Godehard at Hildesheim. Their exteriors are high and bare, like those of Lombardy, with small windows, pilaster strips, and cornices composed of little corbeled arches. The most conspicuous feature of these cathedrals is their towers, of which there are often five, one at each corner and one over

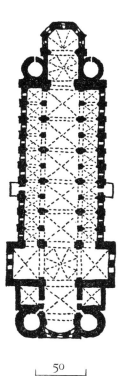

50

Plan of the cathedral at Worms, five towers and two apses.

the crossing. An unusual feature of their plans is that many of them have apses at both ends, which necessitated placing the entrances in the transepts. Their interiors, too, bear a striking resemblance to those of northern Italy. Romanesque continued to be used in Germany until well into the thirteenth century, and the Gothic style was introduced almost suddenly, as a foreign importation, so there are no churches showing a transitional period, as in France and England.

Yet relatively few Gothic churches were built, probably because few were needed after the great building activity of the eleventh and twelfth centuries.

Germany's greatest cathedral is at Cologne. It is very much like the French cathedrals in design and in character, but it has a unity and a finish which are rare in France. This is particularly surprising when one realizes that it was six hundred years in building, having been started in 1248 and not completed until 1880. It is one of the largest of the cathedrals, being 468 feet long and covering 91,000 square feet, and the lofty interior, 155 feet to the crown of the vaulting, is very beautiful even though its proportions are considered to be poor. The exterior, which was largely completed in the nineteenth century, is lavishly decorated with every Gothic ornamental device, executed with an almost machine-like perfection. There are two fine western towers with spires of delicate open stone tracery, and a small flèche over the crossing.

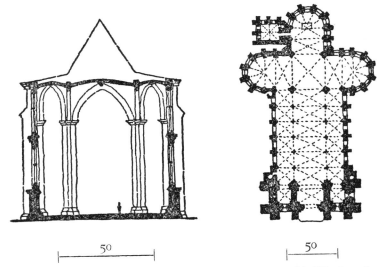

|—————50—————| |——50——|

Plan and section of St. Elizabeth at Marburg, a "hall" church.

The German Gothic builders were responsible for one innovation, which is called the "hall" church. In such a church the nave and the aisles are approximately the same height, doing away with the triforium and the clerestory. St. Elizabeth at Marburg is an example of this type. The interior has the pleasing spaciousness of a great columned hall, 70 feet wide and 67 feet high. Another "hall" church is the famous St. Stephen's at Vienna, which was seriously damaged during the last war. The aisles are nearly the same width as the nave, and all three were covered by one great roof, now destroyed. The entrances are through the transepts, one of which has a very tall and richly decorated spire, which together with the steeply pitched roof formed a beloved landmark for Vienna and all of Austria.

Spanish Gothic

THE GOTHIC BUILDINGS OF SPAIN ARE NOT SO POPULARLY KNOWN AS those of France and England, but they are equally beautiful. The Gothic style was imported from France early in the thirteenth century. It was a period of great national pride and prosperity, for King Ferdinand III had succeeded in winning back much of the country from the Moslems, and had taken the first steps toward welding Spain into a unified nation. The nobility and higher clergy were learned travelers, and they welcomed foreign visitors, ideas, and architects. Don Mauricio, bishop of Burgos, was sent at the head of a mission to bring Beatrice of Swabia to Spain to become the wife of the king. He traveled through France and Germany just at the time when so many cathedrals were being built, and he came back inspired to replace the old cathedral of Burgos with one worthy of its importance as the leading church of Castile. Soon new buildings were rising everywhere, inspired by, if not exactly copied from, the best French work.

Spanish cathedrals generally followed the French plan, having the chevet and other French features, yet there is often a tower over the crossing as in England. The Spaniards were like the Italians in that they were more interested in decoration than in structure, yet

PLATE 47 their Gothic buildings are built with true Gothic construction and possess a great deal of vigor and originality. One characteristic of Spanish architecture of all periods is a dramatic contrasting of areas of profuse ornament with areas of bare wall, a probable result of Moorish influences.

When Seville was recaptured from the Moslems the bishop purified the mosque and dedicated it to God and the Virgin Mary. But by 1400 it was falling into ruins, so the people of the city determined to build a cathedral which should eclipse the glories of even Cologne and Milan. "Let us build such a vast and splendid temple that genera-

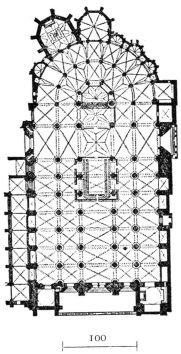

├─────100─────┤

Plan of the cathedral at Toledo, which shows great breadth and massiveness. (Courtesy University Prints.)

tions yet to come will cry of the men of Seville, 'They were mad!' " In this spirit they raised huge sums of money and built the largest cathedral in medieval Europe. It is 430 feet long and 250 feet wide, with two aisles on each side of the great nave 55 feet wide and 130 feet high. A single aisle of Seville is as large as the entire nave and choir of Westminster Abbey. With its patio it covers 198,000 square feet. The interior is French in style, but it has a square apse and a ridge rib like the English churches. It lacks uniformity of design, but with the soft light filtered through the old Flemish glass of the windows, the colossal interior is both marvelous and inspiring.

At Gerona there is an unusual cathedral with a very wide nave and no aisles. The nave extends the full width of the choir and its aisles, making it the widest Gothic vault ever built. Guillem Bofill, the architect, had difficulty persuading the chapter of the cathedral to let him undertake such a daring thing. He argued that not only would it give an unobstructed view of the chancel from every part of the nave, but it would also be cheaper to build. A consultation of the twelve best architects in the country was called for advice. Five of the experts approved of Bofill's plan, but seven thought it unsafe. In spite of that, however, the bishop and the chapter finally agreed to let him have his way. As a result the nave is a magnificent hall 164 feet long, 73 feet wide, and 111 feet high, clear and unobstructed.

Gothic became so completely the accepted manner of building in Spain that there are not only churches, but houses, municipal buildings, hospitals, and fortresses in the style. Many buildings show the influence of the Moors in their design and craftsmanship, for although they had been pushed back into Africa, their skilled Moslem artisans were in great demand wherever fine building was to be done.

Gothic in the Middle East

THERE ARE GOTHIC CHURCHES AND CASTLES IN PRAGUE AND BUDAPEST, and in all the cities and countries of eastern Europe, even in Cracow— in fact, there is a solitary Gothic cathedral in Abo, in faraway Finland. Farther east, they are found as far as Palestine, for when the Crusaders captured the Holy Land in about 1100 they set up a Frankish kingdom there and built churches and forts in the style of their homeland. The Church of the Holy Sepulchre in Jerusalem, begun by Constantine, has a Gothic tower, and in Samaria there is a full-fledged Gothic cathedral. The island of Cyprus was at one time a busy French colony and has two large Gothic cathedrals, one of which is in use today as a mosque. All along the route between the West and the East, followed by Crusaders and traders alike, are the crumbling ruins of Gothic fortresses, each with its little chapel built in the pointed-arch style of France, such as the great stronghold of Krak-des-Chevaliers in Syria. Even on the Acropolis at Athens the high square tower of the Franks stood in front of the Propylaea, until it was demolished less than a hundred years ago.

All during these Gothic centuries Constantinople was still the "Queen City." Even with the great developments of Gothic art and all the monasteries and universities that were founded during the Gothic era, the art and scholarship of Byzantium were still considered the finest in the world, and were still eagerly sought by merchants and scholars from the West. Constantinople did not fall to the Turks until 1453, and at that time the Renaissance had already started in Italy, French Gothic had become Flamboyant, and the old Norman cathedrals of England were being remodeled into the new Perpendicular style. The old Roman empire outlived its own grandchildren.

Castles and Town Houses

FROM THE TIME OF CHARLEMAGNE UNTIL ABOUT 1100, THE TYPICAL baron's castle was a crude affair, consisting of a mound surrounded by a wooden palisade and a ditch filled with water. On top of the mound, protected by another wooden wall, was a small wood building of several rooms. But when the knights traveled eastward on the Crusades they learned from the Eastern empire how to make battering rams and siege machines such as the Romans had used. Wooden walls were no protection against such engines, so fortresses began to be built of stone. The first were massive square towers with few small openings. One is still standing near Orléans. It was soon found that the corners of square towers were vulnerable to battering rams, so round towers were the next development, and with the increase of wealth the towers grew into the great castles of the twelfth and thirteenth centuries. Sometimes they were perched high on an almost inaccessible crag, with only one road of approach. More often they were built on a rise of land with open plains all around, so there was visibility in every direction. There was a moat around the outer circle of stone walls, sometimes dry and sometimes filled with water. Inside the walls were the buildings containing the living quarters of the family and their retainers, a chapel, an armory, stables, and many other service buildings. In some castles there were fine rooms, with spacious courts and gardens. Near the center of the enclosure stood the donjon, a circular tower which formed the last stronghold of the garrison in case the outer walls were breached by an attacking party. These immense towers were damp and gloomy, for the walls were very thick and the windows were only narrow slits. A thirteenth-century donjon is still standing at Coucy-le-Château. It is 100 feet in diameter and 210 feet high, and its walls are 34 feet thick at the base. The Château de Pierrefonds, built late in the fourteenth century and restored in the nineteenth century, stands on a rocky height overlooking its village, with clifflike walls and towers rising over a hundred feet to its picturesque silhouette of turrets, chimneys, and conical roofs.

The later French châteaux retained many of the features of the fortified castle.

In the fifteenth century the increasing use of cannon and gunpowder made even such massive fortresses vulnerable to attack, and their use began to die out. Another contributing factor lay in the social changes that were taking place, for the age of feudalism was passing. Many of the local barons had become little better than brigands, and their castles had become the refuge of criminals and outlaws. Such groups were naturally hostile to both the king and the rising merchant class. The increased power of the king, aided by the wealth of the cities, enabled him to overthrow these local strongholds and to establish once more his power over the land. With less need for such grimly fortified castles, the homes of the upper classes became more open and comfortable, and it became possible to cultivate the amenities of life.

The kings of France built great châteaux as summer palaces, at Blois, Châteaudun, and other places in the pleasant Loire valley. The court and nobles followed them, building spreading mansions which retained some of the architectural features of the fortified castles, but with large windows, wide terraces, and great chambers. Their windows, doorways, chimneys, turrets, and roofs were lavishly decorated with the traceries and spires of the Gothic style of the churches. The dependents and farmers built the little manor houses, farmhouses, stables, and granaries which appeared so romantic to twentieth-century American eyes that for years they were copied for country houses, particularly the farm groups of Normandy and Brittany. Rambling and picturesque to a degree, most of these were built of stone or brick, or a combination of the two. Some were built of heavy timbers, mortised and pegged together, with brick and plaster filling between them. Their roofs were steep and covered with flat red tiles or thatch.

City houses were of similar construction, but of necessity several stories high and crowded together. In order to gain as much room as possible the upper floors were often projected over the streets. On the ground floor was a shop, with a work room at the back. At one side of the shop a narrow stair led to the first floor where were the kitchen PLATE 50 and living rooms for the head of the family. The children, servants, and apprentices occupied the upper floors and the rooms under the steep roof. The ground floor was often built of stone, and the upper stories of timber, the timbers of the street front sometimes being carved and decorated.

The town houses of the nobility and the wealthy merchants were much more elaborate, such as the house of Jacques Coeur at Bourges and the palace of the abbots of Cluny in Paris, now the Cluny Museum. These houses are richly decorated with the tracery and pinnacles of the late Gothic style, with circular staircase towers and tall dormers and chimneys piercing their steep roofs. Inside are handsome rooms with vaulted or carved timber ceilings, great stone mantels, and tapestried walls. It is an ornate style which was often copied for the homes of the wealthy in America in the late nineteenth century.

The city palaces of Italy developed a character distinctly their own. Those of the twelfth and thirteenth centuries are frowning fortress-like buildings with interior courts and few or no openings on the ground floor of the street front, except for the deeply arched portal. The Gothic-arched windows of the two or three tall stories

A town in medieval England, crowded within its protecting walls.

above are subdivided into two or three smaller windows by colonnettes and small pointed arches, and the façade is crowned by a cornice of widely projecting corbels supporting little arches. During the
fourteenth and fifteenth centuries the Venetian Gothic palace developed into one of the most beautiful types of building in Europe.
The Doge's Palace, adjoining San Marco in Venice, is a fairyland-like
structure, its pink and white marble upper walls airily supported by a
lacy system of arches, and the Ca d'Oro, facing on the Grand Canal, PLATE 48
has delicate Gothic-arched galleries, which contrast with the solid
wall at the side. In both buildings the forms of Gothic architecture are
employed in a light-hearted and purely decorative manner, as was
characteristic of the Italian architects.

As the old cities grew they became a crowded maze of narrow
and crooked streets. The garden plots of the older houses were built
upon, until frequently the blocks were built up almost solidly from
street to street. The fortified city walls were the chief cause of the congestion, for no matter how much the town grew, it still had to huddle
within its walls, or build a new circle of walls, only to outgrow them
again. Many towns have their encircling walls still standing, as at
Avignon and at Carcassonne, where they have been restored. But in PLATE 49
the larger cities they have been leveled and transformed into a circle
of boulevards, like those at Paris and Lyons. However, city planning
was not ignored, and new cities were laid out with a rectangular
street plan, with wide avenues leading to the city gates.

Keep, Hall, and Manor

THE ENGLISH CASTLE BEFORE WILLIAM THE CONQUEROR WAS NOTH-
ing more than a wooden house surrounded by earthworks and a
palisade, like those of the same period in France. It was not until
early in the twelfth century that castles were built of stone. They
started with a square tower called a keep, similar to the donjon of
France, protected by a wall and a moat. Sometimes there was a second circle of walls within the outer one. The space inside the walls
was called the bailey. The keep stood near the center or the rear of
the bailey, and against the inside of the walls were the armory,
stables, granary, and storehouses.

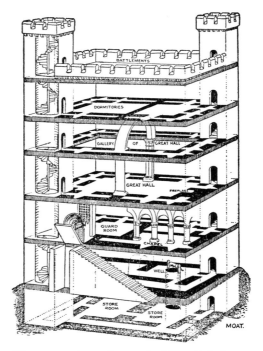

Phantom view of a typical English keep.

The keeps varied in size, but generally they were about 50 or 60 feet square, with walls 12 or 15 feet thick, and slit windows. For security, the entrance was a full story above the ground and it was approached by a ladder or a narrow stone stair. On this main floor was the Great Hall, where the baron, his family, and servants all lived. In a small keep everybody slept in the same room, but in the larger ones there was an upper floor for the baron and his lady. Within the thickness of the walls were small chambers, used for chapel, storage, and visitors' sleeping quarters. The ground floor below could be reached only from the main floor and was used as a cellar. A small circular staircase, within the thickness of the corners of the walls, wound through the height of the tower.

There was no glass in the windows, and leather curtains or wooden shutters were used in the winter, but they shut out the light and air as much as the weather. Cooking and heating depended upon an open fire on a slightly raised hearth in the center of the room, although sometimes the cooking was done in an outbuilding. Occasionally an elegant keep had a fireplace in a recess in the wall, but instead of a chimney there was a funnel-shaped passage behind it

A typical medieval English castle.
(Courtesy Sankey, Hudson & Co.)

through which the smoke was supposed to find its way out. Toilets
consisted of deep pits within the thickness of the walls, or sometimes
tiny chambers projecting on corbels from the outer walls.

During the thirteenth century, the Early English period, as the
military sciences improved, the simple keep surrounded by walls
became a more complex affair. The walls were made higher and
with towers at the corners, and the keep was placed in the center
of an elaborate system of encircling walls, with battlements on top
of them for the archers to hide behind while preparing their bows.
Frequently a projecting stone gallery ran around the top of the walls,
supported on corbels. This is called machicolation. Through holes
in the gallery floor the defenders poured molten lead and liquid fire
down on the heads of the attackers.

A fortified English manor house.

But another type of house began to develop during the fourteenth century as the need for fortifications passed, a manor house
which was sometimes surrounded by a wall but which was laid out
for more comfortable living. The central unit of these houses was
a large room, usually about 25 feet by 40 feet, with a lofty timbered
ceiling. This was the Hall. The entrance was on the side, near a
corner, and the room was protected from drafts by a carved wood

screen extending across the room. Over the screen was a gallery known as the minstrels' gallery. At the other end of the Hall was a low platform called the dais, upon which stood the baron's dining table or "high table." The "low table" for his followers extended down one side of the room. Sometimes there was a wall fireplace, but usually the hearth was in the center of the room, with a louvered cupola in the roof above it. The larger Halls had a great window near the high table where the baron held court. Copied from those in the churches, it was divided by stone mullions and filled with glass.

The Hall was a handsome room, with its fine timbered ceiling, its carved screen, and trophies, banners, and tapestries on the walls. PLATE 51 But it was crowded and dirty, and its stone floor was strewn with rushes, where the dogs and often people slept. There was usually

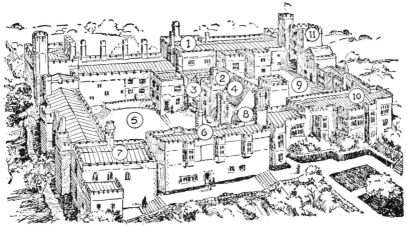

1. Kitchen 2. Pantry 3. Buttery 4. The Hall 5. Lower Courtyard 6. Aviary
7. Chapel 8. Dining Room 9. Upper Courtyard 10. Long Gallery 11. Eagle Tower

Haddon Hall, rambling around its original nucleus, the Hall.
(Courtesy Sankey, Hudson & Co.)

a small wing at each end of the Hall, with the kitchen and buttery beyond the screen, and the baron's withdrawing room, or solar, beyond the dais.

There is the germ of the beginning of the modern house of England and America: the Hall in the center, which was the living portion of the house; the kitchen at one side, with its service rooms; and the solar at the other, where the master could retire with some degree of privacy. For several centuries the Hall remained the center of the house, and as the kitchen grew into an elaborate service wing, and the solar swelled into suites of private apartments, the wings were extended to form one or two hollow squares, with the Hall in the center.

By the fifteenth century the increasing prosperity and the upward social trend led to great strides in planning for privacy and comfort, although convenience was not particularly considered, for servants were plentiful. The interiors were lighter, warmer, and more cheerful, with a fireplace in every principal room, and paneling or tapestries on the walls for warmth. Windows became large, and were usually filled with leaded glass. Many rooms, however, could be entered only from an open court or from another room, and the kitchen was invariably a hundred feet or more from the dining room. The dining room was just coming into being, developing from the "winter parlor," which was the master's study and office. There were still frequent moats and battlemented walls, but more because they were traditional than for any need for defense. The design of the houses began to be something that was studied, the gables and chimneys being placed with an eye for pleasing mass and picturesque effect. For details and ornaments, applied to doorways and windows, the designers naturally turned to the churches. They gained many rich and interesting effects with the use of what was to them a new building material—brick—and before long it became a favorite domestic building material in Britain.

Such were the homes of the great families. The homes of the gentry were similar, and sometimes almost as extensive. Except in districts where the local stone was particularly fine for building purposes, as in the Cotswold Hills, these houses were built primarily of brick or half-timber, or a combination of those materials. Half-timber construction consists of a heavy framework of solid timbers, usually oak in England, mortised and pegged together. It is the actual structure of the house, just as the ribs and piers are the actual structure of the cathedral. The spaces between the upright timbers are filled with brick or with wood laths, and both outside and inside are plastered, although sometimes the brickwork is left exposed on the outside.

Most of the architectural features of the English house as it is

LITTLE MORETON HALL, CHESHIRE

TUDOR INTERIOR

TIMBER HOUSE FRAME

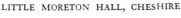

A. Principal Rafters   B. Tie-Beams   c. Collars   D. Roof Plates   E. Purlins   F. Rafters
G. Struts   H. Principal Posts   I. Studs   J. Floor Beams   K. Floor Joists   L. Wall Plates

Details and framing of Elizabethan houses: top left, Little Moreton Hall,
Cheshire; top right, a Tudor interior; bottom, timber house frame.

known today were by now, the fifteenth century, definitely established. Doorways were surmounted by pointed arches which in the
Decorated period were surrounded with mouldings, often with a
bit of foliage carved at the top. In Perpendicular times the flattened
pointed arch was surrounded by a square frame of mouldings. When
houses were built of wood, the wood was carved into the same
forms. Windows grew from single units to large groups of units
framed in stone mullions and transoms. During the Perpendicular
period the windows of many Halls were as large and as handsome
as some of the cathedral windows. In the sixteenth century, or
Tudor period, the bay window developed, usually a tremendous
bank of grouped windows extending from floor to ceiling and pro-

jecting slightly from the face of the wall. Another window development was the oriel, a smaller bay, sometimes semicircular, jutting from an upper story and supported on corbels.

The first fireplaces were simple recesses in the wall, but it was

Details of Tudor buildings.

soon discovered that a projecting hood would catch more smoke, and thus was born the ancestor of the mantelpiece. When the chimney was first carried above the roof, instead of out the side of the wall, it consisted of a single great stack, but as the number of fireplaces multiplied the chimney became a cluster of stacks, each handsomely decorated with twists and spirals formed in the brickwork. One of the dominating features of the houses of the period is the large number of handsome and towering chimneys.

Ceilings and roof construction were of wood; stone vaulting in houses was rare, except over the cellars. At first the ceilings showed the beams and boards of the floor above, but by the end of the fifteenth century they were covered with smooth boarding and paneled with carved and decorated mouldings. The Halls were roofed with trusses, which took many ingenious forms and were handsomely decorated with mouldings, carving, and color. One of the finest types of truss looks like a pointed arch resting on quarter-circular brackets; it is called a hammer-beam truss.

Staircases never developed in medieval times beyond the narrow spiral stairs of the earliest keeps. It was not until the time of Queen Elizabeth that they became the prominent features that they are today. The inside of the walls of the later medieval houses was covered with plaster as a seal against the weather, and fine houses were still better protected with wood paneling from floor to ceiling. Thus the interiors of the medieval houses of England contained many features which have continued in use in both England and America until the present day.

The Architect

IN THE BACKGROUND OF THE BUILDING PROCESSES OF THE MIDDLE Ages stood the almost anonymous architect, creating the design, contriving improved methods of construction, and directing the work. It used to be romantically supposed that the cathedrals were built by untrained masses of devout worshipers, building without plan or forethought, prayerfully putting stone on stone. The form of the great pointed arches was supposed to have been inspired by the upreaching branches of mighty forest trees, or again, by arms upraised in prayer. The belief in such nonsense has been replaced by the knowledge that Gothic architecture is a highly intricate system of construction which was worked out by generations of experts, and that the cathedrals were built by skilled masons and artisans who were paid for their work. They worked from plans and models which had been prepared by architects, and their work was constantly under the architects' supervision. They were not called architects at that time, they were known by various names—master, master mason, master builder, ingeniator, artifex, architectus—but they functioned as architects. Unknown as they generally are, a French scholar claims that the names of twenty-five thousand architects of the Middle Ages have been preserved.

The architects were usually men who rose from the ranks of the building craftsmen because of their creative abilities, and acquiring the necessary education and training they were able to assume the responsibility for the design and erection of large and complex structures. Thus they were accorded high position and ample rewards. They were usually provided with a house rent-free near their building, and were excused from taxes and assessments. Often they were presented with elaborate gifts by a pleased noble or episcopal client. They did not work from a central office, as the professional architect does now, carrying on several commissions at one time. Instead, they undertook only one operation at a time, assuming full charge of it, not only designing the building but actually building it. They were usually paid a daily salary plus an annual retaining fee. The architects were true cosmopolitans, traveling about from one country to another wherever their services were needed. They prepared fairly complete and highly accurate drawings, of which some beautiful examples have been preserved—much of the work of completing the exterior of Cologne Cathedral in the nineteenth century was done from the original thirteenth-century drawings. The drawings were usually on parchment, but sometimes on boards or slabs of plaster. The architects also made accurate scale models. But above all they lived with the job and carefully supervised every detail.

It is true, however, that the individual craftsmen were frequently permitted a great deal of freedom in their work. Where there was a strong local building tradition and highly skilled local craftsmen, as there were in most parts of England and France, the architect often merely indicated on his drawings where ornamental details were to go and what their general nature should be, and left the artisan to devise and execute his own design. That such a high degree of architectural harmony resulted is an indication of the solidity of the craft tradition as fostered by the masons' guilds.

Carefully preserved in the National Library at Paris is a little leather-bound notebook which belonged to Villard de Honnecourt, a French architect of the thirteenth century. It is filled with sketches of figures, plans, and architectural details, recording his extensive travels all over Europe. They indicate that he was not only an excellent draftsman, but skilled also in mathematics and engineering. That he also was possessed of a sense of humor is suggested by the sketch of a lion, beneath which is written, "Know that this lion was drawn from life!"

The writings of Geoffrey Chaucer show such a familiarity with architecture that it has often been supposed that he was an architect. He was not, but he was what would today be called a "clerk of the works," a sort of time- and record-keeper on a construction job. He held this post by royal favor on the building of the Tower of London, Westminster Abbey, and other London buildings.

The credit for a brilliant piece of medieval architecture was so often given to the cleric who promoted it that he was often considered to have actually designed it. The jealousy or indifference of monkish scribes caused them to record and praise the name of the bishop without mention of the name of the true designer and builder. Such was the case of the illustrious William of Wykeham, bishop of Winchester in 1400, who has often been considered the first great English architect. He was not an architect, but he was, however, an excellent business manager and promoter. He had a thorough lay knowledge of architecture, but no technical background, and his great successes were due to his unusual ability in organizing building operations. King Edward III put him in charge of all his work, and under his direction Windsor Castle, portions of Winchester Cathedral, and some of the Oxford colleges were built. Judging by a somewhat ambiguous inscription on one of the towers of Windsor Castle, it was the success of that work which made him the king's favorite. It reads, "This made Wykeham." The real architect of

Winchester was Master William Wynford, whose portrait appears, together with those of the master carpenter and the paymaster, in a stained-glass window in Winchester College Chapel.

Decline of Gothic

GOTHIC ARCHITECTURE developed as the great international Christian style of the West. It had its roots, as did the Church, in Rome. It grew with the Church, and reached its highest development at the time when the Western Church was at the height of its power. It became the accepted manner of building, the outgrowth of centuries of traditions in the crafts, and no one ever thought of building any differently. The structure of Gothic architecture represented a return to the study of science after long ages when all science seemed lost; its decoration represented a return to the study of man after ages when the representation of man seemed stifled by convention. It symbolized the spread of the Christian belief in the majesty and power of God, Who, to the medieval mind, penetrated all beings and all nature.

The early enthusiasm and communal spirit which started the wave of cathedral-building did not last, so most of them were never finished. Beauvais is only a suggestion of what it might have been; no French cathedral ever received all the seven or nine towers which were originally planned. After the thirteenth century, church-building was promoted chiefly by ambitious churchmen and the prosperity and rivalry of the guilds. The Hundred Years' War between France and England in the fourteenth and fifteenth centuries was a further deterrent to building, particularly in France. After that the work of finishing the great churches was carried on primarily by individuals, the royal families, and the wealthy nobles, rather than by communities or groups. The communal effort which built Amiens and Salisbury had died out. The Gothic era had ended.

✳ VIII ✳

Italian Renaissance

LTHOUGH THE Renaissance in architecture may be said to have commenced with the erection of a particular building, the forces and trends of thought which brought it about had been shaping up for at least two hundred years, even while the Gothic era was at its height. Throughout the Middle Ages the memory of the classics lay dormant in the mind of mankind, aroused occasionally to some manifestation, then lapsing again into slumber. At the same time, the Church was losing its grip on the minds of men, the Age of Reason was dawning, and the attacks on Roman Catholicism which ultimately culminated in the Reformation were beginning. The nationalities and the languages of western Europe, as they are known today, were taking shape, and with the decline of the tradition of the empire the real power was passing from the emperors into the hands of the kings of France, England, and Spain, the local princes in Germany, and the self-appointed dukes in the cities of northern Italy.

In the fifteenth and sixteenth centuries northern Italy was divided into a number of independent city-states. Within these states a growing class of newly rich commercial families vied among themselves for power, and whichever one of them could seize authority and hold it obtained control of the government. The heads of these families and their sons were educated and worldly gentlemen who wrote Latin poetry and patronized classical scholars and artists. Although nominally devoted to the Church, they were often crafty and unscrupulous politicians, yet at the same time truly sensitive and accomplished amateurs of the arts. The Church was dominated by men of this type, for the Popes and cardinals were usually members of the great families of Italy, who made a political career of the Church.

The moving spirit of the Renaissance was humanism, which is defined by the *Encyclopaedia Britannica* as ". . . a just perception of the dignity of man as a rational human being, born upon this earth with a right to use it and enjoy it." Thus the Renaissance became the age of the individual, which was as true in the world of the arts as it was in the world of power politics. No longer were the great buildings produced more or less anonymously as the product of traditional methods of building. The individual architect dominated the scene, and scholarship, a knowledge of the buildings of antiquity, became as important a requisite to his art as were creative ability and structural ingenuity.

Italy was rich in its heritage of classic art. Despite hundreds of years of pillage and neglect, remains of Roman buildings were everywhere and many Roman sculptures still stood where they had been placed during the empire. Classic manuscripts were eagerly sought and treasured. The Renaissance in the plastic arts in Italy started in sculpture in the thirteenth century, in painting in the fourteenth century, and in architecture in the fifteenth century. It was, after all, no sudden rebirth, but a gradual development, literary at first, then slowly penetrating into the other arts.

The Duomo of Florence

ARNOLFO DI CAMBIO HAD SHOWN A TRULY ROMAN CONCEPT OF space in planning the cathedral at Florence, but he had not lived to complete it. His plan called for a dome over the crossing which was to span not only the width of the nave but to include the aisles also, a total width of 138 feet. By the beginning of the fifteenth century the prosperity and civic pride of Florence demanded the completion of the dome, so the city fathers announced a competition for de-

signs. Among the contestants were two young students by the names
of Filippo Brunelleschi and Donato di Betto Bardi, called Donatello,
who were destined to become the greatest architect and the greatest

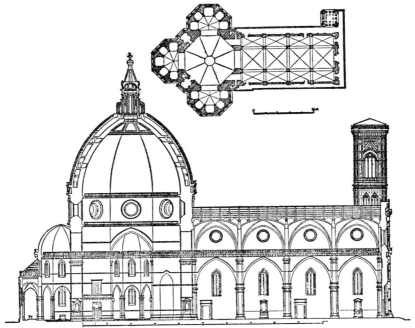

Longitudinal section and plan of the cathedral at Florence. (From
Gromort.)

sculptor of the fifteenth century. Vasari says that they made a trip
to Rome together to study the antiquities, and after their return
Brunelleschi submitted a scheme to complete the dome. It was a
daring solution consisting of two ribbed domes, an outer shell buttressing the thrust of the inner shell, the whole surmounted by a
lantern or cupola 300 feet above the pavement. Although basically
Gothic in structural principle, it was a new approach and a new
form. The city administration favored Brunelleschi's design, but it
hesitated for several years before commissioning him to go ahead with
the work, because of his youth. Work was finally begun in 1419.

Structurally, Brunelleschi's solution is not a dome at all, but a
great cloistered vault, that is, a vault supported by ribs at the angles
of the octagon. Between the ribs is a system of lateral arches which

support the web. The ribs have such a steep curve that the dome was built without the use of centering. Since it is raised on a high drum, not set down on its haunch as was the dome of the Pantheon, it was not possible to buttress it with masses of masonry. The thrust of the ribs of the inner dome is partly taken care of by the weight of the outer dome, but both are tied in by a great chain of timbers with iron connectors, which is embedded in the masonry at the base.

Never before had a vault been called upon to support a great weight like that of the stone lantern. Brunelleschi made a wood model of it, which is still preserved. It is treated with Corinthian pilasters and entablature, one of the first reappearances of a full classic order in a thousand years. From that day until the twentieth century, the classic orders ruled architecture with a supremacy seldom challenged. Brunelleschi's dome has a very fine contour, and its silhouette still serenely dominates the city of Florence today as it did five hundred years ago. Its fame brought the architect many commissions, and not only established him as the leading designer in the new style, but established his city as the center of the new architecture.

Brunelleschi and Florence

FLORENCE HAD become the intellectual capital of italy, as well as a great commercial power. The ruling family was the Medici, headed by Cosimo the Elder, and later by his grandsons Giuliano and Lorenzo. Cosimo was a great man, not only an astute politician but a scholar and a genuine lover of the arts. To encourage classical studies he established schools, founded a library, and ordered the translation of many classic manuscripts. He formed a priceless collection of antique sculptures in his garden, which he opened to young artists for study. He represents the best type of the cultivated Renaissance prince—worldly, sophisticated, sensitive, although at the same time ambitious, unscrupulous, and upon occasion, treacherous. Cosimo was not a true prince, he was only a private citizen, but he completely controlled the nominally republican city government. And as it was with the Medici in Florence, so it was with the Visconti and the Sforza in Milan, the Piccolomini in Siena, and the Borgia in Rome. Some of these "princes" bought titles for themselves from the Pope, but they all held power by force, and they held it only as long as they remained strong.

While the dome was under construction, Brunelleschi designed many other buildings, in all of which he freely used the classic orders, classic mouldings, and classic ornament. Yet with all his careful study of classic forms and his avowed efforts to imitate antiquity, he was not really reproducing ancient Rome, but was creating a new art. The columns, pilasters, and entablatures were combined with a new freedom into forms of which the ancients had never dreamed. They were a fresh mode of decoration. The classic mouldings were given a new elegance of contour, the acanthus leaf, egg and dart, and other Roman decorative motives were highly refined and delicate. This exquisite detail was suggestive of the goldsmith's art, in which, in fact, Brunelleschi had received his early training.

One of Brunelleschi's first designs was an arcade for the front of the Foundling Hospital in Florence, which consists of a series of slender arches resting lightly upon delicate columns. In the spandrel over each column, which is the triangular space between the arches, is a circular plaque in polychromed terra cotta by Andrea della Robbia—the famous *bambini,* the babes in swaddling clothes which have been reproduced so many times. Above them the windows of the second floor are framed in classic mouldings, each surmounted by a little pediment. The surface of the wall is smooth stucco, which contrasts pleasantly with the dark stone trim.

Brunelleschi designed two major churches in Florence—San Lorenzo and Santo Spirito. In these he chose to follow the traditional Early Christian basilica plan, with a flat wooden ceiling over the nave, a small dome on pendentives over the crossing, and vaulted aisles. To lend greater elegance to the Corinthian columns supporting the nave arches, he inserted a full entablature between the capital and the arch above it, as the Romans had done. In the Pazzi Chapel he reached the peak of perfection in his style. This little chapel, only 36 feet by 60 feet, was built by the Pazzi family in the cloister of the church of Santa Croce. It has a dome on pendentives as its central feature, with a smaller dome over the apse. In the decoration of this chapel one may see the freedom and imagination with which the Roman forms were used. Columns and pilasters are nominally Corinthian, but with a delicately simplified capital, and

PLATE 52

PLATE 53

the mouldings of the arches and the wall panels are used with a restrained freedom which was entirely new. Most important of all is the use of the dome as a purely decorative feature, for it is built of wood and plaster. It has no structural value whatsoever; its significance is entirely architectural, as a dome-shaped covering for an interior space.

The first city palaces built in the new style are much like those of Romanesque and Gothic times, with heavy classical cornices supplanting machicolations and battlements, round-arched windows instead of pointed windows, and with symmetry introduced in the grouping of the openings. They are usually three stories high, a hollow square in form, with all rooms opening off the loggia which surrounds the interior court. On the ground floor are an entrance vestibule, service rooms, and stables. An inconspicuous stairway leads to the main floor, the piano nobile, containing the family apartments, and to the second floor, with rooms for servants and retainers. The plans of the Gothic palaces show a haphazard arrangement of rooms, and the new buildings exhibit the benefits of the study of Roman planning, for there is a definite central axis, with balancing chambers arranged symmetrically about it and long vistas from room to room.

The Pitti Palace was built by Luca Pitti, who wanted to eclipse the more modest residence of Cosimo de' Medici. It was long thought to have been designed by Brunelleschi, but is now considered to be the work of Alberti. Construction was abandoned when Luca's conspiracy against Cosimo's son was discovered, and the building was PLATE 54 completed a century later by the Medici. Its tremendous rugged mass is 660 feet long, and although only three stories high, it is 100 feet from the pavement to the cornice. The second and third stories are strongly emphasized by stringcourses supporting balustrades, and all the openings of the street front are massive arches. In this building there is found a surface treatment which is characteristic of Renaissance architecture. It is called "rustication," and consists of emphasizing the joints in the masonry by raising the surface of the stone, leaving the joints recessed. In the Pitti Palace the ground story was given an appearance of great strength and ruggedness by leaving the rusticated surface of the stone almost in the rough state in which it came from the quarry, putting the joints in deep shadow.

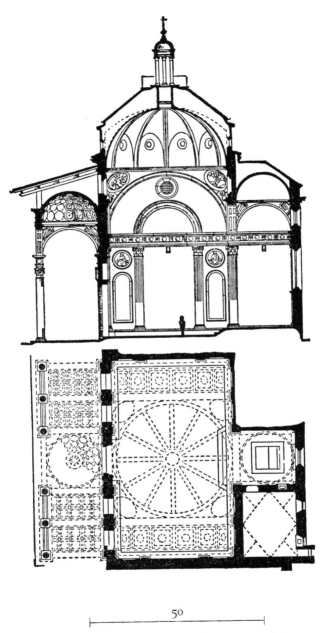

Plan and section of the Pazzi Chapel, Florence, a miniature gem by Brunelleschi. (Courtesy University Prints.)

The stones of the second story have a more even surface, while those of the third story are dressed almost smooth. This is a method of enrichment capable of many variations, lending interest and texture to what might otherwise be blank surfaces.

PLATE 55 It remained to Brunelleschi's pupil Michelozzo to design the palace which became the prototype for all to follow. Built originally for the Medici, it was later occupied by the Riccardi, so it is known by either name. Standing 80 feet high in three great stories, it is crowned with a huge classic cornice projecting 8 feet over the street, enriched with three-foot modillions and an egg-and-dart moulding with eggs as big as a man's head. The ground story has heavy rustications, with windows set into wide arches; the second story has smooth-faced rustications and arched windows which are divided in the center by a colonnette—a harking back to the Gothic traceried window. The third story has smooth stonework, giving a feeling of greater lightness so high in the air.

In the suburbs the patrician families built summer homes, as the ancient Romans had done. They are a far cry from the walled and battlemented castles which had been the country homes of the Middle Ages, for they are open and spacious, with porticoes and loggias overlooking terraces and gardens. From the first they were planned to include the garden as an integral part of the house plan, the loggias and terraces forming a transition from the indoors to the outdoors. The gardens were laid out in formal beds and much use was made of water—in fountains, cascades, and pools. They were not flower gardens, for flowers were incidental, being found only as they occurred on shrubs and vines. They were gardens enriched by the gleam of white marble and pink stucco against the deep green of trimmed shrubbery and dense trees. However, the greatest beauty of the Italian gardens was not to be reached until the Baroque period, two hundred years later.

The Florentine Architect

THERE IS A SEVERITY TO THE CHURCHES AND PALACES OF FIFTEENTH-century Florence which is a contrast to the design of the lesser buildings and the tombs, the altarpieces and monuments. Their decoration is rich and luxuriant, often gay, and by its profusion suggests that the architects were sculptors as well, as many of them were. Glazed terra cotta came into wide use, throughout the cities of northern Italy. The freedom with which this material could be modeled and colored led to an even greater profusion of ornament. In this connection, mention must be made of the della Robbia family, who produced polychromed terra cotta sculpture of great beauty. The work was begun by Lucca della Robbia in the first half of the fifteenth century, and was continued by his nephew Andrea and his sons.

The method by which the artists were trained was largely responsible for their versatility. Most of them, as soon as they showed any artistic talent, were apprenticed to a goldsmith, under whose guidance they learned the bases of design, and how to draw and to model. From this basic training, each went on into his chosen field, but since they all had the same training to start with, many were accomplished in two or three fields. Furthermore, this method of training gave each artist a sympathy and understanding for the other arts, which probably helps to explain why architecture, painting, and sculpture were more closely allied in the production of great works than ever before or since.

The architect of the Italian Renaissance had to be much more than an accomplished designer and builder, for he was frequently called upon to design and construct public works for his city, such as water supply and drainage systems, fortifications, and machines for siege or defense. For the frequent civic and religious festivals, the city and the wealthy families staged great spectacles for the people, and in the fashionable courts of the patricians elaborate pantomimes and dramas were held. In all these affairs it was the architect who arranged and produced them, and devised the realistic effects. For the feast of the Annunciation, which was celebrated in the public square in Florence, Brunelleschi contrived an ingenious apparatus which caused a golden globe surrounded by angels to appear from the heavens, out of which flew the angel Gabriel.

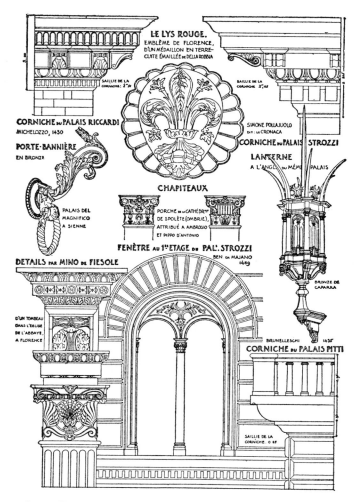

Some Florentine Renaissance details. (From Gromort.)

Alberti

DURING MOST OF THE FOURTEENTH CENTURY THE COURT OF THE Popes was at Avignon, in southern France. They returned to Rome in 1377, but the Church was split by the "Great Schism," which was not healed until 1417. Thus the authority of the Church was at its

BALVSTRADE D'AVTEL
ÉGLISE STMARIA DEI MIRACOLI, A
VENISE, PIETRO ET TULLIO LOMBARDO, 1480-89

PIEDESTAL
PAR ALESSI LEOPARDI, 1488.

MÉDAILLON EN MARBRE
DE COULEUR, CARACTÉ
RISTIQUE DE L'ÉCOLE DES
LOMBARDI.

ATTRIBUÉ A P LOMBARDO

1, 02

SOUBASSEMENT
EGLISE DE LA CHARTREUSE DE PAVIE

FENETRE, COVR DU PALAIS DVCAL A VENISE

COUPE
AB

GR MANTEGAZZA,
GIOV ANT AMADEO,
1491

CHAMBRANLE
PORTE DU PALAIS 'DE VENISE'
A ROME, ATTRIB A G DA MAJANO

PANNEAU, D'UN PIEDESTAL, ÉGLS M DEI MIRACOLI

[STATUE ÉQUESTRE DE BARTOLOMEO
COLLEONE, PAR AND DEL VERROCCHIO,
A VENISE, DEVANT SS GIOVE PAOLO.]

Some North Italian Renaissance details. (From Gromort.)

lowest ebb, and the great city of Rome, without the presence of the papal court, had become little more than a run-down provincial town. In the fifteenth century the Popes were busy reorganizing and rebuilding their spiritual and material empire, and it was late in the century before they set about rebuilding the city itself. Consequently there are few indications of the influence of the early Renaissance in Rome. The style did spread, however, throughout the cities of northern Italy, and up into France where it mingled with the still current Gothic style.

There are early Renaissance buildings in Bologna and Ferrara, and in the northern belt of cities from Milan to Venice. In some cities the buildings are exceedingly ornate, such as the façade which was added to the Gothic church of the Certosa at Pavia, a fantastic and restless composition of Renaissance forms which, like the Gothic façade of the cathedral at Siena, is a screen bearing little relation to the building behind it. To the architects of Venice the style offered new opportunities for surface decoration. They skillfully blended its forms with the use of colored marbles which was their Byzantine heritage. The Vendramini Palace, designed by Pietro Lombardo, has three-storied superposed orders framing arched windows which are divided by center colonnettes, and delicate balconies. The church of Santa Maria dei Miracoli, by the same architect, shows a beautiful blending of the flat "punctured" reliefs and marble-veneered surfaces of the Venetian Byzantine style with the higher reliefs and surfaces divided by pilasters and mouldings of the Florentine style.

The outstanding architect of the mid-fifteenth century was Leon Battista Alberti, a man of many interests and great accomplishments. He was born in Venice, but his buildings are found in many cities. He was a painter, poet, philosopher, and musician, as well as an architect. He was one of the finest organists of his time, and he wrote such perfect Latin verse that one of his dramas was long thought to have been of ancient authorship. It was inevitable that a man of his intellectual ability should think of architecture as something more than mere surface adornment, and in his churches he reintroduced the Roman concept of spatial planning.

On the façade of the Rucellai Palace in Florence he introduced the use of superposed orders, in the form of a flat pilaster treatment, in the usual three stories. He also designed a new façade for the old Gothic church of Santa Maria Novella. Here the high narrow end of the nave is crowned with a classical pediment, and tied to the aisles with two great scrolls. Otherwise the façade is in the old marble-encrusted Florentine manner—probably out of respect for tradition. At Rimini he redesigned the Gothic church of St. Francis

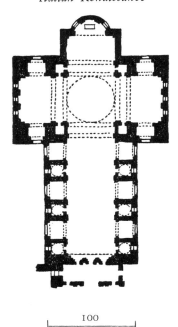

100

Plan of Sant' Andrea at Mantua.

for Sigismondo Malatesta, who dedicated it to his mistress, Isotta. Here Alberti turned away from all fanciful decoration on the exterior, and influenced, no doubt, by Roman remains in Rimini, he relied wholly upon the majestic effect of arches, pilasters, and mouldings, in the true Roman spirit. In this work he foreshadowed the period of the Renaissance that was to come, which centered at Rome and is called the High Renaissance.

In the church of Sant' Andrea at Mantua, with its spacious interior planning and truly monumental character, Alberti again suggests the coming period. This church is cruciform in plan, with no PLATE 56 aisles. Instead, it has a series of barrel vaults at right angles to the nave vaulting, forming side chapels. The walls between them buttress the great barrel vault over the nave, 60 feet wide. Over the crossing is a dome on pendentives, with high barrel vaults over the three other arms of the cross. The effect is spacious and very grand. Other churches had used the barrel vault and the dome, but simply as a handsome covering, whereas here they become the dominant features of the interior, reminiscent of the grandeur of the Basilica of Constantine.

Ever since Brunelleschi, architects had been experimenting with churches planned about a central axis. The basilican plan has a longitudinal axis; a church planned about a central axis would be in the form of a Greek cross, with arms of equal length, or it might be polygonal or circular. Some late Roman and Byzantine buildings followed this plan. It was the only way to obtain the maximum effect of the dome, permitting it to dominate both the interior and the exterior, without being cut off from view by the length of the nave. Brunelleschi's attempt was the little church of Santa Maria degli Angeli in Florence, which is octagonal. He chose, however, to develop the basilican plan, but the great churches of the future were to grow from the Greek cross plan. Alberti designed a church in this manner at Mantua, and Sant' Andrea has some of the features of this plan despite its long nave.

Bramante

POPE NICHOLAS V was a talented and cultivated man, a member of the Florentine humanist group. His ambition was to begin to rebuild the city of Rome on a grander scale than ever before, so it was inevitable that he should send to the North, about 1450, for the outstanding architect, Alberti, thus importing the Florentine style to Rome. Under the influence of the Eternal City, and at the hands of a designer devoted to the severe classic manner, the style quickly took on a more purely Roman character.

Nicholas' most ambitious project was the rebuilding of Constantine's ancient basilica of St. Peter, which was falling into ruin. The apse of the old church was torn down, not without a cry of "sacrilege" from the people, and the foundations for a new apse were put in place. The original tomb of St. Peter was preserved, and a careful examination recently revealed that it apparently has remained intact and unviolated through all the centuries of warfare and pillage. Nicholas died before the apse could be built, and his immediate successors were not particularly interested in the project, so it was another fifty years before the first stone was laid by a new architect.

Following Alberti, other Florentine architects came to Rome, where they erected two or three churches and numerous other buildings. One of these, the palace known as the Cancellaria, built in 1485 as the residence and office for the Chancellor of the Church, has long been ascribed to Bramante, but it is now known that Bramante did not come to Rome until fifteen years later. Its 300-foot façade is both grand and severe, consisting of a rusticated ground floor with small arched openings, a piano nobile with Corinthian pilasters on pedestals, which frame arched windows set in square enclosures in the Florentine manner, and two upper floors which are included in one Corinthian order, as in the Colosseum. A new note appears, for the ends of the long façade are brought forward slightly to form projecting bays, breaking up the planimetric treatment of the façade and forecasting the broken masses that were to come. There are two entrances, the major one leading to the interior court, 63 feet by 103 feet, and the lesser one leading to a church which is incorporated into the building.

After Alberti's death in 1472, the next architectural star to appear on the Roman horizon was Donato Lazzari, who, like so many of his time, became better known by his nickname Bramante, meaning "he who seeks ceaselessly." He was born near Urbino, where he started as a painter, later working under a local architect of great talent. He went to Milan, where he was responsible for the design of portions of two churches, one of which is Santa Maria delle Grazie, to which he added the choir, transepts, and dome. This church is typical northern Italian Renaissance, but there is a new feeling of power in the handling of the dome, which is screened on the exterior by a lofty arcade. The church was damaged, and the two cloisters destroyed, in World War II. It was in the monastery adjoining it that Leonardo da Vinci painted his "Last Supper."

Bramante was about sixty when he came to Rome in 1500, but the ruins of the ancient city inspired him as though he were a young student again; this is reflected in the purely classical manner in which he designed one of his early buildings there, the Tempietto PLATE 57 in the courtyard of the church of San Pietro in Montorio. It is a tiny circular building, only 15 feet in inside diameter, severely Roman in style and mode of construction. It is surrounded by a circular

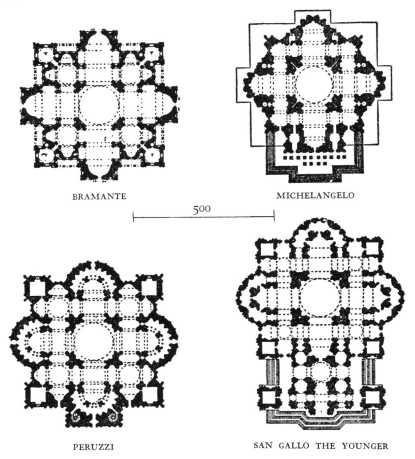

BRAMANTE   MICHELANGELO

500

PERUZZI   SAN GALLO THE YOUNGER

Four plans for St. Peter's. (Courtesy University Prints.)

colonnade of Roman Doric columns, and crowned with a dome
set on a high drum with windows. This little building marked the
turning point in the Roman Renaissance.

Pope Alexander VI, of the hated Borgia family, commissioned
Bramante to unite the straggling buildings of the Vatican Palace,
which was the beginning of the vast palace as it is today. He first
planned the court of San Damaso, adjoining the piazza in front of
the church. Its loggias were decorated by Raphael and his pupils, as
were the adjacent rooms, the famous Raphael Stanze, built by Julius

II as his residence. About a thousand feet away stood the Belvedere, a papal summer villa. Bramante planned two long arcaded wings to connect it with the older buildings adjoining the church. At the far end, backing up against the Belvedere, which stood at an angle, he designed a tremendous niche covered with a great half-dome. On the terrace in front of it stands the ancient bronze pine cone from the atrium of the old basilica. This magnificent court has lost much of its effectiveness, for it has been cut in half by a cross gallery connecting the two sides. Today these chambers house the fabulous treasures of the Vatican, some of the greatest paintings and sculpture and the rarest books and manuscripts in the world.

Alexander died in 1503, and his successor lived for only a month, so much of Bramante's work was carried out under the rule of Julius II, one of the greatest patrons of art and scholarship and architecture. He resolved to undertake at once the reconstruction of St. Peter's, and in 1505 called for an informal competition among the architects, as a result of which Bramante was chosen. Although the building today bears little resemblance to Bramante's design, drawings remain which show it to have been a truly noble conception. Basically the building was a square formed by a cross with arms of equal length, with a dome over the crossing and a half-dome at the end of each of the short arms, the corners between being filled in with sacristies covered with small domes. The plan was splendid, but the exterior would have been disappointing, for apparently Bramante had not yet caught on to the dramatic possibilities of the dome as the dominating exterior feature. His desire to be as Roman as possible led him to hide the low Pantheon-type dome behind a circular colonnade, surmounted by a stepped cone, with a rather squat lantern on top. Even this feature was not allowed to dominate, for a tower rose at each of the four corners to almost the height of the cone.

On April 8, 1506, Julius II descended into the excavation for the apse and ceremoniously laid the first stone. Even though work was pushed, it was a tremendous undertaking, and Julius and Bramante lived only to see some of the piers partially completed. The Pope died in 1513 and the architect a year later. The next Pope turned the work over to Bramante's nephew Raphael, as the most likely to carry on with the master's ideas. That precocious young artist had been introduced to Roman society by his uncle, and had become immensely successful. He and his large school of assistants turned out hundreds of paintings and decorating commissions which were then, as now, passionately acclaimed as near perfection in the painter's art. Raphael was the darling of society and the papal court, and was slated to receive the hat and robes of a cardinal. He lived like a prince, and at the time of his death in 1520 at the age of thirty-seven, he was building himself a palace from his own designs. But he was not the man for such a colossal architectural undertaking as the completion of St. Peter's, even though he was aided by Antonio da Sangallo, a noted architect and engineer, Peruzzi, and others. Sangallo carried on after Raphael's death, but when he died in 1546 the work had progressed but little. Work on the greatest building in Christendom was practically at a standstill.

Michelangelo Buonarotti

MICHELANGELO BUONAROTTI was born near florence in 1475, of good, although not patrician, parentage, and at the age of thirteen he entered the studio of Ghirlandaio, at that time the foremost painter of Florence. His nature seemed to predestine him to sculpture, however, and after a year he left the gentle painter to join the group of young sculptors who were studying under the patronage of Lorenzo de' Medici, in the Medici gardens. His remarkable intellect was quickly recognized by the patron, and the youth was admitted to the household and to the table, which put him in contact with the best minds of the times. While a student there, Michelangelo's nose was broken in a violent quarrel with one of his fellow students, Torrigiano by name, a disfigurement which he was to bear all his life. Lorenzo died three years later, and with civil war threatening in Florence, brought about by Savonarola's fiery preaching, the nineteen-year-old fled to Bologna. He returned a year later, and then went to Rome. After five years of only moderate success there, Michelangelo responded to his aged father's entreaties to return home in 1501, and busied himself with various sculptural commissions, turning out some of the powerful masterpieces which are now in Florence, Bruges, and London.

Meanwhile he had also been busy as a painter, and in 1505 he was commissioned by the Florentine state to paint a companion-piece to a mural being painted by Leonardo da Vinci in the municipal council chamber. He had just completed the sketches of this work, full of the fiery spirit and *terribilità* which accompanied his unrivaled technical mastery, when he was summoned to Rome by Julius II. The Pope wanted a great tomb for himself, to be placed in the new St. Peter's, which Bramante was just beginning. Michelangelo spent six months at the marble quarries at Carrara, getting out the necessary marbles, and fell to work with his usual energy. But the Pope gradually lost interest, for which Michelangelo blamed the jealousy of Bramante, and finally, at Bramante's suggestion, Julius ordered him to interrupt his work to decorate the ceiling of the Sistine Chapel in the Vatican. War diverted Julius' interest again, and to make things worse, the artist found he could not collect payment from the Pope for the work he had done. In disgust he went back to Florence.

His battles won, Julius persuaded Michelangelo to execute a giant bronze statue of himself to be placed in Bologna and to return to Rome, where he found himself faced again with the unwelcome task of the Sistine ceiling. In vain Michelangelo protested that he was not a painter, that sculpture was his business, but to no avail. So, in the face of every difficulty, with no assistants, and having to beg and fight for the necessary money, he commenced the work which was to become his chief title to everlasting fame. Four and a half years later it was completed, one of the greatest works of man.

Julius II died a few months later, and in the next few years Michelangelo managed to complete some of the figures for the tomb, but in 1518 the Medici called him back to Florence to design a fa-çade for Brunelleschi's church of San Lorenzo. When that finally came to naught, the artist found himself besieged with requests for his services from Rome, Bologna, Genoa, and the king of France. He turned them all down and doggedly started four more figures for the tomb of Julius, also designing the architecture and executing the sculpture for the Medici tombs in Florence.

Back in Rome again in 1534, in his sixtieth year, his unwilling services were claimed by the new Pope to paint a "Last Judgment" on the end wall of the Sistine Chapel. This great painting, 33 feet wide and 64 feet high, occupied him for the next seven years, to-

gether with other works of sculpture and painting. An old and somewhat frustrated and embittered man now, he began to express himself in poetry, much of it written to the pious and high-minded widow
whom he loved, to whom he poured out the tempestuous emotions of
his storm-ridden life. Her death in 1547 left him broken in health and
in heart.

Michelangelo and St. Peter's

IT WAS TO THIS OLD GIANT, NOW IN HIS EARLY SEVENTIES, THAT POPE
Julius III turned as the only man who could possibly complete the
church of St. Peter. Again Michelangelo refused the commission,
saying that he was too old, and that he was not an architect anyway. But the Pope felt that he had been inspired to entrust the work
to Michelangelo, and commanded him to undertake it. Again Michelangelo set to work under duress in a field which he considered foreign to him, and again he produced one of the greatest masterpieces
of art.

Michelangelo returned to the basic elements of Bramante's plan,
saying that all changes made by other architects during the past
thirty-five years had been errors. He eliminated many details of
Sangallo's design—the towers, spires, columns, and other features
which would have robbed the church of its classic simplicity. Here
he ran into his first difficulty, for his simplification of the design dis-
pleased the financial administrators of the project, for money was
plentiful and it was to their advantage to see it spent. Michelangelo
went straight to the Pope and demanded full authority to build or to
tear down, as he saw fit. Furthermore, he had it written into his
contract that he served without compensation and "for the love of
God only."

His design set the dome on a drum and raised it to the height of
450 feet to the top of the lantern. The drum is pierced with windows, which are flanked with paired columns on the exterior, appearing as buttresses under the exposed ribs of the dome above. The
dome itself is a double dome, one shell inside the other, like Brunelleschi's, 137½ feet in diameter. Crowning it is a delicate lantern,
which terminates in a short concave spire. Paired columns on the

lantern echo the columns below. The surrounding masses of the church, according to Michelangelo's design, were low, so that from every point of view they built up to the great dome. Unfortunately, the nave was extended and the façade was not carried out as Michelangelo had intended, but from the rear the full effect of his design can be seen. Its great Corinthian pilasters are severe, but there is a nobility of proportions which seems to imbue St. Peter's with that spiritual quality which is characteristic of the churches of the Middle Ages, and which is so conspicuously lacking in most Renaissance churches. The dome still dominates the city of Rome, and may be seen for miles out on the Campagna, and since the Vatican is on a hill west of the city, the sun always sets behind its grand silhouette.

PLATE 58
PLATE 59

Michelangelo died in 1564, when the construction had reached the spring of the vault, but he left a working model which is still preserved. The work was carried on by his favorite pupil, Giacomo della Porta, who introduced a few ideas of his own, chiefly in the lantern. Vignola designed some portions of the church also, but work lagged again until the reign of Pope Sixtus V, who appointed Fontana to complete it. In 1603 the building was finished substantially as Michelangelo had planned it, according to Bramante's original conception of a Greek cross with arms of equal length. This, however, did not mark the end of work on the great church, for several generations of Popes had yet to leave their imprint upon it.

The effects of this design were so far-reaching that from the latter part of the sixteenth century on, no important church was considered complete without a central dome, be it large or small, stone or plaster. In fact, the dome became a "must" for every monumental building, and was transplanted to the shores of the infant United States of America to appear on the Capitol at Washington and on a majority of the state capitols.

Michelangelo designed other buildings in both Florence and Rome, although some were not completed until after his death. In 1524 he designed the New Sacristy for the church of San Lorenzo in Florence, intended as a mausoleum for the Medici family. On these two tombs, in which architecture and sculpture are perfectly blended, are the four magnificent reclining figures known as "Day and Night" and "Evening and Dawn," and the two seated figures of Lorenzo and Giuliano, which are the best-known sculptures of the master. The

PLATE 60

next year he designed the handsome but rather tumultuous staircase and the highly mannerist vestibule for the Laurentian Library in San Lorenzo, which contains the Medici collection of 10,000 Greek and Latin manuscripts. This work was carried out by Vasari from Michelangelo's designs.

Michelangelo's most important architectural work in Rome, other than St. Peter's, was the design for the Capitol, the square crowning the smallest of the ancient hills, where in Roman times the great temple of Jupiter stood. It is approached by a handsome flight of steps, opposite which is the Palace of the Senate, flanked on each PLATE 61 side by a smaller palace. The Palace of the Senate is a medieval structure built on the foundations of the Roman Tabularium. Michelangelo designed a new façade for it, consisting of two-story Corinthian pilasters standing on a high rusticated basement, with true "Michelangelesque" elegance of proportion, the entrance being approached by a superb double staircase with a fountain below. The two flanking palaces repeat the "colossal order" of the Senate, but without the high basement, and with a small Ionic order between them on the ground floor. The handsome Baroque windows of the floor above are later additions.

Michelangelo's work led to a definite Roman school of architecture. Men who had been influenced by him, some his pupils and assistants, tried to carry on in his manner. Therein lies the evil that many a great artist has wrought from his grave. Great men originate, little men imitate. The originality and boldness of Michelangelo's architectural forms became mere novelty and eccentricity in the hands of lesser men. The great brooding, muscular figures which he created in sculpture and in painting, which seem like gods descended to earth, became mere posturing men at the hands of his imitators. Michelangelo started all three arts in a direction which culminated in the Baroque a century later.

Palaces, Fountains, and Villas

IN 1527 ROME WAS SACKED BY THE GERMAN TROOPS OF CHARLES V, BRINGing slaughter, fire, and pillage again to the old city which had seen so much. When this was over, Rome needed rebuilding more than ever, and it was during this period of the High Renaissance that many of the palaces, piazzas, avenues, fountains, and other monuments were built which give the city its principal aspect today. Contemporary with and following Michelangelo were many architects of great ability, most of whom were greatly influenced by his work. One of these was Giorgio Vasari, an architect, painter, and scholar, who through his book *The Lives of the Most Excellent Painters, Sculptors and Architects* is our principal source of knowledge of the lives and activities of Renaissance artists in Italy. Although it repeats many legends and has been found inaccurate in minor details, the book is lively

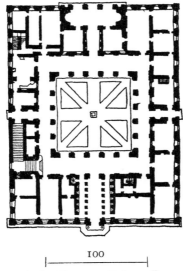

|——————— 100 ———————|

Plan of the Farnese Palace, Rome.

and amusing, and full of information which might otherwise never have been preserved.

Giacomo da Vignola was a scholarly architect who succeeded Michelangelo on the work on St. Peter's, designing two of the smaller domes. His most important building is the Church of the Gesù, the home church of the Jesuit order, which in general follows the pattern of Alberti's Sant' Andrea at Mantua, with a central dome over a barrel-vaulted nave. This church became the type for all Jesuit churches wherever that great missionary order spread. Its interior, as it appears today, is much altered in aspect, as are many of the old churches, by the fanciful Baroque additions of the seventeenth and eighteenth centuries. Vignola's greatest fame, however, comes from his writings. His *Treatise on Architecture* laid down rules for the

Some Roman Renaissance ornaments and mouldings. (From Gromort.)

design of monumental buildings based on the work of Michelangelo. With the aid of many beautiful drawings he reduced the proportions of the five orders of classic architecture to a system of measurements by which they could be faithfully reproduced by even the most backward student. Thus for over three hundred years "Vignola's orders" were the first thing a student of architecture learned, which helped to cast the art of architecture in the classic mould that has confined it until the present day. Now the pendulum of reaction has swung so far in the opposite direction that many a student has never heard of Vignola, and does not know, and thus has little respect for, the beauties of classic architecture.

The palaces of Rome are similar to the palaces of Florence, but they show the imprint of their time in the more regular planning and the greater emphasis upon axes. Their towering façades and great arcaded courts, or cortiles, were invariably designed in three stories, even when there were actually more. The stairway became a grand and monumental affair leading from the ground floor to the piano nobile, and the rooms of that principal floor were decorated with large architectural features and frescoes of classical and allegorical subjects. Such a building is the Farnese Palace, which Antonio da   PLATE 63
Sangallo designed for Paul III while he was still a cardinal. It is an immense building of great monumental dignity, approximately 185 feet by 235 feet, with a cortile 81 feet square. The upper story and the cornice were designed by Michelangelo. The growth of the sense of spatial planning which pervaded the time led to the provision of an open square in front of the palace, to give a proper approach. In the square are two porphyry fountains from the Baths of Caracalla.

As a relief from the formality of life in their official palaces, many of the Popes and cardinals built villas on the edge of the city. These were less pompous in design, often with a gaily designed façade turned upon the terraced garden at the rear. One of the oldest of these villas is the Belvedere, which Bramante incorporated into the buildings of the Vatican Palace, and which now houses the Apollo Belvedere, the Laocoön, and other masterpieces of Greek sculpture. The Villa di Papa Giulio was designed by Vignola in 1550 for Julius III, and displays that master's versatility. Severe and correct as are his formal designs, this summer palace is a free composition based on a semicircular court facing a terraced garden, with a casino and artificial grotto beyond. The living quarters are closely tied to the garden, suggesting an informality appropriate to the summer retreat of a prince.

Rome has always been a well-watered city. The aqueducts still pour thousands of tons of water into the city daily. The Renaissance princes of the Church made full use of this volume of water by building many monumental fountains in the public piazzas and in their private gardens, combining architecture and sculpture. The splashing of these fountains still cools the hot and simmering summer air of the city. The princes also built great avenues leading to the piazzas,

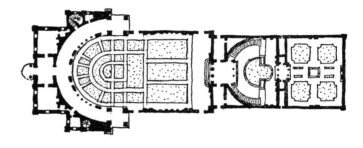

|———— 100 ————|

Plan of the Villa di Papa Giulio in Rome, designed by Vignola as a summer residence for Julius III.

which they named after themselves, and they adorned the squares with sculpture and fountains, framed in terraces, balustrades and staircases.

An idea of the immense building activities of some of the Popes may be gained from a summary of the work initiated by Sixtus V, who ruled only five years. He and his indefatigable architect, Fontana, built the enormous palace within the Vatican which is still the residence of the Popes; the two galleries connecting Bramante's thousand-foot-long wings, now the Vatican library; the Lateran and the Quirinal Palaces, two papal residences; a memorial chapel in the great church of Santa Maria Maggiore; the Via Sistina, which resulted in the opening up of a new section of the city; and at least twenty-five fountains and many obelisks and other monuments.

The country villas became more luxurious than ever before. Near

Tivoli is the Villa d'Este, perhaps the most famous of all. Old engravings show the palace standing at the top of an elaborate terraced garden, with water diverted from the river Anio pouring into hundreds of fountains and cascades and tumbling into pools and basins, amid plots of shrubs and rows of formally planted trees. Today the box and ilex have grown into great luxuriant masses and the towering deep-green cypresses are reflected in the still pools, making this one of the most beautiful spots in the world.

Sansovino and Palladio

IN THE LATTER PART OF THE FIFTEENTH CENTURY FLORENCE PASSED the new Renaissance style on to Rome, and a hundred years later Rome passed it back again, modified and enriched by the genius of the men who fostered it. The influence of Michelangelo was predominant. In Florence, his pupil Vasari designed the Uffizi Palace for the Medici, as their private art gallery and administrative offices. Today one of the great art collections of the world is behind its sober and scholarly façade. In Milan and Genoa, Alessi, another of the master's pupils, designed palaces which are exaggerated in style, chiefly characterized by magnificent staircases and terraced gardens, due to the hilly sites. The Municipal Palace in Genoa has a fine symmetrical plan, and being set into a hill it has an interesting arrangement of interior staircases.

The style of the High Renaissance differed in every city, even though it all emanated from Rome, for the cities themselves were strongly individual. This was especially true in Venice, where the tradition of opulence is evident in both early and late Renaissance buildings. Sansovino brought the Roman Renaissance to Venice. A Florentine by birth, he went to Rome in 1503 as a student and stayed there until 1527, when he fled to Venice to escape the soldiers of Charles V. The city government invited him to stay, and gave him important commissions in both sculpture and architecture. His Roman style soon took on a typical Venetian flavor, characterized by a wealth of finely executed sculpture in high relief and the use of statues to enliven the silhouettes of his buildings. At the foot of the campanile which stands before the church of San Marco he designed

Corner of the Library, Venice.

a little vestibule, known as the Logetta. It is very small in scale, with coupled columns framing its three arches. Between the columns are niches with statues, and there is a very high frieze above with sculpture in relief. Behind the Logetta is the Library, a very long two-story building with a Doric order between the arches of the ground floor and an Ionic order on the upper floor. Above that is a richly garlanded

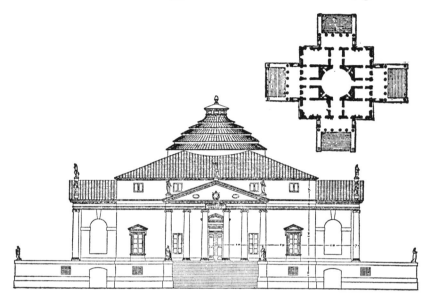

Plan and elevation of Palladio's Villa Capra (Rotonda), Vicenza.

frieze in high relief, which is topped by a balustrade surmounted by nine-foot statues. It is very rich and very Venetian.

Vicenza was the home of Andrea Palladio, an architect who had a very great influence upon architects for the next two hundred years. He filled his city with splendid buildings, of which the best-known is the new front on the medieval municipal basilica. Like Sansovino's Library, it has a Doric order between the open arches of the ground PLATE 64 floor, an Ionic order above, and a balustrade with posturing figures standing on the pedestals. In this building he introduced what has come to be known as the "Palladian motive": a central arch rests on entablatures which form the lintels of two narrower side openings, the entablatures being supported by columns toward the center and pilasters at the sides. The basilica was badly damaged during World War II, the arcades being partially ruined, now restored.

In Venice, Palladio designed palaces and churches, including the church of San Giorgio Maggiore, which stands across the lagoon from San Marco and the Doge's Palace. He also designed many villas, such as the Villa Capra, which is a square building on a high basement, with a dome over a central hall, and a portico with Ionic columns and a pediment on each of the four sides. The design of this villa had a great influence upon the architects of eighteenth-century England and America. Palladio's style is vigorous and original, and he was a prodigious worker. Although, like Vignola, he preached against the use of curves and flowing lines, advocating a return to a stricter classicism, he was too imaginative to follow his own rules. He introduced many novelties, and made much use of the "gigantic order" extending through two or three stories, in conjunction with small orders one story in height. Unfortunately, many of his buildings were built of brick and covered with stucco, and thus they are in a bad state of preservation today.

But Palladio's greatest influence was through the medium of his books. He made and published measured drawings of many of the buildings of antiquity, which constitute the only record we have of some of them. He also published drawings of his own designs and wrote a book entitled *The Four Books of Architecture,* in which he divided all buildings into four groups—public buildings, houses, villas, and churches—laying down rules for the planning and design of each, with many examples. Inigo Jones, the first great British architect of the Renaissance, followed Palladio's style and had his books translated into English. Thus the rules and designs of Palladio were introduced into England and passed from there to the American colonies, where they formed the basis for the American Colonial style.

Baroque and Classic

THE TOWN PLANNING OF THE SIXTEENTH CENTURY CONSISTED PRIMARILY of efforts to make the cities more beautiful, rather than to improve the living conditions of the people, which remained substantially the same as they had been during the Middle Ages. The piazzas, or public squares, which were cleared and embellished before the monumental buildings, were laid out as a result of the return to the ancient Roman planning ideal, the concept of the grand monumental plan, which is a necessary part of any great architecture.

The forms of Renaissance architecture were certainly inspired by those of ancient Rome, but they were seldom actually copied from the antique. With their heritage of medieval structural methods, and their own great vigor and originality, the Renaissance architects modified the forms they borrowed so that they became unmistakably their own. The Renaissance plan was open and symmetrical, with a strong axial emphasis, and monumental or decorative features at the termination of the axes. In other words, the plan compelled the eye to look in a certain direction, and gave it something to look at. It recaptured the ancient sense of interior and exterior mass, as is evidenced by the preference for the central axis type of church plan, as opposed to the basilica plan.

The typical Renaissance façade was divided into a number of more or less self-contained units, vertically by the use of columns and pilasters, or horizontally by cornices and mouldings. The palace, for instance, had base mouldings at the bottom, a cornice at the top, and the stories between were divided by stringcourses into definite horizontal compartments, each designed complete in itself. In most cases it would be almost literally possible to take out one of the intermediate stories and not miss it. Similarly, the monumental building was divided by its orders into bays, each a complete unit with its own central feature.

The Renaissance in architecture started in Florence, and developed there into a delicate method of decoration. Spreading to Rome, it became grander and more structural. In its last phase it developed two trends. One was toward originality and freshness of conception, evidenced by the use of curves, flowing lines, and new forms. Michelangelo and his followers were associated with this trend, and thus fathered the Baroque, which held sway during the next period. The other trend, led by Vignola and Palladio, was toward a stricter classicism, which was to influence the beginnings of the Renaissance in France and England, although ultimately it was overtaken there by the Baroque. Originating in the fifteenth century as the original conception of creative minds, this trend tended to become in the sixteenth century an academic following of rules and formulas.

The Baroque

FOR NEARLY TWO HUNDRED YEARS IT WAS THE FASHION TO DEPRE-
ciate the Baroque, to consider it an aberration to be apologized for, an architectural wild oat to be repented. Even the very word came to be a synonym for artistic extravagance and corrupt taste. But today it is in favor again. Despite the obvious absurdities of Baroque upon occasion, its robust and full-bodied beauties are appreciated and enjoyed. It is the product of a time, the seventeenth century, which was a period of great intellectual liberty when almost anything could be thought or said as long as a minimum of outward convention was observed. Liberty means freedom to some and license to others. Thus in architecture, the spirit of artistic liberty meant an opportunity for originality and invention to some, and for freakish novelty and wearisome over-ornamentation to others.

There are basic differences between the Baroque architecture of the seventeenth century and the classical architecture of the sixteenth century. The latter relies upon mouldings and a flat or linear type of ornament, whereas Baroque architecture leans more to broken masses and a sculptural type of ornament, resulting in a greater play of light and shade. The earlier style is static, and it may be called planimetric in that it deals with the decoration of flat façades; there is a sense of movement in the later style which comes from the play of light and shade, and a feeling of progression from foreground to background which results from spatial planning. The Baroque architects conceived of a building as a three-dimensional volume to be *experienced,* rather than as an arrangement of surfaces to be looked at. This was achieved in exterior design by breaking two wings forward from the central mass of the building, tying them to the immediate foreground with terraces and balustrades, thus creating a three-dimensional composition which could be experienced by walking through it. In interior design it was achieved by the enclosure of space in a monumental and dramatic fashion, so that the space itself is the thing first enjoyed, the decoration of the enclosing walls and ceiling being secondary.

PLATE 1 A reconstruction of the temple at Edfu. *Bettmann Archive*

PLATE 2 The model of the hypostyle hall at Karnak shows the clerestory windows, as well as the all-over painting.

PLATE 3 Sargon's palace at Khorsabad.
Bettmann Archive

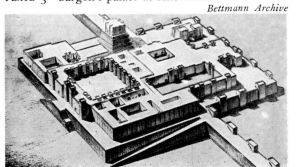

PLATE 4 The restored model of the interior of the Parthenon shows the great statue of Athena.

PLATE 5 The Parthenon.

From "Greece: A Classical Tour with Extras," by Lucile & George Brockway

PLATE 6   The Hephaisteion in Athens is the best-preserved Greek Doric temple.

PLATE 7   The caryatid porch of the Erechtheum.

Great Shambles Press

PLATE 8   The Ionic temple of Niké Apteros.

Great Shambles Press

PLATE 9   The Choragic Monument of
Lysicrates.

PLATE 10   Theater at Epidaurus.   *Great Shambles Press*

PLATE 11   The Maison Carrée at Nîmes.   *Metropolitan Museum of Art*

PLATE 12   The Arch of Septimius Severus.

PLATE 13 Exterior of the Pantheon in Rome.

PLATE 14 Interior of the Pantheon.

PLATE 15 The Baths of Caracalla, reconstruction.

PLATE 16 This reconstruction of the interior of a house at Pompeii shows the atrium, looking towards the peristyle. *Bettmann Archive*

PLATE 17   The interior of Haghia Sophia.

PLATE 18   Haghia Sophia, Istanbul.

PLATE 19   S. Apollinare Nuovo in Ravenna.

PLATE 20   The exterior of San Marco in Venice.

PLATE 21   The interior of the cathedral at Monreale in Sicily.   *Alinari*

PLATE 22   The baptistry, the cathedral, and the campanile at Pisa.

PLATE 23   The portal of St. Trophîme at Arles.

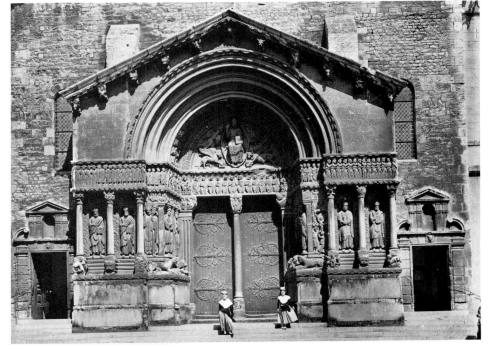

PLATE 24   The nave of St. Sernin at Toulouse.

PLATE 25   The nave at St. Étienne at Caen.

PLATE 26   La Trinité, Caen.

PLATE 27   The nave of the abbey church at Mont St. Michel is Norman Romanesque, but the apse was finished in late Gothic times.

PLATE 28 The interior of Peterborough Cathedral.   *British Information Services*

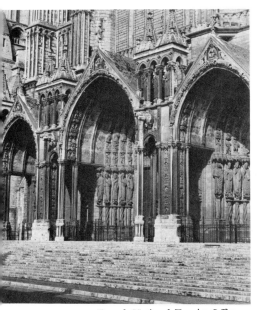

French National Tourist Office

PLATE 29 The south porch of the cathedral at Chartres.

PLATE 30 The interior of the cathedral at Chartres.

PLATE 31 The exterior of the cathedral at Chartres.
Avery Library

PLATE 32 The twelfth-century
Tree of Jesse window, Chartres
Cathedral.

PLATE 33 The window from Le
Mans Cathedral depicting the
Passion and Resurrection.

PLATE 34　The nave of Amiens Cathedral.

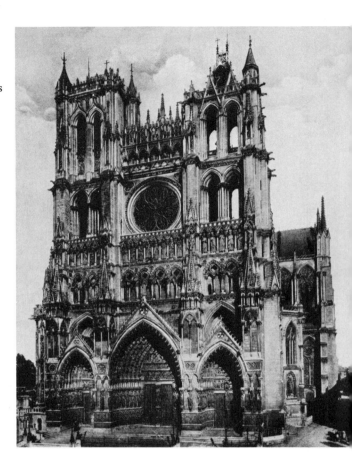

PLATE 35
Façade of Amiens
Cathedral.

PLATE 36　The flying buttresses of Amiens

PLATE 37 The interior of the cathedral of Notre Dame, Paris.

PLATE 38 The interior of Salisbury Cathedral.

Metropolitan Museum of Art

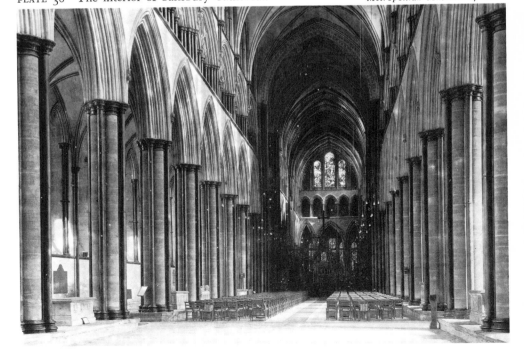

PLATE 39   Salisbury Cathedral.

British Information Services

PLATE 40   Canterbury Cathedral.
        British Information Services

PLATE 41   Lincoln Cathedral.

PLATE 42 Henry VII's chapel, Westminster Abbey.

PLATE 43 The parish church at Feckenham, near Worcester.
Photo by Author

PLATE 46 The cathedral at Worms.

PLATE 47 The interior of the cathedral at Salamanca.
Avery Library

Anderson

PLATE 48   Ca d'Oro, Venice.

PLATE 49   The town of Carcassonne, in southern France.

PLATE 50
The medieval houses of Hildesheim.

PLATE 51   The Hall of Penhurst Place.

From "The Mansions of England in the Olden Time" by Joseph Nash

PLATE 54   The Pitti Palace, Florence.

PLATE 55
The Riccardi Palace, Florence.

PLATE 56 The interior of
Sant' Andrea, Mantua.

Metropolitan Museum of Art

PLATE 57
Bramante's Tempietto, Rome.
Metropolitan Museum of Art

PLATE 58 Section through the dome of St. Peter's, looking into the south transept.

PLATE 59 St. Peter's from the rear shows the noble proportions of Michelangelo's design.
Ewing Galloway

PLATE 60   The New Sacristy in the church of San Lorenzo, Florence.

PLATE 61   The Palace of the Senate, Rome.

PLATE 62   Church of the Gesú, Rome.

PLATE 63   Farnese Palace, Rome.

PLATE 64   Sansovino's Library, Venice.

PLATE 65
The Villa Cors-Salviati near Florence.
Photo by Author

PLATE 66 The baroque façade of St. Peter's and Bernini's colonnade.

PLATE 67 The interior of St. Peter's.

PLATE 68
Santa Maria della Salute,
Venice.

PLATE 69
Francis I's wing of the
château at Blois.

PLATE 70 The château at Chambord.   *French National Tourist Office*

PLATE 71 The château of Chenonceaux displays three periods of French architecture — the medieval donjon, the main building in the style of Francis I, and the wing over the river by de l'Orme.   *French National Tourist Office*

PLATE 72 The palace at Fountainbleau.   *French National Tourist Office*

PLATE 73
The plateresque Casa de
Ayuntamiento, Seville.
Avery Library

PLATE 74   The Escorial.   *University Prints*

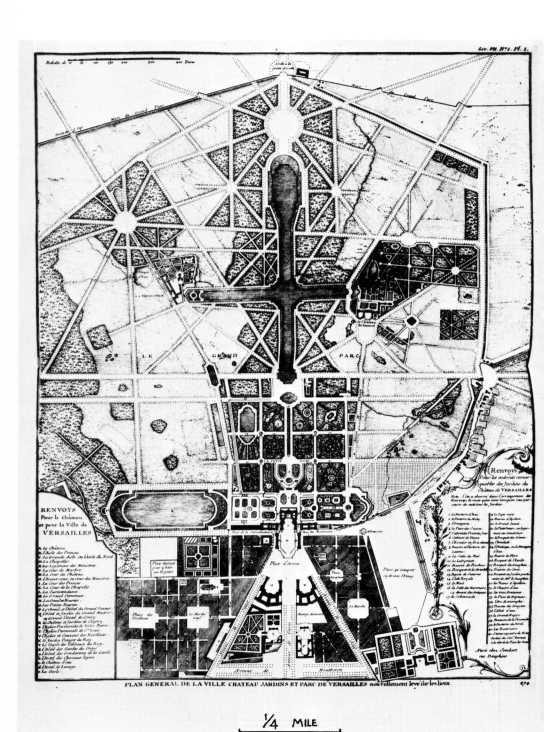

PLATE 75 Le Nôtre's plan of the gardens and the park at Versailles has influenced all formal city planning down to the present day.

French National Tourist Office

PLATE 76 The vast palace at Versailles overlooks many fountains and lagoons.

PLATE 77 The grand vistas and great fountains of Versailles. *French National Tourist Office*

PLATE 78   Royal chapel of the Invalides in Paris.   *French National Tourist Office*

PLATE 79   Perrault's east façade of the Louvre.   *Avery Library*

PLATE 80   The Pantheon, Paris.   *French National Tourist Office*

PLATE 81   The Madeleine, Paris.   *Metropolitan Museum of Art*

PLATE 82   A Louis XV rococo interior.   *Metropolitan Museum of Art*

PLATE 83   An air view shows the Place de la Concorde and the gardens of
the Tuileries, with the outspread arms of the Louvre beyond.   *Metropolitan Museum of Art*

PLATE 84   The Petit Trianon at Versailles.   *Metropolitan Museum of Art*

PLATE 85   The Zwinger, in the fanciful style of the German rococo.

Metropolitan Museum of Art

PLATE 86
The Neumünster in Würzburg.

PLATE 87
The Churrigueresque interior
of the Cartuja at Granada.

PLATE 88   Hampton Court Palace.   *Metropolitan Museum of Art*

PLATE 89   Compton Winyates.   *British Information Services*

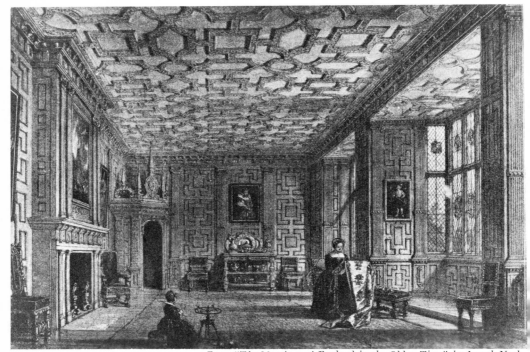

PLATE 90   The late sixteenth-century Renaissance in England produced such richly paneled interiors as the drawing room of Broughton Castle.

PLATE 91   Montacute House.   *British Information Services*

PLATE 92   The Royal Banqueting Hall, Whitehall.

University Prints

PLATE 93   The tower and façade of bombed-out St. Mary-le-Bow.
British Information Services

PLATE 94   The interior of St. Bride's.
British Information Services

PLATE 95   St. Paul's Cathedral from the southeast.   *British Information Services*

PLATE 96   The interior of St. Paul's Cathedral.   *British Information Services*

PLATE 97   The south and east fronts of Hampton Court Palace.   *British Information Services*

PLATE 98   Blenheim Palace.   *British Information Services*

PLATE 99 St. Martins-in-the-Fields.

PLATE 100 The Royal Crescent in Bath, a sweeping semicircle of attached houses.

PLATE 101 Somerset House. The water originally reached to the arches of the basement.

PLATE 102 The smaller Georgian homes of England are simple, well proportioned, and homelike—the best of domestic architecture.
Avery Library

PLATE 103 The interior of the early seventeenth-century New England house was bare and strictly functional.

PLATE 104 The Parson Capen House at Topsfield, Massachusetts.

PLATE 105 The John Ward House in Salem, Massachusetts, built in 1684; its "lucome windows" are restored.
Essex Institute

PLATE 106 The "Old House" at Cutchogue, Long Island, New York; note the unique curved headed doors.
Charles H. Meredith

PLATE 107 St. Luke's near Smithfield, Virginia.

PLATE 108   The Santuario de Ocotlán, at Tlaxcala.

PLATE 109   The McPhedris House in Portsmouth, New Hampshire.

PLATE 110   The Longfellow House at Cambridge, Massachusetts, 1759.

PLATE 115   Independence Hall, Philadelphia.

PLATE 116   The Governor's Palace at Williamsburg.

PLATE 117 The smaller colonial houses of Virginia had steep roofs and great brick end chimneys.

PLATE 118 Westover in Virginia.

Museum of Modern Art

PLATE 119 Mount Vernon, river front.

PLATE 120   The Nathaniel Russell House in Charleston, South Carolina.

PLATE 121   The late colonial room from the home of Samuel Powel in Philadelphia, now in the American Wing of the Metropolitan Museum, displays the refined elegance of the Georgian period.

Metropolitan Museum of Art

PLATE 122   Jefferson's State Capitol at Richmond, Virginia.   *Museum of Modern Art*

PLATE 123   Monticello.

PLATE 124   The mall and library of Jefferson's University of Virginia.

PLATE 125   Colonnades
flanking the mall of the
University of Virginia.
*Historic American
Buildings Survey*

PLATE 126 The Gardner-White-Pingree House in Salem, Massachusetts. *Historic American Buildings Survey*

PLATE 127 First Church of Christ in Lancaster, Massachusetts. *Historic American Buildings Survey*

PLATE 128
City Hall, New York.

PLATE 129 Latrobe's
Bank of Pennsylvania,
Philadelphia. From a
water color by Alexander
Jackson Davis.
Maryland Historical Society

PLATE 130 Girard
College in Philadelphia.
*Detroit Photographic
Company*

PLATE 131 The Ohio State Capitol at Columbus.

PLATE 132 Greek Revival in Racine, Wisconsin.

PLATE 133   The Gothic Revival Grace Church in New York.

PLATE 134 The Paris Opera.   *Metropolitan Museum of Art*

PLATE 135 Boston's Old Museum of Fine Arts

PLATE 136 In the "Italian Style" house everything was high and narrow.

PLATE 137 Some of the houses of the 1880's had no architectural antecedents whatsoever.

PLATE 138   A "French Style" mansion of 1875.

PLATE 139   The suburban house
of 1888 strove for the picturesque
by the use of many materials and
a varied silhouette.

PLATE 140　The W. K. Vanderbilt House, which stood at Fifth Avenue and 52nd Street.

PLATE 141　Richardson's frame house has a Romanesque picturesqueness and ruggedness of texture.

PLATE 142 Trinity Church in Boston.

PLATE 143 Following Richardson, the Romanesque Revival resulted in many rockfaced mansions.

PLATE 144   The Wainwright Building in St. Louis.   *Keystone-Underwood*

PLATE 145 The Carson, Pirie, Scott store in Chicago. *Chicago Architectural Photo Company*

PLATE 146   The Chicago World's Fair, 1893.

PLATE 147   Sullivan's Transportation Building, Chicago World's Fair, 1893.

PLATE 148 The main concourse of the Pennsylvania Station, New York, was modeled closely after the tepidarium of the Baths of Caracalla.

PLATE 149 The Boston Public Library.

PLATE 150   The New York Public Library.

PLATE 151   The Woolworth Building, New York.

PLATE 152   St. Thomas' Church, Fifth Avenue, New York.

PLATE 153 An early McKim, Mead and White seashore "cottage" adapts colonial motives.

PLATE 154 The National Academy of Sciences in Washington is a masterpiece of the classical approach to a modern architecture.

PLATE 155
The Church of the
Sagrada Familia,
Barcelona.   *Mas*

PLATE 156
Casa Milá, Barcelona.
                Mas

PLATE 157   Taliesin, Frank Lloyd Wright's home.   *Museum of Modern Art*

PLATE 158   The Kaufman House at Bear Run, Pennsylvania.
Museum of Modern Art

PLATE 159   The Bauhaus at Dessau.

Museum of Modern Art

PLATE 160   L'Unite d'Habitation in Marseilles, designed by Le Corbusier, is magnificent, sculptural architecture, but failed as an ideal human habitation.

French Embassy Press & Information Division

PLATE 161   The strange and daring form of Le Corbusier's church at Notre Dame du Haut at Ronchamps becomes immediately comprehensible when one experiences the warm sense of devotion in its interior.

PLATE 162   The City Hall in Stockholm.

PLATE 163 The Grundtvig Church in Copenhagen, by P. V. Jensen Klint, is medieval in its spirit, yet daring in its use of new forms.

PLATE 164 The bridge at Saginatobel, Switzerland, designed by Robert Maillart, is an early example of the slender grace made possible by reinforced concrete.

Swiss National Tourist Office

PLATE 165 The interior of the church at Raincy, designed by Auguste Perret.
French Embassy Press & Information Division

PLATE 166 The Chicago Tribune tower.

PLATE 167 The Tabernacle
Church of Christ at
Columbus, Indiana, designed
by the Saarinens, is
characteristic of their
tempered modern spirit.
Hedrich-Blessing

PLATE 168 The Daily News Building in New
York. *Metropolitan Museum of Art*

PLATE 169 The clean, strong lines of the buildings of Rockefeller Center make it one of the finest expressions of the creative approach to the problems of modern architecture.
Rockefeller Center, Inc.

PLATE 170 One of the most distinguished groups of modern buildings is the United Nations complex, on the East River in New York City. It was designed by a group of famous architects under the over-all leadership of Wallace K. Harrison.
United Nations

PLATE 171 Paul Cret's Science Building at the Century of Progress Exposition in 1933 was a brilliant example of the "new architecture."

PLATE 172 The New York World's Fair of 1939. *Museum of the City of New York*

Ezra Stoller Associates

PLATE 173 Eero Saarinen's undoubted masterpiece, the Dulles International Airport in the Virginia countryside near Washington, D.C.

G.M. Research Laboratories

PLATE 174 A modern industrial Versailles—the spreading General Motors Research Center near Detroit, designed by Eero Saarinen.

PLATE 175 The flowing, swirling forms of Saarinen's TWA Terminal at New York's Kennedy International Airport express the fluid material of which they are built— reinforced concrete. *Ezra Stoller Associates*

PLATE 176 Minoru Yamasaki has evolved a style of airy elegance, usually *Balthazar Korab* expressed in marble and fine materials. The McGregor Memorial Conference Center at Wayne State University, Detroit.

PLATE 177 Edward Durrell Stone's first great success: the United States *Rondal Partridge* Embassy at New Delhi, India.

PLATE 178 The now-established Stone style: the model of the John F. Kennedy Center for the Performing Arts in Washington, D.C. *Ezra Stoller Associates*

PLATE 179 Skidmore, Owings and Merrill's Lever House, on Park Avenue, New York, was the pace-setter for the glass and stainless-steel-sheathed office buildings, and has never been equaled. It is especially noteworthy for its generous use of valuable land—the building is set back for light and air all around and the ground floor is open as a pedestrian promenade.
Ezra Stoller Associates

PLATE 180 The Lakeshore Apartments in Chicago, designed by Mies van der Rohe.
Hube Henry, Hedrich-Blessing

PLATE 181   A glass jewel-box in the woods: the Farnsworth House, Plano, Illinois, designed by Mies van der Rohe.

PLATE 182   New York's most distinguished piece of modern design: the Seagram Building on Park Avenue, designed by Mies van der Rohe and Philip Johnson.

PLATE 183 Mies van der Rohe designed the buildings on the new campus of the Illinois Institute of Technology. This is the School of Architecture.

PLATE 184 The IBM Research Center at La Gaude, near Nice, France, designed by Marcel Breuer, with Robert F. Gatje, Associate.

PLATE 185 St. John's Abbey at Collegeville, Minnesota, is a powerful sculptural expression in rough concrete and brick, designed by Marcel Breuer, with Hamilton Smith, Associate.

PLATE 186 A house in Palm Springs, California, by Neutra, is typical of the West Coast modernists.

PLATE 187   Le Corbusier's Carpenter Visual Arts Center, Harvard University.

PLATE 188   Nervi's Olympic Sports Palace in Rome, built for their 1957 games.

Alinari

PLATE 189 The George Washington Bridge Bus Station in New York—
Nervi's only structure in the United States.

PLATE 190 One of the truly elegant tall
buildings of the world, the Pirelli Building in Milan, designed by Gio Ponti and
Pier Luigi Nervi.   *Photo by Author*

PLATE 191 "The Palace of Dawn" is the residence of the President in Brasilia, designed by Niemeyer in the personalized style he evolved for that great new city.

Ezra Stoller Associates

PLATE 192   In the trend for some large corporations to move their offices
from the city to the countryside, the building of the Connecticut General Life
Insurance Co., near Bloomfield, Connecticut, is one of the most handsome.
Skidmore, Owings & Merrill, Architects.

PLATE 193   The International Style has produced a few homes of true
elegance and grace, as in the house in Old Westbury, Long Island, designed
by Edward Stone.

Ezra Stoller Associates

PLATE 194　The new building of the School of Architecture at Yale — *Ezra Stoller Associates*
University was designed by the individualistic head of its school,
Paul Rudolph.

PLATE 195 The scale of the town houses and the apartments in the
background is carefully kept harmonious with that of the old houses of
Philadelphia's Society Hill. I. M. Pei & Partners, Architects.

PLATE 196   The bombed-out center of Rotterdam was rebuilt as one great
modern shopping center, with the old City Hall as a background.

PLATE 197   In Fresno, California, the main
downtown street was closed off and converted
into a shopping mall designed by Victor
Gruen Associates.

PLATE 198   The East Court of Westland Center, Detroit, designed by Victor   *Balthazar Korab*
Gruen Associates, is a great air-conditioned interior mall.

PLATE 199 Constitution Plaza in Hartford, Connecticut, is one of the most successful downtown renewals, grouping several new buildings around a multi-level pedestrian plaza. Charles DuBose was the architect for the over-all design; buildings by several architects.

sculpture in the world. The flawless perfection of its execution is a technical marvel. His masterpiece of architecture is the piazza in front of St. Peter's, but he left many other works. Two which are not left, however, were belfries at the front of St. Peter's, for they fell, and every trace of them has been removed. Urban VIII appointed Bernini superintendent of all construction in Rome, and under his supervision many avenues, fountains, and other public works were built. He designed the architectural decoration of the grand apartments of the Vatican, where his taste for the theatrical was given full reign, and the Scala Regia, the main staircase leading to the Vatican apartments, is a masterpiece of ceremonial and perspective illusion. Besides these activities in architecture and sculpture, Bernini designed and arranged stage scenery, pageants, festivals, fireworks, and funerals. He died, wealthy and loaded with honors, in 1680.

Bernini's rival was the eccentric Borromini, whose designs led the Baroque much further into the realm of curving structural members and confusion of detail. He supplanted Bernini as official architect under another Pope, and many old buildings were modernized into the Baroque style from his designs. One of these is the interior of the venerable old basilica of St. John Lateran, which was given to the early Christians by the Emperor Constantine. Its façade was also modernized early in the eighteenth century, in a manner which is classic enough in its elements, but thoroughly Baroque in scale. The Composite order is 100 feet high, and the gesticulating figures standing on the parapet are 20 feet high. The façade so completely lacks scale that a photograph gives no idea of its true size, unless there are people in the foreground.

Rome was transformed during the Baroque period, which in Italy extended through the eighteenth century. Even with all its ancient buildings, Rome is primarily a Baroque city today. Spreading to other cities, some of the best examples of the style are found in Naples and in the cities of the North. In Venice, the splendor-loving city, it found a second home, and its master there was Longhena. His best work is the church of Santa Maria della Salute, with its fanciful dome PLATE 68 which dominates the skyline of most popular views of Venice. Begun in 1631, as a token of gratitude for the ending of a plague, the church exemplifies the central axis plan, being octagonal in form. The graceful dome is buttressed above the low aisle surrounding it by great volutes which are crowned with the inevitable huge statues. Genoa, the other great maritime city, also had a period of splendor. Michelangelo's pupil Alessi designed palaces there, and also designed the church of Santa Maria in Carignano, in which he tried to follow, even though on a smaller scale, Bramante's conception for St. Peter's.

During the seventeenth century in Italy the architect received official recognition and popular acclaim to an extent never equaled before or since. When Fontana completed the erection of the obelisk in the piazza of St. Peter's, "the artificers, intoxicated with joy, carried Fontana on their shoulders in triumph to his own house, amidst the sound of drums and trumpets and the plaudits of an immense crowd." He was created a Knight of the Golden Spur and a Roman nobleman, given a pension of 2,000 gold crowns for himself and his heirs, and awarded ten knighthoods. Two medals were struck in his honor, and a book was published describing the work in detail. In case this seems exaggerated, it must be remembered that this was a period of flamboyance and display, in which honors and social recognition were eagerly sought after and freely granted.

Bernini was still a young man when his patron became Pope and said to him, "It is fortunate for you that the Cardinal Maffeo Barberini is become Pope; but we are still more so, that the Cavaliere Bernini should live during our pontificate." In 1665 King Louis XIV of France wrote Bernini in person, begging him to come to Paris. His journey there was a triumphal procession; in every city scholars and persons of rank came out to meet him, and the people crowded the streets to catch a glimpse of him—so much so, in fact, that in his diary Bernini compared himself to an elephant or some other curiosity of nature. The king treated him with great esteem, and nobles and ministers vied with each other in paying homage to him. During the eight months he was in France, he received as pay five gold louis a day, and finally a present of 50,000 crowns and an annual pension of 2,000 crowns. Without knowing the exact value of a crown, it can be assumed that it was a considerable sum, for a certain successful Italian architect was lured to England to work for the Prince of Wales with an annual salary of only 800 crowns. When Bernini died, he had received every possible title and honor from the Papacy, and he left an estate of 400,000 crowns.

✽ IX ✽

French Renaissance

I N FRANCE AND the rest of northern and western Europe during the fifteenth century, the wealth and power lay in the hands of the kings and their favorites of the nobility, and a few merchant princes. The immense income of the kings came primarily from taxation, and to a smaller extent from revenue from their many estates. Although Paris was the capital of the kingdom of France, the French kings spent little time there, preferring life on their country estates. They filled in the moats around the old castles, enlarged the windows, built gardens and terraces, and developed a new and more luxurious way of living. Most of these royal and princely country homes were in the valley of the river Loire, about a hundred miles south of Paris, and it was there that the Renaissance in architecture was first manifested in France.

The Renaissance in thought in fifteenth-century France reflected the growing spirit of humanism, as it did in Italy. But in architecture it was definitely an importation, and one which took hold slowly and against considerable resistance. When the brash young French king, Charles VIII, invaded Italy in 1495, he was soon forced to withdraw, but this brief exposure to the new culture of the Italians was an eye opener to him. He and his nobles were tremendously impressed by the new beauties which they saw, and they took quantities of books, paintings, and sculptures back to France with them. Charles assembled a group of twenty artists and sent them to his country residence, the château at Amboise. Their instructions were "to build and work at the orders of the king in the style of Italy." Two of the group were architects, Fra Giocondo and da Cortona; the rest were sculptors, painters, and decorators. Fra Giocondo had made the first translation of Vitruvius into Italian, and had designed the exquisite loggia del Consiglio in Verona in the north Italian style. Upon his return to Italy he worked with Sangallo on St. Peter's.

It is difficult to tell just what these architects did in France. They are supposed to have remodeled Amboise, and to have built the châteaux at Chambord, Gaillon, and Meillant, and a new wing on the château at Blois. But these palaces are so Gothic that it is difficult to believe that a classically trained Italian had anything to do with their designs. The northern climate calls for many fireplaces and steep roofs, consequently there were many chimneys and tall dormer windows. The mass and spirit of the buildings are very Gothic, and only in ornamental details do they show a trace of the Italian influence.

Charles VIII died in 1498, and the only classical touch in the buildings built by his successor, Louis XII, is the manner in which their façades are divided horizontally by stringcourses at each story, with a cornice at the top. It was not until Francis I came to the throne in 1515, a gay and ambitious monarch with a great flair for building, that the French Renaissance may be said to have really begun. Francis brought another group of Italians to France, establishing them at the château at Fontainebleau. These included one architect, Serlio, a couple of first-class painters, Primaticcio and Rosso, and that talented and swaggering sculptor, goldsmith, and diarist, Benvenuto Cellini. Cellini stayed for five years, and returned in disgust to Florence, where he wrote withering comments in his diary on the "barbaric" French court.

Francis I built another wing on the château at Blois, and here for the first time in France is seen a façade divided up with pilasters and PLATE 69 entablatures in the classic manner. Its most striking feature is a polygonal stair tower projecting from the building, a daring and original feature, but definitely not classical despite its Ionic pilasters. The building is profusely ornamented, in a manner reminiscent of some of the north Italian buildings, but it is still French. Resolved to build his own château, Francis chose as a site a clearing on the edge of a swampy forest at Chambord, and there erected an enormous building which set the fashion for the country homes of his court and those of the generation to come. It is not known definitely who designed it. Da Cortona made a model of it, and he may have designed it, or it may have been designed by Pierre Trinqueau, the master builder who built it.

Chambord has a symmetrical plan, in the form of a hollow rectangle 525 feet by 375 feet, with circular towers at the corners. Inside the court, attached to one of the long sides, is a central building 220 feet square containing a double spiral staircase—two spirals starting from the same floor but on opposite sides, so that two groups can ascend at the same time without being able to see each other. The halls and chambers are richly and heavily decorated with classical motives, with great fireplaces everywhere. The exterior walls are comparatively plain, except for the large windows, but above the roof the building breaks into a shimmering silhouette of peaked roofs, chimneys, pinnacled dormers, and a lantern over the spiral staircase, all profusely decorated with somewhat fantastically conceived Renaissance ornamentation.

PLATE 70

There are few known works by the Italian architects who were brought to France by Charles VIII and Francis I. Before he returned to Italy, Fra Giocondo designed the Pont Notre Dame, the bridge over the Seine in front of the cathedral which still carries the busy city traffic. Da Cortona, who chose to remain in France, designed the Hôtel de Ville, or City Hall, in Paris, and he may have designed the church of St. Eustache, one of the few churches built in the sixteenth century. Its vaults and construction are Gothic, but they are clothed in pilasters and entablatures, heavily over-decorated in the "Italian style." Francis' wing of the palace at Fontainebleau was possibly designed by Serlio, but that Italian was not happy in France and soon returned to Italy.

De l'Orme and Lescot

UNTIL THE MIDDLE OF THE SIXTEENTH CENTURY THERE WERE NO French architects equipped to design in the new style. Furthermore, the strongly organized master builders, who still controlled all construction as they had during the Middle Ages, resented the intrusion of the Italian stonecarvers, with their foreign ideas. Enthusiasm for the new style was limited to the world of fashion. During the first half of the century the master builders continued to hold sway and build according to their traditions, permitting the Italians to do only minor decorating. But by 1550, French craftsmen, in spite of themselves, had become well trained in the vocabulary of ornament of the Renaissance, and French architects appeared who had traveled in Italy and had studied classic architecture.

Such was the background of Philibert de l'Orme, son of a mason of Lyons, who had studied and worked in Italy. He became the favorite of Henry II, who succeeded his father, Francis I, in 1547, and thus became a "very great personage," a royal counsellor, abbot of Ivry, and a wealthy man. He was appointed architect for all royal buildings PLATE 72 still under construction, such as the palaces at Fontainebleau, St. Germaine-en-Laye, and others. His fortunes crashed, however, when Henry was accidentally killed in a jousting tournament, for Francis II dismissed him and turned all royal construction over to old Primaticcio, who was a good painter but no architect. Philibert retired and wrote a colossal work on architecture, and before he died he designed buildings for Henry II's widow, Catherine de' Medici, great-great-great-granddaughter of Cosimo de' Medici. The largest building was the Tuileries, a great palace in Paris, with which the queen-mother intended to eclipse the palace of the Louvre which her husband and his mistress had begun. The Tuileries was planned as a vast palace around three courts, forming a rectangle 807 feet by 500 feet, the largest palace designed by one man since the days of imperial Rome. It was only partially built, however, and was burned and almost totally destroyed by the Commune of Paris in 1871. There was no great originality to de l'Orme's designs; he seems to have been satisfied to know and use the orders, as though that were all there was to architecture. PLATE 71 As a constructor, however, he was a brilliant innovator, and in his book he left a legacy of valuable advice to later generations of builders.

Contemporary with de l'Orme was Pierre Lescot, a gentleman of good birth who lived the life of a courtier, and whose design shows his background of breeding and good taste. His most important, and perhaps only, work was the rebuilding of the Louvre, to which he was appointed by Henry II. The Louvre was the old royal palace in Paris, at that time a dark and damp stronghold which had been built in the thirteenth century. Lescot demolished it and began a new palace in the form of a hollow square, which remains as the old portion of the museum of the Louvre today. It is very elegant in design, with fluted Corinthian pilasters and engaged columns, niches with sculpture, and an attic story with delicate reliefs. His collaborator was Jean Goujon, the greatest of the early French Renaissance sculptors, who not only executed the sculpture but may also have had a hand in the design.

Catherine de' Medici had a mania for building, and her husband's mistress, Diane de Poitiers, and other women of the court were also enthusiastic builders, so the art of planning benefited from their influence. Thanks to them, private chambers were given as much consideration as public spaces, service staircases were provided, fireplaces were greatly improved so as not to throw all the heat up the chimneys, and baths and toilets were placed near the bedrooms instead of at the other end of the garden.

Germany and Spain

ITALIAN ARCHITECTS AND ARTISTS, BEARING THE SEEDS OF THE new style, were imported into the rest of continental Europe during the sixteenth century, but their seeds bore little fruit. It was not until a century later that the late Renaissance Baroque style of Italy became thoroughly implanted in the soil. The early Italian influence is most noticeable in Germany, where the most famous sixteenth-century monument is the old portion of Heidelberg Castle, now a vine-covered ruin partially restored for the tourist trade. A picturesque jumble of buildings about an irregular court, it shows no Italian influence in its thoroughly medieval plan. Its three-storied façade is divided by entablatures, and its windows are set apart by niches and pilasters, all elaborately sculptured in a very un-Italian manner. In many of the prosperous cities, guild halls and city halls were built, following a standard type with an arcaded ground floor and five or six stories above, tapering up into a great steeply-pitched gable. The Cloth Hall at Brunswick is such a building, still medieval in form and spirit, but treated with engaged columns and cornices, heavily sculptured and thoroughly Germanic in character. In Cologne a two-story open loggia, in the true Italian manner, was added to the front of the City Hall in 1570, but it was completely destroyed in World War II.

In the latter part of the fifteenth century, Ferdinand and Isabella encouraged a number of foreign artists to come to Spain, but they were from Germany, Burgundy, and Flanders, and were consequently workers in the Gothic tradition. Early in the sixteenth century a designer by the name of Enrique de Egas evolved a system of decoration which shows what seems to be the first use of Italian forms. He may have acquired it from some north Italian marbleworkers who came to Spain to carve reliefs, or possibly from some unknown Spanish artist who had traveled to Milan and Pavia. In any case, his style bears such a resemblance to metalworking that it is called Plateresque, which means "silversmith-like." It involves the use of slender columns whose shafts thicken in a convex curve, with moulded collars separating bands of ornamentation, pilasters decorated with flat arabesques, tiny vaulted niches with figures, candelabra-like forms, and applied to all a relief ornamentation which looks like silver *repoussé*. The first use of Plateresque occurs on several buildings designed by de Egas in Toledo and Salamanca. One of the finest examples is the façade of PLATE 73   the Casa de Ayuntamiento, in Seville.

The Emperor Charles V built an alcazar, or palace, at Granada which marks the first introduction of the Roman Renaissance. Its architect was Pedro de Machuoa, who had been educated in Italy, where he studied the style of Bramante and Raphael. The building is 200 feet square, with a great circular patio, or court, 100 feet in diameter. The walls, both interior and exterior, are treated with severely correct Doric and Ionic orders.

This building was soon eclipsed by the great palace, called the PLATE 74   Escorial, built by Philip II between 1563 and 1584. One of the great palaces of the world, it contains not only chambers, salons, and offices for the court, but a church, a monastery, a library, and a picture gallery. It is a rectangle, 675 feet by 525 feet, with three large courts and ten small courts built on a terrace hewn out of a mountainside, a magnificent and dramatic location. Its plan is the work of a Spanish architect who had worked in Naples. He died soon after the work was begun, and the job was finished by Herrera, the great architect of the Spanish Renaissance. In style the Escorial is very severe, the Doric order being used most frequently throughout. The church follows the type of St. Peter's, but on a greatly reduced scale and with great severity. The entire palace is a work of restraint and dignity.

François Mansart

FRANCE ENTERED ITS GOLDEN AGE IN THE SEVENTEENTH CENTURY, beginning with the reign of Henry IV, "the best King that ever sat on the throne of France." This great period in the arts was continued by his son and grandson, Louis XIII and Louis XIV, and their able ministers, Richelieu, Mazarin, and Colbert. Whereas his predecessors had built to amuse themselves, Henry IV built for the good of the state and to create employment for his people. One of his first undertakings was the revitalization of the city of Paris, which he found in a state of medieval decrepitude. He widened and paved streets, cleared out slums to create new squares and avenues, and had a master plan for the city prepared, which was unfortunately abandoned after the king was assassinated in 1610.

Henry IV completed the Grand Gallery of the Louvre, the wing connecting it with the Tuileries. He added to the château at Fontainebleau, and completed the palace at St. Germaine-en-Laye, both of which had been started by Francis I. He encouraged members of his court to build, and his minister Sully and many others built great country houses. A new and thoroughly French vernacular developed in domestic architecture during the early years of the seventeenth century, largely the result of the need for economy. The lavish ornament of the style of Francis I, with the incessant use of the orders, gave way to a simpler style of brick trimmed with stone. But by the middle of the century the Italian manner took precedence again, as a result of the studies of French architects in Italy under the influence of Vignola.

The great French architect of the seventeenth century was François Mansart. He was born in 1598, the son of the king's carpenter, and little is known of his early training. His greatest asset was his exquisite taste and high intelligence, although on the other hand he was extravagant and independent. Colbert commissioned him to design further additions to the Louvre, but when told he would not

be permitted to make alterations in his design once the work was
started, as he was fond of doing, Mansart refused the work rather
than "give up his freedom." He is generally considered to have been
the originator of the type of roof which bears his name, the mansard
roof, although it seems actually to be a much older form. Mansart's
early work is in Normandy, done in the characteristic brick-and-stone
style. In this style, the corners are formed with stone blocks of alternating lengths, called quoins, and openings are trimmed in the same
manner. The wall between is of brick. There are no pilasters, few
stringcourses, and only the simplest cornice. A classical character pre-
vails, despite the steep roofs, dormers rising flush out of the wall, and
towering chimneys.

The Duke of Orleans commissioned Mansart to rebuild the
château at Blois, and this was followed by the château of Maisons
and many others, including at least ten great houses in Paris. In all
these buildings the "economy style" of Henry IV was abandoned,
and the full Italian style was resumed again. In its free use of classical
forms, this style shows the influence of the Baroque, which was
by that time in full swing in Italy, but at the same time it has a
chastity and dignity which is thoroughly French. Mansart's north
wing at Blois has the orders applied at each floor, in a simple
and severe fashion. It is only in the central pavilion that the
Baroque is revealed in a great shell motive and cartouche over the
main entrance, with surrounding sculpture. One of Mansart's town
houses in Paris, the Hôtel Carnavalet, is chaste classicism supreme,
French only in an undefinable flavor, which is aided by the inevitable
steep roof and by the inclusion of some sculptures of Jean Goujon
which the owner insisted upon using.

Mansart's last work was the design for the church of the Val-de-
Grâce, begun for the queen-mother, Anne of Austria, in 1645. As
usual, Mansart was recklessly extravagant, but his client was timid
and parsimonious, so within a year he was superseded by Lemercier.
Mansart died a few years later, and a period of French architecture
died with him. For sixty years, since the time of Henry IV, French
architecture had followed its own directions, free of royal dictation.
Beginning with the personal rule of Louis XIV, an official style was
decreed and followed.

The façade of the church of the Val-de-Grâce follows the general composition of the Gesù, but on a much smaller scale. The entrance is approached by a flight of steps, and is flanked by coupled Corinthian columns supporting a pediment which breaks forward from the face of the building. At each side is a niche containing sculpture. The high end of the nave above is treated with another Corinthian order and pediment, with the characteristic volutes tying it to the aisles. Over the crossing is a high dome on a drum, which is buttressed by free-standing columns and surmounted by a lantern. The dome is rather fussy in its multiplicity of detail, but the building as a whole is chaste and dignified. The interior has a barrel-vaulted nave pierced by clerestory windows, pilastered piers with arches between, and under the dome is a baldachino, much too large for the little church, with twisted columns in imitation of Bernini's masterpiece.

J. H. Mansart and le Nôtre

THE REIGN OF LOUIS XIV, THE GRAND MONARCH, WAS A PERIOD UN-paralleled in grand construction. Such a huge program required an architect whose abilities were equal to it, and such an architect was Jules Hardouin Mansart. Born Jules Hardouin about 1646, he adopted the surname of his famous great-uncle, François Mansart. Something of a sycophant and not above intrigue, he was still a very able man. He made his way rapidly, designing several fine houses at St. Germain, and soon attracted the attention of the king, so at the age of thirty, Louis XIV commanded him to undertake the vast commission of designing a palace at Versailles, a suburb about eleven miles southwest of Paris. There was a little château there, which had been the favorite hunting box of Louis XIII. In about twenty years it was transformed into the great palace so well known today, at a cost [PLATE 76] which has been estimated at about $65,000,000. With this commission as a springboard, J. H. Mansart literally monopolized the official architecture of France, and a great deal more. In a material sense, he was probably the most successful architect that ever lived, achieving great wealth, receiving every possible honor and title, and being virtual dictator of all the arts in France, through his posts as Director of the Academies of Painting, Sculpture, and Architecture.

The hunting box of Louis XIII was really a good-sized little palace, which had been designed for him by Lemercier in 1627, and during the 1660's Louis XIV had le Vau add two wings to it. Mansart worked on the designs for its extension off and on for the rest of his life, and lesser additions were made by Louis XV and Louis XVI. The purpose of such a vast palace was not only to house the king and his immediate household, but his entire court as well, for Louis XIV required that his nobles be in constant attendance. Hence the hundreds of living apartments, in addition to the many galleries, reception halls, state chambers, and courts. The palace accommodated nearly 10,000 persons, and its façade is over 1,600 feet long. A city grew up around it, for the king gave a piece of land to each of his courtiers, and they in turn built little houses for themselves where they could retire in privacy, away from the strenuous life of the court.

The central portion of the palace, surrounding the Cour de Marbre, is Louis XIII's original château. The wings extending to the east were added by le Vau, and from there to the north and south extend the wings by Mansart and others, leaving a great entrance court between them. One of the most famous chambers of the palace, the Hall of Mirrors, by Mansart, is 240 feet long, 35 feet wide, and 42 feet high. It is most lavishly decorated, with green marble pilasters, gilded ornaments, and a barrel-vaulted ceiling painted by Charles Le Brun, the greatest mural painter of the seventeenth century.

One of the great artists of the latter part of the seventeenth century was André le Nôtre, who would today be called a landscape architect. He was the son of the official gardener of the Tuileries, and studied painting and design before he took over his father's position in 1637. Until his death in 1700, he designed and maintained not only the vast gardens surrounding the palaces of the king, but also those of the members of his court, some of which were as elaborate as the royal gardens. He adapted the Renaissance city planning of Italy to garden planning, conceiving his designs on geometrical lines, with planting laid out in rectangular compartments intersected by walks and avenues, and embellished with sculpture, fountains, lagoons, steps, balustrades, grottoes, and cascades. The whole was framed in artificially planted forests intersected by paths and spotted with marble temples.

The gardens which le Nôtre designed for Versailles are an even

greater sight than the palace. The great terrace on the west has an
enormous circular pool with fountains, and from it an avenue of PLATE 75
grass leads between dense trees to the canal, 200 feet wide and a mile
long. South of the terrace two fine staircases lead down to the
orangery and on to a lake. On the north an avenue lined with fountains leads down to the basin of Neptune, with more sculpture and
more fountains. Throughout the park, alleys ornamented with statues,
urns, and temples are cut through the forest. There are groves, grottoes, and waterfalls, and miles of trimmed yews and hedges. Water
was scarce at Versailles, so to make the fountains possible, it was
brought from the Seine, and when that proved to be insufficient, an
aqueduct was begun to bring water from the river Eure. After spending some $9,000,000 and the lives of several hundred workmen on it,
the aqueduct was abandoned as being impracticable. Finally the surface water drained from a vast area was collected and led by nearly
a hundred miles of channels to the gardens, which are underlaid
with a network of pipes, vaults, and aqueducts. The palace and the
park are a national monument today; when France is prosperous
the great fountains play on Sunday afternoons, and the tourists and PLATE 77
people of Paris roam where once the glittering court of Louis XIV,
le Roi Soleil, promenaded, played, and intrigued.

The Invalides is a great hospital for disabled soldiers which was
founded by Louis XIV. It covers a tremendous area on the left bank of
the Seine in the heart of Paris. Its buildings, grouped around sixteen
courts, were intended to accommodate five thousand veterans. The
original portion was designed by Bruand, but he was soon superseded
by J. H. Mansart, who designed the hospital's dominating feature, the
Royal Chapel, now better known as the tomb of Napoleon. Its fine PLATE 78
gilded dome is set on a very high drum, which in turn rests upon the
crossing of a relatively small Greek-cross-shaped building, treated
with the orders in the most restrained French manner. Not far away,
on the river bank, is the Institut de France, which was designed by
le Vau as the Collège Mazarin. It has a very fine Corinthian portico,
and is topped by the inevitable dome. Paris is full of fine buildings
from the seventeenth century, and the eighteenth century was to
produce still more. These two centuries, with a few important additions of the nineteenth century, produced the Paris that is seen today.

In 1648 the king founded an Academy of Painting and Sculpture

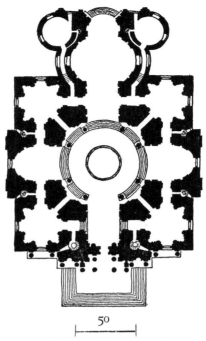

50

The Royal Chapel of the Invalides, now the tomb of Napoleon.

to train artists and set standards for their work. In 1664 the minister Colbert established the French Academy at Rome, in order to have a plentiful supply of classically trained artists and architects to perform for the king. Seven years later he founded the Academy of Architecture to train students and lay down the rules for taste—which was, of course, the king's taste. To settle the controversy between those who wanted to stick to pure classicism and those who preferred the splendors of the Baroque, the Academy decreed that the exterior of buildings should be severely classic, but in the interiors the architects could indulge in all the Baroque freedom they wished!

The Louvre

IN 1665 THE ARCHITECT OF THE LOUVRE WAS LOUIS LE VAU. COLBERT was not pleased with his design of the wing which was projected, so he had a model made of it and asked the architects of Paris for their opinion. They condemned it to a man, and each produced his own design to offer as a substitute. A brilliant amateur architect by the name of Claude Perrault, whose brother was Colbert's secretary, submitted a design anonymously. It was by far the best of the lot, so Colbert sent it to Italy for comment by the Italian masters. At the same time, Louis XIV invited Bernini to come to Paris to settle the controversy.

Bernini was as disloyal to his brother architect as the architects of Paris had been, for he too produced a design of his own. It was accepted by the king, and the cornerstone was actually laid by the king six months later. However, after Bernini's return to Rome the king lost interest in the project in favor of his beloved Versailles. Meanwhile Perrault's brother had been spying on Bernini's design and pointing out its impracticalities to Colbert; furthermore, the Academy resented the foreigner's grand design. So, with both Bernini and the king out of the way, Colbert suddenly discarded the Italian's design and switched to that of Perrault. Thus it came about that an amateur architect, an ardent student of medicine, gets the credit for one of the finest pieces of French Renaissance architecture, the east façade of the Louvre.

PLATE 79

The palace of the Louvre is one of the most important buildings in France, and it portrays the whole story of French Renaissance architecture, from the sixteenth century to the nineteenth. The oldest portion is the completely enclosed court at the east end, of which the southwest corner is the part built by Lescot in 1550 for Francis I, and for Catherine de' Medici in the last years of the sixteenth century. Southward from that corner, and then westward, is the beginning of the wing with which Catherine intended to connect the palace to her Tuileries. Henry IV continued this wing, the "Grand Gallery," westward along the Seine in 1600, but its façades were completely remodeled by Napoleon III in the nineteenth century. Under Louis XIII and Richelieu, Lemercier continued Lescot's courtyard, completing the northwest corner. Then Louis XIV had le Vau complete the court, to which Perrault's external façade was added later. After 1675 nothing much was done to the palace, for Louis XIV was wrapped up in his passion for building Versailles. About 1810 Napoleon I built the other long wing on

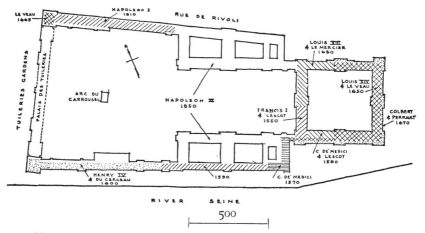

The Louvre was built over a period of three hundred years.

the north connecting the Louvre with the Tuileries, and in 1850 Napoleon III built the central portions, on both the north and south sides, enclosing several smaller courts, and making one building out of the whole thing. When the Tuileries palace was destroyed in 1871, it was necessary to remodel the ends of the two wings of the Louvre where they had joined on to the destroyed building. This work, completed in 1878, was the last in the building of this great palace, now the famous Museum of the Louvre, which covers over 45 acres and stretches for 2,350 feet along the bank of the Seine.

The Eighteenth Century

DURING MOST OF THE EIGHTEENTH CENTURY, FRANCE, EVEN WITH the outward appearance of stability, actually tottered on the verge of bankruptcy and national disaster, heading for the revolution which ultimately came in 1790. The vast building programs of Louis XIV and his never-ending wars, and the extravagance of the court of Louis XV, left the people bitter, miserable, and often openly rebellious, so that the well-intentioned reforms of Louis XVI's minister only stirred up more trouble. In 1789 a middle-class group proclaimed itself a National Assembly, which led into the bloody Revolution and the Reign of Terror, followed by the rise and fall of Napoleon.

Yet during this unstable eighteenth century, aristocratic building went on, although on a reduced scale. During this period, too, the French architects designed many palaces for ambitious princes and bishops in other European countries. Imitations of Versailles were built in Spain, Germany, Austria, Poland, and Russia.

In France the exterior of the buildings generally followed the decree of the Academy that they be severely classic, but in the interior architecture and decoration a new note began to appear, an extreme Baroque style called rococo, in which the rectangularity of architectural lines gave way to an even greater use of curves. In French hands it seldom overstepped the bounds of good taste, but in other countries it produced some fantastic results. This fashion started during the Regency, reached its peak during the reign of Louis XV, and was superseded by a new classicism during the reign of Louis XVI and the *Directoire,* or Directorate, which followed him.

J. H. Mansart's work was carried on by his staff for some time after his death in 1708. The chapel in the palace at Versailles was completed, and palaces at Metz, Bonn, Strasbourg, and Verdun. The outstanding individual architects of the eighteenth century in France were father and son—Jacques Jules Gabriel and Jacques Ange Gabriel. The father was a relative of J. H. Mansart. Under the Regency he designed many fine bridges in various cities, the Place de la Bourse with its surrounding buildings in Bordeaux, and a fine Renaissance cathedral at La Rochelle. Before his death in 1742 he achieved the coveted title of *premier architecte du Roi,* in which position his son succeeded him. Louis XV, Madame de Pompadour, and members of the court kept J. A. Gabriel busy at Versailles and other palaces. It is interesting to note that during the Regency the principal building activity, small as it was, was in public works, while as soon as the king assumed power, the money went once more toward palaces. Money, however, was scarce, and poor Gabriel was plagued and exasperated all his life by being called upon to design grand projects on a penny-pinching budget. At Versailles he remodeled many of the interiors and designed the theater at the end of the north wing. In the gardens he designed the Petit Trianon, a gemlike little palace which Louis XV built for Madame du Barry, of which more will be said later.

In 1748 a competition was held for designs for a monument to Louis XV, in which nearly all the architects of the Academy competed. None of the designs were accepted, but the king appointed Gabriel to take the best ideas from each of the designs and carry out the work. The great public square which resulted, now known as the Place de la Concorde, is one of the handsomest in the world. Three years later Gabriel designed the École Militaire in Paris, a fine piece of classicism in the old tradition which had almost disappeared but which was due for a revival in the latter part of the century. J. A. Gabriel died in 1782, the best French architect of the century and the last of the old school.

About 1760 there was a marked swing back to the Academic and classical style, a movement which reached its height under Napoleon I early in the nineteenth century. In 1784 Soufflot completed the church of St. Geneviève, the patron saint of Paris. During the Revolution it was secularized and renamed the Pantheon, dedicated to all the heroes of France. It is a very handsome cruciform PLATE 80 building with a high triple-shelled dome which is surrounded on the exterior with a circular colonnade. The façade has a broad Corinthian portico with a pediment filled with sculpture in high relief. The interior is dominated by the dome, 200 feet high, and flooded with light from the windows in the drum. Instead of the usual barrel vaults, the nave and the other arms of the cross have low saucer-like domes. A more strictly Roman type of church is the Madeleine, begun by Vignon in 1764, but not completed until the time of Na- PLATE 81 poleon. In form it is a colossal temple, 350 feet long and 147 feet wide, standing on a podium 23 feet high, surrounded entirely by its Corinthian colonnade. The interior is a long nave with three shallow saucer domes and a half-dome over the apse—which comes as something of a surprise after entering under the Roman pediment. The Madeleine has become the favorite church of the people of Paris.

Interior Architecture

THE STYLES IN INTERIOR ARCHITECTURE UNDER THE FOUR KINGS named Louis who ruled France during the seventeenth and eighteenth centuries assumed great popularity during the early part of the twentieth century. Through the whole period there ran the struggle between restraint and license, between official classicism and fantasy. During the period of Louis XIII the forms were taking shape, assuming a definite French character free of the Italianate influence of the time of Henry IV. The trend is indicated by the use of painted panels and shell- and scroll-like decorative forms. During the early years of the long reign of Louis XIV, the fine rooms of the palaces and great houses were treated with pilasters and cornices with a grave and rather pompous dignity, the wall spaces between the pilasters being divided into panels. The mouldings of the panels indicate the trend of fashion, for they gradually became more and more ornate, breaking out into curved and twisted forms at the top, and often they were repeated one within the other. The increasing desire for softness of form led to the use of a cove, a concave moulding, between the cornice and the ceiling, often decorated with a diagonal network pattern. Mantelpieces were curved and bowed, and enormous mirrors were set over them and between the windows.

During the period of the Regency a new freedom, or license, showed itself in the arts, as it did in the life of the court. Gone were the strict formalities, the pompous prudery, and the rigid Academic controls of the days of Louis XIV. Interior architecture turned to fantasy and opulence, pilasters and cornices disappeared, and the paneled walls merged with the ceilings in great decorated coves. The panels were further enriched with more mouldings, and their curved tops were carved and hung with garlands. Instead of being finished in the natural colors of the woods, as they had been previously, the walls were often painted white, with gilding on the mouldings and the ornament. During the reign of Louis XV the rococo reached its height. The love for free curves dominated everything. Panel moulds were not only elaborately curved, but often unsymmetrically. The wall treatment ran right up onto the ceiling, PLATE 82 which was painted with cupids and flowers and allegorical scenes. Richly ornamented as it is, the French rococo has an air of playfulness and charm, and it is never vulgar.

The next trend in interior architecture was the result of two influences. One was the inevitable reaction from the fanciful extravagances of the rococo back to classicism again, and the other was the discovery of Pompeii. The results of the systematic excavation of that buried city aroused great interest throughout Europe, for education was strictly classical, and antique art was still considered the best. Thus the interior architecture of the reign of Louis XVI, the Directoire, and the Napoleonic years was a throwback to the classic mould again. Pilasters and cornices came back, panels became rectangular once more, although often with double or triple mouldings, and ceilings became flat and plain white. Under Napoleon the architects and decorators went back to the style of early imperial Rome for their motives, for the emperor loved to surround himself with the trappings of the Caesars.

City Planning

TOWN PLANNING received considerable attention during the seventeenth and eighteenth centuries in France, although as in Italy it was primarily for beautification rather than for sanitation and the improvement of living conditions. However, it must be said for Henry IV that he built a hydraulic machine on the Pont Neuf in Paris to pump water from the river for sanitary uses, and Louis XIII built the first sewers in the city, ancient stone vaults many of which are still in use. In many cities, squares and boulevards were laid out, after the manner of the improvements the Popes were making in Rome. André le Nôtre was the father of town planning in this sense, and his design for the park at Versailles influenced not only the planning of private parks and gardens all over Europe, but the planning of cities as well. Pierre Charles l'Enfant, French architect and engineer, brought the traditions of le Nôtre and Versailles to America with his plan for the new city of Washington.

The gardens of the Tuileries, in the heart of Paris, were originally planned by le Nôtre as the gardens of the Tuileries palace. Later enlarged, they now cover fifty-six acres, extending all the way to the Place de la Concorde, the great square designed by J. A. Gabriel. PLATE 83 The immense appeal of this square arises not only from its great size, but also from the fine formal planning of its pavements and plantings, which center around an obelisk brought from the temple at Luxor. There is a magnificent vista in each of the four directions: to the north, between two palaces, the Rue Royale leads to the Madeleine, which can be seen in the distance; to the east the vista extends for a half-mile through the gardens of the Tuileries to the Louvre; to the west there is a sweep of a mile up the park-lined Champs Elysées to the Arc de Triomphe; and to the south the Pont de la Concorde carries the view across the Seine to the Chambre des Deputés. The great sense of controlled spaciousness makes this square one of the finest pieces of planning in the world.

Many other cities, and even smaller towns, have fine squares and malls lined with harmoniously designed buildings of even cornice heights, and embellished with sculpture and fountains. One of the best is at Nancy. During the eighteenth century, Stanislas Leczinski, the former king of Poland, who was also the last of the dukes of Lorraine and the father-in-law of Louis XV, built the center of the city. The Place Stanislas is surrounded by handsome buildings designed by Héré, Nancy's own eighteenth-century architect. On the north a triumphal arch, built in honor of Louis XV, leads to the Place de la Carrière, a long mall lined with fine buildings, with the governmental palace at the far end. Nancy is only a provincial city, but its civic center has all the spacious dignity of a capital.

Domestic Architecture

SOME OF THE FINEST BITS OF RENAISSANCE ARCHITECTURE IN FRANCE are relatively little-known—known only, at least, to a few architects and lovers of architecture. They are the little châteaux, manor houses, and town houses of the lesser nobility and the middle-class aristocracy. These houses reflect the quiet and civilized lives of the people who lived in them; they are formal yet suggestive of ease and comfort, elegant yet simple and homelike. An early example of a rural château is the Château de Brécy, near Bayeux, which was designed by François Mansart. The approach is through a long avenue of elms which leads to a handsome Baroque gate through a pilastered brick wall. Beyond is a paved courtyard with the little château at the far end, and the farm buildings along each side. The château is of brick, now covered with stucco, with stone quoins and stone trim around

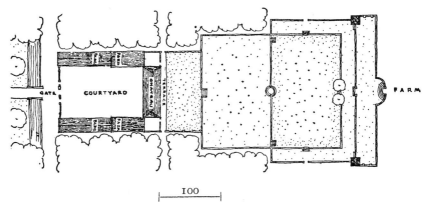

The plan of the Château de Brécy.

The façade of the Château de Brécy shows the simple formality of François Mansart's "economy" style.

the tall windows. It is two stories high, with slender stone dormers rising from the wall into the steep roof. The farm buildings are low, and undecorated except for their stone trim. The other side of the château opens with many windows and French doors onto a paved terrace surrounded by balustrades, which in turn opens onto a series of grassy terraces stepping up the hill toward another handsome gate, which leads to the farm lands beyond. It is a farm, frankly evidenced by the approach through the farmyard, yet in its way it has all the dignity and elegance of a great house.

At number 93 Rue Royale, in Versailles, there is a little Directoire house which is typical of the homes the members of the court built

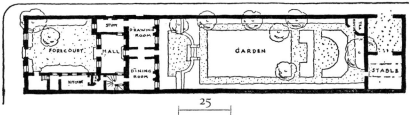

Number 93 Rue Royale, in Versailles.

for themselves as refuges from court life. The corner plot is only 38 feet wide and 188 feet deep, but it has all the appointments of a miniature estate. The house sets back from the street about thirty-five feet, making room for a paved forecourt enclosed by walls on the two street sides and by a one-story kitchen wing coming forward from the house on the other side. The entrance is into a spacious hall, with a study at one side and a stairway, gracefully curved as always, on the other. Opposite the entrance a corridor leads through to the garden door, with a drawing room on the left and the dining room on the right. The second floor contains a library and the master's bedroom and bath, and on the third floor there are two more bedrooms. The drawing room and the dining room open directly out upon the terrace, overlooking the long formally planted garden, which is walled on both sides. Across the back of the property, behind walls, are the buildings that were formerly the stable and the chicken and rabbit yards. Tucked in a corner against the wall is a little tea house. Architecturally, the house has no pretensions whatsoever. Its walls of cool gray stucco are relieved only by stringcourses at each story, relying for interest wholly upon the nice spacing of the casement windows and their slatted shutters. The aspect from the street is formal and reserved, but from the garden the house appears gay and inviting.

The little palace known as the Petit Trianon in the park at Versailles was completed in 1768 from designs by J. A. Gabriel. PLATE 84 Louis XV built it for Madame Pompadour, and upon his succession to the throne, Louis XVI gave it to his young queen, Marie An-

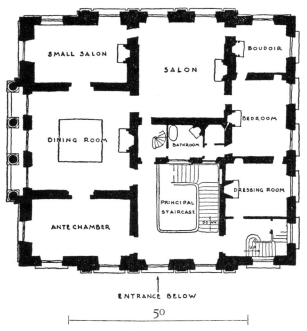

The main floor of the Petit Trianon is devoted to salons and the Queen's Suite.

toinette, with whom it is chiefly associated in history. It is a three-story building, 73 feet by 79 feet, built of cream-colored limestone, standing today in the midst of its gardens just about as it did two hundred years ago. The palace is approached from the south through an entrance court surrounded by walls and beech hedges. The exterior is simple, depending primarily upon good proportion and refinement of detail. The south entrance front and the north front have Corinthian pilasters, the west garden front has a shallow Corinthian portico, all two stories high, standing upon a rusticated basement. The east front has only the finely detailed windows.

The basement or ground floor contains the entrance hall with the principal staircase, a billiard room, and the kitchen and service rooms. The stair hall extends through two stories, with a wide stone staircase and a rich iron rail. On the first or principal story is the salon on the north, two smaller salons in the corners, and the dining room on the west, overlooking the garden. Along the east side is the private apartment of the queen, containing a bedroom, boudoir, and dressing room. This apartment has a lower ceiling than the other rooms, permitting a mezzanine floor above it which contains the king's apartment. The grand staircase terminates at the first floor, and there is a smaller stair going on up to the second floor, which has seven fine bedrooms and six smaller ones around the outer walls, the interior of the building being taken up by closets and corridors.

There are no separate servants' quarters. The kitchen help doubtless slept out of the building, and the personal maids and menservants of the occupants slept in the many sizable closets which serve as antechambers to the bedrooms. The culinary arrangements would seem unsatisfactory to a modern housewife. The enormous kitchen on the ground floor has no direct access to the dining room, the main staircase being the only connection. This difficulty was overcome to some extent by an arrangement which permitted the entire dining table, twelve feet square, to be lowered into the room below, which adjoins the kitchen. Nor would the sanitary arrangements seem satisfactory, for there were none. The king and the queen, to be sure, each had a private toilet room, but the rest of the household and the guests were content with a portable tin tub and a handsome commode—perfectly satisfactory as long as servants were plentiful. There is no doubt that these beautiful palaces were foul-smelling. Viollet-le-Duc, the nineteenth-century writer on architecture, in telling of the palace at Versailles, relates the following anecdote: "One day when I was very young I visited the palace with a respectable old lady who had been at the court of Louis XV. Passing a foul passageway, she could not help but say wistfully, 'Ah, that smell reminds me of the good old days!' "

All the rooms are paneled in oak, which was originally painted a pale shade of bluish green, with the carving picked out in white and touches of gold. In the nineteenth century the woodwork was painted gray-white, and so it remains today. There are no pilasters, and the panels are generally rectangular in form, with semicircular panels over the doors and mirrors in the principal rooms. The dining room, the salons, and the queen's bedroom have very beautiful woodcarving in the dado and the cornice, and in some of the door panels. The paneling in the rest of the rooms is heavily moulded, but otherwise undecorated. The marble mantels are all low, and are curved over the fireplace opening in the characteristic French double-curve.

The west garden is a grassy mall, 100 feet wide and 800 feet long, interrupted about two-thirds of the way down by a little music pavilion. It is enclosed on the sides by alleys of clipped elms, beyond which lie formally grouped shrubs and trees, with geometrically laid out walks leading through tunnels of clipped trees to fountains and other garden features. On the south, screened by trees, are the stables and service buildings, and to the north is the theater where the queen and her friends indulged in amateur dramatics. Off to the northeast is the little hamlet containing farm buildings, a mill, a granary, and caretaker's lodge, where Marie Antoinette and her ladies-in-waiting played at being peasants.

Germany and Spain

IN NORTHERN AND CENTRAL EUROPE, THE BAROQUE HAS LEFT MANY monuments, both splendid and fantastic, many of which were gutted or completely destroyed by the bombings of World War II. Germany was composed of many different kingdoms, electorates, and duchies, so there was none of the uniformity, either political or artistic, that there was in France. On the other hand, the rivalries between the princes was an impetus toward building and toward the seeking of greater and greater novelty. Every little king had to have his Versailles.

In Berlin the Royal Palace dates primarily from the time of

Frederick I of Prussia, which was about 1700. It is a rectangle 650 feet by 380 feet, enclosing two courts. The designs for its best portions were begun by Schlüter and completed by von Goethe in the best Roman Baroque style. The palace was the city home of the German emperor down to World War I, and being in the heart of Berlin, it was largely ruined during World War II. From it the Unter den Linden, a great tree-lined avenue 200 feet wide, laid out in the best Parisian manner, leads for a mile to the Brandenburg Gate, which was built in 1790 in imitation of the Propylaea at Athens.

In near-by Potsdam stands Sans Souci, a palace built by Frederick the Great in 1745. This was another Versailles in miniature. The spreading one-story palace is about 600 feet long, and from it a broad flight of steps descends 66 feet through six terraces to a great fountain. The central pool is surrounded with figures by French sculptors, and its jet of water originally shot 130 feet into the air. A mile west, at the other end of the park, is the New Palace, built by the same emperor twenty years later. It contains a theater seating 500, and a concert hall 100 feet long, for Frederick was a great lover of music and the arts, and something of an amateur musician himself.

Throughout Saxony, Bavaria, Austria, and Hungary are more Baroque churches and palaces than can be mentioned. The style was adopted wholeheartedly and used lavishly, sometimes in the most unrestrained taste, sometimes in a manner both pompous and ornate, and sometimes in a spirit of rich luxuriance that is altogether delightful. At Dresden the once-ruined Hofkirche is a very rich and handsome Baroque church designed by an Italian architect in 1740. Even with its free Baroque details and its seventy-eight statues of saints standing like pinnacles on the parapets and the tower, it had great dignity. Across the square is the Zwinger, badly bombed but now restored, a charming rococo group of buildings which was begun in 1711 by the architect Pöppelmann for Frederick Augustus I, Elector of Saxony and King of Poland. This was intended to be a pleasure palace, with baths in the Roman manner, game rooms, and a race track. All that was built was a forecourt, surrounded on three PLATE 85 sides by a group of airy and fanciful buildings richly overloaded with gorgeous scrolls, volutes, caryatids, cartouches, garlands, urns of fruit, and every conceivable device.

Farther south, in Würzburg, the Neumünster has a façade in the exaggerated Italian Baroque style of Borromini. It follows the PLATE 86

Gesù type, but the central portion curves inward, so that the main pediment and the curved pediment over the door are curved in plan and their outermost columns set at an angle to the building. Furthermore, the corner piers are also set at an angle, so that the entire façade has a sinuous surface. It is a fine illustration of the sense of movement in Baroque architecture. Still farther south, the great capital city of Vienna has churches and palaces in the grand Baroque manner, of which the imperial palace of Schönbrunn is perhaps the best known.

The influence of the Baroque, and its charming but often unruly child, the rococo, extended through Poland and into Russia. Warsaw, with its lovely and thoroughly civilized palaces, destroyed in the war and faithfully rebuilt; the church of St. Andrew the Apostle at Kiev, with its Italianate forms surmounted by the bulbous dome and spires of Russia's Byzantine heritage; the Great Palace of Peter the Great at Peterhof, planned by a French architect in 1715 to be another Versailles, with its enormous cascade; the chaste Alexander Palace and the utterly fantastic Palace of Catherine the Great at Dyetskoye-Selo; and the great Winter Palace at Leningrad, covering twenty-three acres, the Admiralty, and the Smolny monastery, which were designed by an Italian but took on a thoroughly Russian character. All of these were destroyed or badly damaged during the war; several have been rebuilt.

Since Baroque savored of both sensuousness and Catholicism, Protestant Holland showed little interest, and retained the traditional classical Renaissance forms. But in Catholic Belgium the Baroque style was at home. The church of St. Michel in Louvain has a façade which towers up into an extra story, and which is so full of sculpture and exaggerated architectural forms as to be unintelligible. In Brussels, Bruges, and Antwerp there are many houses, guild halls, and town halls covered with engaged columns, caryatids, curved and broken pediments, and pinnacles in fantastic confusion.

The Baroque is said to have come to Spain before the middle of the seventeenth century, with the arrival of a certain Italian architect who came to finish the Escorial. He soon became an important figure and filled the post of superintendent of public buildings, like Herrera before him. His work seems to have been timid enough, but the seed was planted and his followers reaped the harvest. The

Baroque exuberance of Spain is best exemplified by the façade and the exterior of the apse of the old Romanesque cathedral of Santiago. Here the Plateresque elements are intermingled with the Baroque in a richly decorative manner constituting a new style which belongs only to Spain and her colonies. Its luxuriance is never offensive. There is a worldly opulence to the typical Jesuit churches, like the Neumünster, which although handsome, is not always pleasing. The Spanish Baroque churches have a sort of joyous exuberance which perhaps better expresses their purpose than the heavier magnificence of the others.

This Spanish temperament found its best expression in what is known as the Churrigueresque. José de Churriguera, who died in 1725, seems to have been a quiet man, and his own designs are straightforward Baroque, with only a modest dash of originality. But somehow his name came to be attached to the work of a group of men who followed him, in a style capricious and lavish to an extreme. Employing basically the standard Baroque motives of tortured columns, twisted pediments, volutes, caryatids, figures in niches, cartouches, and finials, the Churrigueresque frames them in fantastic scrolls, garlands, shells, and draperies. The effect falls just short of confusion, the basic structure is almost, but never quite, lost in the profusion of play of light and shade. The Churrigueresque recalls the Plateresque in many details, but it is never so delicate, its relief being bold and vigorous.

This rich encrustation was never applied all over a building, but was concentrated at the doorways and the principal windows, and on domes and cupolas. There are fine examples of it in Madrid, Valencia, and Cordova, but the best examples are to be found in the Spanish colonies in the New World. In church interiors this treatment was usually confined to a gorgeous reredos, or screen, over the altar, but there is one instance, at least, where it was applied to an entire interior—the sacristy of the Cartuja at Granada—and a PLATE 87 fantastic and restless interior it is.

As an antidote to the Churrigueresque, the Academic style was carried on too, mostly by French and Italian architects. When Philip V proposed to build a new royal palace at Madrid to replace the old one which had been destroyed by fire in 1734, he brought to Spain a priest named Juvara, who had been a pupil of Bernini. The idea, of course, was to produce another Versailles, and Juvara planned such an ambitious structure that the king and queen were dismayed at the cost. While they were hesitating, Juvara died, so they finally appointed his assistant and another Italian to go ahead with the work. The result was a fine palace 470 feet square and 100 feet high, good in formal design, but cold and lacking in interest. Its coldness is doubtless due partly to the fact that it is built of white granite, which is a forbidding material at best, but it has some very fine interiors. It is interesting to note that the design of the palace is very similar to Bernini's design for the Louvre, which had been rejected by Colbert.

A New Direction in Architecture

THE RENAISSANCE GAVE ARCHITECTURE A NEW DIRECTION. THE architect became an artist whose primary interest was in form and decoration, rather than construction, and these forms and decorations were drawn from a vast vocabulary which was entirely Roman in origin. Yet originality did not suffer; instead, it was given a new impetus and new forms with which to express itself. The Pitti Palace and the Petit Trianon are far apart. Both are classical, both owe the origins of their forms to classic architecture, yet neither could have been designed in Roman times. They are types of the new architecture.

As soon as the new architecture showed signs of becoming academic, stereotyped, too subject to formulas, there were men who revolted, and by their own originality injected new life into the old forms, resulting in the Baroque, the new spirit of freedom. Thus Renaissance architecture became the modern architecture of Europe and America, always changing, never the same in two generations or in two climates, but always classical and subject to the same basic classical formulas. To understand this is to appreciate the new revolt of contemporary architects against those very formulas. The revolt is not necessarily against the forms and the beauties of classical architecture, but against the rigid precepts and strict formulas which it imposes.

❊ X ❊

English Renaissance

HE FIRST HALF of the sixteenth century is called the Tudor period in English architecture, starting with the long reign of Henry VIII, and continuing through the short reigns of his son Edward VI and his daughter Mary. The second half is the Elizabethan period, during the long rule of Elizabeth, from 1558 to 1603. In politics and religious matters, as well as in art and scholarship, this was a century of restless energy. National life was rich and expanding, and the spirit of humanism well suited a people which had thrown off the yoke of papal domination and were developing a new and more secular life. England was closely tied into continental European affairs, and was going through a period of colonial expansion and great national prosperity. Her merchants traded with all the ports of the world, and her privateers plundered the seas, pouring Spanish gold into her coffers. Furthermore, Henry VIII's seizure of the lands and the treasure of the monasteries had tremendously enriched the crown.

It was not a period of church-building, for there was an over-supply of churches from the previous centuries, and men's thoughts were turned more to church reform. More churches were torn down than were built, a few were added to, and many tombs and monuments were erected in the old buildings. It was, however, a period of great activity in house-building, for the new aristocracy which was arising from the merchant class built tremendous houses. Many of them, given titles and estates by the king, added to the feudal buildings, or tore them down and built new houses in the modern style. This prosperity trickled down through the entire social structure, so that new homes were built at all economic levels. Much of what was lost by the churches was gained by the colleges. So much building was done at Oxford, Cambridge, and other universities that the term "collegiate Gothic" has become synonymous with Tudor. For Tudor is essentially a Gothic style, despite its occasional Renaissance details. The three styles, Tudor, Elizabethan, and the Jacobean which followed during the first quarter of the seventeenth century, were the transitional styles in England, as the style of Francis I had been in France.

It was a long time from the first introduction of Italian artists with their designs and details in the new style about 1510, until the first full-fledged Renaissance building was built in 1625. The British building tradition was strong and deeply rooted, the craftsmen were highly skilled in their crafts and firmly set in their way of doing things, and it was only very gradually, and even reluctantly, that they learned the new forms. And even when the woodcarvers and the stonecarvers had learned the new details, they used them to decorate buildings which were still essentially Gothic in form. In fact, the Gothic tradition was carried on by local builders in out-of-the-way places until the end of the seventeenth century.

Henry VIII himself was responsible for the first encouragement of Italian artists. Educated by tutors who were imbued with the Renaissance spirit, he was an accomplished scholar, linguist, musician, and athlete when he came to the throne at the age of eighteen. One of his first official acts was to employ an Italian sculptor to execute a tomb for his father and mother. The sculptor, who had arrived with a company of Florentine merchants about 1510, was none other than the impetuous Torrigiano, he who quarreled with the youthful Michelangelo in the Medici gardens. Thus the tomb of Henry VII, the first full-fledged Renaissance work in England, purely Italian in its design and detail, stands in Henry VII's chapel in Westminster Abbey, one of the last late Perpendicular Gothic structures in England.

Many other Italian sculptors and decorators came to England

during the early 1500's. Little is known of them. Their handiwork and their influence remained, but being good Catholics, they left PLATE 88 the country when the final break with the Church of Rome was made. In 1520, Henry visited Francis I in northern France, their meeting taking place at the famous "Field of the Cloth of Gold," so called because of the lavish display the French monarch laid out to impress and entertain his English cousin. Here Henry and his court picked up many more ideas of what was up-to-date in the world of architecture and decoration. But even before this, Henry's minister, Cardinal Wolsey, a man of great wealth and a fine and cultivated taste, built Hampton Court Palace, showing all the court and even the king, how beautiful a modern house could be.

Much of Wolsey's palace still stands, although part of it was torn down by Sir Christopher Wren in the seventeenth century to make way for his own additions. It is built of warm red brick, laid in a diaper pattern, that is, with dark headers marking out a diamond pattern. It has mullioned windows, battlements, turreted towers, and great clustered chimneys—still definitely a Gothic building. The only indications of the new style are in some modeled terra cotta panels inserted in the walls, bearing the heads of Roman emperors, and in a panel carrying Wolsey's arms, supported by *amorini* or cherubs, and framed by two Corinthian columns and their entablature. The interior was sumptuously fitted with fine furniture and tapestries, and decorated with wall paintings by Italian artists. It may be that the palace aroused Henry's envy, for Wolsey gave it to him after a few years, and the king added more wings, including a chapel and a magnificent banqueting hall with tall mullioned windows and one of the finest hammer-beam trussed roofs in England.

The new security and prosperity, and the example of their royal master, led many of the newly rich and ennobled families to build great homes. There was no need now for moats and fortifications, but battlements and turrets persisted as decorative features because they had become a traditional part of house design, and the British builders shed their traditions slowly. New mansions built on the sites of old houses sometimes retained the moats and bailey walls, for sentiment's sake, and sometimes they were filled and leveled and turned into terraced gardens. The only indications in these houses that the seeds of a new style had already been sown were in little decorative panels, such as those in Wolsey's palace, and in carved details in screens and doorways, which revealed a delicate Florentine pilaster or a bit of egg and dart.

PLATE 89 Of the many Tudor mansions of England, possibly the best-known is Compton Winyates, in Warwickshire. Many Americans are familiar with its handsomest features without knowing it, for they have been copied many times on pseudo-Tudor houses all over the country. The mansion was built in 1520 by Sir William Compton, a London merchant and a favorite of the king. As usual, it is of warm red brick, with stone trim and half-timber in the gables. The popular features are the entrance through a low battlemented tower, the fine mullioned bay window in the court, the richly carved timberwork of the gables, and the clustered chimney stacks with their brick spirals. But few of the modern copies, with their machine-made materials and necessary modern economies, can equal the beauty of color and texture of the old houses, built slowly and carefully by men who had been trained in the ancient traditions of their handcrafts and who knew no other way to build.

Although many of the colleges of England date back to the twelfth and thirteenth centuries, they expanded so greatly during the Tudor period that they present largely a Tudor face today. They were laid out in much the same manner as the larger houses, with a Great Hall and rooms grouped around a quadrangle, and also with many features of the monasteries. The different colleges of the universities of Oxford and Cambridge vary in size and layout; St. John's College, Cambridge, started in 1511, may be taken as fairly typical. The sixteenth-century portion is built of brick and lies around three quadrangles. The entrance from St. John's Street, leading to the first quad, is through a gateway under a tower with the usual turrets at the corners. At the right is the chapel, which was largely rebuilt in the nineteenth century, and on the left are chambers, or dormitories. Across the back is the wing containing the Hall and the kitchen, and beyond this is the second quad, enclosed by more chambers and the Master's Lodge. A gate through another tower leads to the third quad, with the library and the cloister. Beyond that a covered bridge over the river Cam leads to a fourth court, which is modern. The college is a completely self-contained unit. The students and the masters, now as then, live and carry on all their activities within its walls, except for the cricket ground, which is across the river, where each college has its own area for sports.

Many attempts have been made to re-create the atmosphere of these old colleges on college campuses in the United States, by copying their architectural style. Examples are the Harkness Quadrangle at Yale, the entire campus at Duke, dormitories and other groups of buildings at Princeton, Pennsylvania, Cornell, Chicago, and even the skyscraper "Cathedral of Learning" at Pittsburgh. There is incredible beauty and charm in the old-world originals, and there is often beauty in some of their twentieth-century adaptations. But that there is logic and common sense, fitness and economy, in attempting to re-create these styles today, is open to considerable doubt.

The English Architect

THE WAVE OF HOUSE-BUILDING WHICH COMMENCED DURING THE prosperous reign of Henry VIII subsided somewhat during the eleven years of the reigns of Edward VI and Mary, for Henry had left heavy debts, and the times were unsettled, owing to Mary's restoration of the Roman Church and the unpopularity of her Spanish marriage. But when Elizabeth came to the throne at the age of twenty-five, in 1558, England's Golden Age began. This was the age of Drake, Hawkins, and Raleigh, who swept the seas and extended England's supremacy as far as the Pacific. This was the age of Shakespeare, of Spenser, Bacon, and Sidney, and the many classical themes and allusions of these writers set people to reading the classics, arousing a widespread interest in classic art and in contemporary Italian art. The same general influences and tendencies continued during the reign of James I, in the first quarter of the seventeenth century, which is called the Jacobean period, after *Jacob,* the Latin form of James.

The professional architect, as he is known today, was slow in emerging. When cathedral-building ceased, the old type architect seems to have disappeared, or moved on. In Elizabethan times the plans for houses were outlined in a general way by "surveyors," or often by the owners. The owner then provided the materials, letting contracts for labor to the various trades—masons, carpenters, joiners, plasterers, and all the others. Each trade provided its own designs, so that the result was an accumulation of handcraft details, achieving unity only because all the trades had been trained in the same ancient traditions of building. As Renaissance details gradually crept in, they were used, or misused, in such a way as to indicate a complete lack of architectural knowledge, with results which are sometimes handsome in a rugged sort of way, sometimes barbarous, and occasionally fine.

After the Italian craftsmen and decorators left England, they were replaced from about 1550 on by an influx of German and Flemish craftsmen, and it was their version of Renaissance details which prevailed. They brought with them their handbooks of ornament, elaborately engraved pages of caryatids, brackets, finials, carved mouldings, and debased orders. Most of it was crude, some of it ugly. One of their decorative novelties was "strapwork," a system of carving a panel or a surface into an intricate geometric pattern apparently composed of interlacing ribbons or straps attached to the background by elaborate nails. As the British stonecarvers and woodcarvers took over these forms, and the forms of the Italians before them, they became modified and improved to some extent, thanks to the conservative taste of the English, who often showed a fine ingenuity and taste in inventing new forms based on whatever smatterings of classic architecture they picked up.

Soon after the middle of the sixteenth century, English books on architecture began to appear. Some time before that, a certain Dr. Andrew Boorde had published a book which he flowingly subtitled, "A boke for to lerne a man to be wyse in buildyng of his house for the health of his body, i to holde quiyetness for the helth of his soule and body. The Boke for a good husband to lerne." He described the usual plan arrangements of the house of his time, but made no attempt to discuss architecture as an art. John Shute may have been the first English architect, in the modern sense of the word, for he made a study of architectural design, as distinct from construction. He went to Italy about 1550, and in 1563 he published a book dedicated to Queen Elizabeth and entitled, *The First and Chief Groundes of Architecture* "used in all the auncient and famous monymentes: with a farther and more ample discourse uppon the same, than hitherto hath been set out by any other. Published by

John Shute, Paynter and Archytecte." The book contains drawings of the five orders, with rules for determining their proportions, and also translations from Vitruvius and Serlio. In 1611 there appeared an English translation of Serlio's five books on architecture, dealing with geometry, perspective, "Antiquity," the orders in detail, and "diverse formes of Temples." These were important steps, for they gave the English their first look at true classic architecture, and helped put an end to the use of the German handbooks.

There was a man named John Thorpe living and working during the last half of the sixteenth century who may have been an architect who designed and built a prodigious number of great houses, or merely a draftsman and surveyor who measured and made drawings of houses already built by others. In the Soane Museum in London there are 280 sheets of drawings supposedly made by Thorpe—plans, elevations, and details of a great many houses. Whether he designed them all or not, he has left a precious record, for many of the houses have disappeared or have been extensively altered.

At the turn of the century and during the Jacobean period, there were two architects named Smithson, father and son, whose known work shows that the architects of the time were acquiring a better knowledge of Renaissance detail, and at least the beginnings of a grasp of the whole concept, but still their attempts at ambitious projects were a failure. None of the designers so far showed any realization of the fact that Renaissance architecture was something more than another system of decoration, that it was a whole new set of principles of planning and design. They were satisfied if the various parts and features of their buildings were each in themselves pleasing, without regard for the effect as a whole, which is the basic difference between picturesque and formal architecture.

Domestic Architecture

THE HALL RETAINED ITS POSITION IN THE PLAN AS THE CENTRAL feature of the house, but it was no longer the center of the family life. Still a handsome room, with a carved screen and gallery, oak wainscoting and bay window, it served more as an entrance and a connecting link between the wings of the house, and was used only for special festivities or upon state occasions. Sometimes it had the traditional open trussed roof, and sometimes it had a second story over it. The winter parlor now served as the family dining room, and the solar had expanded into a suite of master's rooms, including bedroom and sitting room. The gradual development of gentle manners and the social amenities led to the desire for greater privacy. The family lived apart from the retainers, and the lord had his withdrawing room where he could retire from the family. On the other side of the Hall, the kitchen had grown into an elaborate layout of kitchen offices, with rooms for the steward, butler, and pantler, and larders, sculleries, servants' hall, serving rooms, and storerooms.

A new feature was the great open staircase, broad and handsome, built of wood, leading to the second floor in three or four flights with landings between. It had carved newels with elaborate finials and heavy handrails supported on fat moulded balusters or elaborate pierced strapwork screens. The second floor contained, besides the master's chambers, many more bedrooms and sitting rooms, and another innovation, the long gallery. This was a long and relatively narrow room, often extending entirely across the building, and sometimes it was the most handsomely decorated room in the house, with wainscoted walls, two or three fireplaces with elaborate wood and stone mantels, and a fine moulded plaster ceiling. It is not known for what use the long gallery was originally intended, but it came to serve as the new center of family life and as a promenade among the family art treasures. There apparently was much rivalry among householders as to the length and richness of their long galleries. The gallery at Haddon Hall is 109 feet long, that at Hardwicke Hall is 166 feet long, and at Montacute House 170 feet long by 20 feet wide. Audley End, now destroyed, had a long gallery called in its time the "most cheerful, and one of the best in England." It measured 226 feet long, 32 feet wide, and 24 feet high. Yet one rather obvious convenience was lacking in most houses—corridors or passageways. Most rooms could be entered only by passing through other rooms or from the courtyard. In their striving for comfort and privacy, this seems to have been one of the last things thought of. It remained for Inigo Jones's new concept of planning to introduce this necessity.

As old houses were added to, or as new ones were planned about their Great Hall, they were usually extended by the addition of wings, rather than by enlarging the main block of the house. Thus they formed themselves about courtyards, sometimes extending into two or three. Later, in order to gain more light and air, one side of the court was left off or torn down, so that the houses built during the Elizabethan period generally fall into the H- or E- type plan, which, furthermore, well suited the Renaissance desire for symmetry. The old idea of an approach through a forecourt was retained, however, at least in spirit, by an enclosure in front of the house, bounded sometimes by outbuildings, sometimes by a wall, and sometimes by only a hedge.

Brick was still a favorite building material, and moulded brick mouldings and even window mullions were used a great deal. Many of the brick houses have stepped and curved gables, showing a Dutch influence. Stone, cut in rectangular smooth-faced blocks, or "ashlar," was used in districts where good native building stone was available. In some districts rubble stone was used, with cut stone trim. Occasionally an important house was built of half-timber, such as the well-known Little Moreton Hall, but this was not very common. Roofs, in brick districts, were usually of flat tiles made of the same clay as the bricks, and baked to a rich orange-red of a hundred hues. In stone districts roofs were more apt to be of slate, or even thin slabs of stone held in place by oak pegs. However, there are plenty of examples of tile roofs on stone houses and slate roofs on brick houses. Some of the more faithfully Renaissance houses had flat roofs covered with lead, surrounded with balustrades which were often fanciful in design, some composed of letters spelling out names or Biblical quotations. Thatch, that picturesque roof of the picture post cards, was used only for farm and village cottages. Windows were still narrow casements, with leaded glass set in wood sash, but they were grouped in great square-headed banks and separated by stone or brick mullions and transoms. The bay window increased in popularity, for the Englishman loved sunshine, relatively rare as it is in his climate. There was a curious superstition that the south wind brought harmful "vapours," but in spite of that the great bays were usually placed on the south in order to catch the most sun. As always, the houses were set in walled gardens, with broad flights of terrace stairs, sheltered by hedges of yew, patterned flower beds and long walks and alleys through the trees, and that inevitable fantasy, the labyrinth, formed in clipped yew.

Interior treatment continued much as in Tudor times, but with a greater use of classical and pseudo-classical forms. Walls were wainscoted, often to the ceiling, the paneling being frequently elaborately PLATE 90 designed, sometimes treated with pilasters and arches. The fireplace was the principal feature of every room, usually framed in superposed orders of wood or marble—not simple classic orders, but fanciful orders covered with strapwork or other exotic ornament and supporting entablatures full of figures, masks, grotesques, and more strapwork. Ceilings were flat, sometimes with deep coves where they met the walls. They were plastered, and covered with geometrical patterns formed by small intersecting mouldings, with roses or other ornaments at the intersections, like the late Gothic vaulting. A carry-over from medieval days was the profuse use of color. It was not until the full Renaissance bloomed in England that warm and sensuous color was lost to the cold chastity of the Italian style. The plastered ceilings were painted blue, with gilded roses, and the woodcarving was decorated in red, blue, and yellow, with much gilding, and the family arms emblazoned in full heraldic color. The ceiling of the Hall in one mansion was painted with the signs of the zodiac, "and by means of some ingenious mechanism the sun performed its course across the ceiling, and the stars came out at night."

Furnished with tapestries and heavy, elaborate furniture carved with the same motives found in the woodwork, these handsome but ponderous interiors were a fitting background for the lords and ladies dressed in the heavy brocades and velvets of the day, the gentlemen with slashed doublets, lace collars, and full breeches, the ladies in tight bodices, enormous puffed sleeves, great starched collars, and voluminous skirts of yards and yards of richly embroidered materials. The people may have been heavily upholstered, but they were alert and intelligent, and though their houses were decorated with a heavy hand, they were light and livable. Most of them are in use today, with the addition only of central heating, electric lights, and a bath room. These mechanical conveniences are about all that has been added to housing down to the present day.

Elizabethan and Jacobean Mansions

MONTACUTE HOUSE, BUILT BY SIR EDWARD PHELIPS BETWEEN 1580 and 1600, and probably designed by John Thorpe, is an example of the H plan. The traditional Hall, with its entrance through the screen at one side, often foiled the early architect's struggle for Renaissance symmetry. In Montacute House this problem was overcome by placing the entrance to the Hall in the center, with the Hall on the right side and dining rooms balancing it on the left. In the cross wings the family withdrawing rooms are beyond the Hall, and the kitchens beyond the dining rooms. An unusual arrangement of this house is the placing of the two staircases in the corners of the wings, thus featuring their stepped-up windows on the façade. These stairways lead to the second and third floors, which extend over the entire house, so that even though the house is 160 feet long, it creates a very high exterior mass. Despite the Renaissance symmetry of the plan, the exterior is Gothic in appearance. The windows are square-headed, grouped in mullioned banks, and the walls are plain except for string-courses at each floor. At the roof there are both curved gables and balustrades with pyramidal finials presenting a restless silhouette which is very Gothic. The tall chimney stacks are in the form of Tuscan columns, an amusing use of a fine old Roman detail. Fully three hundred and fifty years old, this house is still the home of the Phelips family.

PLATE 91

There was a popular jingle during the seventeenth century which ran, "Hardwicke Hall, more glass than wall!" and it was quite true, for when Robert Smithson designed and built it during the last quarter of the sixteenth century he achieved as great an area of glass in the walls as in many of today's office buildings or solar houses. Hardwicke Hall is neither H nor E plan, it is a rectangular block three stories high, with two great square bays on each side and one on each end, which are carried up a full story above the roof, forming six towers. The principal rooms are on the third floor, which has a 26-foot ceiling. The long gallery runs the full length of the house, 166 feet, and is 22 feet wide. One long wall is almost entirely tall windows, the other is lined with generations of ancestral portraits. The State Room, 31 feet by 65 feet, plus one of the big bays, has walls covered with tapestries to the height of the wainscot, and above that

and extending to the ceiling is a remarkable modeled plaster frieze
11 feet high. The figures are in high relief and fully colored in low
tones. They represent Diana and her nymphs against a luxuriant
forest background, with lions, elephants, camels, and other exotic
animals. The exterior of the house is severe and boxlike, given scale by
the countless small rectangles of the mullioned windows. There are
stringcourses at each floor and a balustrade at the roof. The parapet of
the towers is an open scrollwork enclosing the initials "E. S.,"
for Elizabeth, Countess of Shrewsbury, for whom the house was
built.

Wollaton Hall, undoubtedly also designed by Robert Smithson,
is a curious departure from the usual type. Basically it is a two-story

HALL

50

The plan of Wollaton Hall, based on the plan in the Soane Collection.

rectangle, with three-story towers projecting at each corner, and
from the center of the rectangle rises a tower-like central mass nearly
a hundred feet high, like the keep of a medieval house. At the very
center of the plan, and at the bottom of the tower, is the Hall, lighted
by clerestory windows 35 feet above the floor. The enormous room in

the tower, above the Hall, was a dormitory for the servants of guests, and was appropriately called "Bedlam." The various rooms of the house surround the Hall on its four sides. The exterior shows that Smithson was a man of originality and ingenuity, but perhaps somewhat lacking in taste. The walls are dressed up with pilasters on pedestals at each floor, badly proportioned and fancifully detailed, and the corner towers are topped with strapwork scrolls supporting a pediment with a figure at its peak. This piece of gingerbread occurs on each of the four faces of each tower, and the chimneys are not only classic columns, but they are formed of three columns in a row with a continuous capital.

As a pleasing contrast, Hatfield House is one of the handsomest Jacobean mansions in England. It was built in 1611 by Robert Cecil, the first Earl of Salisbury, and is still owned by the Cecils. It represented the last word in the taste of a cultivated nobleman. The spreading plan, 275 feet long, is basically an E plan, with only a suggestion of the center wing. The entrance is in the center of the north side, into a hallway which passes through to a long cloister running along the side of the south court. To the right of the entrance are the steward's rooms, with the kitchens beyond; to the left is the Great Hall, extending through two stories. Beyond is the great staircase, and in the east wing beyond it are the drawing rooms and his lordship's suite. In the corresponding west wing is the chapel, with the chaplain's suite adjoining. Several small staircases give access to the second floor from various parts of the house. Over the cloister, the long gallery runs the entire length of the house; at the east end are state bedrooms, including "King James's room," and at the west end are other bedrooms.

The Great Hall is a Renaissance edition of the traditional medieval Hall, purely a hall of state, with a bay and great mullioned windows, a minstrels' gallery, and a coved and modeled plaster ceiling with carved beams. The end of the Hall opposite the gallery is a magnificent carved wood screen two stories high, with Germanic orders employing caryatids and bracketed entablatures framing richly carved paneling and niches. The staircase is broad, ascending in easy stages, with fine carved newels at each landing surmounted by playful figures. Five steps above the floor is the "dog gate," a gate which

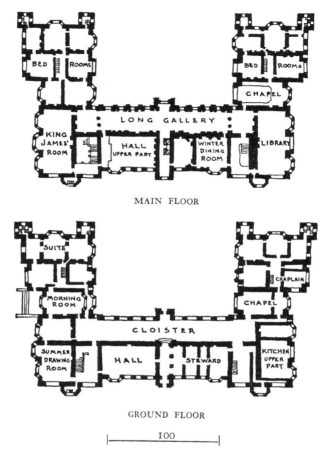

MAIN FLOOR

GROUND FLOOR

|——————100——————|

*The plan of Hatfield House shows the striving for formal arrange-
ment.*

swings across the stair to keep the master's pets confined to their
proper floor. The long gallery, 163 feet in length, is paneled to the
ceiling with a treatment of Ionic pilasters supporting a Doric entablature, and there are two marble chimney pieces and a moulded plaster
ceiling.

The entrance front of Hatfield House is severe. In fact, it looks
very much like a typical American high school built in the 1920's,
for many such schools were dressed up in the Jacobean style.
The plain boxlike mass is broken only by two projecting bays, which

are carried above the parapet as squat towers. Obviously, these bays were introduced only to break the severity of the façade, for they contribute nothing to the plan. Over the entrance, but set well back over the center of the building, is a two-storied tower terminating in an octagonal cupola, probably a later addition, which increases the resemblance to a high school. The material is brick, with stone quoins, window trim, and balustrade; the windows are enormous mullioned and transomed casements. The south front is very different. The cloister is expressed in a fine arcade in the Italian style, with pilasters supporting the second floor which is also pilastered, and a pierced parapet above. The material here is all stone. The central bay projects slightly, with superposed free-standing columns, rising above the main parapet. Above the second floor, framed by the columns, are the finely sculptured arms of the Cecils. Like all fine mansions, Hatfield House is set among formal gardens and terraces, now mellowed and luxuriant after three hundred years of growth and care.

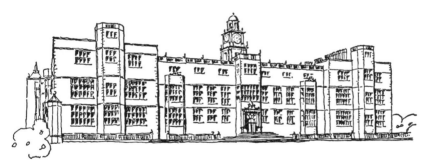

The exterior of Hatfield House presents a balanced yet picturesque composition.

The great Elizabethan and Jacobean mansions, and the Renaissance mansions which followed, are among England's proudest possessions. They are all different, yet all are imbued with that unmistakable quality of homelikeness and good quiet living which is inherent in their bricks and timbers as it is in the British people. A few of the other great houses which are of architectural, as well as historical and literary, interest, are Knole, the seat of the Sackvilles, one of the largest and finest houses in the country; Haddon Hall, containing a whole history of English domestic architecture from the eleventh century to modern times, with its long gallery built by Dorothy Vernon; Burghley House, a vast pile designed by John Thorpe for Sir William Cecil, Queen Elizabeth's minister and treasurer and the father of the Cecil who built Hatfield; Longleat, Bolsover, Charlton, Holland House, and many others. Many of these houses have today been given to the state or to the National Trust, for their hereditary owners can no longer support them; many others are open to the public on certain days for an admission fee, in order to help their owners maintain them. They all represent a way of living which has passed, probably never to return.

The Homes of the Poor

THE PROSPERITY of england during the sixteenth and seventeenth centuries gradually permeated the entire social structure, so that the living conditions of even the humblest people were improved. The serfs of the feudal period, and the farm laborers and poor mechanics of the period which followed, beginning in the fourteenth century, lived for the most part in miserable huts framed with saplings and covered with sod or wattles and clay. Wattles are mats woven from twigs. These one-room hovels were undoubtedly descended directly from the prehistoric dwellings in Britain, and their use persisted for the poorest classes in rural districts through the seventeenth and eighteenth centuries. Even as late as the nineteenth century many were still in use by charcoal burners and other itinerant laborers.

However, by the seventeenth century the farm laborer or village mechanic could boast a tidy little frame cottage of two or three rooms. It was built of heavy timbers, mortised and pegged together, the walls filled in with brick nogging, or with clay or plaster on lath or wattles. The roof was of thatch and the chimney of brick. Only in districts where there was no timber were the houses built of stone. The farm animals were housed in the same building, as they still are in most purely agricultural countries. The people were robust and coarse, by modern standards, and knew nothing of the refinements of life which are considered so essential today—and doubtless would have despised them had they encountered them.

Inigo Jones

AFTER OVER A CENTURY OF THIS HALFHEARTED TOYING WITH REN-aissance architecture, while still clinging to the old traditions, England turned suddenly and completely to the full-fledged Renaissance style as the result of the work of one architect—in fact, as the result of one building. The man was Inigo Jones, one of Britain's two great architects; the building was the Royal Banqueting Hall at Whitehall.

Inigo Jones was born in London in 1573, the son of a poor clothworker. Little is known of his early life, but apparently he was apprenticed to a joiner while quite young. The joiners, members of a trade midway between the carpenters and the cabinetmakers, produced the paneling, wainscoting, and fine woodwork which had become popular. Jones seems to have shown some skill in drawing and painting, as well as proficiency in mathematics. When he was about twenty he went to Italy, spending four or five years in and about Venice, where he acquired his great admiration for the work of Palladio, who had been dead only about twenty years.

He then spent some time in Denmark in the service of the king, who was an ardent amateur architect. The tradition lingers there that Jones designed the Fredericksbörg and Rosenberg palaces, but that seems unlikely. Back in London, he became a designer of stage settings and costumes for masques, the form of theatrical entertainment which was popular with the court. They were written by the best writers of the time, such as Ben Jonson, magnificently staged, and acted by the gentlemen and ladies of the court, including, occasionally, King James himself. With the lessons he had learned in Italy, Jones revolutionized theater design and production in England. The theater of Elizabethan England was a circular or octagonal building open to the sky, with balconies around the sides. The audience stood in the balconies and in the "pit." The Globe, where Shakespeare's plays were produced, was such a theater. The stage was very small, projecting into the pit, only half-covered by a tier of boxes at the rear at the second-balcony level. There was no scenery; a placard gave the locale and the imagination of the audience furnished the rest. Lighting consisted of a few hanging candelabra and candle footlights. Jones enlarged the stage and pushed it back out of the auditorium, enclosing it in an architectural frame, like the proscenium arch of today. He introduced movable scenery, with machinery to operate it, and platforms in the floor of the stage which could be raised and lowered. Although candles and torches were still the only sources of light, Jones massed them in great concealed banks, thus brilliantly lighting the stage. His scenery consisted of elaborate painted architectural backgrounds and a deep vista through a central arch, with perspective artificially contrived to give the illusion of great depth in a short distance. Jones's work on these sumptuous productions, which he carried on nearly all his life, shows that he had fully captured the spirit of the great artists of the Italian Renaissance.

In 1613 he went to Italy again for a couple of years, with a commission to collect antiques for several noblemen, for he was becoming increasingly interested in serious architecture and wanted to study further. In 1615 King James appointed him Surveyor General of the Works, a post which was actually that of royal architect, so at the age of forty-two his career really began.

He prepared designs for several buildings, including the Queen's House at Greenwich Hospital in the Renaissance style, which was not built until twenty years later, and at least two churches in the Gothic style, both of which have been destroyed. He laid out Lincoln's Inn Fields, one of the four ancient Inns of Court which still stand in the very heart of London, their quiet courtyards remote from the noise and bustle of the city. Fortunately World War II damaged only two of them. In 1619 Jones was commanded to design a new royal palace at Whitehall, for like many European monarchs, James I wanted to equal the palaces of the French kings, and upon his death in 1625 his son Charles I ordered Jones to double the size of the palace. Jones and his lifelong assistant, John Webb, turned out a splendid design in the true grand manner of the Renaissance, unequaled in England for scale and originality.

The final plan shows a great rectangle, 1280 feet by 950 feet, with a main court 800 by 400 feet, and six other courts, one of which is circular, 280 feet in diameter. They are arranged with perfect symmetry, and all axes are carefully followed throughout the plan. There are loggias, galleries, grand salons, and presence chambers, scores of living apartments and seventy staircases large and small. The exterior is treated entirely with superposed orders, some with arches between and some without. Some portions are two stories high and others are three, finished off with pediments, cupolas, and statues. All this is known from the plans, which have been preserved. But only one unit was built—the Banqueting Hall—which was com- PLATE 92 pleted in 1625. Construction of the rest was delayed by the unsettled conditions during Charles I's reign which culminated in the Civil War. It was from the middle window of his Banqueting Hall that the king resolutely stepped to the scaffold in 1649, the first European king to be tried, condemned, and executed by his own subjects. "The blow I saw given," wrote an eyewitness, "and can truly say, with a sad heart, there was such a grone by the Thousands then present as I never heard before and desire I may never hear again."

The Banqueting Hall was as fine as anything the master Palladio had done, and every man of taste knew it. From then on there was no more Gothic, no more strapwork, no more caryatids, on any important building in England. From then on, Jones was in demand to design buildings all over the country. When the Earl of Bedford commissioned him to design St. Paul's Church, Covent Garden, he told him to keep it very plain, "not much better than a barn." Jones replied, "You shall have the handsomest barn in Europe," and produced a simple but handsome church which is of particular interest because it has a Tuscan portico, the forerunner of many porticoed churches nearly a century later. St. Mary's Church at Oxford has a magnificent Baroque entrance, with twisted columns and a broken curved pediment, which is the work of Nicholas Stone, a stonecarver and architect who worked closely with Jones. It is thought that Jones gave him the design. Jones was ordered to survey London's old Gothic cathedral of St. Paul, for it was dilapidated and in danger of collapsing. He commenced a scheme of gradually rebuilding it in the new style, but the Civil War put an end to this. His design for the Royal Hospital at Greenwich was very handsome, and one portion, the Queen's House, was built. But Webb, Wren, and other architects all had their hands in it before it was finished. Still standing in an obscure hole at the edge of the Thames, in the heart of London, is the York Water Gate, another joint design of Jones and Stone. In the days when the river was used for pleasure barges, it served as a landing stage for York House, one of the many great mansions which have vanished from the city.

The New Type of House

OTHER ARCHITECTS CONTINUED TO DESIGN TRANSITIONAL HOUSES well along to the middle of the century, but not Inigo Jones. In his design for Raynham Hall, he cast aside the traditional homage to the Great Hall and all other relics of medievalism. The plan is a rectangle, with two wings projecting slightly forward on the entrance front.

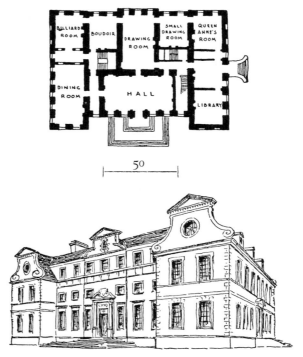

Raynham Hall, designed by Inigo Jones.

The door leads to a hall which is purely an entrance hall—no screen, no minstrels' gallery. Beyond it is the drawing room, and to the left and right are the other rooms of the first floor—the dining room, library, sitting room, and state bedrooms. The tendency of the time was to place all bedrooms on the second floor, and all family day rooms on the first floor, with the kitchen and servants' rooms in the basement. This house still has a bedroom or two on the first floor. There is no grand staircase, instead there are three minor stairs. The grand salon is on the second floor, and the rest of it is given over to family bedrooms, the long gallery having disappeared. The exterior is completely Renaissance, yet certain features seem to make a courtly bow of acknowledgment to their Jacobean forebears. The material is brick, with stone quoins and trim. Windows are framed with simple moulded trims, the entrance has an unassuming Baroque curved and broken pediment, and the cornices are light and simple. The two gables are treated with volutes and big curves, with pediments above, a treatment which is right out of Italy, yet which in England suggests also the curved Jacobean gables. The roof breaks into a minor pediment over the entrance, which is treated with a broken curved pediment supporting a gabled pediment. There is an air of great simplicity and dignity to the design, and through its very restraint it suggests richness. It also has a fine vigor, which is characteristic of all of Jones's work.

In this house is seen for the first time another innovation of the English Renaissance, the sash window, which came from Holland. The old casements, grouped in great banks with mullions and transoms, are gone. The window opening is fairly large, higher than it is wide, and filled with two wood sash which slide vertically. Today they are called double-hung windows. This type of window imposed new limitations upon the designer. The mullioned window could be lengthened or heightened by the addition of more window units, and still be in scale and harmony with the adjoining windows as long as the units were of the same size. But all the sash windows in any one range had to be the same size in order to look right. Thus their size and spacing had to be studied with great care. Many houses derive much of their interest and beauty from their skillfully proportioned fenestration.

Coleshill is another house which illustrates the trend in domestic

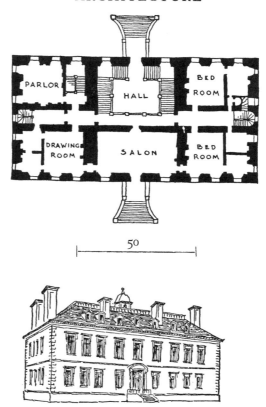

Coleshill.

planning. It is about the same size as Raynham Hall, but was built fifteen years later, and although it has long been attributed to Jones, it is probable that he only consulted on its design. The plan is an unbroken rectangle. In the entrance hall a very grand staircase rises on both sides; beyond is the salon and at one side are the parlor and the drawing room, and at the other are bedrooms, not yet entirely off the first floor. In this house the dining room is on the second floor, an inconvenience which was becoming more uncommon. The exterior is free of all gables or other picturesque features. The roof is hipped, which means that it slopes back from all four walls, with a flat center area surrounded by a rail and with a cupola in the middle. Chimneys are no longer clustered stacks, the many flues being brought together and carried above the roof in a few large chimneys which are located with perfect symmetry. The dormers are no longer continuations of the wall surface. They are built of wood and are set above and back of the cornice, so that they are a part of the roof instead of a part of the wall. The sash windows are large and finely proportioned, and spaced with great care. A modest curved pediment barely emphasizes the entrance. The whole effect is one of restraint and dignity, and possibly of coldness. Coleshill is the best example of the prototype of the Colonial house of eighteenth-century America.

Another of Jones's house designs prepared the way for some of the great spreading houses which were built two or three generations

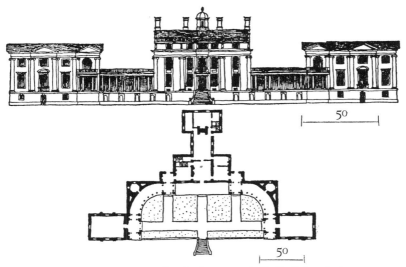

Stoke Park shows the influence of Palladio's designs.

later. Stoke Park was built between 1630 and 1636. It is said that the plan was brought from Italy; whether it was or not, it certainly derives directly from some of Palladio's villas near Vicenza. The main block of the house is three tall stories, with the salon, dining room, and kitchen on the first floor, and bedrooms above. An open one-story loggia curves forward from each front corner of the house, forming a quarter-circle and connecting it with a lower wing on each side, one containing the library and the other the chapel. The exterior is very monumental. The main house has two-story Ionic pilasters supporting a strictly classical cornice, with an attic story above. The two front wings have the same order and pediments. The entire ensemble is set up on a high basement, with a staircase rising to the level of the elevated courtyard between the curved arms of the wings. The spreading plan is 260 feet across the front and 160 feet deep. The greater convenience and comfort of the more functional box type of house are here sacrificed to the desire for monumental effect.

Jones left London during the Civil War, and with other Royalists, hid in the country for two years. In 1646 he was captured and fined, and then apparently allowed to resume his work, but he died six years later. A man of great originality and true genius, he had revolutionized English architecture. He freed it from the merely quaint and picturesque and started it along the path already followed by Italy and France. This he had done not by merely copying the buildings he had seen on the Continent, but by taking what they had to offer him and fusing it with his own genius, turning out something which was in harmony with the advanced thought of his time, yet thoroughly British in character.

His faithful pupil and assistant, John Webb, who was much younger than his master, carried on an independent practice while still assisting Jones. His work has much the same character as Jones's, although possibly lacking somewhat in distinction, and many buildings which have long been considered the work of Jones, are now thought to have been designed by Webb. He lived on to be the connecting link between the great age of Jones and the still greater age of Wren.

Sir Christopher Wren

THE LAST QUARTER OF THE SEVENTEENTH CENTURY AND THE FIRST quarter of the eighteenth were dominated by the figure of Sir Christopher Wren, who was born in 1632. Somewhat of a boy prodigy, his training did not prepare him for architecture, but rather for scientific pursuits. At the age of thirteen he became an assistant to a court physician, preparing anatomical specimens. Entering Oxford at fourteen, he was a brilliant student in mathematics and an inventor of remarkable ingenuity. His inventions covered many fields, such as astronomy, physics, embroidery, submarine navigation, mining, and "new designs tending to strength, convenience, and beauty in building." He had an extraordinary capacity for assimilating knowledge from many sources and putting it to practical use. At the age of twenty-nine he was appointed professor of astronomy at Oxford, and was one of the leaders of the group which founded the Royal Society. In 1661 he was appointed assistant to the Surveyor General of the Works, a gentleman and amateur poet who knew nothing whatever about architecture or construction. The actual work of the office was done by the good John Webb, who had been promised the chief post when next it became vacant, thanks to Inigo Jones's arrangements before his death. Webb's bitterness can be understood then, for when the Surveyor General died a few years later, Wren received the appointment. Poor Webb lacked push, and Wren had plenty of pull. Webb retired and died four years later.

Wren knew nothing of architecture or construction either, but it did not take him long to learn. His first work was Pembroke College Chapel at Cambridge in 1663, designed for his uncle, the bishop of Ely. It is a good and solid piece of design, with Corinthian pilasters, large pediments, and a cupola. Next came the Sheldonian Theater at Oxford, where he showed his skill at engineering by contriving a flat ceiling 68 feet wide, as well as achieving excellent acoustics. In the same year he was appointed to a commission to prepare recommendations for the restoration of St. Paul's Cathedral. In 1665, probably with the realization that it was time he learned something more about architecture, since it appeared that it was going to become his life's work, and possibly also to avoid the Great Plague which swept London that summer, Wren went to France. He spent six or eight months there, seeing and sketching the great buildings of the Renaissance, and meeting the great architects who were working for Colbert on the designs for the Louvre. He wanted to meet Bernini, and that grand personage brusquely granted him a few minutes' interview. Wren never went to Italy, and there has been much speculation as to why not. He had plenty of time and money, so it must have been simply because he felt no need to. He was a thorough scholar, and his library included all the standard works on Palladio and the other

Italian masters, as well as those on the ancient buildings. He was satisfied to know them at second hand.

A few months after his return, the Great Fire of London, in September of 1666, gave Wren one of the greatest opportunities any architect ever had. A lesser man would have been unequal to it. The fire started in a baker's shop near London Bridge early on a Sunday morning, and spread rapidly to adjoining buildings and along the river front, destroying the water wheel which supplied water to that part of the city. It raged for four days, during three of which it was aided by a high wind. When it finally subsided, four-fifths of the City, the old portion of London bounded by the Roman wall, was in ruins. The destruction covered 336 acres, and wiped out over 13,000 houses, 87 churches, and St. Paul's Cathedral, the Royal Exchange, and many other important buildings.

Within a few days after the fire, Wren presented the king with a plan for the rebuilding of the City. It was a fine scheme, in the best tradition of Renaissance city planning. If carried out it would undoubtedly have made London one of the handsomest cities of Europe. It provided for broad avenues radiating from two large squares, intersected by a regular pattern of streets, some of which followed the routes of the old streets. It also provided a fitting setting for a new St. Paul's Cathedral, located at a triangular intersection with open space all around it. The king accepted the plan, but the need for immediate rebuilding, and the great cost and complications of condemnation procedures, prevented it from being carried out.

Wren then undertook the tremendous task of designing the fifty-three churches of the City which are credited to him and his staff, as well as starting the new cathedral, which occupied him off and on for nearly forty years. These churches, of which sixteen were destroyed and three badly damaged in the blitz of 1940, show the incredible fertility of the man's imagination, and his sound common sense. He had little precedent to draw upon, for no Protestant churches had been built in England. Their principal requirement was a large and open auditorium in which the entire congregation could both see and hear the preacher. In a report, Wren wrote, "It would be vain to make a Parish Church larger than that all who are present can both hear and see. The Romanists, indeed, may build larger churches, it is enough if they hear the murmur of the mass and see the Elevation of

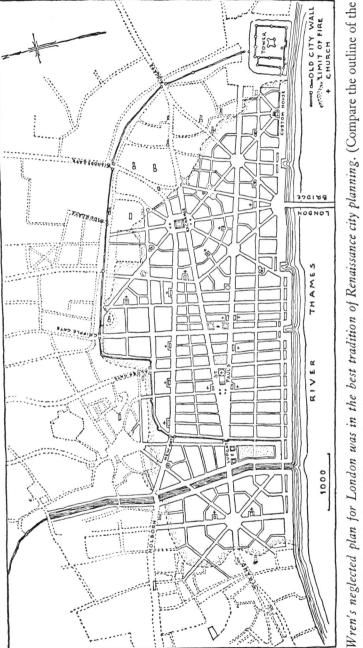

Wren's neglected plan for London was in the best tradition of Renaissance city planning. (Compare the outline of the old City Wall with the view of Roman London on page 57.)

the Host, but ours are fitted for auditories." The long nave and deep chancel of the traditional plan, suited to the processions and the celebration of the Mass of the Roman Church, were not suitable for the new Protestant form of worship. Furthermore, most of the sites were small and irregular—one was only 30 by 60 feet, another was an irregular polygon 55 feet by 85 feet. In some cases he had to adapt his plan to the foundations of the old church, and in all cases he had to make the maximum use of every square foot of the precious ground. There were problems affecting the exterior designs, too. Most sites were on narrow streets and so crowded and hemmed in by other buildings that no general view of the church would be possible. There was no use building an imposing façade if people could get no farther away than fifty feet to see it. And last, but by no means least, there was little money to work with.

In the interiors of the smaller churches, Wren achieved a semblance of a nave and side aisles by the careful placing of as few columns as possible. The exterior walls are pushed out to the property lines, wasting no space on piers and deep-set windows. In many of the larger churches there are balconies over the aisles and across the rear, to increase the seating accommodations. The interiors sometimes seem bare in treatment after the richness and dramatic contrasts of the Gothic churches, but they are handsome and effective. Some have flat ceilings, with a deep cove at the walls, some have plaster domed ceilings, and some have plaster barrel-vaulted ceilings. They all are paneled and coffered, usually richly decorated with carved and modeled plaster ornament. The nave columns are in some cases a single order on a high pedestal, and in others they are piers extending up to the balcony, with columns above. The walls are paneled in wood, and there are finely carved pulpits, altars, organ cases, and other pieces of cabinetwork. The character of these interiors is familiar to Americans from the far simpler white paneled interiors of the Colonial churches, which were derived from Wren's London churches.

On the exteriors, Wren reserved all elaborate treatment for the towers, where it could be seen above the adjoining buildings. Built of brick or gray Portland stone, the churches are solid and dignified, their walls relieved only by the large arched windows filled with wood sash with many small panes, and such simple architectural embellishments as corner quoins and stringcourses. The designs of the towers were largely derived from the Baroque steeples and cupolas of Italy, notably those of Bernini and Alessi. They are attached to the buildings so that they can be seen all the way to the ground, and above the roof of the church they blossom forth into a pilastered treatment. Above that they make a graceful transition to a circular or octagonal plan, and then continue in a series of diminishing stories treated with arches and pilasters and terminating in a spire. One of the astonishing things is the great variety in the treatment of the towers. Wren's freshness and vigor never failed him; no tower is a stale rehash of an earlier one.

Two of the finest and most famous of Wren's towers are those of

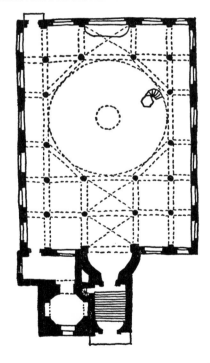

50

The plan of St. Stephen's, Walbrook, shows how **Wren** *achieved a monumental effect in a small rectangular church.*

PLATE 93
PLATE 94

the churches of St. Mary-le-Bow and St. Bride's. The churches were gutted during World War II, but their towers still stand. St. Mary-le-Bow, home of the well-known "Bow bells," was a small church built on an ancient Norman crypt, standing in its churchyard well back from the street. Only the tower, about 30 feet wide at the base and 225 feet high, fronts the street. The unusual feature of the spire is a series of inverted volutes which diminish the upper portion and at the same time buttress the steeple above. St. Bride's, on the other hand, depends for its diminishing entirely upon the setting back of each successive story, like the sections of a telescope. One of the most interesting churches was St. Stephen's, Walbrook, which was completely destroyed. Its open and rectangular interior was broken up into a complex spatial effect by the ingenious placing of a dome over the central area, supported entirely on eight slender columns. The tower was at the front of the church, rising 80 feet as a simple square mass, then above a balustrade it rose another fifty feet in a two-storied composition of engaged columns and pilasters, finishing off in a curious steeple of miniature stories.

St. Paul's Cathedral

MEANWHILE WREN WAS WORKING ON THE NEW ST. PAUL'S CATHEdral. His first effort was to start rebuilding what was left of the old church, but when that fell in 1668, it was decided to make a new start. He prepared several designs. The one which he urged, but which was rejected on ritualistic grounds, was a Greek cross 300 feet across, with the nave lengthened at the west end, a central dome 120 feet in diameter, and four saucer domes in the angles. The exterior had a single tall Corinthian order on a high base, and no cupolas or pinnacles to interfere with the silhouette of the dome. A second scheme, which was accepted by King Charles II, who said it was "very artificial, proper, and useful," had a similar plan, but a curiously freakish dome. A first low dome was cut off about halfway up, and on this ring was set a high drum surmounted by another dome, which was finished off with a fantastic pagoda-like spire. Wren's admirers have had a hard time explaining this design, even going so far as to say that he was playing a little joke. This would seem to be very un-like the amiable and hard-working Wren. It is more likely that he was still feeling his way through the intricacies of the biggest prob-lem he had yet undertaken, for he was only thirty-six and still a comparatively inexperienced architect.

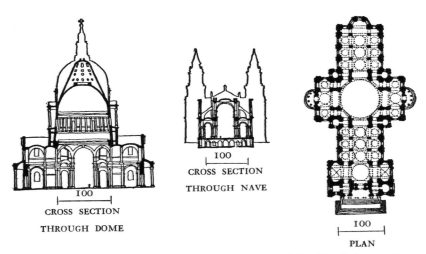

CROSS SECTION
THROUGH DOME

CROSS SECTION
THROUGH NAVE

PLAN

St. Paul's Cathedral is the great masterpiece of the English Renais-sance.

Wren was authorized to make whatever modifications he thought necessary in this accepted design, and the ultimate result was an entirely new plan. There is a central dome over the crossing, a chancel of three bays with a semicircular apse, a nave of three bays with an additional wider bay, and transepts of one bay. Thus the plan is substantially the same as the traditional English Gothic plan, with an over-all length of 514 feet, and an interior width in-cluding the aisles of 116 feet. The dome, 112 feet in diameter, has an inner shell 214 feet high with an opening in the top. Surrounding that is a conical intermediate shell which supports the 850-ton weight of the stone lantern. On the exterior is a timber dome covered with lead, built up to the necessary height to give the proper silhouette. The top of the stone cross is 366 feet above the street. The chancel, PLATE 95

PLATE 96

nave, and transepts are covered with saucer domes 91 feet high, with lower ones over the aisles. The piers are faced with a 50-foot Corinthian order. The effect of the great interior is one of restraint and dignity, almost of coldness, despite the modern mosaics in the vaulting of the chancel. It is in great contrast to the Baroque exuberance of the Italian churches. In recent years the eight piers supporting the dome were found to be cracking, due in part to Wren's unequal distribution on them of the great weight of the dome, and in part to settlement of the foundations, which in turn was caused by the nearby subway—a condition which Sir Christopher could hardly be expected to have foreseen. This was remedied by boring holes in the piers and the foundations and forcing in high-strength liquid concrete.

The exterior has two orders, the Composite superposed upon the Corinthian. It is said that Wren wanted to use one great order, like St. Peter's, but being unable to get stones large enough for the drums of the columns—four feet in diameter—he was forced to modify his design. The central portico of the west façade is flanked by two towers 212 feet high, which are slender enough and far enough away from the dome so as not to compete with it. The dome has a freestanding Corinthian order around the drum, with an attic story above it, surmounted by the fine silhouette of the dome itself and its lantern. There is a feature of the exterior design which is attacked by purists, who say that the second story of the north and south façades, flanking the nave and chancel, is a sham. Since the aisles are low and the nave is high, the outer walls would normally be only one story high, with a roof sloping back to the clerestory, like most Gothic cathedrals. Instead of that, Wren carried the outer wall up the full height of the nave so that its upper story is simply a screen standing free of the clerestory wall. Idealists condemn it, realists defend it. Perhaps it should be said that the architect, of all the artists, must of necessity be a realist. Wren's end justifies his means, for surely he felt that a low one-story façade on a building which has to be viewed from such close quarters would be lacking in the power to achieve a truly monumental effect.

St. Paul's is often compared with St. Peter's, for these are the two greatest monumental buildings of the Renaissance. Yet such a comparison is difficult to make, for they represent two entirely different

national temperaments, as they represent two different religious be-
liefs. St. Peter's is certainly much larger, being about three times the
area of St. Paul's and it is certainly much grander. But St. Paul's
has a greater unity of design, being the work of one architect, one
master mason, and one bishop, from its beginning in the mind of
Christopher Wren in 1668 to its completion when the last stone of the
cupola was set in place by Wren's son in 1710. Both are storied in
stone with the tombs and monuments of great men, and each
has become a symbol for its city and its Church. St. Paul's contains
the tombs of Wellington, Lord Nelson, Dr. Samuel Johnson, Sir
Joshua Reynolds, J. M. W. Turner, and many others. In the crypt,
among the many tablets embedded in the walls, is a simple panel
bearing a Latin inscription to the memory of Christophorus Wren,
ending with the words "Lector, Si Monumentum Requiris, Circum-
spice"—"Reader, If You Wish to See His Monument, Look About
You."

Wren's Long Career

WREN'S CAREER WAS ONE OF INCESSANT LABOR UNTIL ADVANCED
old age. The buildings mentioned so far would have been a busy
life's work for any ordinary man, but Wren was no ordinary man.
His position as Surveyor General included many petty duties such as
the repair of all government buildings, locating lodgings for state
officials, and, at one time, pulling down Dissenting meeting houses
as fast as they were built. In addition, he was responsible for three
royal palaces, two hospitals, many buildings at Oxford and Cambridge, over thirty city halls, many private homes, and numerous
other buildings in London, such as the Monument, Temple Bar, and
the rebuilding of the Temple. He maintained a large staff of assistants, just as any busy modern architect does, but in the case of important buildings he prepared the drawings with his own hands
and personally supervised the construction, although in other cases
he only made sketches which were then further developed and
executed by the men he had trained.

Working closely with Wren was the woodcarver and sculptor,
Grinling Gibbons. He devised a form of carved decoration com-

posed of strings and garlands of flowers, foliage, fruit, birds, and lace, which he executed with the most astonishing delicacy and technical perfection, and massed in large and vigorous compositions. They are found in over-mantels, over-doors, cornices, and other such features in many of the great houses built during his time. He also carved with equal perfection in plaster, and executed the festoons and other ornaments in the choir of St. Paul's.

In his plans for palaces, which were never completed, Wren showed his kinship to the great architects of the Italian and French Renaissance. The royal palace at Winchester, begun for Charles II, was to be another English Versailles, but the king's death put a stop to it. It was a spreading composition, connected by a long avenue to the cathedral, which would have created a superb vista. At Hamp-
PLATE 97 ton Court palace, the quadrangle Wren built for William III was to have been only a part of a great forecourt approached by an avenue sixty yards wide and a mile long. Built in brick, to suit the Dutch king's taste, this palace too was left uncompleted because of the king's death. Wren also had his hand in the group of buildings forming Greenwich Hospital, begun by Jones and Webb, and completed by Wren's successors. In the vestry of St. Paul's there is a drawing showing Wren's scheme for an open square surrounding his cathedral, bordered by an arcade. It was his fate that none of his attempts at planning in the grand manner were ever completely carried out.

There are literally scores of houses, great and small, all over England which are claimed to have been designed by Sir Christopher Wren. It would be a marvel if he had had time to design a fraction of these. If Groombridge Place, however, was not designed by Wren, it could have been. It is a little H-shaped house, built on the site of an older house, and consequently surrounded by a moat. The connecting portion of the H is the Hall, with principal rooms in three of the wing-ends and the kitchen in the fourth. The exterior is exceedingly simple, all in brick, even to the corner quoins. Only the entrance porch is of Portland stone. The steep hipped roof is covered with flat red tiles. The house is approached by a bridge to the forecourt, with the stable yard and service buildings on one side of the little island, and gardens on the others. It is notable for its great restraint, having none of the flamboyance of so many Renaissance houses, even in England.

There are many tales about Wren as a personality, and one of the most revealing follows: When he was building the town hall at Windsor he constructed the main floor as a very flat vault. The commissioners feared that it was not strong enough to stand the heavy floor loads and ordered him to build supporting piers under it, despite his insistence that the floor was strong enough. So, to keep peace, Wren built the piers, and the commissioners were satisfied. But Wren was satisfied too, for when steam-heating pipes were being installed in the old building more than two hundred years later, it was found that the piers stopped six inches short of the vaulting and had never supported it at all!

The jealousy of his rivals clouded the close of Wren's career. George I, the German king, was unsympathetic toward England's greatest architect, and when in 1718 another architect brought charges of mismanagement against Wren, he was dismissed from his post as Surveyor General, after holding it for fifty years. He retired to his home near Hampton Court, and there he died in 1723 at the age of ninety-one, after one of the most productive and influential lives in history. Wren's originality and inventiveness have been emphasized, but the particular, and thoroughly British, character of his work was best expressed by Thomas Carlyle, in his comments on Wren's Chelsea Hospital: "I had passed it, almost daily, for many years without thinking much about it, and one day I began to reflect that it had always been a pleasure to me to see it, and I looked at it more attentively, and saw that it was quiet and dignified and the work of a gentleman."

Much space has been devoted to Jones and Wren, not because they loom so exceedingly large in the entire history of architecture, but because they practically created English Renaissance architecture. Theirs were the creative minds which gave it form, a form which was carried on in devious ways by many brilliant but lesser men. And since this style was the modern mode of the mother country during the busiest years of the settlement and growth of the American colonies, it is of great importance to the story of architecture in America.

The Georgian Architects

THE EIGHTEENTH CENTURY IN ENGLAND IS CALLED THE "GEORGIAN period," for the four Georges ruled from 1714 to 1830. Architecture went through many fads and fashions during those years, from pompous absurdities to the utmost in restraint and refinement, but it never changed completely. The many architects of the period carried on a continuous tradition until it was swamped by the vagaries of the nineteenth century. Jones's career ended with the Revolution and the Commonwealth, during which there was little building, and he left no school. Only Webb carried over into the time of Wren. Sir Christopher, however, left a host of followers, many of whom were his contemporaries.

Nicholas Hawksmoor entered Wren's office in 1679, at the age of eighteen, and worked for him for over twenty years. For another fifteen years he was associated with Vanbrugh. Off and on during those years, and during his later life, he designed many buildings on his own. In 1708, Queen Anne's Act was passed providing for a tax on coal to raise money for building fifty churches in London. Only eight churches were completed, of which Hawksmoor designed at least six. In some of these, for the first time, the portico is found placed on the front of the church, with the tower rising behind it, a form which was to become widely used. Hawksmoor designed some fine quadrangles at Oxford, and he completed, in a heavy-handed Gothic manner, the west façade and towers of Westminster Abbey, which had never been finished. He was an able and conscientious man, having learned almost all he knew from Wren, including the habit of careful study and exacting attention to detail. At the same time he was influenced by the grandiose manner of Vanbrugh, so that his designs often show a rather heavy originality.

Of a very different nature was Sir John Vanbrugh, soldier, gentleman of fashion, dramatist, wit, and architect. He was born in 1664, the son of a rich London sugar baker, and at nineteen was sent to France to study the arts. After two years he entered the army, and ended that part of his career in the Bastille, where he was imprisoned for several years as a spy. While there he wrote his first play, and when he returned to London about 1695 he began his second career as a dramatist and man-about-town. He worked with William Congreve and Colly Cibber in the production of witty farces, meanwhile acquiring a wide reputation as a wit and a good fellow. The attack of moralists on his plays may have been what turned him to a third career, for in 1702 he entered the office of the Royal Works, and in that same year, almost on a dare, he accepted a commission from a fellow member of the Kitcat Club, the Earl of Carlisle, to design him a great "Palladian" castle. To help him in this new field, in which he had some knowledge and many ideas, but no technical background, "Van" lured away Sir Christopher Wren's right-hand man, Nicholas Hawksmoor. The result was Castle Howard, one of the grandest houses in England, and the forerunner of many such monstrous piles.

Vanbrugh thought of architecture as scenery, and planned and designed for effect rather than for comfort. Rooms were placed where monumental mass and rigid symmetry dictated, and everything was conceived on a colossal scale. The plan of Castle Howard goes back to the Palladian type of spreading plan introduced nearly a century

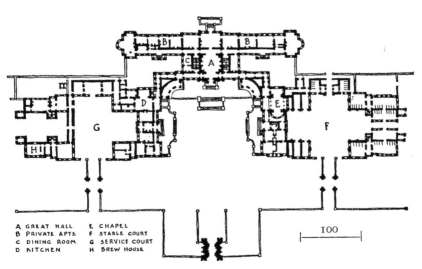

A GREAT HALL   E CHAPEL
B PRIVATE APTS.   F STABLE COURT
C DINING ROOM   G SERVICE COURT
D KITCHEN   H BREW HOUSE

100

In palaces such as Castle Howard, planning in England reached the heights of pompous formality and inconvenience.

before by Inigo Jones at Stoke Park. The central block is connected by curved arcades to lower wings, one containing the kitchen court and the other the stable court. Considerations of economy and domestic efficiency had no bearing upon the plan, for it was based entirely upon the requirements of the grand ceremonial way of life.

Castle Howard was a great social success and it brought Vanbrugh other similar commissions. In 1705 Queen Anne ordered him to prepare designs for the great house which a grateful nation was presenting to the Duke of Marlborough, in appreciation of his brilliant victories over the French. Thus was born Blenheim Palace, the largest and most monumental domestic building in England. It PLATE 98 follows the same type of plan as Castle Howard, with a three-acre forecourt, and it spreads 856 feet from tip of kitchen wing to tip of stable wing. Despite the vast and complicated plan, there is hardly a really handsome room in the building, except for the Hall, which is 71 feet by 44 feet and 67 feet high, and the long gallery, 182 feet by 22 feet. It is interesting to note that these traditional chambers were revived. The exterior is on a colossal scale. The central unit is only two stories, but it is 70 feet high, treated with a giant Corinthian order. Above the pediment rises a still higher mass, with clerestory windows to light the Great Hall, and on its gable ends are gigantic reclining figures which would be twenty feet high if they were to stand erect. On the wings are great towering masses in which the chimneys are concealed, flanked by sweeping buttresses and topped with tremendous urns and finials. It was Blenheim which brought forth the famous rhyme from Alexander Pope, in which he describes the palace and ends with:

> *Thanks, Sir, cried I, 'tis very fine,*
> *But where d'ye sleep, or where d'ye dine?*
> *I find by all you have been telling*
> *That 'tis a house, but not a dwelling!*

With all the obvious faults of his planning and design, the genial Van at least had the true Baroque flair, and his influence did much to limber up British design and keep it from tight provinciality. He died in 1726, and wit as he was, he would surely have appreciated his epitaph: "Lie heavy on him, earth, for he Laid many a heavy load on thee."

James Gibbs studied in Rome, and upon his return to London in 1709 he designed two of the city's best-known churches, St. Mary-le-Strand and St. Martin's-in-the-Fields. The latter church PLATE 99 stood in the country when it was built, but now fronts on busy Trafalgar Square. It is one of the finest churches in the city, with

|— 50 —|

St. Martin's-in-the-Fields set the fashion for the porticoed church.

its broad portico, through which rises its handsome stone tower. Gibbs's best work is the Radcliffe Camera at Oxford. Built as the library, it is a circular building one hundred feet in diameter, crowned with a well-proportioned lead-covered dome of timber construction. Of all the later architects, Gibbs seems to stand closest to the spirit and character of Wren.

Colin Campbell had a waspish temperament, but he was a capable architect. It was he who brought about the aged Wren's dismissal as Surveyor General by a trumped-up charge of mismanagement. Two of his country houses, in the now accepted spread-eagle-type plan, were Wanstead and Houghton, but in Mereworth Castle he reached a new high in inappropriateness. Copied almost literally from Palladio's Villa Capra near Vicenza, its Great Hall is under the central dome, windowless but for four small openings in the dome fifty feet above the floor. Since chimneys, so necessary in England, would have spoiled the Italian design, Campbell, with great ingenuity, brought all the flues to the dome, forming a hollow brick shell which conducted the smoke out through the lantern! However, he performed a great service to architectural history when he compiled and published, in 1715, the first of a series of volumes entitled *Vitruvius Britannicus,* a collection of engravings of the buildings of the best English architects, including, of course, a good many of his own. If it were not for these volumes we should never have known what many a vanished masterpiece looked like. In his opposition to Wren, Campbell included little of that master's work, and thus had much to do with the trend back to a purer Palladianism, after the more personal originality of Sir Christopher.

Just how much of an architect, and how much merely a highly accomplished amateur, was Richard, third Earl of Burlington, has long been a disputed question. However, it seems clear now that he personally designed many fine buildings, generously permitting Campbell or Kent to take the credit for them. At the age of twenty-one, having traveled in Italy and studied Palladio, Lord Burlington tore down the façade of his London house and erected a new one designed in the Palladian manner. Only two of its three stories remain today, but it was unquestionably one of the finest pieces of Renaissance architecture in Europe. Campbell published drawings of it and claimed authorship of the design, but the young lord must get the credit for it.

Burlington's protégé was William Kent, a painter and landscape designer, as well as architect, whom the earl took into his home for nearly thirty years. With Burlington's backing, Kent became fashionable and successful, designing furniture and accessories for his houses, and, for special occasions, even the ladies' gowns. Yet, follower of fashion as he was, he could turn out a substantial design. The Horse Guards in London, is probably his best work.

Later Georgian Architects

THESE MEN were younger contemporaries of sir christopher Wren, but, with the exception of Hawksmoor, they cannot be said to have been carrying on his tradition, which was one of Baroque

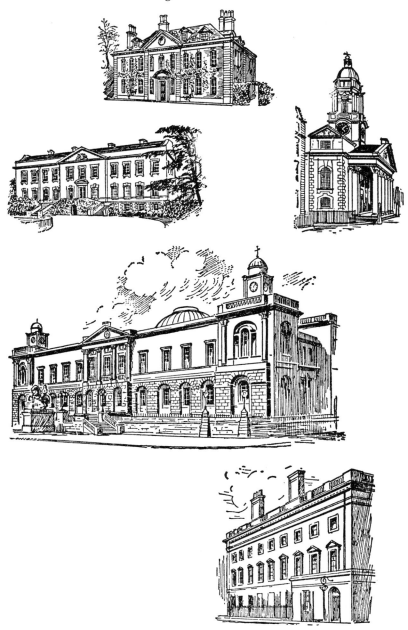

Typical examples of the Georgian style of eighteenth-century England.

vigor. Vanbrugh was the only one with any true originality—the others were followers of Palladian rules—so by the middle of the century architectural design was becoming pretty academic and often dull. Isaac Ware was of this period. His Chesterfield House, in London, is a judicious composition, nicely balanced and above criticism, but it certainly is not inspiring. His best works were his many publications, of which the most important is *The Complete Body of Architecture,* a 748-page folio in which he attempted to gather together all the wisdom of previous writers on architecture, plus plenty of his own. Ware preached a return to more reasonableness in architecture—what today would be called more functional design—and less blind adherence to academic rules. It is good preachment for any age.

All the good architects were not in London. The two John Woods of Bath, father and son, were among the very best of the century. Bath's mineral springs had fallen into disuse since Roman times, but early in the eighteenth century they were promoted as a fashionable resort by Ralph Allen and Beau Nash. John Wood, Senior, came to the city in time to lay out the streets and squares in the grand manner, so that Bath became the only large city in England with a conscious city plan. The designs of the Woods for the buildings of the city, the churches, the elegant baths, and the

PLATE 100 majestic sweep of the colonnaded house around the Royal Crescent, all built of local Bath stone, make Bath the handsomest city in England. It suffered severe damage from air raids during World War II, and many churches, the fine Gothic abbey, the assembly rooms of the baths, and part of the Crescent were damaged or destroyed.

One more architect, whose work has some of the vigor of the Jones-Wren tradition, appeared in London before the close of this period of elegance and pedantry in English architecture. Sir William Chambers started life with the intention of entering his father's mercantile business, but an enthusiasm for art led him to study and work in Paris and Italy. Returning to London in 1755, well-trained but unknown, he was fortunate enough to get the job of art tutor to the Prince of Wales, the future George III. He made an enthusiastic amateur architect and lifelong friend of the young George, and with such a start Chambers reached the pinnacle of success before his death in 1796. His greatest work is Somerset House, a huge building to house government offices. Part of the old Royal Palace was pulled down, as was the old Somerset House, one façade of which PLATE 101 had been designed by Inigo Jones. The scheme called for a frontage on the Thames of eight hundred feet, and it was Chambers' intention to lengthen it still further by a row of private houses on each end, with a continuous façade harmonious in design with Somerset House. The river façade is vigorous and masculine, consisting of two-story engaged Corinthian columns and pilasters standing on a high rusticated and arched basement. Although the Portland stone is now soot-stained and blackened by time, the building still holds its own against the near-by buildings of modern London.

Contemporary and competing with Chambers, but very different in style, were the brothers Adam. The sons of a well-known Scottish architect, all four were brought up in the profession, but Robert and James were the ones who made a tremendous success in London. Robert studied in Italy during the early 1750's, especially seeking out what he could find of Greek and Roman domestic architecture. James also studied in Rome, and the two launched a London practice which became a success almost immediately. About the same time, 1762, Stuart and Revett published the first volume of *The Antiquities of Athens,* which together with the influence of the discoveries at Pompeii and Herculaneum and the writings of Winckelmann and Lessing, brought about a popular craze for Greek and the purest forms of Roman art. The brothers Adam capitalized upon this to the fullest. They devised a method of decoration, for both exterior and interior use, which is refined and restrained to a high degree. Delicate yet rich by contrast with broad smooth surfaces, the style is elegant and highly sophisticated —one might almost call it "slick." It became tremendously popular, and has remained so to this day, as the "Adam style." The Adams were swamped with commissions for all sorts of buildings—country houses, town houses, clubs, theaters, and government buildings.

Just before Chambers began work on Somerset House, the Adams undertook Adelphi Terrace, a similar project facing the river, as a private speculation. Its delicate façades and finely detailed apartments were among the architectural gems of London, and it was occupied by many great people of the literary and theatrical world before it was finally torn down shortly before World War II to make room for modern buildings. One of the Adams' finest works is the completion and decoration of Kedleston Hall, a country house which had been commenced by earlier architects. It

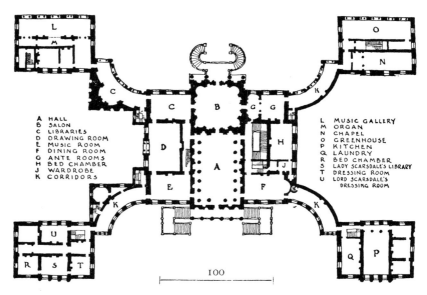

A HALL
B SALON
C LIBRARIES
D DRAWING ROOM
E MUSIC ROOM
F DINING ROOM
G ANTE ROOMS
H BED CHAMBER
J WARDROBE
K CORRIDORS

L MUSIC GALLERY
M ORGAN
N CHAPEL
O GREENHOUSE
P KITCHEN
Q LAUNDRY
R BED CHAMBER
S LADY SCARSDALE'S LIBRARY
T DRESSING ROOM
U LORD SCARSDALE'S
DRESSING ROOM

100

Plan of Kedleston Hall.

has the usual grand plan, with a central block connected by curving wings to four smaller blocks at each of the four corners, of which the two southern units were never built. The magnificent Hall is 69 feet long, 42 feet wide, and 38 feet high, lined on both sides with a fine Corinthian order extending to a coved ceiling decorated with characteristically delicate Adam modeled plaster. The smooth walls behind the columns have niches in which are reproductions of Greek sculpture, and above is a frieze with sculptured panels in low relief. Beyond is the salon, a domed chamber 42 feet in diameter and 50 feet high, chaste and yet rich in its contrast of finely modeled ornament and plain wall surface.

The brothers Adam felt that they were revolutionizing architecture, both in planning and in the use of ornament, and they certainly did shake it out of its Palladian rut. In their great houses they introduced the use of circular and oval rooms, to break the monotony of having one rectangular space after another. The walls are broken with square and semicircular niches and recesses, and they developed even further the emphasis of the axis and the vista. Their grasp of spatial planning shows the influence of their study of late Roman plans. The academic approach to ornament, based on Palladio, was that all ornament had to be elements of the orders. Thus an exterior had to consist basically of a rusticated basement, surmounted by columns, an entablature, and an attic. Interiors had to be miniature versions of the same thing. Openings could be framed only with heavy mouldings or orders, ceilings had to be heavily beamed and coffered.

The Adams swept all this away. Mouldings became light and delicate. Ornament became finely modeled in stucco, based upon Greek motives, such as the honeysuckle, the palmetto, and the fret. The anthemion, the urn, the griffon, swags and ribbons, all these came back into use. New forms were devised from old motives, such as the fanlight in arched openings, and circular, elliptical, and octagonal ceiling panels formed by delicate mouldings and filled with daintily modeled rosettes and classical figures. The extreme delicacy and refinement is almost feminine in character, yet there is a masculine boldness in the manner in which a broad and plain wall surface is relieved only by a deep semicircular niche, in which stands a piece of Greek sculpture. The Adams were excellent self-advertisers, and published books of their designs, which not only brought them more and more commissions, but also made the motives and to some extent the principles of their style available to provincial architects and builders everywhere, in America as well as in England.

Robert Adam died in 1792 and James two years later. They had devised a new method of designing, whereby use no longer had to be cramped into a rigid architectural frame. Instead, a building could now be sensibly planned and then decorated with a judicious application of decorative forms—a sort of architectural cosmetic, beautiful, but only skin deep.

Among the architects who followed the Adams were Henry Holland, George Dance, John Nash, and Sir John Soane. Holland contrived to strike a medium between the old Palladianism of Chambers and the neoclassicism of the Adams, and having traveled in

France, he also introduced some of the flavor of the Directoire style. However, when he was commissioned by the Prince of Wales to remodel Carlton House into a royal palace in 1788, he turned out such a fine and strictly classical design that it aroused admiration from even the opponents of classicism. Horace Walpole, the arch-advocate of romanticism, said, "How sick we shall be after this chaste palace of Mr. Adam's gingerbread and sippets of embroidery!"

Soane was a scrupulously careful and meticulous architect, whose fine houses are exquisitely studied essays in the smooth pseudo-classic style popularized by the brothers Adam. Yet in re-building the Bank of England he showed true creative genius. He treated the windowless exterior walls with a Corinthian order taken from the temple of Vesta at Tivoli, but in the interiors he produced a classical design with hardly a trace of classic detail. It is classical in dignity and spirit, but without orders or mouldings. The plan of one of the banking chambers is a Greek cross, and its arched form suggests a Byzantine church, but instead of a dome resting on pendentives, there is a ring of Greek Ionic columns, with continuous windows behind them, and a flat ceiling above. The grooved soffits of the arches carry right down to the floor without interruption, and the smooth surfaces of the walls and vaults are relieved only by shallow panels. This interior demonstrates that it is possible for the classic tradition to inspire an architect of creative genius to a true and fine originality.

Smaller Georgian Houses

THE GREAT HOUSES OF ENGLAND ARE NOT IN THEMSELVES OF ANY great importance to us today, but they have a spectacular interest, and their architects led the way and formulated the ideas and forms which gradually permeated all English domestic architecture. The most beautiful houses in England are not the great mansions, but the thousands of simple little Georgian houses, with their warm red brick walls and crisp white trim. Their plans are compact and straightforward, their elevations are nicely studied as to fenestration and the placing of their few decorative features, and their interiors are dignified and homelike.

There was a high standard of public taste during the eighteenth century, for every educated man had some knowledge of architecture and a surprisingly well-schooled judgment in matters of design. Rarely did the distinguished London architects unbend enough to design a small house, or a house in a provincial city. They were designed by local architects who may have worked in a great London office for a few years, or they may have had no architect at all, being the work of country builders carrying on the solid tradition of British building, by now completely grounded in the grammar of classical design. These builders were aided, of course, by the many books of designs and handbooks of ornament published by the fashionable architects and their admirers. But without the builders' inherent good taste and good judgment their work could still have been very bad. Nor were the lesser houses of London itself, the homes of the thousands of merchants, clerks, artisans, and tradesmen, designed by architects. Most of them were built speculatively, often in entire blocks at a time, by ambitious building-tradesmen, and designed by themselves or other builders. That they maintained such a high degree of dignity is an indication of the general level of taste of the times.

PLATE 102

The typical city house was a "row house" on a deep and narrow lot. The house was often only two rooms deep, and behind it was the inevitable garden. Back of the garden, for families that could afford it, was the stable and coach house fronting on an alley, or sometimes an annex with additional living rooms. The houses were three, four, and sometimes five stories high. The basement floor was a few steps below the street and contained the kitchen and service rooms, the dining and drawing rooms were on the first floor, then a second and possibly a third floor for bedrooms, and servants' rooms on the top floor. Better-class houses, affording wider plots, left a court at one side of the property, so the house could extend the full depth of the plot, as in the fine house the Adams designed for Lord Derby.

The façade was necessarily high and narrow, usually three or four windows wide, with the entrance at one side. The walls were

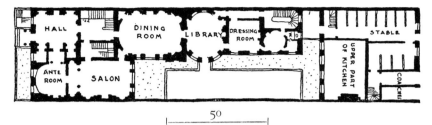

In the plan of Lord Derby's house the Adam brothers achieved much of the sense of spaciousness of a great house, yet on a fifty-foot-wide city lot.

of red or gray brick, and the only ornament was the white wood-work of the window frames, a handsome classic treatment around the entrance door, and the cornice. Building laws, passed in London in 1707 and aimed at restricting the spread of fire, required that window frames, which had always been set flush with the walls, be set back four inches, a custom which is still almost universal. They also stated that "No mundillion or cornish of timber or wood under the eaves shall hereafter be made or suffered." Thus the roof came to be hidden behind a parapet wall and cornices were made of stone or stucco.

Portland stone was seldom used on any but the finer houses, because of the expense, but artificial stone was used a great deal, in stock designs, for cornices and door treatments. During the last quarter of the century, the desire for greater elegance led to the use of stucco, often marked out in jointing to imitate stonework. The Adams used stucco frequently, and their delicately modeled stucco ornaments are very lovely. John Nash, who designed fine rows of houses with continuous façades during the first quarter of the nineteenth century, used stucco almost exclusively.

Middle-class houses in small cities and in the country had all the refinements of those in London, without the disadvantage of being crowded in rows on narrow lots. Their plans were open, usually following the block plan with wings, and occasionally recalling the H or E plan of earlier days. They were set in a garden, screened from the street by a wall or a hedge, often with fine brick gate posts and wrought-iron gates. They were generally built of brick, with wood trim, but frequently with "rubbed" or moulded brick quoins, stringcourses, and cornices. In districts where stone was plentiful, such as near Bath, even the smaller houses were built of native stone. In other districts where there was still a supply of timber, which had long been getting scarce in England, houses were framed in timber as they had been in medieval times, and covered with "weather-boarding," or clapboards, or sometimes with heavy quartered oak shingles which they called "shides." "Tile-hanging" was another method of covering the frames of houses, using the same orange-red flat tiles that were used on the roofs.

Roofs generally continued to be hipped, as they were in Wren's time, often with a spreading pediment in the center of the front. Sometimes the roof rose from a handsome cornice, and sometimes it rose from behind a parapet, in which case there was a light cornice. Occasionally there was a flat roof behind the parapet, and occasionally the roof was not hipped, terminating in pediments at the gable ends. Sometimes, too, instead of such a pediment, the end walls and chimneys were carried up past the roof, forming a sloping or stepped parapet. This last was invariably done when there was a gambrel roof, which is similar to the mansard roof in that it has a steep lower slope and a flatter upper slope. Dormers were no longer architectural features, but were treated simply and in a way to make them blend with the roof. Roofing continued to be tile or slate, with lead on roofs of a very low pitch. Chimneys of the early eighteenth century were paneled and pilastered in brickwork, the last traces of the elaborate treatments of Tudor days. By the latter part of the century they became quite plain, with only stone caps or a few projecting brick courses at the top.

Although the double-hung sash window had first appeared nearly a hundred years before, it was not until the beginning of the eighteenth century that its use became general, and about that time many of the old houses had their windows modernized. The casements of the mullioned windows had been glazed usually with leaded glass, but with the larger units of the sash windows, the designers seem to have found that the leads did not emphasize the divisions between the panes sufficiently to count in the design, so they used moulded wood strips, or muntins, to divide the sash. Today, even though glass can now be made in as large sheets as may be required, the designer of a house in the Georgian style will properly divide the sash with wood muntins, for they are a part of the traditional style and they keep the panes of glass in scale with the other elements of the design.

The windows usually had slatted shutters, but by no means invariably, as is commonly supposed. Sash were seldom paired, but were frequently tripled, with the center unit wider than the side units. However, when grouped windows were designed, the Georgian designers were more apt to form a bay. Brick bay windows often extended through two stories, reminiscent of the bays of Tudor times, and the graceful wood bay windows, either angled or curved, are among the most charming features of the Georgian houses. In connection with the bay windows, mention should be made of the shop fronts, which were typically treated as bay or bow windows, with larger panes than in the houses, grouped in treatment with the entrance doors. The objective was not so much to gain as large a show window as possible, but rather to establish a dignified and inviting character for the front of the shop.

There is a great variety in the treatment of the entrance doorways in Georgian domestic architecture. Generally speaking, the pre-Georgian or Queen Anne entrance had a projecting hood supported on handsomely carved brackets. The hood was sometimes flat and sometimes hemispherical, in which case it frequently had a shell motive carved on the inside. Later came the more strictly classical treatments, either projecting as a porch, with columns, entablature, and pediment, or flat against the building, with pilasters and pediment. The pediment itself was another source of variety, the usual form being varied with broken pediments, curved pediments, and curved and broken pediments. In the latter part of the century two other forms appeared over the doors—cornices supported on consoles or brackets, and arched fanlights with leaded glass patternwork. The character of the early entrances was bold and vigorous, while that of the later entrances tended to become more and more delicate, often so much so as to appear attenuated and wiry. In contrast to the latter were the neoclassic entrances, which employed the Greek orders more or less correctly proportioned. Another feature which appeared about the opening of the nineteenth century and continued in use during the Regency period was the balcony. These delicate platforms of wood or iron, with their graceful railings and slender posts latticed in Greek patterns, supporting a sweeping metal roof, have great charm.

The interior walls of the better middle-class houses were almost universally covered with paneling. Wren had more or less standardized the system, which consisted of a base at the floor, a paneled wainscot to the window-sill height, and large panels above extending to the cornice. Early in the century the paneling was elaborate, with heavy mouldings and raised panels; later the mouldings became very simple and the panels flat, their surface sunk below the surface of the surrounding stiles and rails. Pine and fir, shipped from Baltic ports, were chiefly used for interior woodwork, for good English oak had finally become very scarce and was used only for the finest work. Georgian paneling was almost invariably painted. The Adams introduced plain plaster walls, with a dado at the bottom, thus making all the more effective the rich and delicate ornament on their ceilings and in their friezes and fanlights. Mantels became less overpowering than in the early Renaissance days, and the familiar Georgian mantel began to appear, with its pilasters, fine mouldings, and restrained use of acanthus, honeysuckle, urns, and other classical ornaments. Staircases developed the slender handrail with carved or turned balusters, terminating in a spiral or volute at the bottom, and late in the century the graceful spiral stair became popular, often with a delicate wrought-iron handrail.

For the first time, the beginnings of modern sanitary arrangements began to appear. Lead cisterns in the areaways in front of the houses of London were supplied at certain hours of the day with water from under-street mains laid by private companies. From there it was either dipped out by hand, or pumped by hand to a cistern on the roof, whence it flowed through lead pipes into the house. In country houses, water was similarly carried or hand-pumped from the well. At the rear of the garden, or sometimes attached to the rear of the house, was the commodious "bog house," with a brick-vaulted pit under it which was connected to a brick drain leading to a cesspool. In London many districts had sewers under the streets. In a really fine house, water was piped to flush the drain, but it was not until 1775 that the first water closet, with a trap to seal it, was invented, and three years later an ingenious but dependable valve appeared. Thus it became possible to place the water closet within the house.

The Gothic Revival

THERE WAS A CURIOUS REVIVAL OF INTEREST IN GOTHIC ARCHI-tecture during the last half of the eighteenth century. It started as a literary interest and intellectual fad, more or less paralleling the revived interest in Greek art, and it was the beginning of what is now called the Gothic Revival, which grew to great proportions in England and America during the nineteenth century. Gothic building, as a continuous and genuine tradition, had died out. Jones, Wren, and Hawksmoor had designed churches and collegiate buildings in the Gothic style, probably because it was demanded of them as a carry-over from the previous century. In scattered rural sections, some small Gothic churches were built or rebuilt during the eighteenth century, but they too were the last vestiges of a tradition which died hard.

The growing romantic movement in literature and art was further encouraged by the writing of Horace Walpole, who made a strong plea for a return to the Gothic style in architecture. At the same time he was building Strawberry Hill, his fabulous pseudo-Gothic castle. A few years later James Wyatt, a strange character who had done fine work in the Adam style, designed Fonthill Abbey for a wealthy dilettante. It was a fantastically romantic Gothic monastery, a Hollywood conception in wood and plaster. Meanwhile, wealthy amateurs of the picturesque had long been building little thatched-roof Gothic cottages in the gardens of their estates. Old Gothic churches were being carefully studied and restored, and several new churches were built in a bastard Gothic style, for no architect seemed to understand or care for the Gothic principles. Thus Gothic gradually staged a comeback, not as a living style, but as a conscious style, a fad to please the whims of romantic amateurs.

Landscape Design and Town Planning

TUDOR AND ELIZABETHAN HOUSES HAD ALWAYS BEEN SET SOLIDLY in their surroundings of terraces and geometric gardens, which, stiff as they were, were definitely related to the house and served to frame it. The Dutch influence, which went to extremes of quaintness and charm, was responsible for the exaggerated topiary work, the gardens full of box clipped into the forms of birds and animals, geometric shapes, and ships under full sail. During the seventeenth century the French influence was strong, and Charles II is said to have invited the great le Nôtre to England to design gardens for some of the members of his court. The grandeur of his style, however, with its great fountains and extensive use of sculpture, did not suit the English taste. During the early Georgian period, the British tradition of "informal formal" gardens was established by Bridgman, the royal gardener, who banished the clipped absurdities and geometrical stiffness of the earlier periods, and designed gardens which seemed to grow from the house itself, adhering to axial lines extended from it, but clothing them with a free use of natural-appearing growth.

In the eighteenth century came the influence of the romantic movement, and William Kent and "Capability" Brown designed naturalistic landscapes around the great houses, extending pastures and groves of oaks right up to the very windows of the mansions. This necessitated hidden fences to keep the cattle and the deer from walking in the front door, and thus provided no proper setting to frame the house. Humphrey Repton and his sons, whose practice continued into the nineteenth century, turned English landscape design back to emphasis of the house as the dominating element, surrounding it with formal gardens and connecting it by gradual stages to its natural setting in the countryside.

Town planning was much talked about in England during the seventeenth and eighteenth centuries, but comparatively little was done. When the Earl of Bedford commissioned Inigo Jones to build St. Paul's Church on his property at Covent Garden, he included instructions to build a piazza in the Italian style. Jones produced a very handsome square, with the church on one side and fine Palladian buildings on two sides, fronting on the gardens of Bedford House on the fourth. However, before many years the buildings were remodeled so as to lose their uniformity and the open square was gradually destroyed. Here and there isolated squares were built, such as Lincoln's Inn Fields, in which the design of the houses was uniform, but no effort was made to tie the squares together with avenues or parks. The failure of the Council to put into effect Wren's plan for the rebuilding of the old City lost to London its last chance to capture some of the Renaissance ideal of open spaces and grand avenues.

During the eighteenth century, the work of the Woods in laying out the improvements in the city of Bath was the only large-scale town-planning effort in England. But finally, early in the nineteenth century, a grand scheme was conceived and more or less carried out in the West End of London. The Prince of Wales and John Nash laid out a project for a fine avenue to connect Regent's Park on the north with Carlton House and the government buildings near the Thames. The result was Regent Street and Portland Place, somewhat winding and not too wide, but very handsome. Land was sold to investors, banks, wealthy individuals, and speculative builders, and the buildings were built with a high degree of uniformity of design. Those that were not designed by Nash himself were designed under his control. The curving sweep of Regent Street, now the fashionable shopping center, is very impressive. At the far end of the "Royal mile" is Regent's Park, originally planned to be dotted with villas and royal pavilions. Surrounding the park is a fringe of "terraces"—stone and stucco fronts with great Corinthian orders, sculptured pediments, and massive pavilions, flanked and screened by colonnades and triumphal arches. Much of this, including the fine semicircular Park Crescent, was severely bombed during the last war. Nash later started another scheme which resulted in the clearing of a site and the creation of Trafalgar Square, connected to the Regent Street scheme by Pall Mall. Thus the old and crowded city of London finally achieved in a small way something of the Renaissance grandeur inspired by the capitals of the Continent.

The Golden Age of English Art

THE EIGHTEENTH CENTURY WAS THE GOLDEN AGE IN ARCHITEC-
ture and the arts in England, as it was in France. The forms and
the spirit of the Renaissance became grafted on to the British tradition as firmly as the forms and the spirit of the Gothic Age had
been before. The traditional builder no longer built a Gothic cottage with latticed windows and a Tudor doorway; he produced a
little rectangular brick house with sash windows and a chaste classical entrance, taken from a London pattern book. The great buildings of the English Renaissance take their place beside the great
buildings of the Gothic era before them, and together they form
Britain's heritage in architecture.

The eighteenth century in England closed in an atmosphere
of revolution and change. The war with the colonies led to war with
half of the European world, and to the near disruption of the Empire. At the same time, the French Revolution had sounded a call
for freedom and equality which stirred certain classes in England,
as it did all over Europe. Meanwhile, a more important revolution
was brewing. The application of steam power to industry was bringing about the Industrial Revolution. From 1790 on, the weavers
and spinsters of England were moving from their cottages to the
factories. New cities were growing, dependent upon coal and water
power; and the owners of mines and industries formed a new and
powerful class which chafed under the rule of a Parliament which
represented the old agricultural England. The complex social problems of the nineteenth century were beginning to take shape.

✻ XI ✻

Seventeenth-Century America

THE ENGLISH, whose culture was destined to dominate the North American continent, were the last to settle it. The Spanish were first, building Mexico City in 1521 on the site of the Aztec capital which they had destroyed, and in less than a century they had colonized most of what is now Central America, Florida, Texas, and southwestern United States. Next came the French, founding Quebec in 1608, and spreading through central Canada, the Great Lakes region, and down the Mississippi. In 1624 the Dutch settled New Amsterdam, establishing a feudal domain which extended as far north as Albany.

The English settled Jamestown in 1607, but it was 1620 before another colony was established at Plymouth, and still another ten years before that was followed by the founding of Salem, Charlestown, and Boston. Settlement of the Atlantic coast proceeded rapidly thereafter through the seventeenth century, with the founding of Maryland in 1633, the Carolinas in 1680, and Philadelphia in 1682. The people of each of these English settlements had different social backgrounds, which together with the differences in climate, resulted in differences in their manner of building. But there were two things that all the first settlers had in common: the need for immediate housing and an abundance of wood as a building material. There are very few houses standing today which can be authentically dated as having been built before 1700, and most of them are built of wood.

The first houses were not log cabins. No English settler had ever seen a log cabin, and he could hardly be expected to have invented such a relatively advanced building technique. The log cabin was introduced by the Swedes, who settled along the lower Delaware River in 1638, and it was not until the pioneer expansion westward over the Alleghenies that it came into general use. Few of the first shiploads of English colonists had had anything to do with building construction in England, but all of them were familiar with the huts of the farm laborers, so it was in crude shelters of that type that they lived for several years. They dug pits into the ground about three feet deep, built walls of sod up another three feet, and raised a roof of saplings and wattles. Sometimes the interior was lined with rough boards, and some houses were constructed entirely of wattles and mud. Thus the houses and the churches of Jamestown, Plymouth, Boston, and even as late as Philadelphia, were no more than huts, and even after better houses were built, their use persisted. One was still standing in Philadelphia as late as 1760.

The glowing accounts of the beauties and riches of the new land, which lying adventurers carried back to England, were chiefly responsible for the fact that at nearly every colony, the first shiploads of colonists contained very few building craftsmen, or none at all, and few tools. The second influx, however, usually brought carpenters, joiners, masons, and brick makers—and their tools—and framed houses finished with sawn lumber began to appear within two or three years after the founding of each colony. Thus by 1614 Jamestown had "two fair rowes of houses all of Framed timber (two stories, and an upper garret, or corne loft, high)." Frame houses were built in Plymouth in 1624 and in Salem in 1629; when Governor Winthrop arrived in Charlestown in 1630 he immediately "ordered his house to be cut and framed," and when he moved across the river to Boston shortly after, he took the frame of his house with him. To build frame houses was no innovation for these people, for many of the lower-middle-class Englishmen had always lived in frame houses. With such a wealth of timber at hand it was only natural that they should build houses which were as much as possible like the homes they had left behind, modified only to meet the greater severity of the climate.

Even more than in England, the hearth was the center of the home in seventeenth-century New England. Many houses were begun as only one room, with a great chimney at one end. The entrance was at the chimney end, forming a little vestibule, or "porch," from which a steep and winding stair led to the second floor or garret. The porch, with its door sheltering the room from winter blasts, was the vestige of the screened entrance of the medieval house. The chimney was massive at the base, built of stone in districts where it

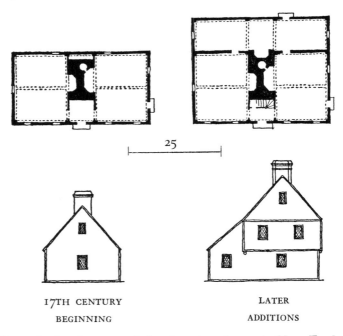

25

17TH CENTURY
BEGINNING

LATER
ADDITIONS

The early development of the American house in New England.

was available, but more usually of brick. It provided a fireplace for each room, that in the kitchen being the largest. Many were 8 or 10 feet wide and 5 feet high, and built into the masonry beside them were circular brick ovens. During the first half of the century, many outside chimneys were built of wood, lined with clay, but they were soon rebuilt in a safer material.

As the family prospered and the need developed for more space, another room was added on the other side of the chimney. If the house was one-storied to start with, a second floor was also added, with a fireplace in each of the new rooms. The final stage in the enlargement was the addition of a one-story leanto at the rear, extending across the full width of the house, and roofed by carrying the main roof down over it in one sweep. This was the origin of the "salt box" house. The larger of the two front rooms was the "hall"

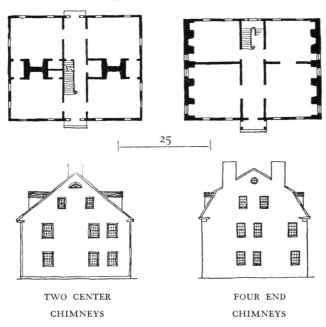

TWO CENTER   FOUR END

CHIMNEYS   CHIMNEYS

The later development of the American house in New England.

or "keeping room," which served as the kitchen and dining room until the leanto was built, and the other was the parlor, usually containing a bed. The second-floor rooms were at first used chiefly for storage. Thus developed the full-fledged early Colonial house, with its center entrance with two windows on each side, and its great central chimney absorbing heat from the fireplaces and radiating it throughout the house.

When a prosperous merchant wanted to build a larger house, he built it two rooms deep, but this type revealed the defect that the rear rooms could be reached only by passing through the front rooms. So the center hall house arrived. The chimney was removed from the center of the house, permitting a wide hallway, with the stair in it, to run through the house from front to back. Two chimneys were built, either inside the house between the front and rear rooms, or on the outside walls. In the latter case, the entire end of the house was sometimes built in brick, since the chimney had to be nearly that wide anyway to accommodate the fireplaces in the four rooms it served.

The ridge of these early houses runs the long way of the house, parallel to the road, and the chimney invariably towers high, in true medieval fashion, often paneled or pilastered in a manner reminiscent of Tudor times. The roof is always steeply pitched, the better to shed the heavy snows and long rains. A few houses have gables toward the front, in order to provide better light and more room for the garret, but they were removed from many houses, probably because of the difficulty of making their intersections with the main roof watertight. These gables are of particular interest because they are descended from the medieval dormers, which ran right up from the face of the wall below. The colonists called them "lucome windows," a name derived from the French word for dormer, *lucarne*. Many seventeenth-century houses have an overhang at the second-floor level extending across the front or the ends, and sometimes both. Some have an overhang at the gable end at the garret-floor level. There could have been no practical need for these overhangs, so they doubtless were intended to be ornamental. They also represent another link to the medieval timbered houses of England. The entrance doorway is always very simple, with a plain and unmoulded trim and a heavy plank door. The windows are small wood casements, although most houses have been re-sashed with double-hung windows. The casements are single or paired, and are glazed with leaded glass in small diamond or rectangular panes. Most of them were filled with oiled paper before 1650, as glass was precious and had to be brought from England.

The houses were framed in the same manner as the half-timber houses of old England. A heavy sill was laid upon the stone foundation, close to the ground, and the floor joists were mortised into it. Few houses have basements. At the corners and near the center, posts were erected, extending the full height of the house (unless there was to be an overhang), with diagonal braces at the corners. Intermediate posts one story high were then placed to frame the openings for the doors and windows. At the second-floor level a girt was mortised into the through posts, carrying all around the house, and a chimney girt was placed on each side of the chimney. A "summer beam" was then placed, spanning either from front to back or from the side girt to the chimney girt, to give intermediate support to the second-floor joists. The second-floor walls were framed like those below, topped by a plate, into which the rafters were heeled. No nails were needed in the frame, for all joints were mortised and secured with oak pegs.

The walls were at first filled with wattles and clay, which could not have stood the weather very well for it was soon replaced by brick filling, plastered on both sides. Even this was found not to stand the extremes of temperature, since the timbers shrank and opened up cracks, so before long all houses were covered on the outside with "very good oak-hart inch board," or clapboards, and wide boards or plaster on the inside. Many of the houses had thatched roofs at first, but these were soon replaced with shingles. Floors were   PLATE 103 covered with wide boards, and partitions were boarded, either horizontally or vertically, whichever best suited the framing members to which they were nailed.

There is the seventeenth-century American house—simple, sturdy, and strictly functional. The only ornamentation is in the frequently elaborate medieval treatment of the chimney, and, on houses with an overhang, the carving of the bottom of the projecting posts into fat knobs or pendants. Some houses have contoured brackets lending apparent support to the overhang, and in later examples there is sometimes a series of corbel-like mouldings under the overhang. Inside the house, the corners of the summer beam and other exposed beams are chamfered, meaning that they are cut off diagonally, and sometimes the chamfers are moulded. The great oak lintel over the fireplace is chamfered, and sometimes carved a bit in a checkerboard pattern, simulating dentils, and the wall boarding is usually chamfered or moulded at the joints. The steep little staircase is enclosed below by vertical boards which extend above the steps, topped with a rail supported by turned or sawn balusters, which ends in a sturdy square newel with a knob on top.

The house described is typical of the Massachusetts houses; those of the rest of New England differ only in minor details. There seem to be no frame houses south of New York which can definitely be ascribed to the seventeenth century, although there are a few which may be of that time. These houses have low sweeping roofs, with small dormers set back from the face of the wall, and great spreading end chimneys.

Brick houses were relatively uncommon at first, chiefly because wood was so abundant and cheap, and because there was in some sections a lack of lime for mortar. The brickmakers and masons were kept busy building chimneys until after 1650, when brick houses began to appear, very few of which are standing today. The story still persists that many houses were built of brick brought as ballast from England and Holland, but outside of New Amsterdam, where a considerable quantity of brick was imported, there seems to be little reason to believe that this is true. Brick was made plentifully in all the colonies almost from the very beginning. Old records indicate that stone was used where it was available; there is a seventeenth-century stone house at Guilford, Connecticut, and there are a few around Philadelphia, where there is an abundance of good building stone.

The New England village of the seventeenth century must have presented a thoroughly medieval appearance, with its steep roofs, many gables and towering chimneys, houses with overhanging stories, some with their half-timber construction exposed, and all with their small leaded casement windows. It was the end of the century before there was any indication of the new architectural style which had been introduced into the mother country fully seventy-five years before by Inigo Jones. Then, gradually, the classic cornice and pilastered entranceway began to appear. Yet, farther back in the hinterland, the medieval methods continued to be used as late as 1750. Curiously enough, there is almost no trace, except in their furniture, of the elaborate and fanciful pseudo-classic Jacobean carved decorations which were the latest fashion at the time the colonists left home. They were for the most part, after all, not a fashionable people, and their houses represent their conservatism and old-fashioned tastes. It was not until some of them began to achieve prosperity and security that they felt the urge to be fashionable, and imported some of the latest ideas from London, which by that time were Georgian.

Massachusetts, Long Island, Philadelphia, and Virginia

IT IS AN UNDERSTANDABLE VANITY ON THE PART OF OWNERS OF OLD houses to claim an age for their homes which is pushed back as far as any shred of evidence will permit. Scholars have to be much more careful. Lacking dates actually carved into the structure of the house, which are rare and even then not entirely dependable, they can be guided only by specific references to the houses in old diaries, court records, deeds, and such papers. Local pride invariably disputes their findings. This scholarly, as opposed to the romantic, approach, puts a very low limit on the known examples of seventeenth-century houses standing today, probably not over twenty-five or thirty.

The Parson Capen House at Topsfield, Massachusetts, is a perfect example of the typical house described above. It was built in 1682, and has been carefully restored to what must be very close to its original condition. It is a four-room house, with an overhang at the front and at the gable ends, and a very tall and handsome chimney. The casement sash are comparatively large, but spaced widely, so the interior is rather dark, as most of them are. Small and few windows and low ceilings were important means of conserving heat. The Fairbanks House at Dedham, also in Massachusetts, is claimed to have been built in 1636, which would make it probably the oldest frame house in the country. Whether this is correct or not, it is certainly very old, and even with later additions it presents a perfect picture of the old four-room two-story house, with its two-room leanto under a great sweeping roof.

In Salem, Massachusetts, that town of many old houses, is the John Ward House, which has been restored by the Essex Institute. It was originally a two-room two-story house, and went through the full development of additions, including the leanto. When it was purchased and moved to its present site for restoration there were no

PLATE 104

PLATE 105

gables on the front, but the framing indicated that it had once had two such gables, so they were rebuilt. The most widely known gabled house is the House of Seven Gables, also in Salem, immortalized by Nathaniel Hawthorne. Its oldest portions may have been built before 1669, and it gets its many-gabled aspect from the fact that an addition was built as almost a separate house. Hemmed in by the city today, it is complete with its old fireplaces, a secret stair, and a dooryard garden. Throughout the coastal towns of New England, such as Duxbury, Plymouth, Old Lyme, and Guilford, to mention only a few, there are many old houses of the seventeenth-century type, some doubtless actually built in that time, and others built later but in the same tradition, innocent of the London fashion.

In the Flatbush section of Brooklyn, on the western end of Long Island, there stood until 1930 an old farmhouse known as the Bergen

The Bergen House, formerly in Flatbush.

House. The date of 1690 was claimed for it, despite later additions, but it also was disputed. In either case, it was a perfect illustration of the New York type of seventeenth-century house. The roof was not so steeply pitched as those of New England, and it swept low to the widely overhanging eaves above the first-floor windows. The chimneys were at each end of the house, fully enclosed within the framework, so that no brick showed until they broke through the roof. There were three small dormers across the front. A wing had a similar but lower roofline, with another overhang sheltering the door and windows. The houses at the eastern end of Long Island, however, are strictly of the New England type. At Cutchogue, almost at the tip of Orient Point, is a house only recently authenticated and restored. Local records indicate that it was originally built in 1649 in near-by Southold, and ten years later the frame was moved to Cutchogue and re-erected where it stands today. It is a four-room two-story house, with no overhangs, and the chimney and entrance are considerably off center. The north wall has some of the original triple casement sash, with fragments of the leaded glass, from which the restored windows were reconstructed. The fine pilastered chimney is completely original. The inside of the exterior walls is plastered between the framing posts, and the fireplace walls are boarded.

PLATE 106

Brick or stone houses were frequently "garrison" houses. The most prosperous family in many settlements built a particularly large and strong house, to which the entire community could retire in case of an attack by the Indians. In most cases they were never needed as a refuge, but their presence must have been comforting. Such a house is the Peter Tufts House, at Medford, Massachusetts, sometimes called the Cradock House. It is a large two-story brick house with a high gambrel roof, being one of the earliest appearances of the gambrel roof in the colonies. It was probably built about 1677, although the date of 1634 is claimed for it. There is another garrison house at Newbury, known as the Spencer-Pierce House, a great structure with granite and brick walls two feet thick. It may or may not have been started as early as 1635, and added to from time to time, but for the most part it clearly belongs to the seventeenth century. It is a long two-story house, with a chimney in the center and another at one end, and a gabled porch wing projecting from the center of the front, giving it an almost Tudor appearance.

According to old records and drawings, all seventeenth-century New England houses were not derived from English cottages. The home of Thomas Hutchinson in Boston, which was built during the 1680's and demolished in 1833, was a fine brick mansion three stories high, with stone Ionic pilasters the full height, a handsome cornice, a balustrade, and a cupola. A contemporary letter says of it, ". . . the structure and inside finishing seemed to be from a design of Inigo Jones or his successor. . . ." The Province House, also in Boston, built in 1679 and burned in 1864, was equally handsome, and furthermore had an entrance porch with columns and entablature and an iron rail above. The stair was a broad flight ascending from landing to landing, with fine turned and twisted balusters, very much like some of Jones's staircases in England.

There are few traces left today of the purely Dutch buildings of the Hudson River valley, but old pictures indicate that as recently as 1820 the streets of Albany were lined with brick houses with stepped Dutch gables and tile roofs. In villages all down the valley, in northeastern New Jersey, and Staten Island, and on western Long Island, are farmhouses which undoubtedly date from the Dutch occupation, or were built later in the Dutch colonial tradition. Most of them have stone first stories, low sweeping roofs with slender dormers, and a low wing at one side. Many have gambrel roofs, which has given rise to the supposition that this form of roof is Dutch colonial. This is not true, of course, for the form developed in both France and England as a practical method of getting more use out of the attic floor, and examples of it are to be found throughout the colonies from New Hampshire to Virginia.

Standing in Fairmount Park in Philadelphia is the William Penn House. It is the same house which was built for Penn before he came to his city in 1682, having been moved from its original downtown location. It is a brick city house, which means that it is narrow and deep. The windows are double-hung, although they may not have been originally. It shows, however, other acknowledgments of the new style in England in its heavily moulded cornice, its wood dormer set back from the face of the wall, and the handsome wood moulding surrounding its fireplace. Standing on Second Street there used to be a fine house which was known as the Slate House, because of its slate roof. The plan was H-shaped, with a hipped roof and massive chimneys. Built of brick, it had white moulded trim and cornice, and originally had mullioned and transomed windows with leaded glass. It was thus a typical transitional English Renaissance house of the style of the early seventeenth century, transplanted to the new colony. William Penn occupied it in 1700 during his second stay in his new city.

At Smith's Fort, in Virginia, stands a house which was built in 1651 by one Thomas Warren. It is of brick, with a high basement, three dormers above low eaves, and a chimney at each end. The interior has handsome woodwork, but it is of a later period. The

The seventeenth-century house in Virginia was usually of brick, with great end chimneys.

most interesting early house in Virginia is Bacon's Castle, in Surry County. It was probably completed about 1670, and is unique because it is really a Jacobean house. The original portion has two rooms on each floor, with a wide passage between which projects to form a porch at the front and a stair tower at the rear. There is a chimney at each end, from each of which three separate stacks rise in true medieval fashion. The brick gable ends are stepped and curved, and the gables over the porch and stair once had Gothic peaks. The windows were originally mullioned and transomed, giving the house the appearance of having been transplanted from late sixteenth-century England. Built originally by a certain Major Arthur Allen, it derived its name from having served as a stronghold during Bacon's Rebellion in 1676.

Of the vanished manor houses of Virginia, Fairfield must have been one of the finest. There are photographs of it showing a long two-storied center portion, with one-story hipped roof wings at each end with triple-stack chimneys like those at Bacon's Castle. One of the wings contained a ballroom, which was described as having a great marble mantel and finely carved woodwork. It was built prior to 1690, and most of it stood until about 1910. Greenspring, near Jamestown, was built by Governor Berkeley in about 1650. It was in the shape of an L, about one hundred feet long, with three large rooms

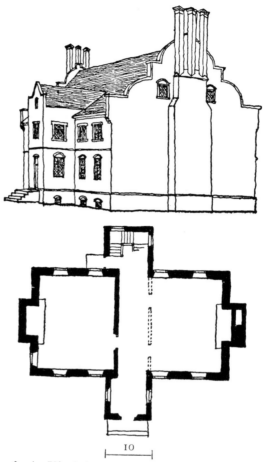

Bacon's Castle, in Virginia, was a true Jacobean house. It has been remodeled into a modern residence.

and a spacious stair hall on the long side and the kitchen in the short wing. There was a rectangular forecourt and a broad entrance gate, and it was probably the finest manor in the colony during the seventeenth century. That these houses were not bare and severe inside, like those of New England, is known from the many fragments of decorative plasterwork which have been found in and near Jamestown. They are elaborately modeled, and show distinct traces of having been polychromed in pink, blue, and green. In South Carolina, on the

Ashley River, stands one wing of Middleton Place, a house that must have equaled in size many of the manor houses of England. Its gable ends are curved and stepped in the Jacobean fashion. The main part of the house was destroyed by General Sherman during the Civil War.

There Are Three Seventeenth-Century Churches

AT SMITHFIELD, VIRGINIA, THERE IS A REMARKABLE CHURCH, FOR IT is the only true Gothic church in the United States. Not that there are not hundreds of "Gothic" churches, but they are products of the Gothic Revival. St. Luke's at Smithfield was built in 1632 in the   PLATE 107 living Gothic style which was still current in the country districts of England. Being Anglican, or Church of England, the plan consists of a rectangular nave with a square tower at the entrance end. The church is built of brick, with brick mullions in the traceried windows, and the gable ends are stepped. It was in use continuously until 1836, when it was abandoned and allowed to fall into disrepair, until its restoration about sixty years ago.

In Philadelphia there is the little church of Gloria Dei, better known as Old Swedes' Church, which was begun in 1698. It is a squat little high-roofed building, built of brick and now covered with ivy, standing alone in its churchyard. Its west tower carries up no higher than the main roof, and is crowned with a modern belfry and short spire. The woodwork, both exterior and interior, is eighteenth century. At Hingham, Massachusetts, is the oldest frame church, known as the "Old Ship." It was built in 1681, with extensions to accommodate galleries added in the middle of the eighteenth century. There were further alterations during the nineteenth century, but in 1930 the Old Ship was restored to its pre-Revolutionary state. It is unique with its foursquare hipped roof, topped by a flat deck with a rail and a cupola. The interior is that of a typical New England meetinghouse, plain and bare, but with box pews and a fine high pulpit with a sounding board above it. The roof is supported by great trusses with curved members which suggest the framing of a ship, hence its name, for it was built by ships' carpenters.

Northern Communities

TOWN LIFE DEVELOPED FROM THE VERY BEGINNING IN THE NORTHERN colonies. The houses were built about a common, which was planted with trees and used as a common grazing ground. Later it became the center of community life, lined not only with the fine houses of the more prosperous village merchants, professional men, and ship owners, but with the churches and public buildings. Each villager had his "out lot," which was his acreage of farm land and woodlot. The size of each town was limited by statute, for no house could be farther from the meetinghouse than a reasonable walking distance. Newcomers were allowed to purchase land only with the approval of the town council, and then upon the condition that they build upon it and use it. Land speculation was unheard of. When a town reached the limit of its size, a new one was started near by—like today's satellite towns.

Later, when the Indian no longer menaced and the road system was better developed, farmhouses began to be built in isolated country locations. They first appeared along the stagecoach roads from town to town, and then as land became more scarce, they were built along the back roads. Today many large and handsome houses are found, often deserted and dilapidated, standing among the crumbled ruins of farm buildings in remote and forgotten spots. The lure of town life has called their owners, and they wait for wearied city-dwellers to respond to their old-world appeal and restore them to warmth and life again, this time the life of the twentieth century.

In describing the buildings of the seventeenth century in the English colonies no distinguished architects have been mentioned, for there were none. The buildings, at least in the northern colonies, were homemade, designed and built by carpenters, masons, and crafts-men. They were completely the outgrowth of the materials at hand and the traditions of the people who produced them. Not since the twelfth and thirteenth centuries had there been such a truly in-digenous architecture. With the coming of the eighteenth century this quality was rapidly lost, for the people became style conscious, and their houses were decorated with architectural motives copied from the latest handbooks received from the mother country. Later in the century the professional architect appeared, trained in the grammar of the Renaissance. This is not to imply that style consciousness resulted in the loss of any fine qualities; on the other hand, it meant a gain in beauty, for certainly the seventeenth-century New England house cannot be called beautiful. But there is a very great appeal in its sturdy integrity, its complete honesty and forthrightness, and its mastery of its limitations.

Mexican Architecture

THE SPANIARDS BROUGHT TRUE SPANISH ARCHITECTURE WITH them, and as they rapidly settled throughout Mexico, they built cities, missions, and churches in contemporary Spanish design. In fact, the designs for buildings of any importance were prepared in Spain, and executed by monks who had been trained in the building arts, or by craftsmen sent over specially for the purpose. The first buildings, erected during the sixteenth century, thus served as a school for colonial designers and Indian craftsmen, so that from then on the Spanish colonial style showed a tendency toward a local provincialism in many districts, side by side with the imported influences from the mother country.

One of the greatest assets to the Spanish builders, besides their own rich architectural heritage and their own highly skilled traditions in the crafts, was the skill of the Indians who formed their laboring class. The Aztecs and the Incas, whom they had conquered, were races who for centuries had had a high degree of skill in sculpture and in masonry construction. So it was necessary for the Spanish to teach them only the new vocabulary of ornament that came with their new religion. The Indians, for their part, contributed in a subtle way some of the strange power of their own genius as sculptors. The result was a beautiful architectural style, or succession of styles, often eclipsing that of Spain itself.

The fortress-like early monasteries and churches built by the monks during the sixteenth century were essentially Gothic structures, even to the vaulted naves of the churches, yet in their decorative features they often employed the Plateresque. Palaces and other secular buildings built at the same time were more up to date, showing little trace of Gothic. The severe High Renaissance style decreed in Spain by Philip II and his architect Herrera, as exemplified by the Escorial, was followed almost reluctantly by the colonists and was soon abandoned for the joys of the Baroque, which suited their temperament much better. And when introduced to the Churrigueresque in the eighteenth century, the Spanish colonials and their faithful Indian converts welcomed it joyously and made it their own. The riotous outbursts of ornament, in either the Baroque or the Churrigueresque styles in the Mexican churches, are a perfect and joyous expression of what their religion meant to them, just as the stark and severe meetinghouses of the Puritans in New England are an expression of what their very different form of Christianity meant to them.

Although at first glance one of these Churrigueresque façades may possibly look like a formless and licentious mass of wriggling shapes, a second look will reveal a strict architectural framework, a rigid symmetry, and an orderly arrangement of parts. Given this logical framework then, the ornament is applied with an imaginative freedom never equaled—figures, cherubs, garlands, fruits, flowers, shells, volutes, scrolls, and urns. As in Spain, this ornament is used with a high sense of dramatic contrast. It is concentrated on the façades of the churches, sometimes on the domes, and always on the upper part of the towers, contrasting sharply with the broad plain surfaces of the walls. Inside, it is usually the *retablo,* or reredos, which receives this gorgeous treatment. Carved in wood or plaster, the effect is further heightened by heavy gilding and a lavish use of color, resulting in an almost incredible intricacy and richness.

Twelve Franciscan friars came to Mexico in 1524, and started building the church and monastery of San Francisco in Mexico City. It grew into a tremendous establishment, the center of the Catholic world in the colonies, with several churches, a school for Indians, a hospital, gardens, and a great cloister. There is little of it left today, for streets have been cut through its site, and most of the buildings have been converted to other uses. However, the fortress church built in 1529 at gay Cuernavaca, where Cortez established his winter palace, is still standing. It has a high barrel-vaulted ceiling, and an elaborate and crudely designed façade which is obviously of Indian workmanship, before the Indians had mastered the new European forms.

Not far northeast of Mexico City is the monastery of San Agustín Acolman, built during the 1540's. The façade is very plain and fortresslike, with battlements and a little triple-arched belfry. The entrance is surrounded with a handsome Plateresque treatment, and its round arch leads into a Gothic nave. The tall arches are simple groin vaults, but the vaulting of the chancel has a rich system of fanlike ribs with liernes such as had been devised in England, and was only then being introduced into Spain, for the cathedrals of Segovia and Salamanca were building at the same time. The arches of the two-story cloister adjoining are heavy and round, supported on short columns which suggest that their builders were thinking more in terms of the old familiar Romanesque forms than they were of the newer Renaissance.

Oaxaca, the most southern of the colonial cities, is in an earthquake zone, so the church of Santo Domingo, one of the largest and most beautiful churches in Mexico, is of exceedingly massive construction. Started very early in the seventeenth century, it has a relatively severe Baroque façade, with two towers which are plain until they reach their top stories, where they blossom out into a rich but rather heavy pilaster treatment surmounted by domes covered with glazed tiles. The great barrel vault of the nave is completely covered with ornament and sculpture in high relief, heavily gilded and polychromed against a white background. It is one of the finest sights in all Mexico.

About halfway between Mexico City and the Gulf of Mexico is the city of Tlaxcala, where is situated one of the most famous shrines in the land. The sanctuary built at the miraculous spring which saved the city from a smallpox plague is the Santuario de Ocotlán, a breath- PLATE 108
taking example of the beauty of the Churrigueresque at its very best. The façade is of gleaming white carved plaster in a typical riot of forms, terminating at the top against a great shell motive which is like a sunburst. The lower portions of the two curiously narrow towers are covered with vermilion tiles in a snakeskin pattern, and their upper stories are in fantastic carved plaster like the façade. It is a startling, shimmering unbelievable sight.

Spanish Missions

IN FLORIDA, LOUISIANA, TEXAS, NEW MEXICO, ARIZONA, AND CALI-
fornia there are many buildings standing today which evidence the
long period of Spanish occupation. Some are in ruins, some have been
restored and are maintained as museums or tourist attractions, and
others are still in actual use. St. Augustine has many old houses, one
of which claims to be the oldest house in the United States, and the
castle of San Marco, now Fort Marion, is without doubt the oldest
fortification in the country, having been started in 1638. The square of
the city is still dominated by the eighteenth-century Spanish cathedral,
with its crude Baroque entrance and its open belfry. There are several
Spanish missions in Texas, of which the most famous is the Alamo in
San Antonio, better known for its historic associations with Davy
Crockett and his frontiersmen than for its heavy Baroque portal. Also
in San Antonio is the ruined San José de Aguayo, built in 1720, which
has a very rich Churrigueresque entrance and fine Baroque details.
In Tucson, Arizona, the old church of San Xavier del Bac shows an
attempt at true Mexican magnificence, with its Churrigueresque portal contrasting with the broad and more severe Baroque towers, which
have been restored.

It was the middle of the eighteenth century before the Spanish
began to push up into *Alta California,* which is now the state of
California. They were alarmed at reports that the Russians were
colonizing Alaska and pushing down the Pacific coast. That meant
not only the advance of a rival nation, but of a rival church. Thus a
series of missions were built ranging up the coast, outposts of Spanish
imperialism and of the Church of Rome. It was the aim of Fra Juní-
pero Serra, who was sent from Spain to organize and build the missions, to establish them one day's march apart.

The mission was a unit of three parts, the presidio, the mission,
and the pueblo. The presidio was the residence of the commandante
and the soldiers, and consisted of a courtyard surrounded by offices, a
dormitory, guard rooms, and armory. The mission was the largest
unit, containing not only the church and the sacristy, with dormitory,
refectory, and cloister for the monks, but also a hospital, guest rooms,

schoolrooms, storerooms, and shops for blacksmithing, carpentry, weaving, tailoring, and many other crafts and trades. Connected with them were corrals and farm buildings, and adjoining were the vast ranges for the herds of cattle and sheep. The pueblo was the living quarters for the converted Indians, who in return for their keep and instruction in the ways of civilization and Christianity, lived a regimented life and performed all the manual labor of the mission.

Architecturally, the missions were in the Spanish tradition of Mexico, but the farther away from the center they were, the simpler and cruder was their style. Those in Texas show that they were built by the same skilled hands that built the churches of Mexico, but those in California are very much more simple, crudely attempting to use the same decorative forms, but omitting the elaborate carving, which was beyond the abilities of the local Indians. In southern California there are San Gabriel Arcángel, near Los Angeles, built in 1771; San Juan Capistrano, halfway between San Diego and Santa Barbara, founded November 1776, four months after the signing of the Declaration of Independence in Philadelphia, three thousand miles away; Santa Bárbara, founded in 1785; and San Francisco de Asís, in San Francisco, of which only the church, started in 1782, remains today.

The mission of Santa Bárbara is one of the most complete and interesting. The church and its adjoining buildings still stand, having been rebuilt several times after damage by earthquake, the last one in 1925. The church is 40 feet wide and 175 feet long, with two solid stone towers flanking the façade. The façade itself is an interesting example of an attempt at classic architecture. The good Padre had in his library a copy of a Spanish translation of Vitruvius—it is still in the mission library—and he chose from it an Ionic portico which he endeavored to copy, with his heavy-handed Indian labor. Considering his handicaps and his remoteness from the centers of learning, he did a creditable job.

The most important cities during the Spanish and Mexican regimes in California were San Diego, the port and principal commercial center; Santa Barbara, because of its beautiful setting the favorite home of the great families; and Monterey, the capital. In all three cities there are houses still standing which were built by the Spanish and the Mexicans early in the nineteenth century.

The typical house is exceedingly simple, built of adobe and whitewashed, with a low-pitched roof covered with tiles. There is an almost complete absence of decoration, the sense of comfort and richness being achieved entirely by the furnishings. The houses are U-shaped, consisting of a series of rooms on three sides of a patio, with a covered but open passage running around it to give access to the rooms. The roof of the passage is lower than the roof of the house, and is supported on wood posts, which may have a little carving at the top. The patio invariably has a fountain and a richly planted garden. The few windows which open on the exterior walls are covered with grilles of wood or iron. Most of the houses have only one story, but when there is a second floor it is usually reached by an outside stair from the patio. Some of the two-story houses have a wood porch or balcony at the second-floor level, projecting on the street front, with the roof of the house extending out over it. Many of the Yankee traders who dealt at the port of San Diego brought their families and settled in this land of sunshine, which may account for the faint suggestion of Georgian architecture that is apparent in the doorways and the window treatments of some of the houses.

Here, as in New England, there arose an indigenous architecture, resulting in buildings which are simple, straightforward, and functional, built out of the materials at hand and given form by the traditions of the people that built them.

The Vieux Carré

ARCHITECTURALLY, TRACES OF FRENCH COLONIZATION ARE relatively few, and their influence has been negligible. Yet they are of such charm as to arouse great interest in those who see them. At Quebec and Montreal there are French manor houses with low hipped roofs and corner towers with conical roofs, and stone town houses with steeply pitched roofs and high gables, widely overhanging eaves, and many dormers. They are bits of Normandy and Brittany transplanted to the interior of a strange continent. It is in New Orleans, however, that one can still capture the atmosphere of France—or is it Spain? Founded by the French in 1718, New Orleans passed to Spain in 1762, so it was French for about forty years, and Spanish for another forty years, before it became an American possession. What is left of the old portion of the city, the Vieux Carré, is thoroughly Latin. On the old Place des Armes, now Jackson Square, stands the Cabildo, the Spanish supreme court building, begun in 1795 in a heavy neoclassic style. The Ursuline Convent was built in 1734, and consequently is thoroughly French. Actually, the majority of the quaint little houses in the Vieux Carré were built in the early part of the nineteenth century, when the Greek Revival was well established, and they reveal it in their detail even when their general aspect is French. These houses have casement windows with shutters in the French manner, lacy wood or iron balconies at the second-floor level, chaste classical cornices, and steep roofs with dormers. The ground-floor front is a shop or business office, with the living quarters on the second floor overlooking the court at the rear, which is a luxuriant garden of royal palms, magnolias, and oleanders. There is a nostalgic old-world charm about these houses which surely cannot hold out much longer against the rising tide of twentieth-century commercialism and "progress."

✻ XII ✻

Eighteenth-Century America

B Y THE BEGINNING of the eighteenth century the pioneering days were over in the established centers along the Atlantic seaboard. The ports of Boston, Newport, New York, Philadelphia, and Charleston were prospering on their export and import trade, and had become centers of social and intellectual activity as well as of business. Between these cities, and some of them inland, many other towns, such as Salem, New Haven, Albany, Trenton, Germantown, Annapolis, and Richmond were increasing in economic and political importance despite the small number of their inhabitants. All the colonies were in close touch with England and with each other, for although land communication was poor, the sea lanes carried heavy traffic. As the merchants of the North and the landowners of the South increased in wealth, it was natural that they should express their affluence and establish their position by the building of fine homes designed in the latest fashion. So the first three-quarters of the eighteenth century was a period of architectural pretension and sophistication, of attempted scholarship and academicism in design.

The gospel of the new style was brought to the colonies by three means. In the newer colonies, such as Pennsylvania and Georgia, it was brought by the new arrivals, who had seen the rebuilding of London after the Great Fire. In all the colonies the busy merchants made frequent trips to London and were fully aware of what was going on, and, furthermore, the royal governors and their officers were usually men of taste, so their first thought was to create for themselves something of the background to which they were accustomed. The third means by which the new style was introduced was books. John Shute's book and the seventeenth-century translations of the Italian writers on architecture were too scholarly for the practical builders, so they were almost unknown here. The books of Kent, Ware, and Gibbs, and Campbell's *Vitruvius Britannicus,* illustrating designs for mansions, were of some help to the few builders who had the opportunity to build on a fairly large scale. But it was the less ambitious publications of lesser men that really gave the colonial builders what they needed.

There were many of these "builder's assistants," by Robert Morris, Abraham Swan, William Halfpenny, and Batty Langley, to name only a few. These men kept their public informed on all the latest changes in fashion, with books illustrated with engravings of treatments for doorways, windows, chimneypieces, ceilings, and cornices, together with plans and façades. These books were the chief sources of American colonial architecture. To the credit of the men who used them, it must be said that the majority showed a high degree of taste and a fine sense of proportion and scale in assembling these parts into a whole.

Drawings, where they existed at all, were simple and crude, usually prepared by a cultivated owner or an accomplished mechanic. But their use was urged by the handbooks. Joseph Moxon's *Mechanick Exercises* says, " 'Tis usual, and also very convenient, for any person before he begins to erect a Building, to have Designs or Draughts made upon Paper or Vellum. . . . The drawing of Draughts is most commonly the work of a Surveyor, although there may be Master Workmen that will contrive a building, and draw the Designs thereof, as well and as curiously, as most Surveyors: Yea, some of them will do it better than some Surveyors; especially those Workmen who understand the Theorick part of Building, as well as the Practick."

There were very few trained architects in the colonies before the Revolution. The buildings were designed, for the most part, by scholarly and talented builders such as Richard Munday and Benjamin Wyatt of Newport, who designed several buildings there; John

Ariss of Virginia, who designed and built perhaps as many as a dozen Virginia mansions, including additions to Mount Vernon; and Ezra Waite, who published an advertisement in the *South Carolina Gazette* in 1769 announcing himself as "Civil Architect, Housebuilder in general, and Carver, from London." On the other hand, John McBean, who designed St. Paul's Chapel in New York City, was said to have worked under Gibbs in London; and Peter Harrison of Newport, who designed many important buildings there and in Boston and Cambridge, was reputed to have worked as an assistant to Vanbrugh on the building of Blenheim Palace.

There were also, as in England, amateur designers whose work has such distinction that they surely warrant the title of "architect-by-courtesy." Among such accomplished amateurs were the portrait painter, John Singleton Copley, who designed his own house in Boston; John Smibert, also a painter, who designed the original portion of Faneuil Hall; Andrew Hamilton, a lawyer, who designed Independence Hall; Dr. John Kearsley, designer of Christ Church, Philadelphia; and Joseph Brown, "merchant, atronomer, philosopher," who designed the First Baptist Church in Providence.

Pre-Revolutionary Eighteenth-Century Houses

WITH THE GENERAL IMPROVEMENT OF LIVING STANDARDS, IT WAS required that the new houses of the eighteenth century have more rooms than the earlier ones, and rooms for special purposes. No longer were the parlor and the bedroom combined. Circulation was improved by the introduction of corridors and secondary staircases, and servants' quarters were separated from those of the master. Plans were chiefly variations of the block plan, as developed by Inigo Jones a hundred years before. These plans placed a principal room in each of the four corners, with the chimneys either between the front and back rooms or on the end walls. The variations arose in the hall, which sometimes extended through the house and sometimes did not, and in the location of the stair, which was sometimes in the center hall and sometimes in a side or rear hall. In the South, with its more aristocratic tradition, the H plan is found in some early houses, and later the block plan tied to flanking buildings by means of walls or loggias, producing a modest version of the spreading plan of some of the great English houses.

Most houses were two stories high, although frequently three in the cities. The hipped roof was very popular, because it permitted a continuous classical cornice. Gabled roofs were usually gambrel, or else they were low-pitched and treated with pediments at the ends. Hipped roofs, which often had a flat deck at the top, were sometimes crowned with a balustrade and a cupola, and on most roofs dormers began to take an important place in the design. The typical dormer was light and slender, with a pediment sometimes supported by delicate pilasters. The functional elements of the façades of the houses, such as the doors and windows, were treated with the standard classical motives, and the wall surfaces were treated with pilasters, quoins, or rustications. As the style developed, an effort was made to gain greater formality by the use of projecting bays. In a block-type house a bay could project but a few inches, but the effect was heightened by the grouping of the pilasters. The Palladian touch is often seen in the use of the colossal order, the pilaster extending the full height of the wall. Rarely, however, did the full entablature of the pilasters extend across the house to form the cornice of the building, for it would cut down the heads of the second-story windows too much. Quoins and rustications, which were strictly of masonry origin, became common in wood; in fact, some houses have an entire wall grooved to imitate rustications, as at Mount Vernon.

In the northern colonies wood was always the favorite material, although brick was used for important houses, and stone in a few localities. Pennsylvania was the only section where stone was used a great deal, and even there the city of Philadelphia was a city of brick houses. Early stone houses in Pennsylvania were built of rubble, often stuccoed to make them more weathertight; later houses were built of ashlar. Few houses of any size in the South were built of frame, brick being used almost exclusively. Stonecarvers were scarce, so there was little stonecarving other than simple mouldings. Carved or rubbed brick was often used for base courses, chimney tops, and sometimes for cornices and doorway treatments.

The entrance doorways of the first quarter of the century were surrounded only by a moulded trim, but after 1725 they came to have a full entablature supported by pilasters or consoles. After the middle of the century engaged and free-standing columns were used, thus leading to the entrance porch. Also during the middle period appeared the Georgian curved, broken, and scrolled pediments, which are so much admired today. The actual door opening was square-headed until the middle of the century, after which it often had a semicircular fanlight above the door. The hall was also lighted by glass in the upper part of the door, or in a rectangular transom above it. There is only one pre-Revolutionary example of either an elliptical fanlight or of sidelights.

Windows were always double-hung, and always divided into small panes with wood muntins, and the panes tended to increase in size through the century. Ordinary windows were only occasionally treated with an entablature or a pediment, but frequently a featured window, such as one over the entrance or on a stair landing, was arched or treated with a Palladian motive. About half the houses had shutters on the windows, and they were almost invariably the fixed slat type, except in the Delaware-Pennsylvania neighborhood, where they were paneled.

After 1700, paneling took the place of boarding on the interior walls. It followed the Wren pattern, having a paneled wainscot or dado, a paneled wall above, and a cornice. Early panels were small, but grew larger as the century progressed. Pilasters were frequently used to frame a mantel or a door, sometimes standing on the dado and sometimes on the floor. Earlier fireplaces were surrounded only by a handsome moulding, sometimes with a simple frieze and a moulded shelf, but more often without. It was not until after 1750 that elaborate overmantels came into use, usually copied right out of a handbook. Wallpapers were used a great deal, in which case the paneling above the dado was omitted. The stairs of the seventeenth century had been the "closed string" type, that is, the ends of the steps were enclosed. But during the eighteenth century they were "open string," with the ends of the steps exposed and frequently treated with projecting blocks or modillion-like scrolls. Balusters became slender and closely spaced, and elaborately turned or twisted. Although the early handrail descended directly to a handsomely carved newel, later rails engaged in a spiral before coming to rest. There was always a paneled wainscot on the wall side of the stair, sloping upward at the same height as the rail. Only in the South were elaborately modeled plaster ceilings in general usage, taken directly out of the handbooks of London and French rococo designs.

The exposed timbers and the pine board wainscoting of the seventeenth-century houses were not painted, and when paneling came into use in the early part of the eighteenth century it was not painted either. Around 1725, painting began to come into fashion, but it was seldom white. The conception of a typical Colonial room as having gleaming white woodwork comes principally from the repainting that was done early in the nineteenth century. The colors were a wide variety of dull shades, such as pearl, cream, buff, gray-green, blue-gray, blue, and a deep Indian red. Occasionally contrasting colors were used, such as brown panels trimmed with white, and, more rarely, the base and mouldings were marbleized. In some particularly fine rooms there were panels painted with classical landscapes and formal decorations, such as garlands, urns, and floral ornaments.

Sanitary arrangements in the houses of the colonies were naturally no better than those in contemporary England. It was early in the nineteenth century before water closets appeared, and later before there were any full-fledged bathrooms, and then only in fine houses. Throughout the eighteenth century, in the larger houses with servants, there were commode chairs in the bedrooms or dressing rooms of the older and more important members of the household. They were emptied by the servants, which was one of the principal reasons for the introduction of service stairs. The remaining members of the household used outhouses, which were usually laid out to accommodate several people, and often they were substantially built of brick and designed to harmonize with the garden houses and other accessory buildings. There was no running water in any city before 1800; city houses got their water from public pumps, and country houses had their own wells and rainwater cisterns. Lighting was still dependent upon candles and whale-oil lamps, but heating had been greatly improved by Benjamin Franklin's invention of the cast-iron stove, which, by placing the fire out in the middle of the room instead of recessed in the wall, was an immense step forward in efficiency for both heating and cooking.

These, then, were the characteristics of the eighteenth-century Colonial style. The term "Colonial" has been used to apply only to buildings built before the Revolution, not only because after the war the country ceased to be a colony, but because during the pre-Revolutionary eighteenth century the architecture was truly colonial in that it reflected completely the current work in the mother country. The majority of the houses in England, except the great mansions, were built by builders who used the same handbooks that were used in America. The Revolutionary War brought no immediate and obvious changes in architectural style, for many houses and churches were built in the after-war years in much the same manner that had been employed a short generation before. Such buildings are called Post-Colonial. However, a new spirit gradually began to manifest itself in architectural design after the formation of the new republic, based primarily upon the innovations of Thomas Jefferson. So as the Post-Colonial tapered off toward the close of the century, the new Early Republican style gradually took hold, until it, too, was superseded in a few years by the Greek Revival, which started as another fashion and came near to developing into an *American* style.

New England, New York, and Philadelphia

PLATE 109 THE OLDEST BRICK HOUSE IN PORTSMOUTH, NEW HAMPSHIRE, IS the McPhedris House, which was completed in 1723. It is a fine solid building with two chimneys at each end connected by a parapet, and a railing and cupola on its gambrel roof. The dormers have alternate triangular and curved pediments, and the curved pediment on the handsome doorway shows a Baroque touch in the manner in which the cornice breaks out over the pilasters below. Another house of considerable elegance is the Royall House at Medford, Massachusetts, which was originally a typical four-room two-story seventeenth-century house built about 1680. It went through several alterations

and ended up in 1740 as a handsome three-story house with brick
end walls and frame front and rear walls. The clapboarded east
front has wood corner quoins and a fine cornice. The windows have
heavily moulded trims, and an added touch of classical formality is
given by the panels between the heads of the first- and second-story
windows and the sills of the windows above.

One of the best-known houses in America is the home of Henry
Wadsworth Longfellow in Cambridge, which was built by a Colonel   PLATE 110
Henry Vassal in 1759. A frame house, it has full-height Ionic pilasters
at the corners and framing the center bay, which projects only
slightly forward and is topped with a pediment. The open porches
on each side are old, but probably not a part of the original design. Such porches were just coming into use, and were considered,
as the painter Copley put it, "very beautiful and convenient." The
Jeremiah Lee House at Marblehead, built in 1768, is an example of
a frame house with its wall surfaces completely covered with
wooden rustications, with wood quoins and even wooden flat arches
over the windows. However, with its hipped roof and pediment over
the central bay, it has as much dignity as any house of its size in England.

Boston's two oldest churches are Old North, 1723, and Old
South, 1729. Built of brick, their wood steeples and paneled interiors
brought the Wren style to America and set the type for the New
England church. Old South was a meetinghouse, used for noisy
political gatherings as well as for Sunday worship, and it is the steeple
of Old North that appears in the story of Paul Revere's ride. The first
Church of England church building was a little frame church built   PLATE 111
in 1688, which was replaced in 1749 by the present stone King's
Chapel, designed by Peter Harrison. Its fortress-like exterior would
look quite different if its steeple had been built as originally planned,
but the interior has all the richness and dignity of a Wren London
church. The First Baptist Meetinghouse in Providence, Rhode Island, is the oldest Baptist church in America, having been founded
by Roger Williams in 1638. The present building was designed by
Joseph Brown and built in 1775, with a very handsome spire which
was obviously taken from Gibbs's *Book of Architecture*. The interior has an elliptical ceiling and, like most meetinghouses, a gallery
at the rear and sides. Throughout New England stand hundreds of

PLATE 112

PLATE 113

town and village churches, the work of unknown designer-builders, a few of them elaborate, most of them simple, but all of them endowed with a dignity and functional forthrightness which gives them a unique place in the history of architecture.

The oldest public building in New England is the Old State House in Boston, built in 1728. Its cupola is graceful, and the sturdy Baroque of its end façade is one of the finest things in the colonies. The stepped gable still has the carved lion and unicorn, symbols of the Crown, and beneath them is a fine doorway with a curved pediment, which opens onto a balcony from which the governor could address the people. Faneuil Hall, the "Cradle of Liberty," given to the city by the prosperous Peter Faneuil, was based upon the form of the old English market, with an arcaded open market place on the ground floor and a public meeting hall above. It was designed by John Smibert, artist, in 1741, and enlarged after the Revolution by Charles Bulfinch, one of the foremost architects of the Early Republic.

There are several pre-Revolutionary houses left in the Hudson River valley. At Albany there is the Schuyler Mansion, built in 1761, a fine and severely formal house different from the New England houses only in that it is seven windows wide instead of the usual five. The Philipse Manor House at Yonkers, built about 1750, is a long and unsymmetrical brick house with a hipped roof and a balustrade at the top. It has some very fine and rather elaborate interiors, including ornamental plaster ceilings in the French rococo style. Overlooking the Harlem River, in New York City, stands the Roger Morris House, also known as the Jumel Mansion, built in 1765, and now used as the summer residence of the mayor of New York City. It has one unique feature, a two-story portico with a pediment, the only one known on a pre-Revolutionary house. The entrance door treatment with its elliptical arch and sidelights was added later.

St. Paul's Chapel, on lower Broadway in New York City, is one of the two finest English Renaissance churches in the United States. It was designed by John McBean and built in 1760. At the Broadway end is a tall Ionic portico, and at the west end is as fine a spire as any in London. The interior has a high vaulted plaster ceiling supported on slender Corinthian columns with full entablatures above them, giving a very light and spacious effect. At the corner of Broad and Pearl Streets, in lower Manhattan, stands Fraunces' Tavern, where General Washington bade a touching farewell to his officers in 1783. Although largely a restoration today, it is still a restaurant and looks much as it did during the Revolution, a sturdy brick building with a handsome cornice, hipped roof with balustrade, and Dutch dormer windows.

Germantown used to be a town near Philadelphia, but it has long been engulfed by that great city. In it are many old stone and brick houses of great architectural interest. Stenton was built in 1728 by James Logan, a brick block-type house, its severe façade relieved only by the curve of the segmental arches over the first-story windows. The roof is hipped, with dormers and two heavy chimneys.

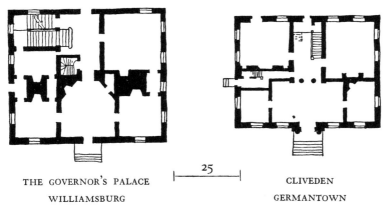

THE GOVERNOR'S PALACE   CLIVEDEN
WILLIAMSBURG   GERMANTOWN

Examples of the center hall mansion: the Governor's Palace at Williamsburg (left) and Cliveden in Germantown (right).

The doorway is wide, with a transom, and is flanked by two narrow windows, probably the forerunner of the door with sidelights. Contrasting with it is Cliveden, built by Chief Justice Benjamin Chew in 1763, a stone house of about the same size but of much greater pretension. It has a gabled roof, with full pediment treatments at the ends. A narrow center bay breaks slightly forward, providing a pediment in the front center, and the doorway is framed by a correct Roman Doric order of engaged columns with pediment. The dormers have round-headed windows under their pediments,

PLATE 114

and as a supreme effort to capture some of the grandeur of the great English houses, there are large stone urns at each corner of the roof and at each end of the ridge. It is a handsome piece of design, over-done only in the use of the urns, and is an interesting contrast to the far greater severity of the earlier house.

The second of the two finest English Renaissance churches in America is Christ Church in downtown Philadelphia, designed by that accomplished amateur, Dr. John Kearsley. It is another Wren-like church, executed largely in brick, even to the mouldings. The tower, which is at the west end, is broad-based and bold in character, not slender and tapering like that of St. Paul's Chapel. The east or chancel end has a great Palladian window, and the height of the nave is expressed above it by a high attic and pediment, while the two-story walls at the sides express the side aisles with the gallery above. The interior has slender Roman Doric columns supporting elliptical arches, the columns standing free of the face of the gallery. The use of the Doric order lends a simplicity to the interior which is often lacking in the more ambitious Renaissance churches.

Philadelphia's other great colonial building, and the finest colonial public building in the country, is the State House, or Inde-

PLATE 115   pendence Hall. It was designed by Andrew Hamilton, a lawyer, and its construction was begun in 1733. The flanking buildings were not built until after the Revolution, but they were part of Hamilton's original scheme. These buildings and the square before them formed one of the first civic groups in America. The main building has great elegance and dignity, with its heavy white wood trim contrasting with the warm red of the brickwork. Instead of a cupola, usual for public buildings, Hamilton had the originality to design a great tower, attached to the building on the south side, creating a space for the monumental staircase and leaving the interior of the building free for fine rooms. The tower, from the Palladian window on the stair landing to the gilded spire, is as virile and vital a piece of de-sign as exists anywhere in the world. The interior is in the same vigorous spirit as the exterior. Richly pilastered and paneled, the use of the Roman Doric order prevents it from becoming ornate. The de-tail is heavy, as befits a public building, yet there is delicate ornament in the Baroque manner where it counts the most. There could not possibly have been a more handsome or fitting background for the great events which took place there.

Contrasting with these buildings, with their splendid, but borrowed, architectural trimmings, are the simple buildings of the "Pennsylvania Dutch," the Germans who settled in Lancaster and Chester Counties of eastern Pennsylvania and up the Delaware River as far as Bethlehem, which they founded. Plain, hard-working, religious people, there is an admirable asceticism in their buildings, as there was in their lives. Built of local stone, they have no ornamentation except the white wood trim, the neat porches, and the little pent roofs which often extend across the front of the house above the windows of the first floor. Here again is a simple and functional indigenous architecture.

Williamsburg, Westover, and Mount Vernon

THE RESTORATION OF COLONIAL WILLIAMSBURG, VIRGINIA, AFfords a unique opportunity to see early eighteenth-century Virginia architecture at its best. Not only a few old buildings, but an entire portion of the city, about a mile long by one-third of a mile wide, has been restored to its condition before 1810. Thus the city plan stands today as it did during the first quarter of the eighteenth century, with Duke of Gloucester Street—nearly a mile long and one hundred feet wide, with the College of William and Mary at the west end and the Capitol at the east end—intersected by the broad Palace Green which extends to the Governor's Palace on the north. Along this street are many old houses and taverns, as well as Bruton Parish Church, carefully rebuilt or restored, completely capturing the atmosphere, as well as the aspect, of the old city.

The three principal buildings are the Governor's Palace, the Capitol, and the College of William and Mary. The College is the oldest, having been started in 1695 from plans alleged to have been prepared in London by Sir Christopher Wren, "adapted to the Nature of the Country by the *Gentlemen* there." It has been through three fires, but retains its original walls, and has been carefully restored with the aid of old engravings, documents, and fragments.

The building is U-shaped, the two wings extending to the rear containing the chapel and the Great Hall. The entrance front is long and high, with tall narrow windows and a steep hipped roof with dormers and a cupola. There is a pediment over a slightly projecting center bay, and above the simple arched doorway is a light wood balcony.

The Capitol was built in 1705, and there is good reason to believe that it too was from Wren's designs. It was twice destroyed by fire, and today's building is entirely a conjectural restoration, built in 1931 upon the old foundations. Here, again, there was documentary and fragmentary evidence as to general appearance and some details, but the largest contribution came from the painstaking scholarship of the architects for the restoration, who quite literally steeped themselves in the traditional architecture of tidewater Virginia. If the handsome paneled interiors of this H-shaped building were not precisely as they are today, they could not have been far different.

PLATE 116   The masterpiece of the group is the Governor's Palace, originally built in 1713, burned to the foundations in 1781, and rebuilt in the same painstaking manner as was the Capitol. It has a block plan, with a one-story ballroom wing extending to the rear, the original of which was added in 1750. The very steep hipped roof is topped by a balustrade and a tall cupola, giving the building a curious verticality; the narrow dormers have hipped roofs, the wood cornice is simple, and the walls are plain. Two low buildings flank it at the front, forming a forecourt which is entered through a fine wrought-iron gate in true English style. The interiors, the furnishings, and the very beautiful gardens of this building have made it a shrine of early Americana.

The wealth of the great landowners of the South made possible the building of mansions which strove in many cases to equal those of England. One of the earliest of these houses is Tuckahoe, in Goochland County, early enough, in fact, to have the Jacobean H plan. The front portion, of four rooms and two floors with a stair hall between, built in 1712, has brick end walls and frame walls at the front and back. The rest of the H was completed in 1730 entirely in frame, the rear wing being a duplication of the front, with a Great Hall on each floor of the connecting wing, resulting in a

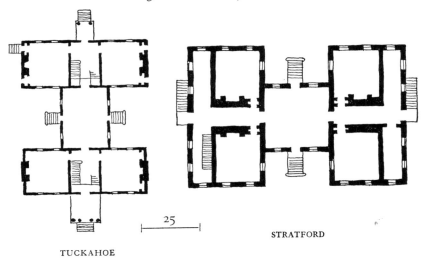

25

STRATFORD

TUCKAHOE

Tuckahoe and Stratford, both in Virginia, are H-plan mansions.

very curious plan. The interiors are finely paneled, some of them clearly copied from one of the most popular handbooks. Another H-plan house is Stratford, the birthplace of Robert E. Lee, built in 1725 in a manner suggesting the work of Vanbrugh. It is of brick, one story high, but placed upon a very high basement. From each wing of the H, four chimneys rise from the low hipped roofs, connected by arches so as to form one tremendous chimney. Set off from the corners of the house are four subsidiary buildings, the library and the kitchen, and the school and the office, thus making a very handsome group.   PLATE 117

One of the finest houses in America, old or modern, is Westover, in Charles City County, built in 1730 by William Byrd on the banks of the James River, and practically unchanged today. It has a block plan, but seven windows wide instead of the usual five, with a low service wing on either side. The hall runs through the house off center, so that the two rooms on one side are larger than those on the other. Plain brick walls are relieved only by a white stonecourse at the second-floor level, and the white wood cornice. The hipped roof rises steeply, and two chimneys at each end tower above it. There are two exceedingly handsome entrance treatments, one   PLATE 118

on each front, of Portland stone brought from England. Both are to
be found in the handbook *Palladio Londinensis,* by William Salmon.

PLATE 119 Mount Vernon, as it appears today, was built over a period of
nearly a hundred years. The original portion was only a story and
a half high, and included the central five windows. It was probably built some time before 1700. In 1758 George Washington increased it to a full two stories high and installed new woodwork
inside and out. The designs seem to have been made by John Ariss,
and the work was supervised by Washington's neighbor and friend,
Lord George William Fairfax. In 1760 Washington apparently
built the two service buildings which flank the entrance front, and
in 1776 he lengthened the house from five windows to nine. The
portico on the side facing the river was added in 1784, and the
cupola in 1787. The house is entirely of frame construction, but the
wood sheathing of the walls is grooved to imitate rustications, its
surface painted and sanded in order to look like stone. The interiors are handsome, although not so elaborate as those of many
Virginia mansions. Only three rooms are paneled, the others having plastered walls, some with paneled wainscots and some with
plaster dadoes with wood chair rails. All the principal rooms have
plaster cornices and mantels with overmantels. The banquet hall,
finished after the Revolution, is one of the handsomest rooms of
its kind. It is 31 feet long, 23 feet wide, and 16 feet high. The walls
are plain plaster, with a wood chair rail and plaster cornice, which
is dropped about two feet below the ceiling to permit a large cove
above it. The cornice, cove, and ceiling are decorated with modeled
plaster in the Adam style, weaving a few agricultural motives, such
as sickles, spades, corn husks, and sheaves of wheat, in with the
classical forms. The principal features of the room are the large
Palladian window on one side and the projecting chimney breast
on the other, with its exquisite marble mantel which was sent as a
gift to Washington from London.

The town houses of the South embody the same plan and general characteristics as the country houses, although frequently of
necessity more compactly. The Brice House and the Paca-Carvel
House in Annapolis are high block-type houses with steep gabled
roofs and low end wings. At Charleston the outstanding feature of
the houses is the use of the double portico, or two-story porch, ele-

gantly and delicately detailed in strict classical fashion. The interiors
and the staircases of the Charleston houses are particularly fine, for   PLATE 120
it was a city of wealth and fashion. It is still a lure to lovers of good
architecture and old houses, with its dignified mansions standing in
their lovely walled gardens.

St. Michael's Church in Charleston, built in 1742, is a handsome
but heavy design copied after the style of James Gibbs. The tower is
massive even though tall, and rises from behind a Doric portico.
Near by is St. Philip's, built a few years later, burned in 1835, and
rebuilt in the original design except that the tower was finished off
with a steeple, whereas it originally had a squat tower with a dome.
The church's unique feature is that it has three porticoes, since it juts
out at a street intersection. The gem of all Southern churches, however, is Christ Church in Lancaster County, built in 1732 by Robert
"King" Carter, one of the richest men in the colony, who also built at
least six mansions for himself and his sons. Probably owing to its remote location, the little church stands today just as it stood two hundred years ago, complete with its high box pews, paneled gallery, and
elevated pulpit with a winding stair and domed sounding board
above. The building is cruciform in plan, with a high hipped roof
which sweeps out in a curve at the eaves. The exterior is severe, with
high brick walls, tall arched windows, and two fine Palladian entrances in moulded brick. There is no tower. It survives as a perfect
example of English Renaissance architecture.

The Post-Colonial

AFTER THE REVOLUTIONARY WAR WAS OVER THERE WAS LITTLE AN-
tagonism toward England. To many men the war had been a fight
of Englishmen against their king for an Englishman's rights, as
guaranteed by Magna Charta. The merchants and shipowners of
New England and the northern coastal cities resumed their trade with
the former mother country, for she was still their best customer. In
these centers English fashion was still followed. It was more in the
South and the inland cities that a strong republican feeling gradually
germinated among the intellectual leaders, and coupled with it was a
turning to France rather than to Britain as a cultural ally. But the
ordinary builders continued to design and build much as they had

before the war, until they were gradually influenced by the ideas and forms originated by their leaders.

The style of the brothers Adam was the fashion which chiefly influenced Post-Colonial architecture, and there were plenty of handbooks to popularize it. In planning this brought a freer approach, better circulation, better orientation, and more privacy. It also brought a use of rooms of contrasting shapes, circular and elliptical rooms, niches and recesses. In exterior decoration it brought a more delicate and refined classicism, a use of shallow recessed arches and panels, stringcourses in the form of flat bands instead of mouldings, and tripled and Palladian windows. The exposed part of the window frames became very narrow and the muntins very slender, and in brick houses there were simple stone lintels over the windows, or flat arches with a projecting keystone. Pediments disappeared from over doorways, and in their stead appeared arched transoms with fanlights, either semicircular or elliptical, with sidelights below, both with designs in leaded glass. After 1790 nearly every house had an entrance porch of some type, usually simply an extension from the wall of the order which framed the doorway, sometimes rectangular and sometimes semicircular in plan. These later led to the use of tall porticoes. Side porches, or piazzas, became common after having been introduced from New York's farmhouses into the more elegant New England style by John Singleton Copley. The railings on the roof of the porches were often filled with "Chinese lattice" instead of the traditional turned balusters. Brick walls came increasingly to be stuccoed or painted, and frame walls were often covered with smooth boards, with the joints concealed as much as possible.

The interior woodwork took on a more refined and delicate character. Paneled walls disappeared, leaving only a plain dado with a chair rail, or nothing but a base at the floor. Ceiling-height pilasters also disappeared, although free-standing columns were frequently used. Curved and spiral staircases, unsupported on the side away from the wall, came into wide use, and some were even completely free of the wall, supported only at the top and the bottom. Turned balusters vanished, becoming plain square or tapered round. Adam friezes, cornices, and "sunbursts" on the ceilings were used until about 1810, when they began to disappear. Principal doorways were framed with handsome trims or pilasters, with friezes and cornices above, and sometimes they were arched. Mantels became even more than before the focal point of the room, but overmantels were rare. Their pilasters and center panels were decorated with carved or composition ornaments, and after 1800 the pilasters were often replaced by slender colonnettes. There were not enough skilled woodcarvers to produce all the fine ornament that was needed, so the use of composition plaster ornaments became widespread, made from moulds often prepared in England. Thus it is not uncommon to find the same ornamental panels in a New England town house and a Virginia mansion. The ornaments were derived from Adam and Louis XVI sources, classical motives, mythological figures, urns, medallions, and garlands. The War of 1812 cut off the supply of such ornaments from England, as well as the desire to use them, and new motives were devised from the American eagle and portrait medallions of American heroes. The flutings and reedings of the Adam style were also used in panels instead of reliefs, ingeniously suggesting festoons and rosettes in the manner in which the flutings were stopped. Augur holes were used too, in patterns suggesting garlands and urns. Thus there developed a thoroughly wooden style of decoration, more suitable to the material than the pre-Revolutionary forms which had been copied from stone motives.

One of the finest Post-Colonial mansions is The Woodlands, standing now in West Philadelphia near the railroad. It was built in its present form by William Hamilton in 1788. Its plan shows great elegance. The entrance is into a circular hall, with engaged columns framing deep niches and arched openings. The arch to the left leads to the stair hall, which is semicircular at both ends so that the stair curves at both top and bottom. Under the stair is the doorway to the elliptical drawing room, which projects from the end of the house as a curved bay. To the right of the entrance hall is the dining room, which has curved ends, providing a curved bay at that end of the house also. Directly back of the hall is the salon, 44 feet long by 22 feet wide, which also has curved ends with niches, and opens out on to the portico overlooking the river. Behind the drawing room is a smaller drawing room, and behind the dining room is the library, with passages connecting them to the front hall so they can be entered without passing through the other rooms. The second floor is given over to eight bedrooms, the principal rooms having closets and recesses for

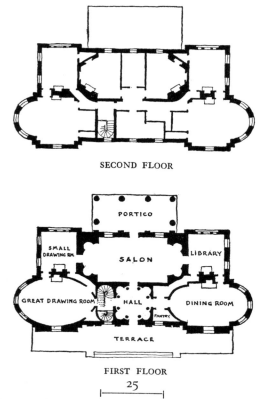

SECOND FLOOR

FIRST FLOOR

The fine formal plan of The Woodlands, in Philadelphia, shows the Adam influence in its use of ovals, niches, and columns.

the beds. The house is an excellent example of the advances made in planning, and the arrangement of the first-floor rooms *en suite* shows the desire for formal elegance.

The entrance front has a central pediment with pilasters in a free version of the Greek Ionic. The house is of fieldstone, but the central bay is stuccoed, with shallow recessed panels under the windows. Window frames show only a narrow line of wood, and the entrance door has a semicircular fanlight, although it retains a curved pediment. On the river front is the portico, flanked by two Palladian windows, set within shallow recessed arches in the stonework. The Woodlands is an exceedingly fine house, clearly illustrating the transi-

tion from the heavy Georgian style of the middle of the century to
the more delicate style of the close of the period.

In New England, one of the best examples of the style is the
Governor Gore House at Waltham, Massachusetts, built between 1799
and 1805 and supposedly designed by Charles Bulfinch. The central
block of the house has long low wings at each side, terminating in
projecting pavilions, and the result is an interestingly varied mass.

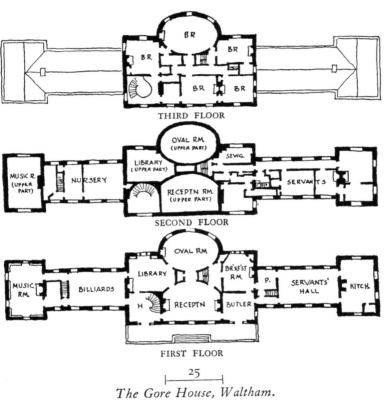

THIRD FLOOR

SECOND FLOOR

FIRST FLOOR

The Gore House, Waltham.

No roofs are visible behind the parapets and balustrades, and the
brick walls are painted gray. The principal rooms are all at the rear of
the house, facing the garden, the central salon being a great elliptical
room nearly two stories high. The entrance is at one side, a simple
shuttered doorway leading into a hall with an exquisite semicircular
stair. A billiard room is contained in the left wing, with the library in

the pavilion beyond, and the wing at the right has a large servants' hall with the kitchen beyond. The exterior is severe, with no applied decoration such as pilasters or stringcourses, and it depends for effect entirely upon the judicious placing and fine proportioning of such functional elements as doors and windows.

Boston, Portsmouth, and particularly Salem, have streets lined with the quiet and dignified houses of the early years of the nineteenth century. From the standpoint of simple good taste, this was perhaps the best period of domestic architecture in the United States. Churches, as well as public buildings, were designed in the same refined spirit, carrying on the Colonial tradition, but without the Georgian vigor. One such church is the Park Street Church in Boston, designed in 1809 by Peter Banner. Its lovely tower has the somewhat attenuated delicacy of its time, set on a square and simple base which is tied to the church itself by curved colonnades of slender engaged columns. Another is South Church, Salem, designed by Samuel McIntire, New England's master woodcarver. With its slender tower rising from a broad pediment, it is the perfect type of New England frame church.

Town Planning

THE EARLY TOWNS AND VILLAGES GREW UP AROUND THEIR COMMON. Some were destined to develop into great cities, such as Boston, and nearly all of them have retained their common, often surrounded now by modern buildings. Some cities, however, were planned as cities to start with, such as the excellent plan of Williamsburg, which, had the little capital been allowed to grow into a great city, would have assured it a broad and handsome mall for its civic buildings. When James Oglethorpe laid out Savannah in Georgia in 1733, he provided for broad straight streets with open squares at frequent and regular intervals. William Penn laid out a gridiron plan for Philadelphia in 1682, with a central square at Broad and Market Streets, four subsidiary open squares, and four main avenues leading from the center. Although the gridiron plan was retained, to prove a strait jacket for twentieth-century traffic, the open squares have decreased in number and in area, and Penn's seventeenth-century narrow streets have proved woefully inadequate. Except for the new city of Washington,

Major L'Enfant's plan for Washington clearly shows the influence of Le Nôtre.

no city was planned in the "grand manner" of the Continent, for apparently no one during the eighteenth century was capable of envisioning to what extent his city and his country might grow.

The American Wing

NO ACCOUNT OF AMERICAN COLONIAL ARCHITECTURE CAN BE COMplete without mention of the American Wing of the Metropolitan Museum of Art in New York City. Here, grouped on three floors representing the three style periods from 1640 to 1825, are rooms from houses and some of them careful reproductions, and each furnished and decorated with the furniture, hangings, china, and silver belonging to the period and locale. The main hall of the third floor has an open trussed roof, the trusses having been copied from those in the Old Ship Meetinghouse in Hingham. There are reproductions of the

entry and kitchen of the Parson Capen House at Topsfield, and the
parlor of a house at Ipswich. There is a 1725 paneled bedroom from
New Hampshire and a fine 1740 paneled room from Woodbury,
Long Island. On the second floor is a splendid ballroom from the old
City Tavern at Alexandria, Virginia, where Washington and others
of the great and near great met and danced. The drawing room from
Marmion, one of the great Virginia mansions, is there, with its land-
PLATE 121   scaped panels, and a beautiful room from the Powel House in Phila-
delphia. The first floor contains four Post-Colonial rooms—one from
Baltimore, one from Petersburg, Virginia, and two from Haverhill,
Massachusetts. Here, as at Williamsburg, one can live for the moment
in the quiet and dignified surroundings of the times which formed
our national architectural heritage.

The Spread of the Style

IN A BRIEF SURVEY IT IS POSSIBLE TO MENTION ONLY A FEW OF THE MOST
outstanding examples of the buildings of a busy century, most of
them located on or near the coast and its cities. But it must be remembered that all through the settled parts of the country, houses and
churches were built which were patterned after the more fashionable
buildings of the cities. In the villages of Massachusetts and Connecticut, in the hills of New Hampshire and Vermont, in the villages of
New York, Pennsylvania, and Virginia, are thousands of sturdy
white houses and simple churches whose good proportions and refined details show them to have been the work of a colonial carpenter-
builder with his tools in one hand and his handbook in the other. It
is interesting to note, too, the cultural lag in the hinterland. As the
traditions and methods of Jacobean England lingered in the houses of
the seventeenth century, so did the traditions and details of the seventeenth-century coastal houses linger in many eighteenth-century
houses inland. There are houses built as late as 1740 deep in New
England which have the overhang and center chimney of the coastal
houses of nearly a century before, and even after 1800 the back-
country carpenter-designers were still using the handbooks which
fathered the Colonial style.

✻ XIII ✻

Nineteenth-Century America
to the Civil War

HE GREATEST SINGLE influence in American architecture after the Revolutionary War was an amateur architect—Thomas Jefferson. Statesman, philosopher, and scholar, Jefferson not only wrote the Declaration of Independence while still a young lawyer, was twice governor of Virginia, ambassador to France, Secretary of State, twice president of the United States, and founder of the University of Virginia; he was also a highly accomplished amateur architect who personally designed many buildings and influenced the design of many more, and was responsible for the adoption of classic Roman architecture for the official buildings of the new republic.

Jefferson was not an artist. His lifelong interest in architecture was that of a scholar and idealist, guided by unerring taste. From the beginning, as he cleared and leveled his hilltop at Monticello in preparation for building his home, he was filled with distaste for both the fanciful Baroque of the Georgian buildings he saw about him, and the delicate fripperies of the Adam style which was the current vogue. The year was 1768, and Jefferson was twenty-five years old. He tried to design his house in the classic style of Palladio, translated into red brick and white woodwork, and his drawings have survived, showing the stages his design went through. When the house was completed in 1772 it was a pure Palladian design, not only in the proportions of its Doric order and its details, but in plan, being a small two-story building with a wing on each side and, presumably, two-storied porticoes of superposed orders at the front and back. It was tied by spreading terraces to octagonal outbuildings, at which points the terraces turned forward to two square buildings, thus making a formal forecourt.

During his five years in France, Jefferson had every opportunity to study the great Renaissance buildings, and he watched the construction of the Pantheon and the buildings facing on the Place de la Concorde. However, it was his visit to the Maison Carrée, the old Roman temple at Nîmes, that inspired him with the conviction that the style of republican Rome should be the style for the new republic in America. While still in Paris, the governor of Virginia asked him for designs for a new state capitol, for the capital had recently been moved from Williamsburg to Richmond. Jefferson's design, which

PLATE 122 he sent to Richmond, was based directly upon the Maison Carrée, being a long building with pediments at both ends, a deep portico at the front, and pilasters on the other three sides. This was a new departure in design, for it was the first temple-type building in America, and it preceded the Madeleine in Paris, the first large-scale building of this kind in modern Europe, by twenty years.

When Jefferson returned to the United States in 1789 he started

PLATE 123 a complete remodeling of Monticello, removing most of the second floor, and extending it on the ground floor, adding the dome and the two porticoes, as it appears today. Its plan is symmetrical, the central mass having a two-storied hall with a gallery, and a tall salon which projects as a bay into the west portico. The wings on each side are not spreading, but are compact though irregular in outline. They contain dining room, library, office, and bedrooms, all of which can be reached by a transverse corridor. The irregularities of the outline of the building are tied together on the exterior by the broad white band of the classic entablature and balustrade and the wide porticoes. The interiors are simple and dignified, with pure classical detail in all the trim, and the elegance of the proportions of the salon make it one of the handsomest rooms in the South.

When the decision was made to build a new capital city on the banks of the Potomac, both Jefferson and Washington were determined that it should have a noble plan, and that its buildings should be in the Roman classic style as the best embodiment of the ideals of the young republic. Major Pierre Charles L'Enfant, a French architect and engineer who had fought in the American Revolution and later established himself in New York, was chosen to lay out the city. Having been well trained in the French tradition of grand planning, L'Enfant created a splendid plan which provided for two great malls, with the Capitol at the end of one and the President's House at the end of the other, the two intersecting in a great plaza overlooking the river. Thus the two principal buildings were given the dominant sites, and the other government buildings were to line the malls. The balance of the city was laid out in the gridiron pattern, which had already become the custom in America, with a system of diagonal avenues superposed upon it, thus creating open squares at their many intersections, with broad vistas in every direction. Even with the great complications wrought by the advent of the railroad and the automobile, the scheme has worked, and had it been more carefully followed during the succeeding hundred years, the city of Washington would be more livable and even more imposing than it is today.

The competitions which were held for designs for the President's House and the Capitol brought forth a large number of designs, some of which were naive and crude, while others indicated a high degree of architectural competence. The winning design for the President's House was by Irish-born James Hoban, who had been trained in architecture in Dublin and had migrated to Charleston before the Revolution. The White House today is in appearance substantially as Hoban designed it, except for the addition of the porticoes. Jefferson submitted a design anonymously, based upon the Villa Capra of Palladio. The winner of the competition for the Capitol was Dr. William Thornton, a physician and widely traveled amateur, born in the West Indies, who came to America in 1793. The original drawings of his winning design have been lost, but it seems to have been in the form of a great classic temple. Construction of the design was carried out with the assistance of the second-place winner, a Frenchman by the name of Stephen Hallet. The building, after being burned by the British in the War of 1812, was rebuilt and altered by other architects, so that it is largely their work today, but the hand and the mind of Thomas Jefferson were ever-present. His correspondence shows that he was always in close touch with the architects who worked in Washington, guiding them and influencing them, and being influenced by them. He was as pro-American in his architecture as he was in his politics, determined that no suggestion of English Renaissance architecture should creep into the nation's capital city.

All through his career, Jefferson was a dominant influence in American architecture. In the seven or eight Virginia mansions which he designed between 1790 and 1820, besides Monticello, he was striving toward the ideal Palladian plan of the central axis, as represented by the Villa Capra, and the full portico, which he applied to all his designs, came to be widely accepted throughout the South. As early as 1779 he had made studies for remodeling the Governor's Palace at Williamsburg, adding a portico to both fronts, and four years later he had sketched a plan for the governor's house at Richmond, in the form of a central domed rotunda surrounded by four corner chambers with corridors on the axes.

The University of Virginia was in every way Jefferson's creation. He conceived the idea, persuaded the state to finance it, organized it and selected its faculty, and designed and built the buildings. This campus is today one of the most beautiful in the country. At one end PLATE 124 of a long mall is the library, a circular domed building with a tall Corinthian portico, the Pantheon of Rome reduced in size and executed in red brick and white woodwork. Like the Virginia state capitol, the library was an innovation, for nothing like it had ever been PLATE 125 seen by the American people. Flanking the two long sides of the mall are a series of temple-like buildings connected by colonnades, each unit a faculty residence with class rooms. Each is an essay in classic architecture, one representing the Doric of the Baths of Diocletian, another the Ionic of the temple of Fortuna Virilis, a third the Corinthian of Palladio, and so on for ten buildings. Despite his innovations, there is little real originality in Jefferson's architecture, but there is great beauty, and considering the times there was great fitness, for certainly the "Roman Revival" was more appropriate for the young republic than a mere extension of Georgian and Adam architecture would have been. Jefferson's influence upon public architecture has lasted to the present day, and the majority of government buildings and state capitols all over the country have been designed in a modified Roman style.

Boston and New York

SAMUEL McINTIRE OF SALEM, MASSACHUSETTS, WAS THE GREATEST of the carpenter-architects. He was born in 1757 and spent his life in Salem, designing and building houses in the Colonial and Adam traditions, almost untouched by Jefferson's Roman and republican ideals. He was personally a woodcarver of consummate skill, and proud are the Salem residents today who can boast McIntire gateposts with their delicate urns, a McIntire doorway with its rich scrolled and broken pediment and fat pineapple finial, and a McIntire mantel with its fine American eagle and delicate basket of fruit. The typical Salem houses, built when the city was at the peak of its prosperity as a shipping center, are rectangular boxes five windows wide and three stories high, often without the grace of good proportion or the interest of broken masses. However, in their careful fenestration and good detail many of them are very handsome. The Pierce-Nichols House is an early McIntire house, and shows his attempt to achieve the monumental. It is a clapboard house with a little Doric entrance porch, entablatures over the windows, massive Doric pilasters at the corners, entirely out of scale with the house, and an entablature with triglyphs half as big as the third-story windows. The Gardner-White-Pingree House, built later in 1805, shows how greatly   PLATE 126
McIntire had advanced in taste and understanding of design. Built of brick, it is still in the standard Salem type, but has a delicate semicircular porch, white stone flat arches and sills at the windows, a cornice with modillions and a balustrade above, and no other decoration beyond plain stone bands at each floor level.

McIntire was able to think in other terms as is evidenced by his design for the Lyman House in Waltham, which has a central block with wings, and an elliptical salon projecting on the garden side. Pilasters are confined to the second floor, and the rest of the house is very severe, but has interest because of its good proportions. McIntire submitted a design in the competition for the national Capitol which

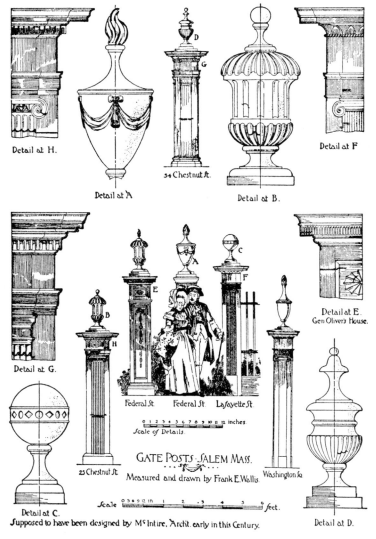

Detail at H.

Detail at F

34 Chestnut St.

Detail at A

Detail at B.

Detail at E.
Gen Oliver's House.

Detail at G.

Federal St. Federal St. Lafayette St.

0 1 2 3 4 5 6 7 8 9 10 11 12 inches
Scale of Details.

GATE POSTS · SALEM MASS.
· · · · · ·

23 Chestnut St.

Measured and drawn by Frank E. Wallis.

Washington Sq

Scale 0 3 6 9 12 in. 1 2 3 4 5 6 feet.

Supposed to have been designed by Mc Intire, Archt. early in this Century.

Detail at C.

Detail at D.

The handsome McIntire gateposts of Salem.

shows his real quality, for it is well planned and well organized as to details, in the manner of Sir William Chambers, although not truly monumental in character. It was not what Washington and Jefferson were looking for, but it does great credit to the woodcarver of Salem.

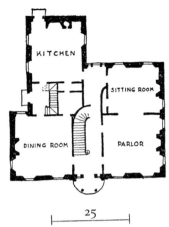

25

The Gardner-White-Pingree House, Salem.

The greatest of the New England architects was Charles Bulfinch, born in 1763 of an aristocratic Boston family. He graduated from Harvard, traveled abroad, and designed his first houses as an amateur, until family misfortunes forced him to turn professional. The first phase of his work is purely in the Post-Colonial manner, as evidenced by the State House at Hartford, Connecticut, and the Boston State House, both built before 1800. They are colonial but not provincial, and the latter in particular has a monumental scale which shows the results of Bulfinch's European study. His Harrison Gray Otis House, on Mount Vernon Street, Boston, is a three-storied city house, with shallow segmental arches framing the first-floor openings in the Adam manner, and fluted Corinthian pilasters extending through the two upper stories to the entablature and balustrade. Bulfinch's judicious designs for many houses on Park Street, Beacon Hill, and his Franklin Crescent are largely responsible for the appearance of old Boston today, for his style was followed by many contemporaries.

The second phase of Bulfinch's work was under the influence of Jefferson and his Early Republican style. In 1817 Bulfinch was called to Washington to take charge of the reconstruction of the Capitol, after its burning in 1814. He remained there until 1830, and the front of the Capitol facing the mall, with its great portico, is largely his work. During this period he designed one of New England's most

The *"Bulfinch Front"* of the Boston State House, as it appeared in *1831.*

PLATE 127 beautiful churches, the First Church of Christ in Lancaster, Massachusetts. The clean strong brick arches of its portico with their simple pilasters and pediment, and the daring simplicity of the tower, terminating in a little dome, show how he strove to combine the traditional New England Colonial church style with the new Early Republican spirit. Bulfinch lived on until 1844, entering a third phase upon his return to Boston in 1830, for the Greek Revival was under way and he participated fully in it.

Asher Benjamin of Greenfield, Massachusetts, was probably responsible for more Post-Colonial houses and churches than any other architect, yet he personally designed only a few. In 1796 he published *The Country Builder's Assistant,* in which he set forth façades, doorways, windows, cornices, mantels, and mouldings from which hundreds of buildings were designed almost to the middle of the nineteenth century. His designs are excellent, and they represent no slavish copying of English work, for they show a definite attempt to modify and scale them to American needs. In one of his prefaces he says: "We do not conceive it essentially necessary to adhere exactly to any particular order, provided the proportion and harmony of the parts be carefully preserved. . . ." During the first quarter of the nineteenth century he issued several new books following the trend of fashion into the Greek Revival, with designs which were always scholarly yet original, and always in excellent taste.

In New York, the leading architect and builder after the Revolution was John McComb, who designed many churches and houses in the Post-Colonial style, following the traditions of the Adams and Sir William Chambers rather than the lead of Thomas Jefferson. His greatest work is the old City Hall, built in 1803, with the collaboration   PLATE 128 of a French architect, Joseph Mangin. This accounts for the decidedly French character of the delicate arches and the graceful curved double staircase under the rotunda. Here and there an occasional McComb house has survived, and New York lost one of its finest churches when his St. John's Church on Varick Street was destroyed about fifty years ago to make way for the extension of Seventh Avenue. Lesser-known examples of McComb's more utilitarian work are the old fort on the Battery which later became Castle Garden, then the Aquarium, and now awaits an undecided fate, and the famous lighthouse at Montauk Point, on the easternmost tip of Long Island.

Benjamin Henry Latrobe

DR. WILLIAM THORNTON, THE PHYSICIAN WHO WON THE competition for the design of the Capitol at Washington, designed several residences. They are definitely in the Post-Colonial style, despite his close contacts with Jefferson and the fountainhead of the Early Republican. He is supposed to have designed James Madison's Virginia home, Montpelier, a spreading mansion to which Madison, at Jefferson's suggestion, later added a very wide and tall portico. One of the finest houses of the period, designed by Thornton in Washington, is now known as the Octagon, the home of the American Institute of Architects. In front a semicircular bay extends the full three stories, a fashion introduced by Jefferson and popularized by Bulfinch. The entrance porch is a chaste Greek Ionic order, the second-floor stringcourse is a plain white band, and there are white stone panels under the third-story windows in the Adam manner. The interiors are simple, yet with rich detail which has the

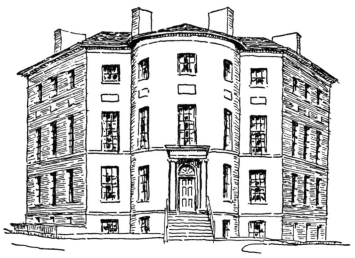

The Octagon, designed by Dr. William Thornton in Washington, D.C., is now the headquarters of the American Institute of Architects.

somewhat wiry character of the style. This versatile Quaker doctor also designed the Library of Philadelphia, and ended his days as the first Commissioner of Patents at Washington.

The real founder of the architectural profession in the United States was Benjamin Henry Latrobe, who was born in England in 1764. He was thoroughly trained as an architect, and achieved considerable success in London, where his work showed that he was following the same path as Sir John Soane, away from the niceties of the Adams toward a deeper understanding of monumental forms, strongly influenced by the current fashion for Greek detail. Coming to America early in the 1790's, his first important work was the Bank of Pennsylvania in Philadelphia, 1798. It was in a style completely new to Americans, and was a tremendous popular success. A small building with a low dome and porticoes front and back, it was clean and smooth and devoid of ornament. The order of the porticoes was Greek Ionic, and there was not another piece of carving on the bank; even the mouldings of the entablature flattened into mere bands before they continued around the building. Because he used the Greek order, Latrobe is often said to have originated

PLATE 129

the Greek Revival in America. But this building was Greek only in spirit, and the Greek Revival was reaching American shores anyway, for it was the latest fashion sweeping Europe.

Latrobe's houses were designed in the same simple and functional manner, with no pilasters, no cornices, no stringcourses, and only occasionally a portico, which, when it occurred, was pure Greek. They were thoroughly up-to-date in their planning, with clean-cut circulation, dressing rooms and closets for all bedrooms, and even, in the Markoe House in Philadelphia, a bathroom complete with tub, basin, and water closet—in 1810! For the architect Latrobe was also the engineer Latrobe who in 1800 designed and installed Philadelphia's municipal water works, the first in America. When he was called upon to design a Roman Catholic cathedral for Baltimore, he submitted two designs, one Gothic and one classical. The bishop chose the classical design, but the inclusion of a Gothic design is interesting, for it indicates that even the best American minds were already veering toward eclecticism, the dominant characteristic of American architecture later in the century. As a matter of fact, it might be said that Latrobe also originated the Gothic Revival in America, for as early as 1799 he designed a suburban house for a wealthy Philadelphia merchant in the Gothic style—the romantic kind of Gothic of Walpole and Fonthill Abbey —and years later he designed two Gothic churches.

Latrobe designed many important buildings in many cities, as far west as Kentucky and as far south as New Orleans. But his most important work began in 1803, when he was put in charge of completing the Capitol at Washington. Politically and structurally it was in a state of confusion. Some walls were completed, other foundations had been put in and abandoned. Latrobe had a firm hand, and managed to carry the Capitol along toward completion, following Thornton's plan but modifying the doctor's delicate Adam-like design as best he could into something more to his and to Jefferson's taste. Then the retreating British burned the Capitol in 1814, and Latrobe was able to rebuild much of the interior. His design can be seen today in Statuary Hall, originally the House of Representatives, and the Old Supreme Court Room, which was the original Senate Chamber, and their adjoining spaces. His efforts to create a purely American style of ornament, though cast in a classic mould, can be seen in the columns of the Senate entrance—which have Corinthian-like capitals using ears of corn as the decorative form—and those of the Senate rotunda, which employ tobacco leaves. Latrobe resigned in 1817, and Bulfinch was put in charge; he completed the central rotunda with a low dome according to Latrobe's design, and carried out the main portico.

Latrobe's influence was great, not only because of the high quality and fresh though classical originality of his design, but also because he was the first American architect who had not started as either an amateur or a builder. He came to his work with a thorough professional training in his art, and was well grounded in both scholarship and engineering, those important tools of the architect. His influence was continued and extended by the younger men who received their training in his office, the most important of whom were Robert Mills and William Strickland.

The Greek Revival

THE GREEK REVIVAL APPEARED IN ENGLAND IN ITS INFLUENCE upon the work of the brothers Adam and Sir John Soane, and in the popular interest aroused by the publication of Stuart and Revett's *Antiquities of Athens* and other books on Greek culture. It was at this time that Lord Elgin brought to England some of the metopes and pediment sculptures from the Parthenon, and Byron stimulated the cult of things Grecian with his poetry and romantic escapades. The Greek Ionic front of the British Museum and many other Greek-style buildings and monuments were built as a result of this fad. Enthusiasm was not limited to England. With the exception of France, where both the Republic and the Empire adhered to the Roman classic style as their expressions of the classic revival, the Greek style was enthusiastically adopted all over Europe. The result was such great buildings as the Court Theater in Berlin, the Pinakothek at Munich, the Valhalla at Regensburg, the Thorvaldsen Museum in Denmark, the Admiralty in Leningrad, and many more, all modern buildings dressed in the sometimes ill-fitting garments of ancient Greece.

The Roman classic revival in France resulted in the Pantheon and the Madeleine, and continued in the great buildings of Napoleon —the Bourse and the new Chamber of Deputies, with their great Roman colonnades. Still later, the Arc de Triomphe was built, in a classicism which is not truly Roman but thoroughly French. Napoleon revived the Royal Academy of Architecture in 1816 by establishing the École des Beaux Arts, which for over a hundred years was to be the mecca of students of architecture from all over the world. Here they were taught the fundamentals of architecture on the sound Roman principles of broad planning for use and for beauty.

Architecture was becoming diffuse. All over the Western world new types of buildings were needed. No longer were kings and courtiers, churches and cities the only clients to call upon the architect for great buildings. The architects of the nineteenth century were called upon to design factories and warehouses, railroad stations and hotels, banks and commercial buildings, as well as residences and government buildings. In all of them they were expected to take full advantage of the latest developments in construction, sanitation, and mechanical equipment, and all buildings had to be planned economically and functionally. The improvement of facilities for travel, and the invention of the camera and methods of picture reproduction created a public which was aware of all the architectural periods of the past and demanded an ever-increasing eclecticism in design. Architects came to realize that if they could resurrect Greek and Roman architecture, that if they could build in the Gothic style, they could also design buildings for modern uses, built of modern materials, and dressed in any style—Egyptian, Moorish, Romanesque, and Byzantine—without limit. Each innovation was hailed by a public eager for novelties; countless individuals and organizations, newly wealthy from the rapid growth of commerce and industry, and devoid of the settled traditions that bring culture and sound taste, made demands upon architecture to supply them with the unusual and the bizarre, the grandiose and the picturesque. The fact that they got it is another evidence of the axiom that architecture is always a reflection of its times.

The Greek Revival in America

THE FAD OF THE GREEK REVIVAL HIT THE AMERICAN CITIES IN ABOUT 1820, the year of Benjamin Latrobe's death. Before that, work which had been done in the Greek manner, such as Latrobe's, was not so much the response to a fad, but a sincere effort to create something new and suitable to America, and it served to prepare the public for what was to come. As early as 1806, Nicholas Biddle, a wealthy Philadelphia banker and a vivid and influential personality, had visited Greece and become enthusiastic over Greek art. He published an article urging the adoption of Greek forms as the most suitable for American architecture, and it had a great influence in Philadelphia, which was still the cultural center of the country. The War of 1812 and the burning of Washington had done much to turn the public away from England, and had created a desire for a truly American culture. During the 1820's, the fierce Greek wars of independence further kindled the popular enthusiasm for things Greek, for the American people pictured the Greek people as going through what they themselves had just been through. A country colonel said, "Give me six hundred mountaineers with two pounds of beans and a gallon of whiskey a day for each, and we'll lick the Turks in forty-eight hours." So the Greek Revival was essentially a part of the romantic spirit of the times, a movement in which the people led and the architect followed the demands of their taste. It was genuinely popular in all classes of society, and as it died out on the upper level, overcome by the desire for follies and fripperies, it lived on vigorously at the lower level throughout the westward-expanding nation down to the eve of the Civil War. The names of the new towns in the Western Reserve, the Middle West, and the Northwest show the dominance of classic ideals—Athens, Elmira, Ypsilanti, Corinth, Rome, Carthage, Cincinnati, Sparta, Cairo, and Euclid, all with their simple Greek revival houses, churches, and court houses.

For a generation the Greek Revival almost completely superseded the Roman classicism of Jefferson's Early Republican style: yet as the Greek Revival faded out of sight over the Alleghenies in about 1850, the Roman style was carried on in official and governmental buildings, and has continued to recent years. For a while it looked as though the Greek Revival might become the basis of a new and truly American style, for it became deeply rooted in the American mind and well adapted to American needs. But it was finally engulfed by the growing demand for variety and display, the new taste for the picturesque and the grandiose.

Mills, Strickland, and Walter Were Great Planners and Engineers

AS A YOUNG MAN, ROBERT MILLS WORKED AS A DRAFTSMAN FOR Jefferson for two or three years. Then, upon Jefferson's advice, he went into Latrobe's office in Philadelphia to complete his training. He was a serious-minded man, deeply interested in social and economic problems, and chiefly concerned with planning his buildings in a straightforward and functional manner, expressing those plans in designs which were both simple and honest. It was only natural that his architectural forms should be those that were popular in his time. He followed the trend into Greek classicism, and designed in the Gothic style occasionally when called upon to do so. But he never followed these styles slavishly, always putting the function of the building first. In an introduction to a proposed book illustrating his works, Mills said, "Utility and economy will be found to have entered into most of the studies of the author, and little sacrifice to display; at the same time his endeavors were to produce as much harmony and beauty of arrangement as practicable. The principle assumed and acted upon was that beauty is founded upon order, and that convenience and utility were constituent parts. . . . The author has made it a rule never to consult books when he had to design a building. His considerations were—first, the object of the building; second, the means appropriated for its construction; third, the situation it was to occupy; these served as guides in forming the outline of his plan." Good architectural gospel for any age.

During the first half of the nineteenth century a vast number of important buildings were constructed, many of them new types for new uses. Mills had a large share in that widespread activity be-

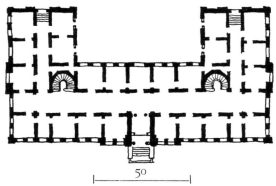

Robert Mills's building for the Post Office Department at Washington shows simple and straightforward planning.

fore his death in 1855. In Washington he designed the office buildings for the Treasury Department, the Post Office, and the Patent Office; in Charleston, the Record Offices. These buildings were all of fireproof construction. He is said to have designed a system for warming and cooling air, which was later installed in the Capitol, although it appears never to have been used. He developed the auditorium type of church, round or octagonal in plan, building two in Philadelphia and one in Richmond. He designed the customhouse at New Bedford, Massachusetts, a hospital at Columbia, South Carolina, buildings for the University of South Carolina, the United States Marine Hospital at Mobile, and houses and other buildings all over the East and the South. He also designed one of the best-loved structures in the land—the Washington Monument—yet not one person in ten thousand who admires it knows the name of the architect. It was designed in 1833, begun in 1848, and completed in 1884. The original plan called for an elliptical Greek Doric temple at its base, surmounted by a sculptural group representing Washington in a triumphal chariot with six horses driven by Victory. Possibly even Mills would feel that the monument is better the way it is, in the clean beauty of its geometric form.

William Strickland was another man of Mills's caliber, although of a very different personality. He, too, had his training in Latrobe's office, but as Mills had been a dependable plodder, Strickland was a brilliant scatterbrain. In 1810 he designed his first building, a

Masonic Hall in Philadelphia decorated in the Gothic style, of which the city was very proud. After that he deserted architecture and worked as a landscape painter, engraver, and scenic artist in New York until 1818, when he returned to Philadelphia and to architecture. Settled and sobered, he developed into a great architect and engineer. His first success was the Second Bank of the United States, 1819, now the Custom House. At the direction of Nicholas Biddle, he

Strickland's Second Bank of the United States in Philadelphia was the country's first full-fledged Greek temple.

designed it as a Greek Doric temple, with full porticoes at both ends, and a well-planned and fireproof interior. It was the first full-fledged Greek temple the American public had seen, and its popularity established the Greek Revival style.

Strickland's planning was as practical and straightforward as Mills's, and his structures were as solid and as fireproof. Their difference lies in their design, for Strickland showed a greater delicacy and elegance, and more reliance upon archaeological Greek detail. His share of the important buildings of the period was as great as Mills's. In Philadelphia he designed the United States Mint, the graceful Merchants' Exchange, now restored and standing, almost alone in a vast restoration project, and the great Naval Hospital. Among other buildings are the Athenaeum at Providence, the Mint at New Orleans, now the city jail, two churches in Nashville, and the Tennessee State Capitol. The capitol shows his adherence to traditional forms, for although its plan is ingenious and thoroughly practical, the exterior has Greek Ionic porticoes and is surmounted by a cupola in the form of a colossal adaptation of the Choragic Monument of Lysicrates.

Two other architects who had a wide influence had their training in Strickland's office. One is Gideon Shryock, son of a Kentucky builder-architect, who took the Greek Revival back to his native state, which was then the "far west." In 1825 he designed the Kentucky State Capitol, an Ionic temple with a small domed cupola, a design far ahead of its time for the unsophisticated West. The other architect is Thomas U. Walter. After early ventures in the Gothic and the Egyptian styles, Walter turned to a modified and rather heavy-handed practical adaptation of the Greek style which he used on hospitals, churches, and other Philadelphia buildings. Of special PLATE 130 interest is his design for Girard College. Stephen Girard, banker, miser, and agnostic, left in his will a tremendous sum of money to the city of Philadelphia to establish a college for orphan boys. The terms of the will were very explicit, outlining even the dimensions of the buildings that were to be built, and further requiring that no clergyman of any faith ever be permitted to put his foot inside the gates of the college. Nicholas Biddle, that lover of everything Greek, who was president of the board of trustees, dictated to Walter that the college be designed in the Greek temple style. Within this rigid framework of requirements, Walter designed in 1833 the great marble Corinthian temple that stands today. Completely surrounded by its tall columns, the windows are practically useless, but the strong and fireproof construction is a monument to the structural ingenuity of its architect.

Before the advent of iron and steel construction, buildings could be made fireproof only by employing groined and barrel vaulting for the floor construction. In a building three or four stories high, therefore, it took great skill to devise vaults which were flat enough not to require great story heights, and to concentrate all the loads on piers so the interior of the building would not have to be filled up with massive bearing walls. Mills, Strickland, and Walter proved themselves masters at solving such structural problems.

After a sojourn in South America, where he designed harbor works and fortifications, Walter returned to the United States and culminated his career between 1855 and 1865 by completing the dome of the national Capitol and designing the two wings which house the Senate and the House of Representatives. Here he made use of iron, the newest contribution of industry to the art of building. The great dome of painted cast iron may not be defensible on purely esthetic grounds, for it masquerades as stonework, but the existing foundations would not have supported a true dome of masonry construction, so the practical compromise does great credit to Walter's ingenuity. Its splendid silhouette and majestic circular colonnade form a magnificent crown to one of the great buildings of the world, of which certainly Jefferson, Thornton, Latrobe, and Bulfinch would be proud.

About twenty states have capitols which were built during the period of the Greek Revival, and there are innumerable county court houses. A few of the capitols are still in use, but many of them have been superseded by newer and larger buildings. Other than those already mentioned, a few of particular interest are: the capitol at Raleigh and the old capitols at Springfield and Indianapolis, which were designed by Town and Davis of New York; the old capitol at

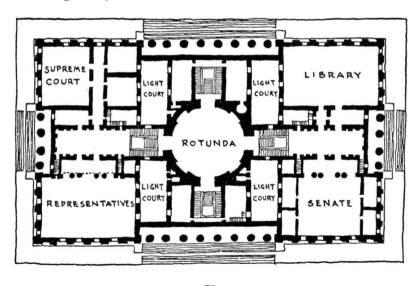

First floor plan of the Ohio State Capitol at Columbus.

Little Rock, by Gideon Shryock; and the old capitols at Jefferson
City, Iowa City, Jackson, and Albany. Even the first capitol of California was a little Greek building with a wooden Ionic order, built
in 1853 at Benicia. When Ohio held a competition for designs for a
capitol in 1838, over fifty designs were received. Before the building
was completed in 1860, at least seven architects had had their fin-
gers in its design, including Thomas U. Walter, A. J. Davis, Richard
Upjohn, and Isaiah Rogers. The general design, however, is usually
PLATE 131   credited to Henry Walter of Cincinnati, the winner of the competition, and it is considered one of the finest public buildings of the
Greek Revival.

Hotels and Houses

IN THE NORTH, THE GREEK REVIVAL WAS CARRIED ON BY A LARGE
number of busy architects, for it was a period of great building activity there too. In Boston, Bulfinch's later work shows the Greek
touch in its refined details, and his houses retained the aristocratic
elegance and quiet harmony which had distinguished them earlier
in the century. The houses of Alexander Parris are similar to those
of Bulfinch, with brick fronts, round bays, white panels, and chaste
detail. Self-taught, as most Boston architects were, Parris had started
as a schoolteacher, and ended his days as a civil engineer in charge
of Portsmouth Navy Yard. Apparently the Yankee architects were
still jacks-of-all-trades, for Solomon Willard started as a carpenter,
attended Asher Benjamin's school for architectural drafting, turned
to woodcarving, then to sculpture and model-making, made two
trips to the South, settled down as an architect for a few years and
then switched to quarrying granite, and finally died in 1861 as a
scientific farmer. He brought the use of granite into Boston architecture, using it in his severe buildings, decorated only by their Doric
columns. His most famous work was the design for the Bunker Hill
Monument. The purest example of the Greek Revival in Boston is
the granite Custom House, designed in 1837 by Ammi B. Young,
who later became supervising architect for the Treasury Department,
and in that capacity designed custom houses all over the country.

The first hotel specialist developed out of this group of Boston

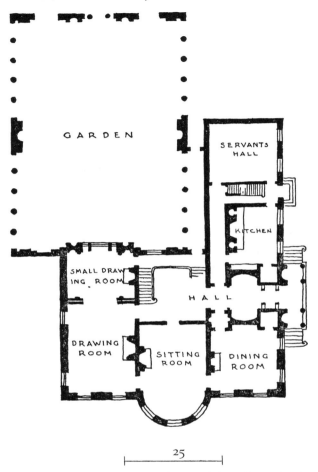

GARDEN

SERVANTS HALL

KITCHEN

SMALL DRAW ING ROOM

HALL

DRAWING ROOM

SITTING ROOM

DINING ROOM

25

The Sears House in Boston was designed by Alexander Parris, a contemporary of Bulfinch.

architects, a man who introduced what were then revolutionary ideas. Isaiah Rogers was the son of a shipbuilder and he drifted into architecture through carpentry. In 1828, two years after he had opened his own office as architect, he had the good fortune to be com- missioned to design the Tremont House, which he made the first modern hotel in America. A three-story building standing on a high basement, its exterior treatment was very simple, with plain walls, end pilasters with an entablature which extended across the entire

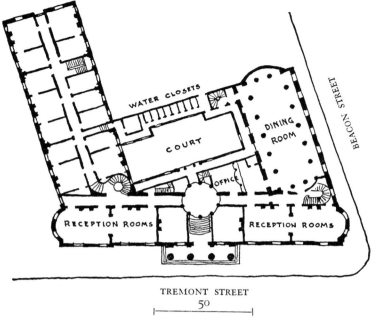

The Tremont House in Boston, by Isaiah Rogers, was the first modern hotel.

building, and a small Doric portico without a pediment. It was in the planning and appointments that the building was revolutionary, for it had a handsome public lobby and office, a suite of sumptuous reception rooms, a large and handsome main dining room, and bedrooms, single and *en suite,* arranged along straight corridors with ample exit stairs. The entire building was lighted by gas, and on the ground floor there was a battery of screened water closets and bathrooms with running water. But even these were not the greatest innovation, for in the Tremont House, for the first time in any hotel, a guest could rent a single room all for himself instead of having to double up with one or more strangers!

The fame of this hotel put Rogers in great demand, and he was called to New York in 1832 to design the Astor House. It exceeded the Tremont House in size, luxury of appointments, and mechanical conveniences, for there were bathrooms and toilet rooms on each floor. Nearly every large hotel built in the country until Isaiah

Rogers' death in 1869 was henceforth designed by him—in Charleston, New Orleans, Cincinnati, Louisville, Nashville, and many other cities. These hotels illustrate one of the new types of buildings for which the need arose, and the manner in which ingenious architects, with no past experience to draw upon, filled those needs. The buildings themselves were not a product of the Greek Revival, they were

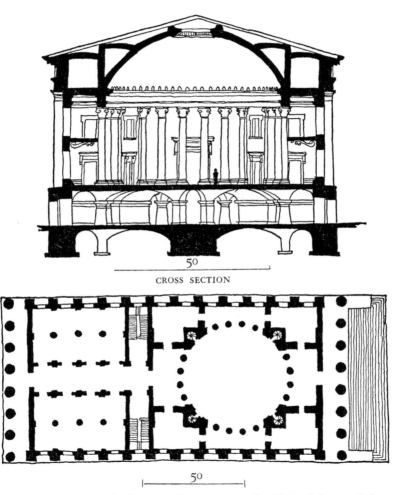

CROSS SECTION

The old New York Custom House, now the United States Sub-Treasury, still stands on Wall Street.

a product of the economic life of their times, and they represent the solution of an economic problem. They were dressed up in Greek Revival garments because that happened to be the fashion at the time—which was fortunate because it was an appropriate style, being clean and strong and simple.

During the late 1820's in New York, while John McComb was still designing his delicate Post-Colonial houses, many other architects and builder-architects were introducing the new fashion. The most outstanding of these were Ithiel Town and A. J. Davis, two brilliant and accomplished men whose partnership seems to have been loosely organized, for many buildings are credited to but one of them. They designed the Custom House, which is now the Sub-Treasury, standing on Wall Street at the head of Broad Street. It is another Greek Doric temple, archaeologically correct on the exterior, and brilliantly planned and constructed in the interior. It has a low domed rotunda, the dome being entirely under the temple roof, and is entirely of fireproof construction, the dome and all floors and ceilings being of cut stone vaulting. Martin Thompson, at some times a partner with Town and Davis, designed the Bank of the United States, of which the graceful English Renaissance front now forms one of the court façades of the American Wing of the Metropolitan Museum of Art. Around the city there are still warehouses and other old buildings of indeterminate uses, as well as a few churches, which were designed by members of this firm, also many rows of houses such as those gracious homes which are fast disappearing from Washington Square.

The typical New York city house became fairly well standardized. It was two or three stories high, and only 20 or 25 feet wide, for the city had been laid out on the basis of lots of those widths by 100 feet deep. The first floor was about a half-story above the street level, and the fanlighted entrance door was usually the only decorated part of the simple red brick façade. The house was two rooms deep, with a hall at one side running through it, the stair at the back, and a covered passage leading to the privy at the rear of the property. The front room on the first floor was the parlor, with a wide and handsomely trimmed doorway, with sliding doors, connecting it with the dining room at the rear. On the basement floor the kitchen was at the back, and the family sitting room at the front.

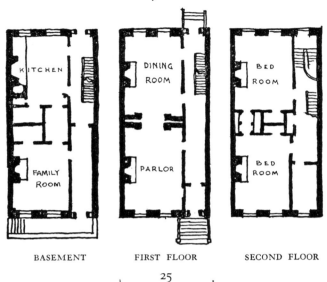

BASEMENT   FIRST FLOOR   SECOND FLOOR

Plan of a typical New York City house of the early nineteenth century.

The second floor, and sometimes a third, had two bedrooms, one front and one back, with a small "hall bedroom" at the front of the stair hall. As bathrooms were gradually introduced, it was usually the hall bedroom that was converted. The servants' rooms were in the attic. Mantels were simple but handsome, often of marble, and door and window trim was ordinarily a wide and deeply moulded casing, with square carved blocks at the corners.

Minard Lafever of New York was another Asher Benjamin. In 1829 he published *The Young Builder's General Instructor,* and followed it in a few years with two more such books. They, together with the books of a few others, were the chief means by which the Greek Revival was broadcast over the rapidly expanding nation, to cities and villages far beyond the reach of the professional architect. Lafever was one of the most accomplished architectural decorators of his time. His exquisite engravings of entrances, cornices, capitals, mantels, and mouldings are beautiful essays in adapted Greek forms. His books also included house plans based upon the Greek temple, some with wings and porches, together with nicely studied elevations for them, which show a remarkable inventiveness and impeccable taste. Thanks to the handbooks, there are countless examples of the Greek Revival in houses, churches, and town buildings throughout upper New York State, Pennsylvania, Ohio, Indiana, Michigan, on west through Iowa and Missouri, and even in Oregon.

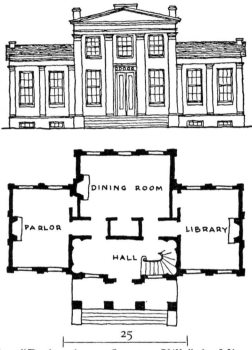

Tracing of a "Design for a Country Villa" in Minard Lafever's Modern Builder's Guide, *1833.*

PLATE 132   The characteristic feature is the gable facing the street, with heavy Greek mouldings. There may or may not be a portico, and the columns may be square for economy's sake. There is apt to be a low wing on one side, often on both sides, with its ridge at right angles to the main ridge. The door is set between sidelights, with a rectangular transom above; an elaborate entrance may have fluted engaged columns between the door and the sidelights, a simple one will have square posts. The whole is framed in a heavily moulded trim, or it may have pilasters with a broad entablature. If the house

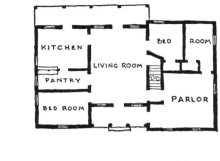

25

A typical Greek Revival house in the Middle West.

has an air of quiet dignity and the charm of good proportions and refined detail, it is probably from one of the handbooks of Minard Lafever, Asher Benjamin, or George Biddle.

The Gothic Revival

THE GOTHIC REVIVAL BEGAN IN ENGLAND DURING THE EIGHTeenth century, starting as an offshoot of the romantic movement in literature, and resulting in rich men's fancies like Strawberry Hill, Fonthill Abbey, and Gothic cottages in the park. It turned out to be more than a passing fad, however, and continued to grow, fostered by writers such as Scott, whose discovery of England's medieval past was enchanting to people weary of the often pompous formalities of an imported classical culture. So, side by side with the Classic Revival, grew the Gothic Revival. The English people seemed to find in the resurrected medieval forms a sense of continuity with their past, giving them a feeling of national security at a time when the Continent was torn by the Napoleonic wars. Since this was an age of individualism, when the artist strove to express his own emotions rather than the polite conventions of society, many people were stirred by the emotional appeal of Gothic architecture.

A. W. Pugin, an architect of the second quarter of the nineteenth century, wrote books ridiculing classical design and advocating honesty of structure and materials, and published volumes of beautiful drawings of Gothic details from the old churches. During the last half of the century the writer and critic John Ruskin wielded a tremendous influence with his essays urging a return to Gothic art and the medieval spirit. The best results of the Gothic Revival in England were in the field of religious architecture, and in that field it is still alive. The worst results were in domestic architecture, and there it fortunately died by the end of the century. Castellated houses and Gothic mansions were built, with exaggerated pointed windows, crude tracery, buttressed towers, and alternating stripes of light and dark stone or brick in the Italian Gothic style urged by Ruskin. Their falsity was only too apparent, and Victorian Gothic died with the Victorian Age. Several public buildings were built in this exaggerated style, such as the Albert Memorial in London. The one great exception is the Houses of Parliament, designed in the Gothic style at the instance of Queen Victoria, by Sir Charles Barry, with the assistance of Pugin on the detailing, and built between 1840 and 1860. The building has been much criticized but more generally admired, and certainly the view from the Thames reveals a great structure of real beauty.

The Gothic churches of Street, Bodley, and Bentley successfully capture the spirit of the medieval churches, even though scholars criticize their detail and purists decry their plaster vaulting. Sir George Gilbert Scott designed the Albert Memorial, the St. Pancras Hotel and Station, and "restored" a large number of the English cathedrals and abbeys. His grandson, Sir Giles Gilbert Scott, has carried on the finest of the Gothic Revival tradition with his magnificent designs for Liverpool Cathedral, which is still under construction.

In Germany and central Europe the Gothic Revival had much the same causes behind it as in England. A wave of restoration swept the land, and many medieval buildings were completed, sometimes from the actual ancient drawings which had been almost miraculously preserved, as in the case of the west front of Cologne Cathedral. New Gothic churches, city halls, and "castles" were built, but often in a sadly debased style, even employing imitation stonecarving made of cast iron. It was characteristic of most of the architects of the Gothic Revival in every land not to appreciate the true structural meaning of medieval Gothic, and to be satisfied to obtain merely its appearance, often by the use of sham materials.

France had a great student of the Middle Ages in the architect and scholar Viollet-le-Duc, who alone seemed to realize that a real return to medievalism was impossible. In spite of France's preoccupation with the Empire style of Napoleon III, his writings aroused people to some appreciation of the glory of their great cathedrals, and the government commissioned him to restore many medieval buildings, including the cathedrals of Notre Dame and Amiens, the château of Pierrefonds, and the walled city of Carcassonne.

The Gothic Revival in America

NATURALLY, A MOVEMENT AS WIDESPREAD AS THE GOTHIC REVIVAL in Europe was bound to be felt in the United States. Its first indications here, very early in the nineteenth century, appeared as a mere novelty in the beginning, but rapidly assumed a greater significance. Probably the first Gothic Revival building was Sedgley, the house Latrobe designed near Philadelphia in 1799. Mills designed a building for the Bank of Philadelphia in 1809 which had a Gothic front, and the next year Strickland turned out his Gothic Masonic Hall. Meanwhile, lesser architects were designing buildings and houses which followed conventional forms, except that they were tricked out with pointed arches and fussy finials. By the 1820's they had become quite common, and by the 1840's the movement was at its peak.

Washington Irving's "Sunnyside," on the Hudson River above Tarrytown, was an old Dutch stone farmhouse which he remodeled into a romantic and ivy-covered Gothic cottage. A so-called "English cottage style" was popularized by A. J. Downing in a book of

Robert Mills's Bank of Philadelphia was a strange Gothic.

house designs, which also included examples in the styles of the
Italian villa and the Swiss chalet. A. J. Davis designed several mansions with turrets and battlements, pointed arches and traceried windows, all carefully copied out of Pugin. It was all bastard Gothic,
yet it cannot be denied that many of these buildings have a singular
charm, especially those in wood, with their steep roofs and scrolled
gable ends, their high and narrow windows in the board walls with
batten strips over the joints, and their fanciful Gothic entrances and
porches, sometimes in scroll-sawed wood and sometimes in cast iron.

Out of this pseudo-Gothic hodgepodge, however, three men
appeared to design Gothic churches which, despite their obvious
faults, are beautiful even to today's critical eyes. And probably thanks
to them, the revived Gothic has remained the favorite, although by
no means the only, style for Christian churches. They are Richard
Upjohn, James Renwick, and none other than Minard Lafever.
Richard Upjohn was born in England in 1802 and came to America
in 1829, entering Bulfinch's office in Boston. Transferring to New
York, he received the commission in 1846 to design the new Trinity
Church on Broadway at Rector Street, in the English Perpendicular
style, which paved the way for many more. Upjohn was the first

president of the American Institute of Architects and the founder of a famous architectural family now in its fourth generation. James Renwick was New York born and educated, and in 1843 won the competition for the design of Grace Church, on Broadway at Tenth Street, when he was only twenty-five years old. The success of this richly beautiful little Episcopal church brought him several more churches and great fame, and during the 1850's he won the competition for the design of St. Patrick's Roman Catholic Cathedral on Fifth Avenue. Despite its coarse detail and plaster vaulting, this great church, more or less patterned after St. Ouen at Rouen, has many beauties and still holds its own against the tall buildings which surround it. Renwick also designed many hotels, theaters, and fashionable houses in New York, and the Smithsonian Institution in Washington.

PLATE 133

Minard Lafever started life as a carpenter in upstate New York, and after going to New York City in 1828 he worked as a draftsman for various builders. Finding this work unrewarding, he started on his famous books of Greek Revival details, which undoubtedly educated him to become the imaginative and creative artist he soon showed himself to be. During the 1840's he designed two churches in Brooklyn which showed that he had assimilated the Gothic style as thoroughly as he had the Greek, using its forms with the same exquisite taste and originality. These are the Church of the Holy Trinity and the Church of the Saviour. He also designed Packer Collegiate Institute and other buildings in both classical and Gothic styles, which have been destroyed.

As in the field of domestic architecture, the Gothic Revival left many of its most interesting churches in small towns. Side by side with the churches of the Greek Revival, stand little stone or wooden churches, their towers and pointed windows indicating that they are attempting to reflect some of the glories of the medieval past. They are usually simple buildings of the meetinghouse type, with a square tower at the front. In stone, they have tall and narrow pointed windows with wood tracery, the doorway through the tower may be recessed, enriched by a few mouldings, and the tower topped with battlements or a wood spire. A characteristic of the simpler frame churches is the use of vertical battens over the joints in the sheathing boards, and a few Gothic trimmings executed in wood. There are also some churches which naively combine both Greek and Gothic forms, resulting in windows with triangular heads and Colonial-type towers decorated with finials and bits of tracery. It is snobbery to subject these little buildings to harsh architectural criticism. They have virtues which are often lacking in more pretentious and archaeologically correct churches. Their charm lies in the fact that they are simple and honest building, created by a provincial people to fill their need, using what smatterings they had of traditional forms.

The Growth of Cities

THERE FIRST APPEARED IN CHICAGO IN 1833 A NEW METHOD OF house-building which was destined to change the face of America, by making possible the relatively quick and cheap erection of frame houses. The exact origins of the balloon frame are obscure, but its time and place are fairly definite, and from there it spread over the land, so that its use was almost universal by 1870. The invention of the balloon frame was of necessity preceded by the invention of machine-made nails, and improvements in sawmill machinery coincided with it.

The time-honored method of framing a house depended upon the use of heavy timbers with mortised and tenoned joints, held together with hardwood pegs, a method which was slow and becoming increasingly expensive. The balloon frame substituted the use of light strips of sawn lumber, pieces 2″ by 4″ being the standard for the framing of walls, extending through the entire height of the building, and held together entirely by nails. Such a framework could be rapidly assembled on the ground and then raised to an upright position by a few hands, which was probably the origin of the name. This method, together with the growing availability of sawn lumber and its widespread distribution by rail, made possible the building of houses by the thousands in the ever-expanding cities and the new industrial centers.

The beginning of the age of industrialism brought the founding and rapid growth of many new communities. The engineer took the place of the architect in the laying out of new cities, and at the behest of the promoter and the land speculator he laid out mile after mile of gridiron streets, with the land cut up into narrow lots which could be bought and sold and gambled with. Little thought was given to open spaces for recreation and settings for public buildings. Older cities which may have had the beginnings of a good plan were often robbed of it. Even the plan of Washington was disregarded by permitting the railroad to lay its tracks across the Mall, and by the placing of new government buildings in the center of it. Growth and the attraction of business, in order to increase land values, seemed to be the only function of a city, and the possibilities of growth seemed unlimited. The concept of a city as a healthy, convenient, and beautiful place in which to live and work occurred only to a few prophets who cried in vain.

Detroit went through stages in its growth which were typical of many cities. The old city was completely destroyed by fire in 1805, and a grandiose new plan was prepared for rebuilding. It was based upon intersecting radial streets, but carried to the point of absurdity. Twenty-five years later a new plan was adopted, omitting some of the radial avenues, and in 1853 a gridiron plan was established for the area surrounding the already built-up section, thus cutting off many of the radial avenues leading out from the congested downtown area. Fort Wayne, Indiana, is an example of a city which grew by the simple extension of its straight streets and square blocks from the original nucleus of the city on the banks of its two winding rivers. The result today is a neglected river front and a congested business district of narrow streets and high land values, with no means of expediting traffic to and away from the center. Buffalo, New York, was more fortunate, for its original plan of wide avenues radiating from Niagara Square was not completely lost, and as a result it has today a number of thoroughfares leading out from the center of the city, connecting with a system of parks and boulevards for which provision was wisely made long ago.

One great gain in American cities was the advent of public sewers and the provision of gas and water supplies. Although the use of backyard privies continued in some of the more solidly built-up cities, like Philadelphia, down to the present century, the water supply was no longer dependent upon individual wells. Gas was introduced for lighting into the better houses and all public and commercial buildings, and street lighting appeared. This last was an important step, for it made the public streets relatively safe for the first time from the footpads and hoodlums who had always roamed them under cover of darkness. One of the last improvements in the cities was the paving of the principal streets, which did not become general until the end of the century.

Age of Restlessness

THE GREEK AND THE GOTHIC REVIVALS WERE INDICATIVE OF THE restlessness which was becoming a part of the American nature, a malady, in fact, from which most of Europe was suffering too. At the root of this restlessness was a desire for permanence and stability, which manifested itself by a reaching into history for architectural expressions which, being age-old, might seem to offer a tie to the permanence and continuity of the past. Yet the gratification of this desire was thwarted by the swiftness with which fundamental changes took place, due to the rapid growth of invention and industry, and by a constant striving for novelty. Architects and people who thought about architecture were trying, first in one direction and then in another, to find or create overnight a style of architecture which would suit America and all its needs. Rapid growth and quick change had robbed the nation of the benefits of a slow maturing. The country abounded in anachronisms and contrasts. The shining new marble capitol of a mid-western state, with its great portico and gleaming dome, stood face-to-face with the ramshackle huts of the pioneers, surrounded by a sea of muddy roads. This is a disease from which we are still suffering. Time alone, with its generations of thoughtful men, will bring the answers to the architectural, as well as the social, problems which have plagued us since the acceleration of change wrought by the industrial revolution.

Modern architecture, like the modern architect, was born in the first half of the nineteenth century. New demands for new types of buildings were thrust upon the architect faster than he could give them serious thought. It was enough to solve the practical problem, and that he did well, the esthetic problem would have to wait. Within one generation the hotel grew from an unheated, unlighted, over-sized house, centering around a taproom, to Isaiah Rogers' luxurious palaces, heated, lighted, and equipped with conveniences which most guests had never dreamed of. These architects planned well, their hotels, banks, railroad stations, and factories were thoroughly practical and functioned well according to the needs of the day. Their application of an archaic architectural decoration to these new forms of buildings was the best that could be expected of them under the circumstances, for the changes were taking place so rapidly that no one mind could encompass their true meanings. A truly integrated and honest architecture could develop only with time. But it did not develop. The restlessness of the age swept the architects on and plunged them into the fripperies and absurdities of the post-Civil War era.

❈ XIV ❈

Civil War to Depression

THE CIVIL WAR accelerated the breaking up of architectural traditions, a process which had been going on for a long time. The war was followed in the industrial North and Middle West by periods of prosperity and expansion, interrupted by depressions and panics. Every year hundreds of thousands of hopeful immigrants arrived to furnish manpower for the ever-increasing mills, mines, and factories. The concentration of thousands of families in industrial areas created housing and social problems which still exist. Rows upon rows of flimsy houses were thrown together to accommodate the workers, and with the exception of a few in New England, the mill-owners felt that the problem had been taken care of. City tenements crowded as many people as possible into as little space as possible, often with interior rooms with no windows at all. Speed and greed seem to have become the controlling motives in industrial life, and industrial life was becoming the very life of the nation. Great buildings were needed, but they were needed quickly and cheaply, for tomorrow's changes might render them obsolete and appearances did not matter. The architect lost ground to the engineer, whose training equipped him to solve structural and mechanical problems rapidly and economically, without particular regard for esthetic or social consequences.

The rise of the engineer was partly due to the development of the use of iron, and later steel, for building construction. During the 1840's mills had been built with cast-iron columns and beams to support the floor construction, and when wrought-iron beams were manufactured a decade later, they made possible the design of trusses and built-up girders, satisfying the demands of the railroads for cheap and quickly fabricated bridges, and of the manufacturers for wide floor areas without the obstruction of columns and piers. All this became the engineer's work, and as a result there gradually grew a cleavage between the work of the architect and the work of the engineer. The architect had developed from the master builder, but in this new rush for purely utilitarian structures he was no longer the master. Beauty was the last concern of the engineer, yet when a piece of engineering was carried to its perfect solution it was inevitably beautiful, as evidenced by Roebling's Brooklyn Bridge, which was begun in 1869, and Eiffel's tower in Paris, 1889.

Out of this industrial scramble grew the great corporations and vast personal fortunes which became such controlling factors in the American scene for the next two generations. One step below them were the thousands of newly rich men who dominated their own industry or their own city, and it was these men who, directly or indirectly, were to be the clients of the architects of the future. Education, beyond their most immediate needs, had not been necessary to them to attain their position, and it was not until they relaxed their push and drive that they began to realize that perhaps they had missed something. The parvenu in search of a background, and willing to pay good money for it, thus became the patron of the architect.

With a few exceptions, the architect of the post-Civil War period was little different from his clients. Since both the tradition of the architect as master builder and the tradition of the amateur architect had broken down, men of training and skill in architecture were rare. The first school of architecture in the country was established in 1866 at the Massachusetts Institute of Technology, to be followed in a few years by schools at Illinois, Cornell, Columbia, and Harvard. But it was still to be several years before the graduates of these schools could acquire the experience to assume leadership. The small handful of men who had traveled abroad or studied at the École des Beaux Arts in Paris were the only men who had the equipment to meet the task. And they, too, were only products of their time, torn between the traditions of the past and the demands of the present, between what they knew to be right and good in architecture and what they knew their clients expected of them.

The architecture of the more important buildings of the period from 1865 to 1895 was subject to two major influences from abroad. One was the continuing Gothic Revival in England, which through the persuasive writing of Ruskin, and the revolt of the artists of the Pre-Raphaelite Brotherhood, had grown into a full-fledged rebellion against classicism. William Morris' attempts to re-establish the medieval crafts, and his protests against the characterless products of the machine, had aroused a wide following among intellectuals and artists, including such architects as Philip Webb and Norman Shaw, who designed country houses which were medieval in form, and also attempted to recapture the medieval delight in the beauty and texture of hand-wrought materials. Their work was thoroughly romantic and the antithesis of the products of the new machine age.

The other influences came from Paris, which was again being rebuilt. Work on the Louvre had been resumed, to complete the scheme begun over three centuries before; the style of the new work was a rich and elegant classicism, new in spirit yet harmonizing with the old. Charles Garnier designed the great Opera, supremely logical in its planning and conception, basically classical in its use of traditional forms, and richly sculptural in its magnificent decoration. It represented the very best of modern architecture as taught by the École des Beaux Arts. Under the direction of Baron Haussmann, new boulevards had been cut through the center of the city to relieve congestion, and encircling boulevards were built on the sites of the old city walls, thus creating new sites for public buildings, monuments, and fountains. Yet the new architecture of France was eclectic too. Buildings were built following the Gothic, Romanesque, and Byzantine styles, such as the church of Sacré Coeur, which lifts its white domes above the heights of Montmartre.

Other countries of Europe were following with great buildings in the free classical style, such as the florid Imperial Museums in Vienna, the picturesque city hall in Leipzig, and the huge Palais de Justice in Brussels. Already the influence of the École des Beaux Arts was being felt, in the old capitals of Europe and the new capitals of

PLATE 134

South America, as young architects came home and attempted to recreate some of the splendors they had seen and helped to build in Paris. It was inevitable that some of this influence should reach the United States.

Another influence working on the American architect was the client himself. The grand tour of Europe had become an essential to everyone who aspired to any degree of culture, and after the parvenu, and especially his wife, had visited Paris, Venice, and Florence, he came home full of vague recollections of the gardens of Versailles, the palazzos of Venice, and the villas of Tuscany, and the desire to recreate them at home. Furthermore, with his hastily acquired background in such matters, he saw no reason why he should not have some of the more delightful features of several of these styles all in one building, and cheap too, for so much fine marble and carved stone could easily be imitated in wood, cast iron, and sheet metal.

Late Victorian Buildings

ECLECTICISM MEANS A REACHING HERE AND THERE FOR PARTS OR for ideas. It had come into American architecture with the Greek and Gothic Revivals, and it apparently came to stay. The peak of eclecticism occurred during the early 1900's, and the reaction against it began slowly to get under way during the 1930's, although the first revolts came forty years earlier. The eclecticism of the post-Civil War period had many fantastic results, and a few which were fine in spite of their period.

The first Grand Central Station in New York was opened in 1871. The trains came into a great train shed two hundred feet wide, roofed with arched iron trusses covered with glass. This was fronted by a three-story building of red brick with stone and cast-iron trim, in the French manner, with tall pavilions topped with bulging curved mansard roofs with dormers. In Boston, the old Museum of Fine   PLATE 135 Arts was designed by one of the city's most distinguished architects in the Gothic style. The almost continuous windows of the first floor had pointed arches resting on slender colonnettes, the brickwork of the blank second-story wall was paneled with stone, and the roof broke out into a picturesque silhouette of gables, dormers, and finials.

The city hall in Buffalo was designed in a more or less Romanesque style in 1876. There were little round towers at each of the many corners, terminating in turrets, tall narrow windows with round arches, and a massive fortress-like tower with machicolations, projecting turreted corners, and a lumpy clock tower covered with slate.

Philadelphia's city hall is a huge and restless pile of superposed orders and mansard roofs begun in 1872, topped by a tower 548 feet high on which stands a gigantic figure of William Penn. Designed by John McArthur, Jr., it was thirty years abuilding. Thus, public buildings nearly everywhere were built to be as showy as possible, with little regard to what was fitting or traditional. Be it said, however, on behalf of the federal and state governments, that in general they stuck quite successfully to a classical style. The federal buildings and the state capitols are often heavy and ornate, but they seldom wandered too far from the basic type originated by Jefferson and the architects of the early republic. Even the new capitol at Hartford, Connecticut, designed by the son of Richard Upjohn and completed in 1880, retained the classical form and a tall domed cupola, though the detail of the building is Gothic.

PLATE 136   The greatest variety appears in the houses of the time. There is the "Italian Style," which was usually an L-shaped house with a square tower in the angle. It stands high, with tall and narrow windows, and arched porch under the tower; there may be projecting balconies and canopies at some of the second-story windows, and widely overhanging eaves and gable ends supported by jigsawed wood brackets. The tower runs up into a third and sometimes a fourth story, with a low hipped roof. Every so often one of these houses has an air of quiet dignity, with simple well-spaced windows and a classic cornice, but usually they are restless and striving. Then there is the "Gothic Style," Victorian Gothic, it should be called, to separate it from the quaint houses of the earlier Gothic Revival. In this style irregular masses break out into a jumble of steep roofs, gables, dormers, and cupolas, all with wide overhangs tricked out with a pseudo-structural network of carved and turned posts and beams supported on fancy brackets. The roofs are of slate, with patterns worked in red and blue. The windows are high and narrow, often completely darkened on the first floor by wide porches surrounding the house, offering another opportunity for turned posts, carved brackets, and spiky finials. It is difficult to find one of these houses about which anything good can be said.

The "French Style" was perhaps the most popular. A stone city   PLATE 138 house in this style, influenced by the misunderstood elegance of the work of Charles Garnier, has a certain heavy dignity, but it is also ponderous and ugly. The walls of the first story may be rusticated, with strange carvings about the large plate-glass windows. There is a heavy stringcourse at the second-floor level, and the windows above are framed with stumpy Corinthian-type columns and a caricature of an entablature. Above a heavy cornice rises a mansard roof, covered with patterned slate and ending in another cornice, this time of sheet metal and topped by an iron railing with spikes and curlicues. The projecting entrance pavilion forms a tower, with a series of grotesque superposed orders, and ending at the top in another steep mansard roof, with a crown of sheet-metal garlands and cornices and iron spikes. Frame houses in the same style show less restraint, for the cheaper and more workable material afforded an even greater opportunity for the use of bays, brackets, quoins, finials, and pilasters, none of them simple forms, but all of them carved, chamfered, and jigsawed into the most elaborate and unusual forms imaginable.   PLATE 139 These houses stood well back from the street, with a driveway sweeping up through the porte-cochere, a cast-iron fountain in front, and cast-iron deer and dogs and beds of cannas scattered about the immaculate lawn.

There is an enjoyable exuberance and vigor to all these houses, despite their lack of more architectural virtues. They are the perfect expressions of what Veblen called "conspicuous display." Each house   PLATE 137 tried to eclipse its neighbors by being taller and more elaborate. The interiors are in the same spirit as the exteriors. There is an entrance hall, with a reception room on one side and a parlor on the other. The hall widens into a stair hall in the center of the house, with a passage leading to a side entrance. Back of the stair hall is a library, in the center is the sitting room, and on the other side is the dining room. Off to the side are dark passages leading to a nursery, kitchen, butler's pantry, laundry, servants' rooms, and service stairs. Upstairs are five or six bedrooms of irregular shapes, a private bath, and a hall bath.

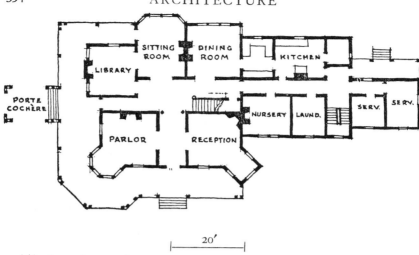

The late nineteenth-century house was spreading and spacious, but its plan lacked convenience and order.

The multiplicity of rooms would not in itself be bad, if there were any possible need for them all, but there is neither convenience nor order in their arrangement.

The ceilings are high, doors and windows are tall and narrow, often with panes of colored glass, and the marble mantels have small arched openings for the cast-iron grates. Woodwork is of walnut or oak, dark and heavy, chamfered, turned and carved in a clumsy style known as "Eastlake," after the English architect who originated it. The wallpaper is striped or diaper-patterned, the cornice is a heavy moulded cove, and in the center of the ceiling is an elaborate plaster rosette from which hangs the gaslit chandelier, with brass chains, crystal pendants, and etched and colored glass globes.

There were a few rays of light in this architectural dark age, and one of them was Richard Morris Hunt. Of a well-to-do Vermont family, Hunt was one of the first Americans to study at the École des Beaux Arts and work in the office of a Parisian architect. He returned to New York in 1855 and practiced for forty years, trying, together with a few kindred spirits, to uphold the traditions of the art of architecture and the standards of the profession. He achieved great success as an architect of fashion, and received every possible honor. He became the architect for the rising dynasties of the financial aristocracy, designing homes on Fifth Avenue, palaces in North Carolina, and villas in Newport for the Vanderbilts, the Astors, and the Goelets. Often falling into the popular mansard roof vernacular, Hunt nevertheless never forgot his training, and gave his clients houses which were costly and ostentatious, but always grammatical and well composed. Standing until forty years ago were two houses nearly opposite each other on Fifth Avenue, which showed both his eclecticism and his good taste. The W. K. Vanderbilt House was an exquisite French   PLATE 140 mansion in the style of Francis I, with the delicate traceries and classic stringcourses of the period, corbeled turrets and oriels, and steep roof with great stone *lucarnes*. The other house was a double house known as the "Marble Twins," four stories of white marble classicism, with an arched and rusticated ground floor, two-story Corinthian pilasters and a great modillioned cornice with a balustrade above.

Another ray of light was Henry Hobson Richardson. "Light" is the last word that could be applied to his architecture, for it was dark and ponderous to an extreme, but in his sincere originality there was a great deal of light and hope for the future. He was born in Louisiana, graduated from Harvard in 1859, and spent several years in Paris at the Beaux Arts and in architects' offices. His first works were churches in the Gothic style, and in 1872 he won the competition for the design of Trinity Church, Phillips Brooks's great church   PLATE 142 in Boston. His finally completed design was a sensation which swept the country. It is in a highly personalized Romanesque style, cruciform in plan with a massive central tower. The mass and composition are superb, and the detail is appropriate, well-placed and lovely. The interior glows richly with subdued color, there being murals by John LaFarge and stained-glass windows designed by Sir Edwin Burne-Jones of the Pre-Raphaelite Brotherhood and executed by William Morris and LaFarge. Thenceforth commissions were showered upon Richardson from all over the country, particularly the growing and culture-seeking Middle West, for libraries, railroad stations, court houses, business buildings, college buildings, and residences. His style   PLATE 141 is low and massive, with "rock faced" stone walls, small and deeply set windows, heavy arches, no cornices, round towers with conical roofs, and a minimum of ornament. Its virtues lie in its fine sense of mass and its absolute honesty of materials, for Richardson would stand for no shams.

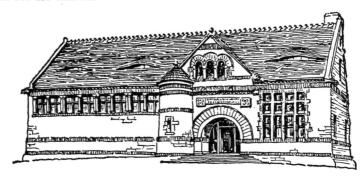

The Crane Memorial Library at Quincy, Massachusetts, is typical of Richardson's personal Romanesque style.

Richardson's warehouse building for Marshall Field in Chicago was a skyscraper in its time, and exerted a great influence upon later design. It was seven stories high, which was about as high as the exterior walls could be carried in solid masonry, without such excessive thickness at the ground floor as to be economically impractical. The interior walls and floors were supported by iron beams and cast-iron columns, but the principle of supporting the exterior walls in such a manner had not yet been fully developed. Richardson died while only forty-eight, having popularized a new style, the "Richardson Romanesque," which in the hands of his imitators degenerated into just another bad style. But the greatest benefits of his influence came from the impress of his vital and rugged personality on the young men who surrounded him, and his constant war against the debased standards of the jerry-builders, with their tricks of cheap imitation and gimcrack ornaments. He was at heart a builder, not a decorator, which probably accounts for his turning to the Romanesque, it being an unformed and elemental style with no rules of grammar and etiquette, which he felt he could shape into a style suitable for the as yet unformed culture of his own country. That he had a true feeling for the basic quality of functionalism is indicated by his remark to his biographer: "The things I want most to design are a grain elevator and the interior of a great river steamboat."

PLATE 143

The first step in the architectural education of the American people, although it was not intended as such, was the Centennial Exposition in Philadelphia in 1876, one of the first of the "World's Fairs." The majority of the buildings were no better than the taste of the times, and they were arranged with little thought for grouping or monumental effect. Still, they were great buildings—the main exhibition building was 1880 feet long and 465 feet wide—and the beautiful exhibits of the foreign countries opened the eyes of the 10,164,489 American visitors to the art and products of the rest of the world. Furthermore, one or two of the buildings of the exposition, such as Horticultural Hall and especially the Fine Arts Building, were well designed in the classical style, and helped to pave the way for what was to come. For the battle of the styles was nearly over, and the classical was about to be declared the winner.

The First Skyscrapers

IRON HAD BEEN USED IN THE CONSTRUCTION OF FACTORIES AND WARE-houses since the 1840's, and by means of brick arches resting on iron beams a type of construction was developed which was considered "fireproof." Steel beams and columns began to come into use after 1875. Paxton's famous "Crystal Palace," erected for the Exhibition of 1851 in London, was a great iron framework covered with glass, like a gigantic greenhouse. Several such structures were built in the United States in connection with fairs and exhibitions. A number of disastrous fires in these iron-framed buildings taught the engineers and architects the fallacy of the "fireproof" building. A beam of iron or steel will not burn, but heat so weakens it that it deforms and collapses. A wood beam may often burn halfway through before it will collapse. Thus the lesson was learned that iron and steel must be protected with a covering of masonry to insulate them from the heat of fire.

Elevators had been in use in factories in Europe since the 1820's, but it was not until 1852 that Elisha Otis perfected a safety device to prevent the car from falling, which made elevators safe to use in buildings higher than two or three stories. Edison had not only invented the electric light in 1879, but he had also developed the central generating plant and the underground cable, making possible the distribution of power without overhead wires. The principle of heating buildings by passing steam through pipes was first expounded by Tredgold in 1836, and had had many successful adaptations. Systems of water supply and sewage disposal were already installed in all principal cities. Urban congestion had increased land values to such a point that landowners were crying for more income out of their properties, but six or seven stories seemed to be the structural-economic limit of the height of buildings. The stage was all set for the skyscraper. But nobody stopped to think what the effect would be on the transportation facilities and living conditions of a city if a thousand people were crowded onto the same plot of ground that had held a hundred before.

The Home Insurance Building in Chicago, designed by W. L. Jenney and begun in 1884, seems to have been the first building employing true skeleton frame construction. It was twelve stories high, and the street fronts received a simple treatment more or less Romanesque in style. The new principle that made the height possible was that the exterior walls were supported at each floor by iron beams, which were in turn supported by iron columns encased in masonry piers. Thus the walls supported nothing but their own weight, and since each separate wall section was only one story high, they needed only enough thickness to keep out the weather, eight to twelve inches. All the great loads of the structure were supported on the iron columns, which could be small enough not to interfere with the precious floor space. The basic similarity to the principle of rib and pier of Gothic architecture is obvious. This fundamental change came about so suddenly that few architects realized that they had an entirely new system of construction at their disposal, which called for a new expression in architectural design. The principle of eclecticism and of veneering the fronts of buildings with fragments of the historical styles had become so deeply rooted that most designers went right on, digging deeper into their books to find more Romanesque or classic details to spread over the façades that were now rising twenty and more stories in the air.

There was at least one architect, however, who gave a great deal of thought to the esthetic implications of the revolution which had come into building construction, and he was Louis Henri Sullivan.

He had been born in Boston, and after reaching manhood he drifted about for several years, including a year or two at the École in Paris, before he went to Chicago in about 1879, still in his early twenties. Soon becoming a partner in the firm of Adler and Sullivan, he designed many buildings in the fast-growing city, which was still recovering from the fire of '71 and the panic of '73. He was influenced by the integrity of Richardson's work, and during the 1880's he gradually evolved his own version of Richardson's Romanesque, a style less heavy and more suitable to tall buildings. He also devised a very beautiful system of foliate ornament in low relief, executed in terra cotta, which was fully expressive of the fact that it was a surface veneer. His first skeleton frame building was the Wainwright Build-   PLATE 144 ing in St. Louis, 1891, in which he achieved the appearance of light-ness by accenting the vertical piers, which also served to suggest the columns behind them. The base of the building is quite plain, and the top has a rich terra cotta frieze modeled in Sullivan's characteristic flat foliate ornament. By 1899, in the building now occupied by the Carson Pirie Scott department store in Chicago, Sullivan showed the   PLATE 145 full development of his theory that the design of a building should express its construction and its function. The store building is a per-fect expression of the skeleton frame which supports it. Neither hor-izontal nor vertical lines are emphasized, although the horizontals predominate because the beams are spaced more closely than the columns. The amount of masonry surrounding the steel frame is re-duced to a minimum, and the spaces between are all windows. The first two floors, being visible from the street, are a veneer of plate glass and delicate cast-iron ornament, and the cornice at the top is only a slim projecting member. It was the first building in what is today proudly called the "Modern" style, and Louis Sullivan is con-sidered to have been the father of the "Modern" movement. For a few years he had a great influence in the Midwest, and it began to look as though Chicago might be the birthplace of a new style of architecture, not only truly expressive of its day but also truly expres-sive of America.

However, Sullivan's forms were doomed to be superseded soon by the classical style, and his theories to be not understood. His now-famous slogan, "Form follows function," fell unheeded on all but a few ears. With the great popularity of the classical style, Sullivan's commissions gradually faded away, and a few minor buildings in the Middle West are all that there were after 1900. Forgotten by all but a few, he lived on until 1924. Today his buildings and more particularly his words are the gospel of the new generation.

There were two other firms of architects who wielded great influence in these formative days of modern American architecture, one in Chicago and one in New York. The Chicago firm was Burnham and Root, led by Daniel H. Burnham, a great executive and a man of fine appreciations, but not a designer. This lack was made up by the brilliant accomplishments of his partner. The firm had the largest practice in the country, following along in the Romanesque fashion of the time, yet somewhat timidly trying out some of Sullivan's theories. The New York firm was McKim, Mead and White, a great organization which led and dominated the classical architectural tradition in the country until the middle of the 1920's. Both McKim and White had studied at the École and had worked for Richardson, but they chose to work in the classic and Renaissance styles.

The Chicago World's Fair

THE CHICAGO WORLD'S FAIR, PROPERLY KNOWN AS THE World's Columbian Exposition of 1893, was what finally turned the tide in favor of classicism, and sounded the death knell for Victorian Gothic, Richardson Romanesque, and Louis Sullivan. Here in this great formal grouping of gleaming white classical buildings, magnificently set among lagoons and fountains, the American people saw architecture in the grand manner for the first time. They came, they marveled and they went home, and in a very few years the country was sprinkled with classical façades, towering buildings with temples on top, and formal groups of civic buildings struggling to assert themselves amid straggling slums and warehouses. The exposition was a triumph which profoundly affected the entire course of American architecture. It resulted in countless wonderful and beautiful buildings during the next four decades, yet there are those who say it was a calamity which stopped the progress of American architecture, binding it with the shackles of a beautiful but dead classicism, and stifling all originality and logical growth.

The organizing genius of Daniel H. Burnham was responsible for directing the designing and construction of the fair buildings. Five of the best firms of architects in the country were called in to design the principal buildings, including Richard M. Hunt and McKim, Mead and White; and five Chicago architects, one of them Louis Sullivan. Frederick L. Olmsted was the landscape architect. All agreed on the basic elements of the great plan, but when the discussion turned to style it was apparent immediately that the cards were stacked by the architects from the East who favored the classical style instead of following Chicago's more progressive trends. Sullivan argued in vain. It was voted that the exposition was to be classical, with uniform cornice heights, and all buildings were to be white.

Burnham appointed Augustus Saint-Gaudens to take charge of the sculpture and Frank Millet to take charge of mural painting. Each man was at the top of his field, and called in the best talent in the country. As a result, the fair was not only a great artistic achievement; it represented a collaboration of all three of the arts such as had rarely been seen since the height of the Renaissance in Europe. Thus PLATE 146 it was an even greater lesson to the public, most of whom had never seen any great painting or sculpture, especially in combination with architecture. The architecture of the exposition was magnificent, of course, although today much of it would seem trite and over-decorated. But it must be judged against its time, and from that point of view, triumph or calamity, it was still magnificent.

And Louis Sullivan? The architectural commission made a special exception in his case, and permitted him to use his own style and his own color. His Transportation Building was the one truly original PLATE 147 building at the fair, and a great popular as well as artistic success. There were no orders and no domes. The flat façade was treated in colored stucco as frankly a veneer, making no attempt to look like permanent marble, as in the other buildings. And the great golden arch of the entrance, with its delicately modeled surface ornament, was a new and beautiful form. Sullivan was not as articulate as many of his later followers have been, but his autobiography shows that he was deeply concerned not only with the esthetic implications of the new system of construction, but with its social effects as well. He was concerned with what the skyscraper and its resultant congestion were going to do to humanity. He had a profound belief in American democracy—he was an architectural Walt Whitman—and he was striving for a form of architecture which would express American ideals. One cannot but wonder what the fair would have been, and what the future of American architecture would have been if Louis Sullivan had been the guiding spirit instead of Burnham and McKim.

Modern Buildings Were Clothed in the Styles of the Past

TO FOLLOW THE PROGRESS OF AMERICAN ARCHITECTURE THROUGH the first quarter of the twentieth century would involve a long list of celebrated names and a longer list of great buildings, for once the path was chosen it was followed with a vigor that may never be equaled. By 1900 there were hundreds of competent architects in all the cities of the country. The means of a sound architectural education had been multiplied by the establishment of schools of architecture in colleges and universities everywhere. As a more strictly classical balance to the École des Beaux Arts in Paris, Charles F. McKim had been instrumental in founding the American Academy at Rome in 1894. Both of these great schools admitted many American students every year, and offered scholarships for which there were annual competitions among young architects. For those who could not go to college, the graduates of the École established the Beaux Arts Institute of Design, which conducted a full course in architectural design for men employed in architects' offices. In all major cities there was at least one atelier, with a local graduate of the École as patron, where practicing architects gave their time night after night to help train the younger men, in an atmosphere of enthusiastic camaraderie similar to that of the ateliers of Paris. To work a few years in the office of one of the great architects, and to travel and sketch for a few months in Europe, was the goal of every young architect in the country, and thousands of them achieved it. Returning to their home cities they carried on unquestioningly in the tradition they had been taught, most of them in mediocre fashion, a few of them with brilliance. The architect had regained his position of leadership.

McKim, Mead and White continued in pre-eminence, so much so that books devoted to their work were used as references in the schools of architecture, side by side with the books of classic and Renaissance architecture. The building which had first brought them prominence was the Boston Public Library, completed in 1895, a modified version of a library in Paris which had been built twenty years before. In New York there is the University Club, 1900, at Fifth Avenue and Fifty-fourth Street, a magnificent Florentine palace; and the Pennsylvania Railroad Station, completed in 1910, a great Roman bath of tremendous scale. Yes, McKim, Mead and White were copyists, but what splendid copyists! Their taste and their skill never faltered, and every one of their works is as near perfection as a piece of classic or Renaissance architecture could be.

PLATE 149

PLATE 148

Classical buildings dotted the streets of every city. Skyscrapers were coated with superposed orders, or designed on the principle of the column, with a heavy base, a plain "shaft" extending upward for many stories, and a "capital" consisting of decorated upper stories and a huge projecting cornice. And all their beautiful detail was copied out of the books of ancient buildings.

The French school of classicism had its followers too, in the architects who designed in the manner of the late French Renaissance. Their work was apt to have more originality and vigor, but since it was less bound by the rules of academicism it was also apt to run to the garish and over-ornate. One of the finest examples of the work of this group is the Grand Central Station in New York, 1914, designed by Warren and Wetmore. The functional planning and spatial conception is superb, and its great concourse has tremendous scale and dignity, making it one of the finest interiors of any age. The New York Public Library, by Carrère and Hastings, is a beautiful example of the French Renaissance style at its best. But there are also many buildings in which Beaux Arts vigor was uncontrolled, overloaded with great cartouches, garlands, and fantastic copper cornices and roof ornaments.

PLATE 150

With the Woolworth Building, completed in 1913, a new note came into American eclecticism, a note which was radical at the time. Designed to be the tallest building in the world, Cass Gilbert conceived it on the lines of a Gothic cathedral tower. Reasoning that by

PLATE 151

its very height the skyscraper tends to soar, he emphasized the vertical lines to make it appear to soar all the more. It may be just as illogical to dress a modern building in Gothic as it is in Doric, but the result is certainly more unified and more beautiful. Thenceforth, many tall buildings appeared in Gothic dress.

In the field of church design the leaders were Cram, Goodhue and Ferguson. Cram was a Gothic scholar, Goodhue a creative designer. Their churches are equal to the finest in Europe, old or modern, and they are built in true Gothic construction, with no plaster PLATE 152 "vaulting." Their works include St. Thomas' Church, in New York, the chapel and other buildings at the United States Military Academy at West Point, the First Baptist Church in Pittsburgh and the Episcopal Cathedral of Maryland at Baltimore. Ten years before Goodhue's premature death in 1924, he broke away from his partners and designed many more churches, residences, and public buildings in his personalized version of the Gothic and the Spanish Renaissance styles. Several of his buildings show that his creative mind was working toward a new and definite style which did not turn its back upon the past, but rather assimilated and synthesized it. Examples of his work in this spirit are the Los Angeles Public Library, the National PLATE 154 Academy of Sciences at Washington, and the Nebraska State Capitol.

Colleges went in for great campus plans and groups of buildings in beautiful and expensive styles, such as the incredible but exquisite Gothic Harkness Quadrangle at Yale and the fine Georgian buildings at Harvard. For some reason, public-school buildings seem to have run to either the Colonial or the Jacobean styles, the latter lending itself particularly well to the large banks of windows that were needed. Moving picture theaters went in for everything from the perfectly beautiful to the utterly fantastic, but always rich and lush. The theory seems to have been that since the movie is a dream world, the architecture of the theater must be as lavish and unworldly as possible. In the vast field of industrial buildings the engineer usually held sway, but sometimes the architect was permitted to come in with his cornices or pointed arches. However, the work of Albert Kahn on the buildings for the Ford Motor Company in Detroit, and of Cass Gilbert on the United States Army Base in Brooklyn, showed that some architects could restrain their hand and let simple mass and functional openings dominate.

Apartment houses were nothing new, for multi-family dwellings of several stories had been built in ancient Rome and ever since. But they took on a new importance in American urban life, and their growth was one of the most typically American aspects of early twentieth-century architecture. From the three-story six-family walk-ups of the suburbs and small cities, to the great twenty-story de luxe apartments covering half a city block, they created a new way of living, and a way of living which thousands of families seemed to prefer. Probably at least half of the apartment houses built were not put up in congested areas where there was an economic justification for them; they were built in areas where there was plenty of space and low-cost land, because there was a demand from families who preferred them to houses. They were planned with great skill, from the standpoint of getting the maximum amount of rental out of a given area of land, but most of them were failures as adequate human abodes. Handsome façades, marble foyers, and uniformed doormen were poor substitutes for fresh air, sunshine, and space for recreation.

Structural and mechanical engineers were far ahead of the architects. The structural system of a skyscraper, the heating, ventilating, plumbing, and electrical systems of a city hotel, were incredibly intricate, but the engineers produced solutions for every problem which were efficient and clear-cut. The absurdity of clothing these structurally and mechanically perfect machines in terra cotta and plaster Romanesque, Spanish Renaissance, or Louis XIV ornaments seemed to occur to few people. Building construction had become a highly organized assembly procedure, requiring the architects and the general contractors to maintain large and efficient organizations. All of the structural and mechanical parts of a building, and much of the decoration and fittings, were fabricated in remote factories, delivered to the job according to a predetermined schedule, and assembled into the building. The amount of on-the-job handcraft that went into a building was very small, and was confined to such elemental trades as bricklaying and plastering. Even in the factories, with modern methods of production, the amount of hand labor was kept as low as possible. So the erection of a large building became an assembly job, and the individual workman lost contact with the job as a whole, with a consequent loss of pride and quality in workmanship.

The use of reinforced concrete for building construction became more general. It had been highly developed in the construction of dams, bridges, and industrial plants, and by the mid-1920's it was sometimes applied to buildings ten or twelve stories high. In Europe concrete was frequently used for fine finished work, such as thin projecting balconies and canopies, slender spiral staircases, and even for the entire structure of a church. But in the United States its use was for the most part still confined to the elaborate footings and underpinnings often necessary, and to warehouses and an occasional apartment house. It proved itself, however, a material of great potential possibilities.

Domestic Architecture

IN THE FIELD OF DOMESTIC ARCHITECTURE THERE WAS A TREMENDOUS improvement during the first quarter-century. As mechanical appliances for the home improved and multiplied, the standards of home planning were raised higher and higher, until the average American small house had more comforts and greater privacy than the homes of the wealthy had had a generation before. That the average home was not better built than its predecessors was due to the fact that probably seventy-five per cent of them were built by speculative builders. That the average home was of mediocre design was due to the fact that the post-Civil War period was still only one generation behind, the period when the continuity of the American architectural tradition had been broken, and architects, builders, and their public alike all lost their heads in a scramble for novelty and display.

However, good taste in house design began to reappear occasionally during the 1880's and the 1890's, in picturesque houses which were free from any "style" tags. In shingle and stone, they had irregular roofs, circular towers, and spreading porches with wide shingled arches. The plans were spacious and open, and there were abundant windows. Many of the early McKim, Mead and White houses were in this picturesque and comfortable style. The typical suburban house of 1900 was a frame house, although it may have had a stone tower with a candle-snuffer roof. There were still many gables and dormers, often widely overhanging. There was a porch which extended around two or even three sides of the house, and it was apt to have classical columns and a railing with Renaissance balusters. In fact, there was quite a fashion for the "Colonial" house for a few PLATE 153 years, but the word *Colonial* applied only to details which were lavishly applied to basically picturesque houses—gate posts with urns, porches with rich entablatures, elaborately detailed Post-Colonial entrances, and Palladian windows in the peaks of the gables. The interiors had imposing staircases with turned balusters and handsome newels, and chimneypieces with full columns and delicate composition ornament. The plans of the houses, however, were more sensible than their exteriors, with wide openings, large windows without muntins, many projecting bays, and large and sunny rooms. These houses are "old-fashioned" today, but they were well-planned for their time and are still comfortable.

In the decades before and after the first World War, eclecticism reached its greatest height in domestic architecture. With two or three possible exceptions, there were no traces of regional traditions. Colonial houses, Tudor houses, Spanish houses, French houses, were built everywhere from New York to California. Yet, beneath their archaeological skins, they were all basically alike. In a land where a traveler could eat the same breakfast foods, see the same billboards, buy the same hats, and read the same news, in cities three thousand miles apart, he could also visit in the same houses. Mass education, mass advertising, mass circulation of magazines, and mass production of building materials and accessories were responsible for that. In the north-eastern states, especially in New England, the Colonial house was the most popular, for there was a natural feeling that it belonged there, even though many a man who built one had no colonial ancestors. In southern California the Spanish colonial tradition survived, as it should, for it had a traditional meaning there. In southern Florida, which did not begin to grow until the promoters took it over early in the 1920's, the Spanish style was resurrected from the seventeenth century, to which it had some traditional claim. However, at least half of the houses built had no style whatsoever, and never came from an architect's drawing board. They were just plain houses, square little boxes with porches, forthright and functional even though dull, and as such they were better architecture than many more pretentious and expensive attempts at "style."

However, in the homes of the wealthy and the well-to-do, there was a great deal of beauty. In the New York area, Dwight James Baum set a high standard with his smaller Colonial houses, Delano and Aldrich's exquisitely studied Georgian houses are as fine architecture as has ever been done, John Russell Pope took time off from his classical buildings to design picturesquely beautiful Elizabethan mansions, and Harrie T. Lindeberg designed original and romantic houses which exhibit a medieval delight in textured materials and irregular forms. Around Philadelphia, Mellor, Meigs and Howe's houses and farm groups, built in the local stone, recall the rural charm of Normandy and Brittany.

In Florida, Addison Mizner was one of the architects responsible for the nostalgic beauty of Spanish cloisters and red tile roofs, and in Chicago, David Adler showed his perfect taste and refined detail in houses in the style of eighteenth-century France. If a medal were to be awarded to the area which maintained the highest standard in domestic architecture, it would probably go to southern California. The free and modernized version of the Spanish colonial which was evolved there is suitable, usually simple and restrained, and often very beautiful. Bertram Goodhue of New York, who had a home there, was one of the men responsible for the development of the style, which was carried on by Reginald Johnson, George Washington Smith, and many others.

In domestic architecture, more than in any other field of architecture, these traditional styles are by now deeply rooted in the hearts of the American people. Although a new style has developed, based upon new planning concepts and new materials and new uses for old materials, and even though the new developments are taking place in domestic architecture more rapidly than in other fields, it will remain the field of architecture in which tradition will die the hardest, if ever.

City Planning

ACTIVITY IN CITY PLANNING WAS STIMULATED ALL OVER THE country by the revival of L'Enfant's plan for Washington. In 1900 Congress appointed a commission with Burnham as chairman, and composed of McKim, Saint-Gaudens, and F. L. Olmsted, Jr. They drew up a plan which improved and extended L'Enfant's plan, accommodating it to the great modern city which Washington had grown to be. The Pennsylvania Railroad was persuaded to remove its station from the center of the Mall and reroute its tracks. A new station was built, designed by Burnham, in back of the Capitol. Old government buildings obstructing the clean sweep of the Mall were to be replaced with new classical structures along the sides, facing upon it. A memorial to Abraham Lincoln was to be built at the river end of the long axis—the later Lincoln Memorial, designed by Henry Bacon. And so through the years the plan for Washington has gradually taken shape, making the center of the capital of our country one of the handsomest groups of buildings in the world. The fact that it is bordered by slums and its avenues choked with traffic is only typical of our country. We are just beginning to catch up on such matters. The Washington plan is a Renaissance conception of broad avenues, magnificent vistas, and great buildings. That used to be all there was to city planning. The automobile and the social conscience were to come later.

Chicago, Cleveland, Denver, and other cities adopted city plans, meaning that they planned monumental groups of civic buildings and laid out parks and playgrounds. This was the "City Beautiful" movement. Gradually, however, the evil of the slums became so apparent that the larger cities were forced to undertake slum clearance programs, building in their stead fireproof and sanitary apartments, with playgrounds and space for the free circulation of air and sunshine. The extreme congestion of traffic caused by the concentration of so many people in such small areas led many cities to condemn and clear built-up land in order to build avenues and parkways to move traffic faster to and from the business centers.

Led by New York and Chicago, the larger cities adopted zoning ordinances which either limited the height of buildings, or required that they set back from the street after attaining a certain height, and

continue to set back at a certain angle, in order to insure light and air
for the lower stories and for the streets below. This accounts for the
stepped silhouette of most of the more recent tall buildings in New
York and Chicago. All cities, and nearly all towns and many suburban districts, adopted zoning ordinances which restricted the uses of
all areas, setting aside some for business, some for industry, and
others for residence use, in order to control population densities and
to preserve the character of neighborhoods. Proper zoning should be
based upon a long-range "master plan" for the entire area, which has
not always been done, so as a result much zoning has been stupid and
even harmful. However, in principle, zoning is beneficial to all and
is the only means of preventing conditions from getting worse than
they have been.

Such measures did not remove the causes of congestion and
slums, they were only an effort to improve conditions that were becoming intolerable. It began to be realized that the whole organization of the modern city was wrong, and a school of planners arose
who advocated decentralization as the city's only hope for survival.
The concept of garden cities and satellite cities was originated in England. The garden city was a city planned to a definite size, with areas
allocated to industry, business, residence, and recreation—almost a
return to the principles of the early New England village. The satellite city was a large urban business and manufacturing center surrounded by a ring of residential towns, with a "green belt" separating
them, all limited to the size to which they might grow. The social
conscience had finally awakened, and was trying to create better living and working conditions for all men.

The Generation of the Giants

THE FIRST THIRTY YEARS OF THE TWENTIETH CENTURY SAW THE
United States built as it appears today. It was a generation of immense
building activity. Cities built office buildings, hotels, and department
stores, apartment houses, schools, and hospitals. Towns built banks,
stores, and schools, and often proudly a ten-story office building, for
emulation of the great city was the civic ideal everywhere. Real estate

developments multiplied around the cities, following the lines of transportation, often growing into new towns, some well-planned with winding roads away from main traffic arteries, and provision for schools, community centers, and shops. Others were laid out only to obtain the quickest and cheapest dollar from the investment, with monotonous rows of almost identical houses on straight streets. In these the future community as a whole was left the problems of traffic, play areas, and transportation. Great manufacturing plants multiplied and became cities in themselves, the centers of the lives of thousands of people. "Progress" was the watchword everywhere.

The giants of architecture, the "grand old men" of the profession, were the men mentioned above—Burnham, McKim, Gilbert, and Goodhue, and many others such as Charles A. Platt, H. VanBuren Magonigle, Whitney Warren, Howard Shaw, Grosvenor Atterbury, Ernest Graham, George B. Post, Henry Hornbostel, Paul Cret. These men were the inheritors of the traditions of Brunelleschi, Bramante, and Mansart, of Jones, Wren, and Latrobe. They were men of vision and powerful imagination, great artists and influential personalities. Consciously or not, they all followed Burnham's counsel, "Make no little plans, they have no magic to stir men's blood."

The architects of the younger generation had highly developed esthetic and social consciences, and they were also highly articulate. It has become something of a fashion to decry the great architects of a generation ago, accusing them of perpetrating and perpetuating a colossal fraud upon the American people, of raising false standards and crushing true and original expressions. This is shallow and intolerant thinking, influenced perhaps by resentment at the rejection of Louis Sullivan. These men were the product of their time and their background, great planners and sincere artists. Some of them may have had doubts as to the suitability of the manner in which they were designing, for the evolution of the work of some of them shows that they were striving toward new expressions. But most were content to create beauty as they conceived it, believing firmly in the progress of ideas, and convinced that they were contributing toward the gradual evolution of a new architecture.

During these years Europe was going through the same social and artistic evolution as the United States. The trends and influences were the same, only the names were different. The advanced building techniques developed in the United States had considerable influence abroad, but Europe still set the artistic standards. It was from Europe that Americans were to hear the song of a new architecture, for the few who sang it here were unheard or misunderstood. They were heard abroad, however, and all the time the American architects were zealously designing their classical and Gothic façades, new ideas and forms were shaping in Europe which soon were to crystallize in new schools of architectural thought and new trends in architectural design. A new generation of giants was in the making.

✻ XV ✻

Contemporary Architecture

THE SPIRIT which urged Richardson and Sullivan to think differently from their fellows was not confined to them, nor did it originate with them. In all ages there are individuals who are dissatisfied with the accepted thought of their time, who are thinking, talking, and writing far ahead of their generation. Even now the seeds of popular thought a generation hence are being planted, we know not by whom. By the time a new movement appears in concrete form it may have lived a long evolution in men's minds. Brunelleschi's dome was a new form, but it was the product of nearly two hundred years of gradually awakening interest in ancient culture by a small but ever-increasing number of people.

Many nineteenth-century idealists were searching for a way toward a better integrated life. Fourier in France, Robert Owen and William Morris in England, Bronson Alcott and Horace Greeley in the United States wrote of utopias, and some tried to establish them. The expression of this movement in the arts was encouraged by the writings of such men as Ruskin and Viollet-le-Duc, and its effect upon some architects was an urge to seek an appropriate and meaningful architecture, free from the restraints of tradition. William Morris' arts and crafts movement in England and the Art Nouveau movement in France were manifestations in the decorative arts of this spirit of protest. The Art Nouveau had a brief vogue about the

[373]

turn of the century, and several buildings were built under its influence, even in New York. Its ideal was a truthful expression of structure, and in its ornament it employed natural forms, often sinuous and intertwining. Not consciously a part of this movement, but a product of the same influences, were the buildings of Antoni Gaudí, a strongly individualist Spanish architect who devised daring vaults and undulating concrete surfaces which presaged some of the more advanced thin-shell vaults and poured concrete structures of today.

PLATE 155
PLATE 156
The church of the Sagrada Familia and Casa Milá, an apartment house, both in Barcelona, are his best-known works.

Even though Louis Sullivan gave up the fight, there were a few young men who had worked with him who did not. Of these the foremost was Frank Lloyd Wright. A magnificent non-conformist, for seventy years he carried on the fight, writing, teaching, and designing buildings which were often so radically different that in his earlier years many people considered him merely an eccentric.

PLATE 157
Wright's rebellion was, of course, against eclecticism and slavery to tradition, but he did more than rebel, which is negative; he produced, which is positive. He believed that architecture exists for people and that it should give them the opportunity for the fullest possible life.

PLATE 158
He believed that buildings should be a part of their environment, not a denial of it; that the form and construction of a building are one; and that buildings should not only shelter the human body but nourish the human spirit. Wright died in 1959, just a few days short of 95, the most widely known architect in the world—and still probably the least understood. Despite the great range of his work and the many new forms and approaches he devised, it is probable that his greatest influence has been upon domestic architecture. The whole concept of "open planning" in residential architecture was first exemplified in his "prairie houses" of the 1890's. His critics—and no architect ever had more—called him, even as late as the 1950's, the "greatest architect of the nineteenth century." Intended unkindly, it is close to the truth, for he was the sole connecting link which carried over into the twentieth century the principles of integrity and functionalism that Louis Sullivan had instilled in him.

Wright's early works and writings had a great influence in Europe, especially in Germany, Austria, and France, where in the

Berlage in The Hague, Otto Wagner in Vienna, and Peter Behrens in Berlin were arriving at a twentieth-century architecture based upon twentieth-century methods of construction. Young American architects traveling abroad after the war saw the work of these architects and many others; they stayed to study and work with them, and at the *Bauhaus,* or workshop, of Walter Gropius at Weimar and later at Dessau. During the 1920's some of the European architects, such as Richard Neutra of Vienna, came to the United States, and during the 1930's there was a greater influx of them, accelerated by the spread of nazism. These men, then, became the new generation of old masters.   PLATE 159

Europe, however, had its single great individual too—Le Corbusier, another uncompromising individualist. Architect, sculptor, painter, draftsman, his versatility was amazing, his conceptions always grand. It is also true that they didn't always work, but neither did Wright's. His great apartment house in Marseilles, l'Unité   PLATE 160 d'Habitation (1947–52) was the progenitor of all "slab" type apartment houses built anywhere since. His little parish church, Notre Dame du Haut at Ronchamps (1955), with its great upsweeping   PLATE 161 concrete roof and its devout interior atmosphere, is one of the great buildings of the century. His rugged concrete style was brought to the United States in his design for the Carpenter Visual Arts Center   PLATE 187 at Harvard University in 1962, and carried into the East in his plan and design for Chandigarh, the new capital city of the Punjab in India. Le Corbusier died in 1965.

There were many different schools of thought and of design in Europe during the twenty years before World War II. They ranged from the purely mechanistic group, who seemed to consider a building purely as abstract form, to those who were interested in achieving picturesque results with a revival of handcraft methods applied to new materials and new forms. In 1927 Sweden sent to New York an exhibition of arts and crafts, consisting of glass, ceramics, textiles, and woodwork of beautiful designs and exquisite workmanship which aroused much popular enthusiasm. The City Hall in Stock-   PLATE 162 holm, designed by Ragnar Ostberg, is an example of this approach applied to a major building. It is essentially medieval in its form and use of brick and stone textures, and its great hall glows richly with magnificent mosaics, yet there is not a Gothic detail in the

PLATE 163

PLATE 164

PLATE 165

building. On the other hand, there are groups of workers' housing in Sweden, Finland, and Holland which are strictly functional, depending only upon the color and texture of their materials for life and interest; and there are factories and stores in Germany of glass and brick and concrete in which the walls are mere screens, for the structure is carried entirely upon the beams and columns. One of the better-known buildings of this time is the Town Hall at Hilversum, in Holland, designed by W. M. Dudok in 1928. Its simple brick forms are geometric yet picturesque in their massing, dominated by a striking asymmetrical tower.

Reinforced concrete came into wide use in Europe long before its use became prevalent in the United States. The slender and graceful bridge spans designed by the French engineer Robert Maillart have not been excelled even in these days of prestressed concrete. The church at Raincy designed by Auguste Perret has almost flat concrete vaulting, slender concrete columns, and huge windows filled with concrete latticework; nowhere is there the slightest attempt to imitate Gothic forms, yet its interior has a definite Gothic mood. The real leadership came from Germany and Austria, before the masters went to England and the United States. The municipal housing in many cities, such as Berlin and Frankfort, is sharp and efficient-looking, all glass and stucco, as are the department stores and office buildings. They have not worn very well, however, and after thirty years they look barren, stained, and weary. During these prewar years a large number of modern buildings were built all over Europe, and they served as a proving ground for what was to come. American architects still seemed to feel the need to turn to Europe, not, as in the days of eclecticism, for details to copy, but for guidance in approach and confirmation of principles.

The American Skyscraper

MEANWHILE, THE AMERICAN ARCHITECTS WERE ARRIVING AT A SOLUtion of their own special problem, the designing of the skyscraper. Their solution was not satisfactory to Europe's contemporary old masters, but it was eminently satisfactory to the American people, who were trailing conservatively a generation behind the intellectually more progressive Europeans. The building boom of the 1920's was under way in all American cities. The race to build the biggest or the highest building was not urged so much by economic necessity, the sole justification for the skyscraper, as it was by the desire for its sensational advertising value.

A competition for designs for the *Chicago Tribune* Building brought submissions from all over the world. It was won by Raymond Hood and John Mead Howells of New York. Hood was an PLATE 166 architect hitherto little known to the public, a graduate of the École des Beaux Arts. His building had clean, strong, vertical lines which swept upward without the interruption of horizontal accents; to be sure, they blossomed out into Gothic buttresses and tracery at the top, but the design would probably not have won the competition without some concession to tradition. But it was the never-built second prize that created a sensation in the architectural world. Designed by a Finn, Eliel Saarinen, its upward sweep and gently telescoping mass was a new and free conception, softened and enriched by a sparing use of original ornamental forms. Both designs, especially the second-prize design, had a wide influence. Traditional forms almost completely disappeared, and in their stead the flat piers of tall buildings were allowed to sweep upward, sometimes with simple ornamental panels in the spandrels under the windows, and invariably with spots of ornament between the piers at the top. The fundamental change lay in the fact that the emphasis was upon mass rather than upon surface decoration. Instead of being accepted as an ungainly bulk to be covered with a decorative veneer, the skyscraper was moulded into a fine mass and treated with pronounced vertical lines to give an upward movement. The new zoning ordinances, first introduced in New York in 1916, had a pronounced effect upon the silhouettes of new buildings; they required that a tall building be set back from the street progressively as it went up in height, in order to preserve light and air for the street and the lower stories.

Eliel Saarinen came to the United States in 1923. He designed the buildings for Cranbrook Academy of Art at Bloomfield Hills, Michigan, and became its head. With his son Eero, he designed the Tabernacle Church of Christ in Columbus, Indiana (1942), one of PLATE 167 the first truly contemporary churches in this country, and the famous Crow Island School in Winnetka, Illinois (1940, in collaboration with Perkins, Wheeler and Will), which became the prototype of the modern one-story, spreading school building. Eliel Saarinen died in 1950.

PLATE 168 In 1930, Raymond Hood designed the *Daily News* Building in New York, a more advanced design with no concessions to tradition. It has no ornament whatsoever, depending entirely upon its effective masses and the strongly emphasized verticals which simply stop when they come to the top. In his McGraw-Hill Building he tried a horizontal emphasis instead of the vertical. This is more defensible logically, for it expresses the fact that the building is, after all, a succession of stories; but it is less successful esthetically, and it completely lacks the dynamic quality which is so impressive in the *Daily News* Building.

The Empire State Building, by Shreve, Lamb and Harmon, is one of the two masterpieces of the period. Its complete simplicity, sparing use of detail, and fine silhouette give it a majesty that befits what is still, after nearly forty years, the tallest building in the world. The other masterpiece is the group of buildings known as PLATE 169 Rockefeller Center, or Radio City. The nucleus of the group, the tall, thin RCA Building, was designed by an association of architects of which Hood was the designing spirit. Hood died an untimely death in 1934; the remaining buildings were designed by the rest of the group and by other architects, but they all adhered closely to the spirit and form of the RCA Building. The original area of the Center has been greatly enlarged over the years, and buildings are still being added to it, but none of them violate the style. However, the great contribution of Rockefeller Center to architecture, to city planning, and to New York City, was the concept of the open urban square, full of lively activity, surrounded by handsome and harmonious buildings. It has inspired many similar attempts, but it has never been bettered. These buildings, completed in the early 1930's, were the last skyscrapers of the booming 1920's. To many they seemed to mark the end of the skyscraper era. But twenty years later the race was on again.

The Depression and the Fairs

THE DEPRESSION, WHICH BEGAN IN 1930 AND LASTED ABOUT FIVE years, gave the architects an unwelcome pause and a chance to look back over past progress, or the lack of it, and to think about the future. It also brought in new influences. The sound of the rivet hammer ceased after having echoed constantly through the cities for ten years, and all building activity gradually came to a standstill. The architects were among the first to feel the effects of the Depression; in a few months the majority found themselves with no work whatsoever. Under the work relief programs of the Roosevelt administration many of them found work at teaching, making a survey of historic American buildings, or working in the architectural offices of the federal government. For this became the day of the federal project. Post offices, libraries, schools, and other public buildings were built with federal funds. Those few not designed in government offices were designed by local architects in government-approved styles. This official architectural dictatorship was no doubt unintentional on the part of the authorities, but it was inherent in the setup. Fortunately, it was in general a beneficent dictatorship, for it was largely administered by younger men who had been exposed to the new trends of thought. Most of the buildings were of simple design, often quite dull, representing a conservative and rather insipid attempt at a modernism which was essentially classical in spirit, if not in detail.

One of the developments during these lean years was the reintroduction of the mural painter and the sculptor into the activities of the architect. For many years the architects had neglected them—with a few notable exceptions, such as Goodhue's reliance upon Lee Lawrie for the sculpture which was a very part of the essence of his architecture. Painted panels and sculptured decorations had been turned over to commercial art studios and stonecutters rather than to artists. The new government-sponsored buildings were filled with work-relief murals, reliefs, and figures, good, bad, and indifferent; but their quality was not so important as their quantity, for they re-accustomed the public to seeing the three major visual arts in full collaboration, as they always had been during the great historical periods. Thus a new generation of architects cut their teeth on these federal projects, a generation which has furnished most of the new old masters of the 1960's.

Another architectural influence arising out of federal activities during the Depression and which proved to be far-reaching was the attention paid to housing. The broad social policies of the New Deal focused public attention upon the need for improving the living conditions of thousands of families living in sub-standard tenements in the cities and in shack towns everywhere. The new homes that were built for them, whether they were multi-story apartments or two- and three-story walk-ups, were planned to insure proper sunlight, ventilation, sanitation, and privacy. They were intended to be set in landscaped grounds with play areas for the children; a few of them were, but most were placed in barren plots in which grass would not grow and children could not play because of high wire fences and "Keep Off the Grass" signs. However, this was also the era of Radburn and the Greenbelt towns, Baldwin Hills Village in California and Chatham Village near Pittsburgh—communities planned for people and children, with the automobile separated from the pedestrian and with green open spaces for human enjoyment.

The aristocratic conception of city planning was abandoned with the growing realization that perhaps the whole method by which cities grew was basically wrong. The architects and the public turned their attention to community planning on a broad scale. It was discovered that the countries of Europe were far ahead of the United States in this respect too, and groups went to Germany, Holland, and England to study their accomplishments in housing and town planning. A second influx of European architects took place, bringing with them not only their thoroughly modern conception of the function of the architect as the planner of living in the broad sense, but their highly advanced theories of design as well. These Europeans became a major influence in the reshaping of the aims of American architecture, especially since so many of them became professors in the schools of architecture. The schools themselves underwent a major overhauling, and curricula were revised to meet the new trends of thought. Emphasis on the study of architectural history was dropped, and the stress was placed upon social needs and community planning. Students were allowed greater freedom of expression in their design problems, and as a result traditional architecture disappeared from the schools entirely.

Two more great world's fairs came and went, leaving their influences behind them: Chicago's Century of Progress Exposition in 1933 and the New York World's Fair in 1939. At Chicago the public saw for the first time what the modern-minded architects had been talking about, and in general they liked it. What they saw was a broad sweep of mass and color. There were many kinds of buildings, from the balanced masses and studied detail of the converted classicists to the often ungainly and strictly functional masses of the Internationalists. Varied as the buildings were, they were   PLATE 171 unified by skillful group planning, largely the work of Raymond Hood, and a tremendously effective use of color and illumination as integral parts of the design. From the public there was both condemnation and praise, as might be expected, but an important piece of missionary work had been accomplished. What is probably most significant is the fact that when the promoters and the architects first met to discuss plans, there seemed to be no question in anybody's mind but that the style should be "modern."

The New York World's Fair was more successful architecturally, but not such a great surprise to the public, for during the years since 1933 many minor buildings had been built in the new style. The Fair was particularly notable for its great formal plan, with   PLATE 172 true Renaissance magnificence and its splendid use of fountains and falling waters, another effect revived from the Renaissance. It must be noted, however, that the finest individual buildings were among the foreign exhibits, notably the Swiss, Brazilian, French, Belgian, and Polish pavilions.

Contemporary Architecture

THIS, THEN, IS THE BACKGROUND OUT OF WHICH POST-WAR "CONTEMporary" architecture developed. At first feeling their way cautiously, the architects of the late 1940's and the early 1950's gained confidence and authority. There were many, like Eero Saarinen, son of the

Finnish architect, who probed every problem deeply, finding the solutions of some in daring new structural forms like the great PLATE 173 building at Dulles International Airport in Washington, or in the PLATE 174 trim classic lines of the General Motors Research Center near Detroit. PLATE 175 There were many others who sought only novelty, employing every structural trick to create innovations which would startle and draw attention. And there were also some who developed a more or less PLATE 176 personal style, usually of prettiness, like Minoru Yamasaki and PLATE 177 Edward Stone, using it on all types of buildings, no matter what PLATE 178 their function. Architecture was becoming a popular art, and it became the goal of many architects to attract attention, constantly striving for novelty. The popular magazines devoted many pages of color photography to the latest buildings and their creators, and several times architects achieved that zenith of popular fame—the cover of *Time* magazine.

Commercial architecture became subject to fadism. The completion of Lever House on Park Avenue in New York in 1952, by PLATE 179 Skidmore, Owings and Merrill, a beautiful irregular mass set back from the corner, sheathed in green glass panels and stainless steel, set the fashion for a countless horde of similar glass and plastic-paneled buildings, not one of which had the quality of its progenitor. The reaction against the "curtain wall"—the glass paneled facade—set in by 1960, and precast concrete panels became the fashion. There had been a cry for "sculptured" facades, for "texture," instead of for a smooth and shiny glassiness. It was probably Paul Rudolph who led the way, with his rugged concrete textures and bold forms. By the middle 1960's this too was being done to death. At this date of writing, it is hard to foresee what will replace them.

Post-war architecture became truly "international." Architec-PLATE 170 tural students from Europe and Asia studied in American universities; students from the United States and South America traveled abroad and worked for architects of many countries. As a result, nationalism and regionalism in architecture began to disappear. Architects followed the cult of the individual or the will-o'-the-wisp of their own imagination rather than the tradition of their own country. Young designers in Bangkok and Ghana designed steel and glass buildings like those they saw in the monthly magazines from abroad but which their countries were ill-equipped to build. New structural methods were devised, new materials were perfected, mechanical equipment was vastly improved, engineers learned how to perform daring feats undreamed of a generation before—and architects were liberated into a new world of possibilities. Scores of "leaders of the profession" appeared in Europe, the Americas, and the Far East. And every "leader" had a hundred followers. Only a few of the leaders can be mentioned here, and none of the followers. Some of the leaders were very great artists.

Wright and Le Corbusier we have already met. Walter Gropius is professor emeritus at the School of Architecture at Harvard University and founder of The Architects Collaborative, a firm which has maintained a consistently high standard of design. One of Gropius' best-known works is the Harvard Graduate Center. Mies van der Rohe became head of the School of Architecture at the   PLATE 183 Illinois Institute of Technology. He retired in 1958, to practice architecture in Chicago. His chaste, carefully studied creations in steel and glass are jewel-like in their perfection. Examples are the Lake-   PLATE 180 shore Apartments in Chicago, the Farnsworth house in Plano,   PLATE 181 Illinois, and an urban renewal project, LaFayette Park in Detroit. In collaboration with Philip Johnson, he designed the Seagram Building in New York, a building of such great distinction of design   PLATE 182 that the city levied a special tax on it! Marcel Breuer's finest works have been the IBM Research Center at la Gaude, near Nice in   PLATE 184 southern France, and St. John's Abbey at Collegeville, Minnesota.   PLATE 185 His giant curved building in Washington for the new Department of Housing and Urban Development is still under construction at this writing. In 30 years of practice in California, Richard Neutra   PLATE 186 has designed some of the most restrained and elegant domestic architecture in the country, as well as other public work of great originality, such as the Visitors' Center at Gettysburg, Pennsylvania.

There are, of course, European, Asian, and South American architects who must be listed among today's "greats." Alvar Aalto of Finland is one of them. His town hall at Saynatsalo, his industrial plants, his apartment buildings in the new towns in the pine forests of his native land, and his curving dormitory building for MIT in Cambridge, Massachusetts are perhaps severe, yet they are rich in textured brickwork and eminently suited to the character of their sites. Pier Luigi Nervi of Italy is not, strictly speaking, an architect.

He is an engineer and a contractor, yet he is one of the great artists of our time. He has developed a system of spanning great spaces with an intricate network of precast concrete ribs which are as beautiful, and as strictly functional, as the ribs of Gothic architecture.

PLATE 188 His Olympic Sports Palace in Rome (1957) is one of his most admired structures, as is his bus terminal at the east end of the George

PLATE 189 Washington Bridge in New York. The United States no longer has a corner on skyscrapers. Many have been built in the cities

PLATE 190 of Europe and some in Asia. The Pirelli Building in Milan, designed by Gio Ponti with Nervi as engineer, is one of the few truly elegant tall buildings in the world, and its reinforced concrete structure is most unique.

South Americans produced some very progressive architecture during the 1950's and 1960's. After designing many advanced buildings, Lucio Costa achieved international fame as the planner of Brasília, the new inland capital of Brazil conceived and nearly completed by Jan Kubichek, the country's progressive President. Bra-

PLATE 191 sília's buildings were designed by Oscar Niemeyer, who, after a frivolous architectural career, settled down and designed some of the great buildings of his generation. Affonso Reidy, also a Brazilian, has designed significant buildings, notably the Museum of Modern Art in Rio de Janeiro. Felix Candela of Mexico developed a system of thin-shell concrete vaulting—rooted undoubtedly in his country's long tradition of vaulting with thin, flat bricks—which has enabled him to design some daring and delightful structures.

Antonin Raymond, an Austrian-born American, is closely associated with the architecture of Japan, where he has practiced for many years—even though living in New Hope, Pennsylvania. He has succeeded in combining the spirit of traditional Japanese architecture with the techniques of modern European and American construction. Among Japan's own contemporary architects perhaps the greatest is Kenzo Tange, a quiet little man who is a very great influence indeed. His reinforced concrete structures show the influence of Le Corbusier, but thoroughly assimilated into the Japanese idiom. One of his most interesting recent proposals was a vast scheme for extending and building Tokyo out over its harbor, in an effort to find space for that ever-crowded city.

In the United States, perhaps the most creative architect of the current generation has been Eero Saarinen, who, unfortunately, died in 1961; his work is being carried on by his former associates. Certainly the most prolific firm of architects of the mid-twentieth century has been Skidmore, Owings and Merrill—popularly known as SOM. Probably their most competent design partners are Gordon Bunshaft and Walter Netsch. SOM's particular achievement has been to demonstrate that a really large architectural office can turn out superlative work, which they have done over a period of years. Their fine attention to detail is equaled by only a few—and much smaller—offices. Lever House has been mentioned. Their spreading building for the Connecticut General Life Insurance Company, PLATE 192 fitted to the rolling Connecticut countryside near Bloomfield, has the restrained elegance of a contemporary palace. Their design for the United States Air Force Academy near Colorado Springs has been criticized because it brings the city to the great open spaces— but it is a beautiful city, and its unconventional aluminum-spired chapel has silenced its critics with its daring beauty.

One of the most interesting and original architects is Philip PLATE 193 Johnson. His beautifully studied work varies in mannerisms from the cold, bare elegance of his own steel and glass house in New Canaan, Connecticut, to the curious but delightful semi-byzantine domed glass cylinders he designed for the Museum of Pre-Columbian Art at Dumbarton Oaks in Washington, D.C. Of a more profound nature is Louis I. Kahn of Philadelphia; he has done relatively few buildings, but those few have had a great influence. Like most of the best architects today, he is a teacher as well as a practitioner, and it is through his students that he is making his greatest impact upon the world. Paul Rudolph rose to fame by a few daring designs in Florida and became the head of the School of Architecture at Yale, from which he has subsequently resigned. His design tech- PLATE 194 nique involves the use of reinforced concrete in bold and rugged forms, with the surface left naturally rough as it comes from the forms. One might say that his design is at the opposite pole from that of Philip Johnson, whose work is invariably exquisitely finished. To complete this all-too-brief catalog of outstanding mid-century architects, there is Io Ming Pei, best known for his office buildings and tall apartment houses, such as those at Mile High Center in Denver, the Society Hill Towers in Philadelphia, the Ville St.

Marie in Montreal, and the Capitol Park Apartments in Washington, D.C. Strictly commercial buildings, they stand as proof that good architecture and a low building budget are not incompatible.

Domestic architecture in the United States remains in a state of confused eclecticism. Of the hundreds of thousands of builders' houses that have been built to accommodate the middle classes which have been expanding and fleeing the city, only a handful here and there show even a trace of architectural distinction—notably in the Pacific Northwest and in the San Francisco Bay area. Others are a jumble of "Colonial" motives, low "ranch" roof lines, modernistic angles, and picture windows. They may have had honest builders, but they never had honest designers; they are the illegitimate off-spring of a striving for the ambitious and the ostentatious, and a longing for the cosy, the quaint, and the conservative. Religious architecture is in almost as bad a state. Surprisingly enough, the majority of the churches and synagogues that have been built during the 1950's and 1960's are not traditional in design but quite modern —too "modern." There are, of course, a few perfectly beautiful exceptions across the country, but most of them are guilty of extreme structural stuntism, violently contrasting materials, and plain bad

PLATE 195   taste. One of the most interesting recent developments has been the shopping center. At its best, it is a vision of the world of tomorrow,

PLATE 196   beautifully planned for the automobile age—sometimes even covered
PLATE 197   and air-conditioned; at its worst it is a dull collection of barren store buildings perilously situated in a sea of automobile tops.

A Broader Field for the Architects

SINCE WORLD WAR II, AND ESPECIALLY SINCE THE MIDDLE 1950's, the architects have been increasingly called upon to undertake planning in a very broad sense. With the tremendous growth of the cities and the great expansion of many institutions such as state universities and research centers, there has arisen a great need for men capable of long-range planning of a large area for a complex diversity of uses, as well as planning on a regional scale for the future development of whole counties. There has been indeed a planning profession, but it has been limited in numbers, and most of its members have been employees of planning offices in local, state, and federal governments. Historically, of course, city planning was always a part of the architects' work, and in the early twentieth century most of the planners of Britain's "New Towns" and of the new civic developments on the Continent were architects. During the 1920's there was a small group of architect-planners in New York who laid the groundwork for the gradual growth of interest and abilities in planning on the part of many members of the architectural profession. Among these pioneers were Clarence Stein, Henry Wright, Henry S. Churchill, and Frederick L. Ackerman; working with them were such non-architects as Lewis Mumford and Benton MacKaye. One of the early influences was the Regional Plan Association, which developed and preached broad planning on a truly regional basis.

During the Depression years, as we have already noted, Radburn and the Greenbelt towns were designed and at least partially built as towns for the motor age. The first regional plan on a great scale was carried out by the TVA Authority in Tennessee. Abroad, Le Corbusier planned Chandigarh and Lucio Costa planned Brasília. By 1960 scores of architectural offices all over the western world included planning as a regular part of their work, and nearly all schools of architecture added departments of planning to their curricula. Many planners also came from the field of landscape architecture, and with the growth of urban renewal programs and the expansion of metropolitan areas all over the country, planning became not just a matter of physical arrangement of buildings, streets, and open spaces, but a complex of problems involving the sociologists, the psychiatrists, the cultural anthropologists, the economists, the ecologists, and the traffic engineers. The modern planning office—like that of the Greek architect Constantinos A. Doxiadis—whether originated by an architect or a sociologist, has come to include experts from all the humanities, for the problem of human settlements and the population explosion calls for men and women trained in all disciplines.

The exciting plans that have been created for new communities PLATE 198 and for the rebuilding of old communities during the 1960's are a topic for a separate study. In this field unquestionably lies the greatest PLATE 199 work of the architect of the future. Beautiful buildings, functional buildings, efficient buildings will always be needed, of course, but we now realize that these are only units in an over-all environment, and it is the creation of a beautiful, functional, and efficient environment that is the goal toward which society is now striving. The decay of the cities and the tremendous social problems involved in rebuilding them; the inevitable building of entirely new cities in virgin territory; the preservation of what few ancient and historic buildings and sites we have left; and the conservation of nature and the beauty of the countryside—all these are the paramount problems today, and the members of the design professions and their allies have ahead of them the greatest creative opportunities the world has ever seen.

Additional Reading

FOR THOSE wishing to read further, there follows a list of nontechnical books which will be found highly informative and thoroughly readable. Nearly all should be obtainable in most college or city libraries, and many are available in paperback editions.
(Prepared with the assistance of George E. Pettengill, Librarian of the American Institute of Architects)

GENERAL

    Banister Fletcher, *A History of Architecture* (Scribner's)

    Sigfried Giedion, *Space, Time and Architecture* (Harvard)

    John Gloag, *Guide to Western Architecture* (Macmillan)

    The Great Ages of World Architecture [11 slim volumes] (Braziller)

    Talbot F. Hamlin, *Architecture: An Art for All Men* (Putnam's)

    Talbot F. Hamlin, *Architecture Through the Ages* (Putnam's)

    Henry-Russell Hitchcock et al., *World Architecture—A Pictorial History* (McGraw-Hill)

    Henry A. Millon and Alfred Frazer, *Key Monuments of the History of Architecture* (Abrams)

    Nikolaus Pevsner, *An Outline of European Architecture* (Penguin)

ANCIENT

    Helmut Berve and Gottfried Gruben, *Greek Temples, Theaters, and Shrines* (Abrams)

    William Bell Dinsmoor, *The Architecture of Ancient Greece* (Batsford)

    James Walter Graham, *The Palaces of Crete* (Princeton)

    Paul MacKendrick, *The Greek Stones Speak* (St. Martin's)

MEDIEVAL

    Henry Adams, *Mont-Saint-Michel and Chartres* (Heritage)

    Henri Focillon, *Art of the West in the Middle Ages* (Phaidon)

    Paul Frankl, *Gothic Architecture* (Penguin)

    Jean Gimpel, *The Cathedral Builders* (Grove)

    Allan Temko, *Notre-Dame of Paris* (Viking)

RENAISSANCE

James S. Ackerman, *The Architecture of Michelangelo* (Viking)

Bruce Allsopp, *A History of Renaissance Architecture* (Pitman)

Mary McCarthy, *The Stones of Florence* (Harcourt, Brace & World)

Peter J. Murray, *The Architecture of the Italian Renaissance* (Schocken)

John Summerson, *Georgian London* (Penguin)

AMERICAN ARCHITECTURE

Wayne Andrews, *Architecture in America* (Atheneum)

John Burchard and Albert Bush-Brown, *The Architecture of America: A Social and Cultural History* (Little, Brown)

James Marston Fitch, *American Building* (Houghton Mifflin)

Alan Gowans, *Images of American Living: Four Centuries of Architecture and Furniture as Cultural Expression* (Lippincott)

Talbot F. Hamlin, *Greek Revival Architecture in America* (Dover)

Hugh Morrison, *Early American Architecture: From the First Colonial Settlements to the National Period* (Oxford)

Lewis Mumford, *The Roots of Contemporary American Architecture* (Dover)

Trent E. Sanford, *The Story of Architecture in Mexico* (Norton)

CONTEMPORARY ARCHITECTURE

The Best in 20th Century Architecture (Reynal)

Peter Blake, *The Master Builders* (Knopf)

Encyclopedia of Modern Architecture (Abrams)

Henry-Russell Hitchcock, *Architecture: 19th and 20th Centuries* (Penguin)

Henry-Russell Hitchcock and Philip Johnson, *The International Style* (Norton)

Le Corbusier, *Towards a New Architecture* (Praeger)

Masters of World Architecture [11 slim volumes] (Braziller)

John Peter, *Masters of Modern Architecture* (Braziller)

Frank Lloyd Wright, *The Future of Architecture* (Horizon)

Frank Lloyd Wright: Writings and Buildings, selected by Edgar Kaufmann, Jr.

UNDERSTANDING ARCHITECTURE

James Marston Fitch, *Architecture and the Esthetics of Plenty* (Columbia)

Walter Gropius, *Scope of Total Architecture* (Collier)

Alfred Browning Parker, *You and Architecture* (Delacorte)

Steen Eiler Rasmussen, *Experiencing Architecture* (M.I.T.)

THE CITY

Henry S. Churchill, *The City Is the People* (Norton)

Victor Gruen, *The Heart of Our Cities* (Simon and Schuster)

Lewis Mumford, *The City in History* (Harcourt, Brace & World)

Eliel Saarinen, *The City* (M.I.T.)

Wolf Schneider, *Babylon Is Everywhere: The City As Man's Fate* (McGraw-Hill)

Paul D. Spreiregen, *Urban Design—The Architecture of Towns and Cities* (McGraw-Hill)

Christopher Tunnard, *The City of Man* (Scribner's)

Index